AF829800

Varieties of Capitalism Over Time

This book looks at how varieties of capitalism emerge over time and across different geographies, and is comprised of submissions from scholars around the globe. Covering a wide range of territories including Europe, the Americas, Africa, and Asia across both the nineteenth and twentieth centuries, this edited volume considers the roles that the state and business working together play in the emergence of different economic systems. Whilst most analyses focus on identifying different types of capitalism, the chapters in this volume instead focus on how these different types develop, the drivers of their emergence, and the people and organisations behind the developments. The geographical spread of analyses allows the reader to delve into how different countries have managed and even created their economic systems providing comparative insights into our understanding of how different national economic models develop over time.

This book was originally published as a special issue of *Business History*.

Niall G. MacKenzie is Professor of Entrepreneurship and Business History at Adam Smith Business School at the University of Glasgow, Scotland, UK.

Andrew Perchard is Professor of Industry & Society at Newcastle Business School, Northumbria University, England, UK, and Honorary Research Professor at Otago Business School, University of Otago, New Zealand.

Christopher Miller is Lecturer in Economic and Social History at the University of Glasgow, Scotland, UK.

Neil Forbes is Professor of International History at Coventry University, England, UK.

Varieties of Capitalism Over Time

Edited by
Niall G. MacKenzie, Andrew Perchard, Christopher Miller and Neil Forbes

Routledge
Taylor & Francis Group
LONDON AND NEW YORK

First published 2023
by Routledge
4 Park Square, Milton Park, Abingdon, Oxon, OX14 4RN

and by Routledge
605 Third Avenue, New York, NY 10158

Routledge is an imprint of the Taylor & Francis Group, an informa business

Introduction, Chapters 2–4 and 7–9 © 2023 Taylor & Francis

Chapter 1 © 2019 Martin Shanahan and Susanna Fellman. Originally published as Open Access.

Chapter 5 © 2020 Pasi Nevalainen and Ville Yliaska. Originally published as Open Access.

Chapter 6 © 2020 Martin Eriksson, Lena Andersson-Skog and Josefin Sabo. Originally published as Open Access.

With the exception of Chapters 1, 5 and 6, no part of this book may be reprinted or reproduced or utilised in any form or by any electronic, mechanical, or other means, now known or hereafter invented, including photocopying and recording, or in any information storage or retrieval system, without permission in writing from the publishers. For details on the rights for Chapters 1, 5 and 6, please see the chapters' Open Access footnotes.

Trademark notice: Product or corporate names may be trademarks or registered trademarks and are used only for identification and explanation without intent to infringe.

British Library Cataloguing-in-Publication Data
A catalogue record for this book is available from the British Library

ISBN13: 978-1-032-36983-9 (hbk)
ISBN13: 978-1-032-36984-6 (pbk)
ISBN13: 978-1-003-33478-1 (ebk)

DOI: 10.4324/9781003334781

Typeset in Myriad Pro
by codeMantra

Publisher's Note
The publisher accepts responsibility for any inconsistencies that may have arisen during the conversion of this book from journal articles to book chapters, namely the inclusion of journal terminology.

Disclaimer
Every effort has been made to contact copyright holders for their permission to reprint material in this book. The publishers would be grateful to hear from any copyright holder who is not here acknowledged and will undertake to rectify any errors or omissions in future editions of this book.

Contents

Citation Information

The following chapters were originally published in the journal *Business History*, volume 63, issue 8 (2021). When citing this material, please use the original page numbering for each article, as follows:

Chapter 1

Shifts in government business relations: Assessing change using the restrictive business registers in the OECD, 1945-1995
Martin Shanahan and Susanna Fellman
Business History, volume 63, issue 8 (2021) pp. 1253–1272

Chapter 2

Shaping the rules of the game: Spanish capitalism and the publishing industry under dictatorship (1939–1975)
Maria Fernandez-Moya and Nuria Puig
Business History, volume 63, issue 8 (2021) pp. 1273–1292

Chapter 3

'No mutiny will be allowed': business, the tax system and the Greek version of Mediterranean capitalism during dictatorship, 1967-1974
Zoi Pittaki
Business History, volume 63, issue 8 (2021) pp. 1293–1308

Chapter 4

State intervention in East Asia's varieties of capitalism: A case study of the electric power industry in China and Japan, 1882–1951
Chenxiao Xia
Business History, volume 63, issue 8 (2021) pp. 1309–1326

Chapter 5

From state-owned smokestacks to post-industrial dreams: The Finnish government in business, 1970–2010
Pasi Nevalainen and Ville Yliaska
Business History, volume 63, issue 8 (2021) pp. 1327–1356

Chapter 6

National institutions, regional outcomes. The political economy of post-war Swedish regional policy
Martin Eriksson, Lena Andersson-Skog and Josefin Sabo
Business History, volume 63, issue 8 (2021) pp. 1357–1370

Chapter 7

Only one way to raise capital? Colombian business groups and the dawn of internal markets
Beatriz Rodriguez-Satizabal
Business History, volume 63, issue 8 (2021) pp. 1371–1392

Chapter 8

Varieties of capitalism, competition policy and the UK alcoholic beverages industry
Julie Bower
Business History, volume 63, issue 8 (2021) pp. 1393–1412

Chapter 9

'Settlers and comrades'. The variety of capitalism in South Africa, 1910–2016
Grietjie Verhoef
Business History, volume 63, issue 8 (2021) pp. 1413–1446

For any permission-related enquiries please visit:
http://www.tandfonline.com/page/help/permissions

Notes on Contributors

Lena Andersson-Skog is Professor of Economic History at Umeå University, Sweden.

Julie Bower is an independent scholar and former alcoholic beverages industry analyst in London, UK.

Martin Eriksson is a research fellow in Economic History in the Department of Economic History at Umeå University, Sweden.

Susanna Fellman is Professor of Business History at the School of Business Economics and Law at the University of Gothenburg, Sweden, and Visiting Professor within Helsinki University Humanities (HUH) Program at the University of Helsinki, Finland.

Maria Fernandez-Moya is Associate Professor of Economic History and Management at Colegio Universitario de Estudios Financieros (CUNEF), Spain.

Neil Forbes is Professor of International History at Coventry University, England, UK.

Niall G. MacKenzie is Professor of Entrepreneurship and Business History at Adam Smith Business School at the University of Glasgow, Scotland, UK.

Christopher Miller is Lecturer in Economic and Social History at the University of Glasgow, Scotland, UK.

Pasi Nevalainen is a postdoctoral researcher at the University of Jyväskylä, Finland.

Andrew Perchard is Professor of Industry & Society at Newcastle Business School, Northumbria University, England, UK, and Honorary Research Professor at Otago Business School, University of Otago, New Zealand.

Zoi Pittaki is Lecturer in Creativity and Entrepreneurship at Brunel Business School at Brunel University London, UK.

Nuria Puig is Professor of Economic History and Institutions at the Universidad Complutense de Madrid (UCM), Spain.

Beatriz Rodriguez-Satizabal is a PhD candidate (2020) at the School of Business and Management at the Queen Mary University of London (QMUL), UK.

Josefin Sabo is a researcher in Economic History at Umeå University, Sweden.

Martin Shanahan is Professor of Economic and Business History at the University of South Australia, Australia, and Visiting Professor at the University of Gothenburg, Sweden.

Grietjie Verhoef is Professor of Economic and Business History at the College of Business and Economics at the University of Johannesburg, South Africa.

Chenxiao Xia is Lecturer in Economic History at the Graduate School of Economics at Osaka University, Japan.

Ville Yliaska is an Administrative Science student at the University of Lapland, Rovaniemi, Finland.

Introduction: Varieties of Capitalism Over Time

Niall G. MacKenzie, Andrew Perchard, Christopher Miller and Neil Forbes

Introduction and rationale

Hall and Soskice's cornerstone work *Varieties of Capitalism* (2001) aimed to 'elaborate a new framework for understanding the institutional similarities and differences among the developed economies' (pg.1). As they acknowledged, the work formed part of a longer tradition of examining comparative business systems (CBS). In their view, this started with Andrew Shonfield's classic 1965 work on state planning, and the success of such institutional levers in France and Japan in economic development as contrasted with the UK (along with a large cast in the subsequent decades preceding VoC within the CBS tradition, including Goldthorpe, 1984; Piore and Sabel, 1984; Lazonick, 1991; Herrigel, 1996; and Whitley, 1999), followed by the work of Acemoglu and Robinson (2012).

In developing their framework, Hall and Soskice identify firm capabilities as relational in nature and therefore subject to co-ordination challenges. They then detail five spheres where firms must develop relationships to resolve co-ordination problems in their core competencies to operate effectively within capitalist systems. These five spheres are industrial relations; training and education; corporate governance; inter-firm relations; and employee relations. In so doing, Hall and Soskice defined two 'ideal types' of market economy, the 'liberal market economy' (LME), and the 'coordinated market economy' (CME). The former was best characterised by the variety of capitalism found not only in the United States but also typically included Britain, Australasia, and Canada, while the latter was best typified by Germany and the Nordic countries, and to a lesser extent, Japan. The power of such characterisations, the authors argued, lay in being not only able to define how certain economies were structured but also to explain existing strengths and weaknesses and crucially to *predict* future successes. CMEs, for example, with more emphasis on long-term stable collaboration via business groups and trades unions, would in theory be better at 'socialised' or incremental innovation, rather than the radical innovation more likely to be fostered in LMEs. This in turn tilted such economies towards the development of certain kinds of products and services, and thus dominance in specific sectors of national and global markets. As we show in this edited collection, this has not been received without some significant criticism and pushback, though the influence of Hall and Soskice's theories on management and economics literature is undeniable.

As Hall and Soskice paid tribute to the antecedents of VoC, so we too acknowledge the valuable contribution of this work. As Mira Wilkins (2010) subsequently observed, VoC was successful in assuming the mantle of a broader literature with a catchy title. Despite the shortcomings of the VoC approach, which are discussed below and by the contributors to this collection, Hall and Soskice's contribution has been to provide a synthesis of the CBS tradition and a systematic approach to consider the interplay of these factors on the development of industrial economies and the firm.

The intention of this collected volume is to complement and extend an extant work on the topic, including in an important roundtable special issue on VoC in *Business History Review* (BHR) in 2010. This roundtable brought together a group of prominent business historians to consider how business history can contribute to the VoC literature, which, the editors noted, was 'conventionally criticized as ahistorical, at least in its original formulation' (pg.638). What we have sought to do with this collection is to explore how VoC has emerged over time and in different ways and has added, thereby, historical, geographical, and business-government relations to the discussion.

The work in this collection helps delve deeper into our understanding of how VoC emerge and continue through the prism of business-government relations as the two principal actors in capitalist development. In doing so it builds on and extends work by Thomas and Westerhuis on corporate governance and national economic models (2014). The focus of much of the existing canon on varieties of capitalism is centred on aggregated models of institutional environments. Consequently, VoC analyses have tended to focus on the characterisation of systems, rather than on the interactions between actors within such systems, and what impact this has upon innovation and economic development. We take the cue from emerging work on the state and business in business history then to consider what this means for VoC and to what end. In doing so, this collection bridges a number of different literatures, including those in business and economic history, economics, development studies, political economy, and political science, to consider how 'varieties of capitalism' (VoC) shape, and are structured by, government-business relations.

The visible hand of Chandler is present in much of business history, and relevant to this collection in particular is his superficial treatment of the role of government vis-à-vis business. In the decades following Chandler's seminal works, business historians have greatly expanded the understanding of different sectors and firms in different national environments, including looking at business-government relations. Nevertheless, Kipping's assertion that a better grasp of the business-politics nexus requires more work still stands (2003). Business historians have increasingly recognised the value of better understanding business-government relations; various studies have emerged in recent years that have added to the wider body of knowledge on the effects business has on the state and vice versa (MacKenzie, 2012, 2018; Perchard, 2012, 2019; Rollings, 2014; Perchard and MacKenzie, 2020). This body of work is the platform for our contention that such interactions are key to understanding VoC and that historical research can go a long way to addressing some of the criticisms levelled at existing scholarship on the topic.

Critiques of varieties of capitalism

Hall and Soskice's original premise has been criticised for, among other things, its generally narrow focus on mature industrialised nations; its determinism and rigidity; and, more specifically, the absence of actors, process, and a limited conceptualisation of institutions (Howell, 2003; Hancké et al., 2008). Despite these critiques, Howell (2003) claimed, with some assurance, that 'something approaching a consensus' (pg.103) had been reached around distinctive national capitalisms. This was followed by a further body of work, which has sought to question Hall and Soskice's conceptualisation and refine their original rubric of LMEs and CMEs to include such typologies as hierarchical and mixed market economies; southern European, Latin American, and Nordic capitalisms (Amable, 2003; Hancké et al., 2008; Fellman, et al., 2009; Schneider, 2009); and more recently variations in regional capitalisms (Ebner, 2016). Political scientists Jackson and Deeg (2008, 2012), adopting more explicitly historical approaches, have sought to introduce greater distinction into the comparative capitalism literature, including in the consideration of emergent markets. Meanwhile, Mahoney and Thelen (2010) promote their definition of a more nuanced understanding of incrementalism within institutions in conceptualisations of change over time in a correction to what they perceive to be the tendency of 'historical institutionalists' to view institutions as operating in a state of endogenous stasis. In a similar vein, scholars have sought to challenge the extent to which VoC's typologies are capable of predicting kinds of innovation within a given economy (Akkermans et al., 2008). For scholars looking to understand different aspects of economic and business development, VoC offers a route in but problems nevertheless persist in the mechanics of how such development is operationalised rather than abstract characterisations.

Notwithstanding a nod in the direction of the work of Douglass North, in particular his definition of institution (1991), Hall and Soskice's original work focuses overly on what North defined as 'formal rules (constitutions, laws, property rights)' at the expense of North's equal emphasis of 'informal constraints (sanctions, taboos, customs, traditions, and codes of conduct)' (pg.97). North identified the importance of the 'rules of the game' in shaping business activity; such rules are usually set by governments but rarely without engagement with firms. In fact, recent work by business historians has identified that when it comes to business, the state is 'always in' (Scranton and Fridenson, 2013; MacKenzie et al., 2020). By looking at business-government relations we can start to unpick the nature, structure, flows, and intensity of interactions between firms and governments across different contexts and time as a way of explaining the development of different forms of capitalism.

Moreover, given the critiques of how the original VoC framework was conceptualised, It Is noteworthy that initial conceptual flaws were replicated and reinforced in subsequent work responding to such criticisms whereby

> a proliferation of additional types of national political economies, such as mixed-market economies, Mediterranean and East Asian capitalisms, and hierarchical market economies (in Latin America). Such departures from parsimony have not made the new types any better at explaining changes within systems that run contrary to the direction encouraged by complementary institutions. Refinements of the typology, in other words, have not made the types themselves less rigid and focused on stability and reproduction rather than change (Herrigel and Zeitlin, 2010, pg. 671).

The same shortcomings identified by Herrigel and Zeitlin are evident in new contributions to the VoC literature (for example, Kiran, 2018). VoC has become the dominant paradigm in comparative political economy but remains lacking in historical perspective and research – Fast describes it as 'insufficiently historical and causally thin' (2016). Business historians are thus well-positioned to help fill significant gaps identified in the literature, particularly in relation to better understanding the mechanics of business-government interactions to explicate the how and why of the development of different types of capitalism over time. This would go some way towards addressing the conceptual flaws present in VoC and, simultaneously, providing stronger evidential analysis to mitigate the ahistorical approach often taken.

Contribution of this collection

This collection is therefore intended to address identified deficiencies, at least in part, as well as recognize that business history has its own shortcomings in this area. As Herrigel and Zeitlin also pointed out in the 2010 BHR roundtable discussion on VoCs, business history's own tradition of CBS analysis still needed to overcome its own constraints (p.667):

> In order to contribute fruitfully to the understanding of the variety-producing dynamics of capitalist development, business historians need to shed—if they have not done so already—the old Chandlerian paradigm of a teleological hierarchy among global business systems, where the best and most competitive paths lead in the direction that the United States has already traversed.

This is partly in response to the constraints presented by classic business history literature that details the emergence of modern capitalist systems (Chandler, 1990; McCraw, 1997; Wilkins and Hill, 2011), literature that has been criticised for largely focusing on the creation and development of American capitalism and that is therefore not necessarily reflective of other forms of national capitalisms (Kipping and Bjarnar, 1998).

An important corrective to the large literature on the efficacy of US capitalism is the work undertaken by Fellman et al. (2009) on the development of Nordic capitalism, not least owing to its identification of the central role of the interaction between business and the state in developing a system of capitalism which competes globally while providing strong social safety nets. Other business historians have also explored the development of alternative models of capitalism that are in many respects markedly different from the American story. For example, Cassis (2002), Carreras and Tafunell (1997), Fear (2005), Fellman et al. (2009), Schmidt (2003), Sluyterman (2014), Stokes (1988), and Tooze (2006) have all explored the development of different types of European capitalism in detail. Crucially, these consider the central role of government-business relations, national culture, and specific historical context that are distinct from the American story. Despite some work on Africa, Asia, and Latin America (for example, Austin, 2016; Stockwell, 2000; White, 1996; Musacchio and Lazzarini, 2014), the limitations of the geographical scope of case studies of the development of capitalism and business systems have also been criticised (Radice, 2015).

This has begun to be addressed recently, in particular with the emergence of the 'History of Capitalism' stream of scholarship and the establishment in 2020 of *Capitalism: a Journal of History and Economics*. Both of these initiatives have sought to move away from a US-centric focus by bringing a more nuanced understanding of how capitalist systems emerge and develop over time. These developments themselves build upon a growing literature on non-US economic and business systems that explores more holistically how different actors and structures are created, developed, and interacted to create and develop capitalist and, more recently, non-capitalist systems (Scranton, 2018, 2019).

The contributions to this collection provide a strong set of historical analyses that are wide-ranging in geographical scope and therefore shed light on how capitalism has developed in both Western and non-Western countries. They illustrate the ways in which business historians can contribute to the understanding and methods of VoC. All of the articles within the collection identify – as a central methodological approach – the problems with understanding the construction and development of national or comparative business systems without the consideration of changing historical context. As Mira Wilkins noted in her contribution to the *BHR* roundtable of 2010 (pg.639):

> … no economic historian ever had the illusion that all capitalist systems were identical (alike perhaps, but far from the same). Moreover, and of great importance, with the passage of time, every economic historian has come to recognize that capitalism took on different forms, not only between different countries but also within individual countries.

This collection illustrates Wilkins's point by providing in-depth analyses of the emergence of a range of different capitalist systems across and within very different geographies and industries, moving away from overly deterministic teleological characterisations to more nuanced and considered portrayals of the principal actors in such developments.

By examining business-government relations in different national (and indeed transnational) contexts and demonstrating how historical analysis of business can facilitate a more complex and nuanced understanding of national economic models and CBS, the articles presented here highlight vital methodological considerations that need to be addressed in any interdisciplinary work involving history. Recognising changing context over time and contingency within historical research methodologies (Perchard et al., 2017) can act as a valuable corrective to the often overly rigid scholarly understanding of systems, while at the same time underpinning the need to bridge the language of disciplines through respectful engagement (Maclean et al., 2016).

Synopses

As Martin Shanahan and Susanna Fellman demonstrate in their contribution to this volume, criticisms of Hall and Soskice's historical periodisation and its generalisability have not been confined to historians. Building on earlier work by Kipping and Bjarnar (1998), Schröter (2005), and others, Shanahan and Fellman analyse business-government relations and VoCs through the lens of cartel registers across 13 OECD countries between 1945 and 1995, challenging narratives of the Americanisation of European competition rules and the conduct of business, and demonstrating not just national distinctions but differing national agendas and distinct periods of development. As Shanahan and Fellman observe, these do not conform to existing, typically static, VoC conceptual frameworks due to their dynamic and changing nature. Similarly, their article throws into relief questions of how multinationals working across national economic systems fit into such static conceptualisations, raised within the 2010 roundtable, as a number of single transnational and historical industry studies have sought to show in relation to cartels (Ingulstad et al., 2014; Storli, 2014; Bertilorenzi, 2015).

María Fernández-Moya and Núria Puig's and Zoi Pittaki's papers, respectively, on the publishing industry in Francoist Spain and taxation under Greece's military junta, expose the problems of the rigidity and definitions of institutions within existing VoC models and how institutional change can affect and effect changes in economic systems. Equally, Chenxiao Xia's rich comparative study of the electric power industries in China and Japan explores the role of state capitalism and domestic agendas of national defence and unification, in the context of imperial expansion and occupation, in shaping national economic systems. In so doing, these articles also contribute to a rich body of historical work on business (both local and multinational) engagement with dictatorships and with political risk (Forbes, 2000, 2007, 2019; Tooze, 2006; Wubs, 2008; Scherner, 2013; Frøland et al., 2016). Fernández-Moya and Puig's exploration of the shaping of the institutions and processes governing publishing within different phases of economic transformation and industrialisation under Francoism illustrates the complexity of changes within national economic systems. Engaging with Royo's VoC literature on Spain (2002, 2006), they also closely examine the motivations and actions of particular actors against this changing context even under dictatorship. The focus of Moya and Puig's contribution provides vital clues as to the importance of 'informal constraints' in capitalist development. Xia's paper also uses the case study approach to explore East Asian VoCs and the place of the state in these.

Pasi Nevalainen and Ville Yliasko's work concerns the re-emergence of state ownership in Finland since the 1970s. They show that the standard view of Finnish reforms vis-à-vis business, namely privatisation and the breaking up of monopolies, overstates the extent to which government gave up state-owned enterprises (SOEs) and became an enthusiastic supporter of the free market. Instead, they argue the picture was rather more complex, insofar as the government in many cases never fully relinquished ownership of key firms but instead sought to safeguard the domestic competitiveness of firms through 'ownership steering'. As such, preferential intervention in the economy was retained in some important respects. In sum, Nevalainen and Yliasko's research has important implications for recent trends in 'Nordic' capitalism, building upon earlier key work by one of the collection's other contributors, Susanna Fellman et al. (2009).

Martin Eriksson, Lena Andersson-Skog and Josefin Sabo's article considers the regional and national aspects of VoC over time. It presents an historical analysis of the changing nature of business-government relations in Sweden, encompassing a strong spatial aspect through examination of the emergence and development of regional policy in the country. Looking specifically at the loan guarantee system that emerged in 20th-century Sweden, they find that regional imbalances of spatial development in the country required an interaction between business and government which informed the development of a CME in Sweden. By connecting spatiality and temporality they meet the call of Peck and Theodore (2007) for more nuanced understanding of how the two interact in capitalist development, while at the same time extending existing analyses of regional and national economic development to encompass the firm-level and national priorities. On this basis their work speaks to the emerging research on regional varieties of capitalism, illustrating the spatial challenges central governments face in pursuing economic development and the requirement of different actors' input at different times. Their focus on the long-term development of regional policy in Sweden provides an angle that is often missed in the literature.

Beatriz Rodriguez-Satizabal's piece considers the relationship between sources of capital and the creation of new internal capital markets in Colombia by focusing on the country's largest business groups during the pivotal decades from the 1950s to the 1970s. In common with other papers in this collection, it stresses the importance of institutions and policies in shaping firms' access to (and creation of) markets and highlights in particular the key role of financial liberalisation both from within Colombia by the government (e.g. the establishment of building societies) and from outside (principally through the World Bank's survey mission of 1951). Rodriguez-Satizabal thus shows how new financial legislation laid the foundations of larger internal capital markets that provided the key source of funding to Colombia's hitherto capital-starved firms and helped to fuel growth in the period from 1965. While the pattern was in some senses similar to that experienced by firms in Chile and Mexico, the piece is careful to highlight some significant differences and in so doing sheds light on similarities and variances within the still poorly understood 'varieties' of Latin American capitalism.

Julie Bower's piece examines an important area of UK industry, the alcoholic beverages sector, and how competition policy was developed over time. Bower points out that the UK was comparatively 'late' in becoming a full-throated advocate of market competition, something which indeed emerged only under Thatcher, despite a series of developments – largely along American lines – in the years since WWII that anticipated this. In this sense, evolving British competition policy since WWII, and especially in regard to mergers, in Bower's view, has had 'arguably a more fundamental impact on the... UK brewing industry than any other domestic industry'. This can be witnessed in the post-war history of the sector, from small-scale vertical ties to pub ownership to the later free-market specialisation that has created massive conglomerates like Diageo and expansive retail chains of pubs across the British Isles. Yet, as Bower shows, the recent reinvigoration of small-scale family brewing indicates that such a process is not linear or necessarily smooth and, crucially, that this case study reaffirms Wilkins (2010) arguments for the ability of several 'types' of capitalism to co-exist within the same regulatory framework and/or to vary over a relatively short time.

Grietjie Verhoef takes a quite different tack to the other articles in this collection by focusing on how business-government relations in South Africa developed over time, in particular the ways in which racial aspects constituted part of the development of a market economy. Her article considers the pre- and post-1990 periods separately. Consistent within this analysis is an exploration of how the South African VoC developed into what Verhoef terms a 'Racial Market Economy' (RME) as a variation on a CME, reflecting the shift from minority white rule to a black majority coalition, which she characterises as a 'heavily interventionist redistributive state'. This extends the VoC literature by offering an analysis that moves beyond the original binary definitions of LME or CME to encompass racial politics. In this sense it is an exploration of the role that business and political elites play in the development of economies, contributing to a long-standing area of business history investigation and interest, as well as shedding light on how the activities of elites can shape the development of capitalist systems. The South African example is a particular one but nevertheless instructive in showing how the lasting effects of colonisation, inequality, and changing institutional environments shape and are shaped by business.

These articles also speak to existing literature in a number of other areas, for instance: on the importance of considering the role of business leaders as political actors (Turner, 1984; Phillips-Fein and Zelizer, 2012; John and Phillips-Fein, 2016); on the enduring influence of national defence considerations in affecting planning structures and the relationship between business and government (Edgerton, 2005; Peden, 2007; Sparrow, 2011; Perchard, 2012, 2019; Miller, 2016, 2017, 2018; Wilson, 2016); and on the role of state intervention and the state as entrepreneur (Millward, 2005; Amatori et al., 2011; MacKenzie, 2018; MacKenzie et al., 2020). Taken together, they provide geographic range and various industrial foci, as well as a clear articulation of the importance of how business, national, and transnational actors interact in the formation, development, and operation of VoC that extends the concept while retaining a focus on historical perspectives.

Areas for future research

The concept of VoC is not an end in itself but an attempt to typologise the characteristics of different strands of capitalism while also explaining developments within nation states. Yet because economic and business systems are complex, multi-dimensional ideas, they inevitably do not fit neatly into simple categorisation. Cognisant of this, we have sought to provide a range of geographic and industrial coverage in this collection. Nevertheless, we are acutely aware that it provides only a snapshot of the wider potential of business history to expand, explain, and better understand VoC and its linkages to studies of business-government relations.

There are thus a number of areas where business history has developed deep knowledge and strong competences that can be applied to this end. We offer suggestions on some areas where we believe historical research can be most fruitful. Perhaps most pertinently, there have been myriad recent studies on the role of the state as entrepreneur and as an engine for innovation (most prominently, Mazzucato, 2013, 2022) and the relative roles that private industry and states or institutions play in creating and growing markets by 'pushing out' or 'pulling in' resources (Christensen et al., 2019). Growing in some ways from established work on national systems of innovation (NSI), these works implicitly touch on and challenge Hall and Soskice's assertion that certain kinds of technological innovation (radical or incremental) are better served by one or other variety of capitalism. Christensen et al. in particular are critical of the bulk of multinational enterprises, which have come in recent years to focus on 'efficiency' and 'sustaining' innovations for known groups of consumers over more radical (but riskier) attempts to create new markets. In so doing, Christensen et al. implicitly reject such typologies of market economies, albeit without reference to VoC, arguing the problem is now much worse in Mexico or the UK, where Ford and Nissan have accepted government incentives to relocate plants, than it is in Japan or South Korea. The result then is literatures on innovation, business-government relations, and VoC that do not talk well or often enough to each other and crucially lack much historical contextualisation to augment theories which seek to explain and later predict the course of industrial economies.

This is far from the only case where such research could yield results. Another pertinent and timely area for further exploration by business historians would be to look more closely at other ways in which VoC emerge and develop over time. These include transnational flows of capital, offshoring, business ethics (which typically do not consider the profound economic, environmental, and social legacies of industrial closures and therefore the social import of these), and industrial politics. This follows a growing literature in the field of deindustrialisation studies (Cowie, 1999; Cowie and Heathcott, 2003; High, 2003; Anastakis, 2013; and High et al., 2017). In the context of the election of Donald Trump in the US, Brexit in the UK, and the rise of Far-Right parties in Western Europe, it is clear that politics plays a crucial role in the development of capitalist societies, but business historians have to date largely been shy to investigate these relationships more closely.

A recent exception to this is a seven-year (2020–2027) transnational study undertaken by scholars in Canada, France, Germany, Italy, the UK, and the US (including one of the editors of this volume, Perchard), funded by the Social Sciences and Humanities Research Council of Canada and entitled 'Deindustrialization and the Politics of Our Time'. This project offers a significant opportunity for business historians to analyse the relationship between politics and capitalism and the effects thereof more critically. This is an area that we think business historians should be looking closely at, not least because of the insights such investigations could yield for our understanding of the machinations and outcomes of capitalist behaviours across national boundaries.

Due to existing VoC frameworks' inability to sufficiently and accurately capture MNE behaviour, historians who are interested in the practice and evolution of Corporate Social Responsibility (CSR) and the (un)ethical behaviour of MNEs should consider the relationship between MNE behaviour, which on one level has the potential to spread sets and subsets of corporate values to new and emerging markets across the world and existing characterisations of VoC – particularly where government-business relations are concerned.

This can be seen in several areas, with behaviour being driven by businesses and governments alike. The most obvious is through the conventional (and long-standing) practice of outsourcing and offshoring, particularly in cases where host nations 'attract' foreign firms with lower environmental standards than their home countries (Stokes and Miller, 2018), or by 'greenwashing' harmful practices through focusing exclusively on the areas in which firms go further than current regulations demand. This said can also be seen in the rather more positive light of large foreign firms helping to normalise, support, or insist upon drives for race, gender, and LGBT equality in otherwise more heavily restrictive political environments – for example, by regulating and scrutinising indigenous contractors within supply chains. This has been characterised as a kind of greenwashing or social washing of its own, however: Apple's suppliers are required to subscribe to a strict code of conduct with requirements (for example) on working conditions, respect, and dignity, though the spate of worker suicides brought on by extreme pressures within its key Chinese supplier, Foxconn, have thrown those commitments into question in recent years (*The Observer*, 2017).

Thus, in an era where political leadership in the BRICs and other emerging economies have attacked the 'West' for alleged hypocrisy in demanding higher global environmental or labour standards than they themselves held during their own phases of rapid industrialisation in the 19th and earlier 20th centuries, the behaviour of such 'Western' multinational enterprises up and down their own supply and value chains is worthy of note: while Brazilian President Jair Bolsonaro argued in 2019 that his country 'owes nothing to the world with regard to environmental preservation' and it was 'concerned only with economic development',[1] dozens of large multinationals operating in Brazil publicly pledged to support the Paris Climate Accord's targets of limiting carbon emissions (Viola and Gonçalves, 2019). Indeed, as attempts to bind nations to agreed minimums on corporate taxation appear to be bearing fruit as of 2022, it is likely that the future battleground for host nations seeking FDI will be environmental and social regulation (or the lack thereof), rather than financial incentives. How firms respond to this, and what it means for the various kinds of market economies, remains to be seen.

Finally, ongoing streams of work in colonialism and postcolonialism (as mentioned by Verhoef) offer rich potential to understand the effects of such imperialism and race on modern-day economic and business systems and vice versa. Stockwell (2000) and White (1996, 2004) have produced excellent grounded studies of business and empire (and decolonisation), and most recently, Enstad (2018) has explored the intersections of business, colonialism, race, and gender in the global tobacco industry. Similarly, the growing interest in the longer-term effects of slavery will be vitally important areas for business historians to engage with and informing debates over VoCs, for example, in relation to insights into the development (or not) of modern economies as a direct result of the transatlantic slave trade (for example, Mullen, 2013, 2020; Haggerty and Seymour, 2018). Verhoef's contribution to this collection also points to the importance of exploring alternative economic models in the face of racialised states or structural racism, which has also been explored in relation to the US by Prieto and Phipps in their recent *African American Management History* (2019). This is an area that requires substantial further research and one that also touches upon the continued importance of exploring alternative economic models. These examples are, of course, illustrative and not exhaustive.

To conclude, the rationale for this collection was to engage with the concept of VoCs as business historians, and, more broadly, to consider how we conceive of the business-political ecosystem and the role of business in society. Besides providing a fertile ground for local, as well as national and transnational, studies, this collection offers a variety of fresh perspectives, including those from often peripheralised voices in business history. We hope this encourages historians to reach out to social scientists (and vice versa) in undertaking research in this area and on cognate subjects. Realising this objective will require us to undertake vital exploratory discussions about epistemological and methodological considerations. In so doing, perhaps we can arrive at more nuanced and sophisticated understandings of the nature of business and political ecosystems and of the impact that such assumptions can have on economic and social development, policy, politics, sustainability, and the environment. Business history is currently in a phase where its research output is beginning to be noticed in other disciplines. We hope by offering this collection of work that we can demonstrate the wider value still of business historical approaches to understanding the world around us yesterday, today, and in the future.

Note

1. 'Bolsonaro says Brazil owes world nothing on environment' https://www.france24.com/en/20190323-bolsonaro-says-brazil-owes-world-nothing-environment [accessed 20 August 2020].

Acknowledgements

The editors would like to extend their thanks to Business History and Stirling Management School, and to Sharon Bolton, Martin Chick, Gillian Geddes, and Ray Stokes for their support in supporting the Paper Development Workshop held at Stirling Management School in 2018.

References

Acemoglu, D. and Robinson, J.A. (2012). *Why Nations Fail: The Origins of Power, Prosperity, and Poverty*, (Crown Business, New York).

Akkermans, D.H.M., Castaldi, C. and Los, B. (2008). Do 'liberal market economies' really innovate more radically than 'coordinated market economies'? Hall & Soskice reconsidered. *Research Policy*, Vol. 38, No. 1, pp.181–191.

Amable, B. (2003). *The Diversity of Modern Capitalism*, (Oxford University Press, Oxford).
Amatori, F., Millward, R. and Toninelli, P.A. (eds.) (2011). *Reappraising Sate-Owned Enterprise: A Comparison of the UK and Italy*, (Routledge, London).
Anastakis, D. (2013). *Autonomous State: The Struggle for a Canadian Car Industry from OPEC to Free Trade*, (University of Toronto Press, Toronto).
Austin, G. (2016). Is Africa too late for "late development"? Gerschenkron south of the Sahara. In Andersson, M. and Axelsson, T. (eds.) *Diverse Development Paths and Structural Transformation in the Escape from Poverty*, (Oxford University Press, Oxford), pp.206–235.
Bertilorenzi, M. (2015). *The International Aluminium Cartel: The Business and Politics of a Cooperative Industrial Institution*, (Routledge, New York).
Carreras, A and Tafunell, X. (1997). Spain: Big manufacturing firms between state and market, 1917–1990. In Chandler, A.D., Amatori, F. and Hikino, T. (eds.) *Big Business and the Wealth of Nations*, (Cambridge University Press, Cambridge), pp.277–304.
Cassis, Y. (2002). *Finance and Financiers in European History, 1880-1960*, (Cambridge University Press, Cambridge).
Chandler, A. D. & T. Hikino (1990). Scale and Scope: The Dynamics of Industrial Capitalism. · Harvard University Press, Cambridge, Mass.
Christensen, C.M., Ojomo, E. and Dillon, K. (2019). *The Prosperity Paradox: How Innovation Can Lift Nations Out of Poverty*, (Harper Business, New York).
Cowie, J. (1999). *Capital Moves: RCA's Seventy-Year Quest for Cheap Labor*, (Cornell University Press, Ithaca, NY).
Cowie, J and Heathcott, J. (eds.) (2003). *Beyond the Ruins: The Meanings of Deindustrialization*, (Cornell University Press, Ithaca, NY).
Ebner, A. (2016). Editorial: Exploring regional varieties of capitalism. *Regional Studies*, Vol. 50, No. 1, pp.3–6.
Edgerton, D.H. (2005). *Warfare State: Britain 1920-1970*, (Cambridge University Press, Cambridge).
Enstad, N. (2018). *Cigarettes, Inc. An Intimate History of Corporate Imperialism*, (Chicago University Press, Chicago, IL).
Fear, J.R. (2005) *Organizing Control: August Thyssen and the Construction of German Corporate Management*, (Harvard University Press: Cambridge, MA).
Fellman, S., Iversen, M., Sjörgen, H. and Thue, L. (eds.) (2009). *Creating Nordic Capitalism: The Development of a Competitive Periphery*, (Macmillan, London).
Forbes, N. (2000). *Doing Business with the Nazis: Britain's Economic and Financial Relations with Germany 1931–1939*, (Routledge, London).
———. (2007). Multinational enterprise, 'corporate responsibility' and the nazi dictatorship: The case of Unilever and Germany in the 1930s. *Contemporary European History*, Vol. 16, No. 2, pp.149–167.
———. (2019). Reinventing the Rio Tinto Company: Spain, political risk and corporate strategy before and after the Second World War. In Forbes, N., Kurosawa, T. and Wubs, B. (eds.) *Multinational Enterprise, Political Risk and Organisational Change: From Total War to Cold War* (Routledge, London). 134–153.
Frøland, H.O., Ingulstad, M. and Scherner, J. (eds.) (2016). *Industrial Collaboration in Nazi-occupied Europe: Norway in Context*, (Palgrave, London).
Goldthorpe, J.H. (1984). *Order and Conflict in Contemporary Capitalism*, (Clarendon, Oxford).
Haggerty, S. and Seymour, S. (2018). Imperial careering and enslavement in the long eighteenth-century: The Bentinck Family, 1710–1830s. *Slavery & Abolition*, Vol.39, No. 4, pp.642–662.
Hall, P.A. and Soskice, D. (eds.) (2001). *Varieties of Capitalism: The Institutional Foundations of Comparative Advantage*, (Oxford University Press, Oxford).
Hall, P.A. and Gingerich, D.W. (2009). Varieties of capitalism and institutional complementarities in the political economy. *British Journal of Political Science*, Vol.39, No. 3, pp.449–482.
Hancké, B., Rhodes, M. and Thatcher, M. (eds.) (2008). *Beyond Varieties of Capitalism: Conflict, Contradictions and Complementarities*, (Oxford University Press, Oxford).
Herrigel, G. (1996). *Industrial Constructions. The Sources of German Industrial Power*, (Cambridge University Press, Cambridge).

Herrigel, G. and Zeitlin, J. (2010). Alternatives to varieties of capitalism. *Business History Review*, Vol. 84, (Winter), pp.667–674.
High, S. (2003). *Industrial Sunset: The Making of North America's Rust Belt, 1969–1984*, (University of Toronto Press, Toronto).
High, S., MacKinnon, L. and Perchard, A. (eds.) (2017). *The Deindustrialized World: Confronting Ruination in Postindustrial Place*, (University of British Columbia Press, Vancouver).
Howell, C. (2003). Review: Varieties of capitalism: And then there was one? *Comparative Politics*, Vol. 36, No. 1, pp.103–124.
Ingulstad, M., Perchard, A. and Storli, E. (eds.) (2014). *Tin and Global Capitalism, 1850–2000: A History of the "Devil's Metal"*, (Routledge, New York).
Jackson, G. and Deeg, R. (2008). Comparing capitalisms: Understanding institutional diversity and its implications for international business. *Journal of International Business Studies*, Vol. 39, No. 4, pp.540–561.
———. (2012). The long-term trajectories of institutional change in European capitalism. *Journal of European Public Policy* Vol. 19, No. 8, pp.1109–1125.
Kipping, M. (2003). Business-government relations: Beyond performance issues. In Amatori, F. and Jones, G. (eds.) *Business History Around the World: Comparative Perspectives in Business History*, (Cambridge University Press, Cambridge). pp.372–393.
Kipping, M. and Bjarnar, O. (eds.) (1998). *The Americanisation of European Business: The Marshall Plan and the Transfer of US Management Models*, (Routledge, New York).
Kiran, J. (2018). Expanding the framework of the varieties of capitalism. Turkey as a hierarchical market economy. *Journal of Eurasian Studies*, Vol. 9, No. 1, pp.42–51.
John, R.R. and Phillips-Fein, K. (eds.) (2016). *Capital Gains: Business and Politics in Twentieth-Century America*, (University of Pennsylvania Press, Philadelphia).
Lazonick, W. (1991). *Business Organization and the Myth of the Market Economy*, (Cambridge University Press, Cambridge).
MacKenzie, N.G. (2012). Be careful what you wish for: Comparative advantage and the Wilson Smelters Project, 1967–82. In Frøland, H.O. and Ingulstad, M. (eds.) *From Warfare to Welfare: Business-Government Relations in the Aluminium Industry*, (Tapir Akademisk Førlag, Trondheim). 163–198.
———. (2018). Creating market failure: Business-government relations in the British paper-pulp industry, 1950–1980. *Business History Review*, Vol. 52, No. 4, pp.719–741.
MacKenzie, N.G., Knox, S. and Hannon, M. (2020). Fast breeder technology and the entrepreneurial state in the UK. *Business History*. Special Issue Paper in the Atomic Business: Structures and Strategies.
Merchant, B. (2017). Life and death in apple's forbidden City. *The Observer*, 18th June 2017.
Mahoney, J. and Thelen, K. (eds.) (2010). *Explaining Institutional Change: Ambiguity, Agency, and Power*, (Cambridge University Press, Cambridge).
Mazzucato, M. (2013) *The Entrepreneurial State: Debunking Public vs. Private Sector Myths*, (Anthem Press, London).
McCraw, T. K. *Creating Modern Capitalism: How Entrepreneurs, Companies, and Countries Triumphed in Three Industrial Revolutions*. (Harvard University Press, 1997).
———. (2022). *The Mission Economy: A Moonshot Guide to Changing Capitalism*, (Penguin, London).
Miller, C.W. (2016) British naval armaments, cartels, and defence planning between the world wars. *Entreprises et histoire*, 85 (1), pp. 70–87.
———. 2017) Extraordinary Gentlemen: the Economic League, business networks, and organised labour in war planning and rearmament. *Scottish Labour History*, Vol. 52, pp. 120–151.
———. (2018). *Planning and Profits: British Naval Armaments and the Military-Industrial Complex*, (Liverpool University Press, Liverpool).
Millward, R. (2005). *Private and Public Enterprise in Europe: Energy, Telecommunications and Transport, 1830–1990*, (Cambridge University Press, Cambridge).
Mullen, S. (2013). A Glasgow-West India Merchant House and the imperial dividend, 1779–1867. *Journal of Scottish Historical Studies*, Vol. 33, No. 2, pp.196–233.

———. (2020). The rise of James Watt: Enlightenment, commerce, and industry in a British Atlantic merchant city, 1736–74. In Dick, M. and Archer-Parré, C. (eds.) *James Watt (1736 – 1819): Culture, Innovation and Enlightenment*, (Liverpool University Press, Liverpool), pp.39–61.

Musacchio, A. and Lazzarini, S.G. (2014). *Reinventing State Capitalism: Leviathan in Business, Brazil and Beyond*, (Harvard University Press, Cambridge, MA).

North, D.C. (1991). Institutions. *Journal of Economic Perspectives*, Vol.5, No.1, pp.97–112.

Peden, G.C. (2007). *Arms, Economics and British Strategy: From Dreadnoughts to Hydrogen Bombs*, (Cambridge University Press, Cambridge).

Perchard, A. (2012). *Aluminiumville: Government, Global Business and the Scottish Highlands*, (Carnegie, Lancaster).

———. (2019). This thing called goodwill: The Reynolds metals company and political networking in wartime America. *Enterprise & Society*, Vol.20, No. 4, pp.1044–1083.

Perchard, A and MacKenzie, N.G. (2020). Aligning to disadvantage: How corporate political activity and strategic homophily create path dependence in the firm. *Human Relations*. Vol. 74, No. 7, pp.978–1006.

Perchard, A., MacKenzie, N.G., Decker, S., and Favero, G. (2017). Clio in the business school: Historical approaches in strategy, international business and entrepreneurship. *Business History*, Vol.59, No. 6, pp.904–927.

Phillips-Fein, K. and Zelizer, J.E. (eds.) (2012). *What's Good for Business: Business and American Politics since World War II*. (Oxford University Press, Oxford).

Piore, M.J. and Sabel, C.F. (1984). *The Second Industrial Divide*, (Basic Books, New York).

Prieto, L.C. and Phipps, S.T.A. (2019). *African American Management History: Insights on Gaining a Cooperative Advantage*, (Emerald, London).

Radice, H. (2015). *Global Capitalism: Selected Essays*, (Routledge, London).

Rollings, N. (2014). The twilight world of British business politics: The Spring Sunningdale conferences since the 1960s. *Business History*, Vol. 56, No. 6, pp.915–935.

Scherner, J. (2013). Armament in the depth or armament in the breadth? German investments pattern and rearmament during the Nazi period. *Economic History Review*, Vol. 66, No.2, pp.497–517.

Schmidt, V. (2003). French capitalism transformed, yet still a third variety of capitalism. *Economy and society*, Vol. 32, No. 4, pp.526–554.

Schneider, B.R. (2009). Hierarchical market economies and varieties of capitalism in Latin America. *Journal of Latin American Studies*, Vol. 41, No. 3, pp.553–575.

Scranton, P. (2018). Managing communist enterprises: Poland, Hungary, and Czechoslovakia, 1945–1970. *Enterprise & Society*, Vol. 19, No. 3, pp.492–537.

———. (2019). You can trust the communists, really.... *Entreprises et histoire*, Vol. 94, No. 1, pp.207–208.

Scranton, P. and Fridenson, P. (2013). *Reimagining Business History*. John Hopkins University Press, Baltimore.

Shonfield, A. (1965). *Modern Capitalism – The Changing Balance of Public & Private Power*, (Oxford University Press, Oxford).

Sluyterman, K. (ed.) (2015). *Varieties of Capitalism and Business History: The Dutch Case*, (Routledge, New York).

Sparrow, J.T. (2011). *Warfare State: World War II Americans and the Age of Big Government*, (Oxford University Press, New York).

Stockwell, S. (2000). *The Business of Decolonisation. British Business Strategies in the Gold Coast*, (Oxford University Press, Oxford).

Stokes, R.G. (1988). *Divide and Prosper: The Heirs of I.G. Farben Under Allied Authority, 1945–1951*, (University of California Press, Berkeley).

Stokes, R.G. and Miller, C.W. (2018) Pollution and climate change. In da Silva Lopes, T., Lubinski, C. and Tworek, H. (eds.) *The Routledge Companion to the Makers of Global Business* (Routledge, Abingdon). 564–577.

Storli, E. (2014). Cartel theory and cartel practice: The case of the international aluminum cartels, 1901–1940. *Business History Review*, Vol. 88, No. 3, pp.445–467.

Thomas, D. and Westerhuis, G. (2014). *The Power of Corporate Networks: A Comparative and Historical Perspective*, (Routledge, London).

Tooze, A. (2006). *The Wages of Destruction: The Making and Breaking of the Nazi Economy*, (Allen Lane, London).

Turner, J. (ed.) (1984). *Businessmen and Politics: Studies of Business Activity in British Politics 1900–1945*, (Heinemann, London).

Viola, E., and Gonçalves, VK. (2019). Brazil ups and downs in global environmental governance in the 21st century. *Revista Brasileira de Política Internacional*, Vol. 62, No. 2, p. e010.

White, N.J. (1996). *Business, Government, and the End of Empire: Malaya, 1942–1957*, (Oxford University Press, Oxford).

———. (2004). *British Business in Post-Colonial Malaysia, 1957–70: Neo-colonialism or Disengagement?* (Routledge, London).

Whitley, R. (1999). *Divergent Capitalisms: The Social Structuring and Change of Business Systems*, (Oxford University Press, Oxford).

Wilkins, M. (2010). Multinational enterprises and the varieties of capitalism. *Business History Review*, Vol. 84, (Winter), pp.638–645.

Wilkins, M. and Hill, F.E. (2011). *American Business Abroad: Ford on Six Continents*, (Cambridge University Press, Cambridge).

Wilson, M.R. (2016). *Destructive Creation: American Business and the Winning of World War II*. (University of Pennsylvania Press, Philadelphia).

Wubs, B. (2008). *International Business and National War Interests: Unilever Between Reich and Empire*, (Routledge, London).

OPEN ACCESS

Shifts in government business relations: Assessing change using the restrictive business registers in the OECD, 1945–1995

Martin Shanahan and Susanna Fellman

ABSTRACT

The varieties of capitalism framework highlights the governance of firms' competitive behaviour as a key aspect of state-business relations. This article examines changes in the scope, intensity and transparency of cartel registers in 13 OECD countries in the half century following World War II. Quantifying these policy aspects over five decades using the OECD's 2013 *New Indicators of Competition Law and Policy* reveals changes in government-business relations over time, with different approaches evident in each country. The results reveal complex interactions effect policy in each country and challenge a simple 'Americanisation' explanation for changes in cartel policy and the static typology of the VoC literature.

Introduction

How governments regulate the behaviour of firms in market-based economies is at the heart of the relationship between capitalism and the state. This study examines the variation and development of a key policy instrument, the 'cartel register' that was used in many countries in the mid-20th century to identify and constrain anti-competitive behaviour. Our aim is to investigate how this instrument reflects the differing and gradual transitions in state-business relations from initially tolerant attitudes towards anti-competitive agreements to regulations that were intolerant of cartels and their activities. This policy, and its evolution serves as an explicit case-study of the relationship between the government and private sector

The varieties of capitalism (VoC) literature, most closely associated with the work of Hall and Soskice, and expanded by Hanke and others, examines patterns in countries' institutional and governance frameworks that organise capitalistic markets within their own boarders (Hall & Soskice, 2001; Hanke, Rhodes, & Thatcher, 2008). As part of a broader literature on comparative capitalism the VoC literature attempts to explain variations in economic performance using a framework that goes beyond a nation's proximity to the technological frontier or simple adherence to market-based solutions (Jackson & Deeg, 2006). The central

This is an Open Access article distributed under the terms of the Creative Commons Attribution-NonCommercial-NoDerivatives License (http://creativecommons.org/licenses/by-nc-nd/4.0/), which permits non-commercial re-use, distribution, and reproduction in any medium, provided the original work is properly cited, and is not altered, transformed, or built upon in any way.

idea is that institutions can provide a comparative advantage to an economy (or conversely produce a comparative disadvantage) and so affect economic performance.

> Something approaching a consensus has now emerged around the notion that national capitalisms are distinguished one from another by particular configurations of interlocking and interdependent political-economic institutions that produce different forms of behaviour on the part of economic actors, different economic and social outcomes, and different patterns of economic development. These distinct national capitalisms are quite resistant to pressures towards convergence upon a single model of capitalism (Howell et al., 2003, p. 103).

Institutions are important, not because they operate as individual elements in the economy, but because they have impact on the strategic interactions between firms and economic actors affecting the level of decentralised cooperation required to solve collective problems. In their original work, Hall and Soskice advanced the notion of two distinct classes of national capitalism; one that tended towards a liberal market economy (LME), captured in the examples of Australia, Canada, Ireland, New Zealand, the UK and the US and another class that tended toward a coordinated market economy (CME). The membership of this group included Austria, Belgium, Denmark, Finland, Iceland, Germany, Japan, The Netherlands, Norway, Sweden and Switzerland. Differences in institutional structures and processes resulted in different responses to economic stresses and different 'patterns' of capitalism. For example, liberal market economies could be characterised as being able to make relatively rapid adjustments in their capital and labour markets. Driven more by markets, competitive pressures and with economic actors more at 'arms' length' such economies are heavily influenced by market mechanisms and shaped by market outcomes. Coordinated market economies, however, are characterised as those where firms have a more 'connected' and 'committed' relationship to each other, and to other actors in the economy. The state can also be quite active in coordinating the market mechanism. The result is a slower ability to respond to market signals, but higher quality labour and productivity outcomes because of their enhanced consultative processes and more interconnected links between labour and capital. The LME and CME both represent 'ideal types' and the variations between countries can be considerable.

Despite the insights of their approach, however, there are difficulties with the VoC approach. As recently noted, determining which institutions are critical in these comparative studies, and then delimiting their individual areas of influence using a comprehensive model, is challenging (Rougier & Combarnous, 2017, p. 71). In broad terms, the VoC model identified as critical: 1) industrial and labour relations; 2) corporate governance and finance; 3) product market regulation and inter-firm relations; 4) training and education systems; and 5) level and type of social protection (Rougier & Combarnous, 2017, p. 71). Clearly, identifying and separating these categories is not always simple; for example, delineating corporate governance from inter-firm relations; or labour relations from a nation's social protection system, may result in arbitrary (and potentially false) differences being identified between nations. This has led some researchers to include additional sectors.[1]

The organising concepts behind the models, such as a sector's 'governance mechanisms' may also be vague and difficult to define. For example, given Douglass North's definition of what institutions are, such categories need to be broad enough to include both formal institutional structures and national attitudes. Efforts to measure 'institutions' have revealed the difficulty of producing commonly accepted estimates of institutions; or that other factors (such as human capital) appear to be more fundamental (Glaeser, La Porta, Lopez-de-Silanes, & Shleifer, 2004; North, 1990).

Other criticisms of the VoC literature are that it is 'incomplete' (underestimating the multiple roles of the state); path-dependent and overly static; 'mechanistic' in its determinism, overly simple, and with a heavy bias toward countries and institutions with a significant manufacturing sector (Hanke, Rhodes, & Thatcher, 2008, pp. 6–9). It has also been suggested that the varieties of capitalism thesis is time dependent (Howell, 2003) as the thesis better explains the stable 1990s than the unstable 1970s.

Ahlquist and Christian undertook a careful review of the original country clusters posited by Hall and Soskice (Ahlquist & Breunig, 2009). Using a mixed-model clustering analysis, they examined the stability and consistency of the identified clusters in three different periods; 1980–1984; 1990–1994 and 2000–2003. They found that not only did the number of 'like' clusters (based on statistical measures of association) vary over these periods but also that individual countries shifted between clusters in different periods. They concluded that while they had not disproved the varieties of capitalism literature, they had shown that the clusters were not as stable or consistent as the literature implied, and that great care needed to be taken to avoid circular reasoning.[2] They suggested the characterisation of countries as CME or LME should be considered as ideal-types that could alert researchers to look for patterns of 'institutional complementarities' to explain different outcomes - but that the differences may be in more specific areas (such as wages or monetary policy). Examining the historical development of LME and CME countries from 1900 onwards, others found little evidence that the characteristics associated with each ideal-type persisted over time, strengthening the argument that the patterns proposed by the VoC literature are period specific (Schneider & Paunescu, 2012; Shanahan, 2012).

Research question and approach

Our research takes its point of departure from these debates. Separate from the VoC literature are current historical interpretations of economic development of advanced economies in the decades after WWII and the importance of American attitudes towards markets, competition and trade in shaping those economies. As one aspect of this, it has been suggested that the competition and cartel policies in many countries (and especially many OECD countries) after World War II were a direct result of their Americanisation. It is suggested that America's strong anti-trust approach to cartels something that developed in the United States in the 1890s, was transferred to many European and developed countries, directly for example, through the US occupation in Germany and later via consultants and experts in European institutions. American attitudes and models also penetrated Europe indirectly suggesting to some interpreters that the process was inevitable and occurred in a relatively similar manner across a range of countries (Djelic, 2002; Edwards, 1967; Leucht, 2009; Leucht & Marquis, 2013; Schröter, 2005, 2010).

By showing the varied paths and occasionally slow transitions towards less tolerant attitudes regarding anti-competitive behaviour, this article challenges the static VoC categories and the 'inevitable' Americanisation interpretation of Europe's competition policy history. While the overall significance of American influence is clear, and international convergence on economic models and competition policy obvious, the transition has been complex and followed national paths.

Despite the insights provided by the VoC approach there are problems with identifying the critical patterns of similarity or difference in governance mechanisms that ultimately impact on economic performance. The critical literature suggests the results depend on the time period selected and the breadth of institutions analysed. One way forward would be to examine an extended period (perhaps 50 years), but focus on a comparatively narrow, but critical aspect in state-business relations. Given a sufficient number of studies that examine particular aspects of state-business relations, or individual aspects of wage setting, or financial markets it would be possible to construct a more nuanced analysis of the similarities and differences between nations and the changes in these areas over time.

Similarly, the Americanisation interpretation of European nations' competition policy fails to take account of the important variations between countries' economies, political parties, and national histories (Segreto & Wubs, 2014). After WWII, different countries faced different economic and social challenges, and there was considerable variation in national attitudes towards cartels and other forms of cooperative behaviour. Moreover, competition legislation was the focus of strong lobbying from various economic sectors and industries, often dressed as being in the 'national interest', and which affected the outcome of the legislation. A close examination of the transition of national policies governing anti-competitive behaviour would reveal whether nations were simply 'swept along' in their adoption of American style anti-trust legislation, or whether their paths of policy development were more unique.

This article investigates how and when the content, enforcement and transparency of cartel registers changed after World War II. We do this by creating a form of 'tolerance index' for the individual countries, at specific points of time. While the end-point in most countries was the adoption of legislation that criminalised or heavily punished cartel-like behaviour, the results show that the path to this final position varied greatly between nations. We demonstrate this historical journey in national competition policies and how anti-cartel policies differed between countries in ways that were not always consistent with the VoC framework.

The article is in four sections. The first briefly introduces the cartel registers, explains their aims and methods and demonstrates the degree of national variation between them, despite their relatively common objectives. Section two discusses the recent OECD competition indicator that we adapt to measure change in the register-legislation and the data sources on which this assessment is based (Alemani, Klein, Koske, Vitale, & Wanner, 2013). Section three presents the results of this analysis for 13 countries over the five decades of the second half of the twentieth century. Finally, section four presents our conclusions and overall assessment development of policies designed to inhibit anti-competitive business practices in the OECD.

Cartel registers

The Sherman Act of 1890 and the Clayton Act of 1914 are usually taken as delineating the starting date of American's strong anti-cartel (anti-trust) attitudes. The Europeans, by contrast, were less antagonistic towards cartels, probably because of the proportion of family businesses in Europe and the perception that only cooperation could help European businesses compete against their US counterparts.[3] The European approach attempted to balance the potentially harmful activities of cartels against the benefits of cooperation they might create (Edwards, 1967; Thorelli, 1959; Timberg, 1953). The inter-war period is seen as the highpoint for cartels in Europe and countries outside the American sphere of influence. Inter-firm collaborations were frequently regarded as promoting stability and cooperation, especially via export cartels that advanced the national interest. Many forms of business collaboration and restrictive practices were not targeted by governments and were occasionally promoted in times of crises and wars (Bertilorenzi, 2016).

This approach did not go completely unchallenged, however. While the cooperative movement expressed its concern about the impact of cartels on smaller firms and consumers, and legal and economic experts too expressed their reservations, the consensus of the 1927 League of Nations report was that business combinations were not necessarily bad, but must be judged by their impact (Hirsch, 1926). They recommended a policy of watching and learning (Bertilorenzi, 2016). Four years later, however, the reports of another international committee suggest the tide had turned against cartels and recommended publicly identifying offenders and their agreements (McGowan, 2010).[4] The dominance of the US economy after WWII, with its free-enterprise approach and trade liberalisation, and cartels' close association with fascist systems saw attitudes shift against anti-competitive practices. For nations to participate in the modern, international economy required the old rules of comfortable business arrangements be overturned, especially if they might hamper change or cause inflationary pressures. As a consequence, several European countries introduced competition legislation, although these usually did not ban anti-competitive agreements outright.

Influenced by their previous interactions with business, European regulators focused more on the effects of the anti-competitive practices than on the agreements themselves, balancing the pros and cons of cartel behaviour, frequently on a case-by-case basis (Harding & Joshua, 2010, p. 40.) Consideration was given to the public interest, business and consumer interests, as well as economic and political goals. Through the 1950s, 1960s and 1970s, balancing such considerations also saw modifications to the cartel legislation – as each nation followed the path it viewed as best serving its own interests. By the last two decades of the 20th century, however, supranational policies (such as those required by EU membership) required individual nations to meet externally imposed standards when tackling non-competitive agreements within their own borders. Harsher legislation directly prohibiting firm cooperation became the new norm.

While the national attitude to cartels when legislation was introduced can reveal how tolerant (or not) government regulators were, it is also possible to use the modifications made to the legislation after it became enacted, as a measure of change in national business-government relations, and the degree to which countries solved the 'coordination problem' between market processes and market outcomes. If the legislation governing firms' anti-competitive behaviour remained relatively unchanged, for example, this suggests a relatively static government-business relationship and perhaps that the internal national vested interests are influential. If there were real modifications to the initial legislative settings, it may be that the business-state relationship is more dynamic than proposed by the VoC framework, or that factors external to the nation (i.e. trade openness) are (or become) influential. In any case, overlooking legislative and regulatory change reduces our understanding of how business-government relationships vary over time and how market economies transform. Change is usually a gradual rather than revolutionary process.

Business regulations and the rules designed to promote competition are the outcome of many influences including a nation's traditional attitudes to competition ('competition culture') and the role of the state, the relative importance of particular industries, pressure groups, individual actors, international trends and the overall balance between the economy, development and standard of living. They are also a critical element in defining the relationship between government and business – a dimension at the core of the VoC literature.

Cartel registers were one form of regulation that occurred in many nations in the twentieth century. These registers, which existed to chronicle anti-competitive agreements, adopted a wide variety of approaches, revealing a broad range of potential influences (Fellman & Shanahan, 2016). The term 'cartel register' or 'restrictive practices register' refers to the instrument that recorded restrictive trade practices used by businesses to manipulate their markets and lessen competitive forces. These instruments frequently formed one element of a government's broader competition policy.[5] For example, some reflected agreements which were under government control (an approach labelled 'anti-abuse' or 'tolerant') while others only recorded agreements exempt from overall prohibition (an 'anti-trust' or a 'non-tolerant' approach) (Schröter, 2010). Some jurisdictions were legalistic in their enforcement, while others were informal or even 'voluntary'. Some registers were designed to publicise market manipulation; others were secret registers not open to the public. All were designed, however, to govern in some way, anticompetitive business agreements. Given such variation, cartel registers and their content can reveal aspects of the central relationship between governments and the capitalist actors (firms) and markets within their jurisdiction.

This article takes advantage of the variation in regulation of cartel behaviour to detect whether there was any association between this variation and a country's classification as a liberal market economy or a coordinated market economy. Finding only circumstantial evidence of an association we quantify dimensions of the anti-competitive regulations, and their changes over time, to detect whether these shifts to cartel register legislation appear to be the result of the 'coordination' mechanism associated with being either a CME or LME economy, or whether the changes are clearly consistent with an American-type 'anti-trust', pro-competition influence.

More than a simple record and monitor, the registers were also used by some competition authorities as a mechanism to alter firms' behaviour. This variation around a common legislative form can be compared against the VoC categories of a nation being either a coordinated market economy (CME) or a liberal market economy (LME). Table 1 reports the dates when cartel registers were introduced, (as early as 1920 in Norway, and as late as 1967 in Australia). It is also classifies whether the initial legislation (which changed over the decades) was initially highly tolerant, tolerant, intolerant or very intolerant of business behaviour that was anti-competitive, by identifying how restrictive was the initial form of legislation. This categorisation is of course a crude first-estimate (based on earlier assessment of each country's attitudes) and our further calculations from the model developed here will provide a more fine-grained picture (Fellman & Shanahan, 2016). Finally, it reports Hall and Soskice's classification of each nation as either LME or CME.

As is clear from the table, despite the register being a common form of governance of firm behaviour, there is no clear pattern of adoption by either the LME or CME coded nations. Our data set, which collected records from countries where information about the register was available for an extended period, suggests that both coordinated and liberal market

Table 1. Thirteen OECD countries with cartel registers in the 20th century and the VoC categorisation.

Country	Original legislation	Tolerance of restrictive practices (year legislation introduced)	Type of register	Liberal Market or Coordinated Market Economy
Norway	Price Regulation Act	Tolerant (1920)	Public	CME
Denmark	Law on Price Agreements; replaced by Monopolies Supervision Act 1955	Highly Tolerant (1937)	Public	CME
Sweden	Act on Probation on Restrictive Business Practices	Highly Tolerant (1946)	Public	CME
Japan	Act on Prohibition of Private Monopolization and Maintenance of Fair Trade	Highly Intolerant (1947/1953)	Public	CME
United Kingdom	Monopolies and Restrictive Practices (Inquiry and Control) Act	Intolerant (1956)	Public	LME
Germany	Law against Restraints in Competition	Intolerant (1957)	Public	CME
Finland	Act on the Control of Practices Restricting Economic Competition	Highly Tolerant (1957)	Public	CME
Netherlands	Economic Competition Act	Highly Tolerant (1958)	Secret	CME
New Zealand	Trade Practices Act	Intolerant (1958)	Public	LME
Austria	Cartels Act	Tolerant (1951)	Public	CME
Israel	Restrictive Trade Practices Act	Intolerant (1959)	Public	n.c
Spain	Act to Afford Protection Against Activities that Reduce Competition	Intolerant (1963)	Public	n.c
Australia	Trade Practices Act	Highly Tolerant (1967)	Secret	LME

Note: Of the 35 current members of the OECD, more than 14 had cartel registers during the 20th century. Other countries that had cartel registers include Hungary, Poland, Czechoslovakia, Yugoslavia and Italy and Bulgaria, but these are omitted from this analysis due to lack of information about the content of their registers. The registers in the Eastern European countries were abolished after WWII, when these countries became part of the socialist bloc.

Degrees of tolerance: Highly tolerant (ban no restrictive practices; only control); tolerant (bans some specific practices; no general ban); intolerant (in principle bans; allow exemptions); highly intolerant (ban most; few exceptions).

n.c. – not originally classified by Hall and Soskice Varieties of Capitalism.

Sources: As in Table 2 plus Borrel, 1998; Hunter, 1963; Thorelli, 1959; Rampilla, 1989.

Table 2. Dates cartel registers were introduced and ended in selected OECD countries.

Country	Register first considered (ie first mentioned in debates)	Register legislation created	Register began operation	Year ended	Years in existence
Norway	1919	1920	1920	1993	73
Denmark	1920/1930	1937	1938	1989	52
Sweden	1936	1946	1947	1993	47
Japan	1952	1953	1954	1999	46
Austria	1898/1948	1951	1952	2006	55
United Kingdom	1955	1956	1956	1989	33
Germany	1923/1952	1957	1958	1985	28
Finland	1952	1957	1959	1992	35
Netherlands	1941/1956	1958	1959	1998	40
New Zealand	Na	1958	1958	1961	3
Israel	1956	1960	1960	1988	28
Spain	1962	1963	1964	1989	26
Australia	1959	1965	1967	1975	9

Sources: Compiled from: Bhattacharjea, 2012; Collinge, 1969; Edwards, 1967; Hunter, 1961; Jaffe, 1967; Kestenbaum, 1973; OECD, 1964, 1971, 1978b; OECD, 1967–1975; OECD, 1978a; OECD, 1987, 1991, 1993, 1995, 1997, 2007; OECD, 1998.

economies used registers as a policy instrument. Half of Hall and Soskice's original six LME nations (Australia, New Zealand and the United Kingdom) and almost three quarters of their CME nations (Austria, Denmark, Finland, Germany, Japan, The Netherlands, Norway, and Sweden) adopted a register.[6] While most of the countries that were tolerant towards cartels when the register legislation was introduced were also coordinated economies, the link between intolerance and categorisation as a liberal market economy is not as clear-cut. There were only two cases where the register documentation was not made public; one case was in the Netherlands (a CME) and the other case was in Australia (an LME).

One interpretation of these patterns is that the cartel register is not, as is claimed, an insightful tool by which to identify countries' governance of businesses and the role of markets. Given that the legislation establishing a register is directly focused on identifying (and in some cases reducing) firms' anti-competitive activities, this interpretation does not seem reasonable. A second interpretation is that the link between government, business and markets is more complex than the binary categorisation proposed under the VoC. It is assumed here that the interaction between the state, business and markets is relatively complex, changes over time, and is influenced by the history and the particular institutional circumstances found in each nation.

Variation between nations

While the label 'restrictive practices register' or 'cartel register' identifies a policy mechanism that dealt with firms' anti-competitive activities, there was considerable variation in how the various registers operated. As already highlighted by the categorisation of legislation as ranging from highly tolerant to highly intolerant, government policies varied in the type of activities they targeted, how they were used by the authorities, and the vigour with which they were implemented.

The activities and forms of anti-competitive behaviour included in the registers also differed. In some countries, it included virtually all anti-competitive agreements, as well as mergers and acquisitions and firms in dominant market positions, while in others only vertical and horizontal agreements were registered. Resale price maintenance, which directly impacted on consumers, was often made an offence, but not in every jurisdiction. In some nations, the registers recorded firms with written agreements to engage in anti-competitive behaviour; in others, all known agreements were recorded. In some countries, the records included firms that had restrictive agreements, while in others the registers recorded firms granted exemption from prosecution for being involved in such agreements. At least some of these variations were likely due to the impact of lobbying on the policy creators and the politics associated with creating legislation. This has been discussed elsewhere (Fellman & Shanahan, 2018).

Table 3 provides a simplified categorisation of the possible variations in form, content, and approach associated with the regulatory instrument labelled a 'cartel register'. Within this narrow slice of competition policy, the variation in these dimensions represents the range of potential 'solutions' to what has been termed 'the coordination problems' facing both LME and CME countries (Hall & Soskice, 2001).

Method

In 2013, OECD researchers proposed a set of competition law and policy indicators (Alemani et al., 2013).[7] We essentially follow a modified version of their approach in the analysis that follows. This reveals the extent to which national legislation is tolerant (or not) toward restrictive business practices as well as categorising aspects of the complexity of such legislation.

Table 3. Categorisation of variation in range of aims, contents and enforcement of cartel registers in the 20th century.

	Possible range of variation	
Aim of Register	Prohibit outright (intolerant)	Prevent Abuse (tolerant of existence)
Types of agreements	All forms (written or verbal)	Only written included
Content of Register/Forms of agreement	All forms of market manipulation prohibited	Selected forms of manipulation
	Horizontal. Vertical, full-price forcing, market sharing, tender rigging,	Typically horizontal agreements
	Include merger and acquisitions	Excludes mergers and acquisitions
Enforcement mechanisms	Public exposure (shaming)	Authorities record (have a record)
	Use of law courts (prosecution)	Quiet discussion (persuasion)
	Vigorous pursuit	Minimal efforts to enforce policy
Level of transparency	Transparent (publicly accessible)	Not transparent (closed)
Coverage	Entire economy (including export industries)	Partial coverage of select industries

Source: Fellman and Shanahan 'Regulating Competition'.

Even countries that have adopted strictly non-tolerant policies over the past two decades often adopt different targets, and practices in enforcing their policies. The OECD report focuses first on the scope of action of the authorities (legal powers to investigate, impose sanctions or block mergers or other anti-competitive behaviour); secondly on their policies toward anti-competitive behaviour (methods to counter or reveal various forms of anti-competitive behaviour); and thirdly, on their probity of investigation (independence and accountability of authorities and their fairness in their actions). Thus, modern analysis of contemporary competition policies sees the focus increasingly on the efficiency of the authorities and their independence from interest groups and their influence, and less on the formal legislation itself. The 2013 report concludes that the competition regimes in the OECD are broadly similar and close to 'best practice', while the real differences between jurisdictions lie in the implementation of their legislation (Alemani et al., 2013). Their method of assessing the relationship between government and business, in the field of competition policy, lends itself to examining changes in the efficacy and impact of cartel registers in the decades after WWII, although it has to be simplified for our historical investigation.[8]

The indicators proposed by the 2013 OECD study that focus on the scope of policies are the most useful for our analysis of cartel register policies. A diagrammatic representation of the indicators' categories, and their sub-elements used in this study is reflected in Figure 1. For example, the 'scope' of any country's cartel register is assessed against four elements, that include: the number of sectors of the economy the legislation covered; the percentage of restrictive agreements included; whether international agreements were included, and whether the activities of foreign-owned companies operating inside a country were required to be included on the register. Each element is given a value ranging from zero (not required) to a maximum of six (for sectors covered).[9] The values and meanings of each element are given in detail in Appendix 1.

For our purposes, this approach quantifies changes in one important governance relationship between the government and the private sector and provides the case-study evidence with which to assess the consistency of VoC categorisations. The results also allow us to examine the path state-government relations travelled in this field of regulation and assess whether the changes appear to be a direct consequence of the 'Americanisation' of competition policy. Beginning with either a tolerant or non-tolerant attitude to cartels, the evidence reveals the comparative changes to the duration, scope, activities and transparency of the registers over almost 50 years of regulation.

Competition Indicators

Scope of Action	Activity Registered	Transparency of Register
Elements within each indicator		
No. of Sectors covered	Horizontal Agreements	Public or Secret
% of restrictive agreements included	Vertical Agreements	Vigour of application
Inclusion of international agreements	Refusal to deal/boycott	
Inclusion of foreign owned companies	Excusive Dealing	
	Dominant firm	
	Resale Price maintenance	
Number of Years Legislation in Operation*	Mergers & Acquisitions	

Figure 1. Overview of Register indicators. Source: Based on OECD study by Alemani et al. (2013). Notes: *This category was classified as a separate competition indicator in the scales that follow.

Having collected data from historical documents relating to the registers, we tabulate and rank each country's register along the three dimensions of scope, activity and transparency in each decade from 1950 to 2000.[10] Given the variation in start and end dates, not every country appears in each panel. While many elements may trigger change in government policy, and cause a modification of the register, our focus is on the relative changes that occurred in different dimensions of the registers themselves.

The key data source for this approach is the series of OECD publications on restrictive business practices published regularly since the 1960s. These present summaries of member countries' legislation together with regular follow-ups of any legislative changes. These are supplemented with reports from individual countries, and analysis by contemporary commentators, to construct a series of observations on the registers in 13 countries.

The balance in the instrument's measures of duration, scope, activity and transparency is reflected in the maximum aggregates possible for each indicator: 10 for duration; 11 for scope; 7 for activity and 2 for transparency. The total score is expressed as a percentage to assist comparisons.[11]

Results

Tables 4a and 4b report the key variations in the legislation covering restrictive trade practices legislation in 13 OECD countries for the decades of the 1950s, 1960s, 1970s, 1980s, and 1990s. Collectively Table 4 incorporates the four most important dimensions of the administrative and legislative permutations within each register policy and quantifies these into four simple numerical scores to improve comparability.[12] A total percentage score is recorded as a summary of all four dimensions. The results are a relative measure of the collective 'impact' of a nation's register policy. As the registers changed over time, we report scores,

Table 4a. Relative impact of national anti-competition registers.

	1950s					1960s				
Impact measure	Duration	Scope	Activity	Transp.	Total	Duration	Scope	Activity	Transp.	Total
Max score	**10**	**11**	**7**	**2**	**100**	**10**	**11**	**7**	**2**	**100**
Norway	10	6	6	2	**80.0**	10	6	6	2	**80.0**
Denmark	10	5	5	2	**73.3**	10	5	5	2	**73.3**
Sweden	10	6	5	2	**76.7**	10	6	6	2	**80.0**
Austria	8	5	5	2	**66.7**	10	5	5	2	**73.3**
Japan	6	8	7	1	**73.3**	10	7	7	1	**83.3**
UK.	4	3	3	1	**36.7**	10	3	6	2	**70.0**
Germany	2	4	6	2	**46.7**	10	4	6	2	**73.3**
Finland	1	5	3	1	**33.3**	10	5	4	1	**66.7**
Netherlands	1	6	4		**36.7**	10	6	4	1	**70.0**
New Zealand	2	6	7	1	**53.3**	1	6	7	1	**50.0**
Israel						10	6	6	1	**76.7**
Spain						6	5	4	1	**53.3**
Australia						3	5	5	1	**46.7**
	1970s					**1980s**				
Impact measure	Duration	Scope	Activity	Transp.	Total	Duration	Scope	Activity	Transp.	Total
Norway	**10**	6	5	2	**76.7**	**10**	7	6	2	**83.3**
Denmark	10	5	5	2	**73.3**	9	5	5	2	**70.0**
Sweden	10	7	6	2	**83.3**	10	7	6	2	**83.3**
Austria	10	6	6	2	**80.0**	10	7	6	2	**83.3**
Japan	10	7	6	1	**80.0**	10	8	7	2	**90.0**
UK.	10	6	6	2	**80.0**	9	8	6	2	**83.3**
Germany	10	4	6	2	**73.3**	10	4	5	1	**66.7**
Finland	10	6	6	2	**80.0**	10	4	5	1	**66.7**
Netherlands	10	6	4	1	**70.0**	10	6	4	1	**70.0**
New Zealand										
Israel	10	8	6	1	**83.3**	8	8	7	1	**80.0**
Spain	10	6	6	1	**76.7**	9	6	6	1	**73.3**
Australia	5	6	6	1	**60.0**					

Notes: Adapted from Alemani et al. (2013) and Lee (2007). For details of values, see Appendix 1.
Sources: See Tables 1 and 2.

Table 4b. Relative impact of national anti-competition registers.

	1990s				
Impact measure	Duration	Scope	Activity	Transp.	Total
Max score	**10**	**11**	**7**	**2**	**100**
Norway	3	8	6	2	**63.3**
Denmark					
Sweden	3	7	6	2	**60.0**
Austria	10	8	6	2	**86.7**
Japan	9	10	7	2	**93.3**
UK.					
Germany					
Finland	2	7	6	2	**56.7**
Netherlands	8	8	7	1	**80.0**
New Zealand					
Israel					
Spain					
Australia					

Notes: Adapted from Alemani et al. (2013) and Lee (2007). For details of values, see Appendix 1.
Sources: See Tables 1 and 2.

for each decade of the 1950s to 1990s, capturing the change in each country's policy over time. The scores are mostly comparable within the period to which they refer, as legislative changes over time redefined activities (usually broadening the mandated behaviour). This is even though the number of activities proscribed in legislation increased over time in most jurisdictions. One issue is that when some types of agreements were eventually banned, they disappeared from the legislation as such behaviour was no longer registered. In our model these behaviours also disappear, as our focus is to reveal changes to the cartel legislation and its scope, implementation and transparency, rather than measure a nation's entire statutory transition toward more anti-cartel legislation.[13] On the repeal of the entire register legislation, the jurisdiction disappears from our measure entirely.

It is immediately obvious that the use of the cartel register as a form of governance, while used extensively in the 1950s, reached its peak in our 13 sampled OECD countries in the 1960s, diminishing only marginally in the 1970s and the 1980s. By the 1990s, however, the use of the register as a form of anti-cartel policy had disappeared from the statute books of most of our sampled countries.

Japan achieved the legislation with the widest scope (achieving 10/11 in the 1990s), while many of the Nordic countries' legislation was broadly applied for several decades. Countries that exhibited the narrowest range of areas covered by the legislation were Germany, which exempted many sectors from the legislation, Australia (and briefly) New Zealand. The United Kingdom went from an initially narrow scope (score 3) to the 1980s when it achieved a score of 8. Overall the scope of coverage generally enlarged over the decades.

The measure 'activity' which takes account of the various types of agreements covered within the sectors covered by the legislation was generally sustained through the decades. The exceptions were the UK and Finland which started with a relatively low number of agreements in the 1950s.[14] Again Japan scored highly in this field, as did the Netherlands in the 1990s. As with the results for scope, activity scores generally increased over the decades.

Transparency (with a maximum score of 2) was mostly impacted by the legislative requirement that the registers were either public documents or secretly recorded. In all cases where the registers were initially secret, they remained so over the period of the legislation. The vigour with which the legislation was enforced (also included in this category) also increased over time (and the exception, however, is Spain).

Calculating scores for four dimensions immediately highlights the importance of continuity in regulatory regimes. Countries where the registers existed for extended periods (e.g. Austria, Norway, Denmark, Japan) were likely more influential in shaping firms' behaviour than countries where the register existed for only a short period. This is not equivalent to saying there was necessarily less anti-competitive behaviour as a result, but rather, that the longer a regime is in place, the more firms are likely to modify (in one way or another) their behaviour. A more embedded 'competition culture' develops. Consumers and other interest groups in the market also adapt their expectations to the view that collusion and anti-competitive behaviour is not acceptable. To determine whether the regulatory framework produced relatively more intense pressure on firms, however, requires consideration of the other dimensions of application – such as the range of sectors covered, the activities included in the register and the degree to which firms' behaviour was revealed publicly. This is the intention behind quantifying these other dimensions.

The transition towards less tolerant legislation took a variety of paths. Based on the scores for legislative scope, activity and transparency reported in Tables 4a and 4b, Figure 2 depicts changes in the 'tolerance index' and reveals the various paths followed by each nation; and that each country gradually shifted from more to less tolerant cartel registration legislation

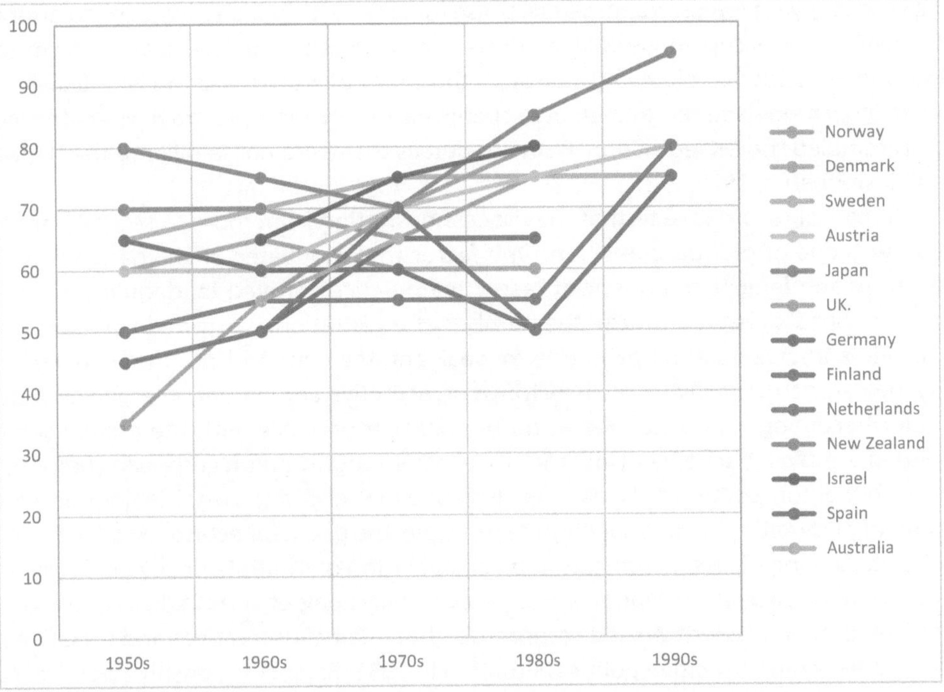

Figure 2. Trends in the scope, activity and transparency of anti-competitive business registers in 13 OECD countries after WWII.
Note: Based on total scores for each country reported in Tables 4a and 4b, but excluding scores for duration. Several countries prohibited anti-competitive behaviour outright in the 1980s. Including varying low duration scores in this decade misrepresents the shift to less tolerant legislation.

over 50 years. Some nations were 'early adopters', but it took a long time for them to 'toughen' their approach. This is best exemplified by Norway, which first legislated in 1920 but only adopted zero-tolerance legislation in the 1990s. On the other hand, the Norwegian legislation was not completely toothless compared, for example, to Finland or Sweden during the first decades. Finland was included by Thorelli among the early starters, but the first statute was especially weak and remained so for a long time. On some occasions, the direction of change was reversed and legislation impeding anti-competitive practices was weakened, as in Japan in 1953 (Ohata & Kurosawa, 2016). Finally, there were other examples (i.e. Spain) where intolerant legislation was so meekly enforced as to make the actual policy environment quite accepting of anti-competitive practices. In other situations (e.g. Australia) the proposed legislation was successfully opposed for several years before an acceptable (weakened) consensus emerged, while in other countries such as New Zealand, comparatively strong legislation was passed only to be quickly (within three years) taken off the statute books.

Countries which held public accountability in high regard mostly created registers that were open to public inspection (e.g. Sweden, Denmark, Norway) while more secretive approaches were adopted in Australia and the Netherlands. To judge a strong anti-trust framework as definitive of the actual competitive environment or to equate the development of such a framework with the process of modernisation is thus overly simplistic.

The influence of America's antitrust fervour also differed between countries. In the case of Japan and Germany the rapid implementation of an anti-cartel policy was a direct result of the US occupying forces. Nonetheless, these initially harsh policies were eased after the withdrawal of the occupying administrations. In many cases countries learned from their neighbours (like the Nordic countries, or in the cases of Australia and New Zealand) or adopted legal models suited to their own circumstance, for example Israel where the legislation resembled the UK legislation, but with details that were not familiar to the UK legislation (Kestenbaum, 1973).

The historical record reveals that the process of shifting from more to less tolerant legislation was one of gradual transition. One factor that motivated such change was that registration and lenient treatment of restrictive practices proved inadequate to trigger changes in firms' behaviour. Often the number of registrations remained very low, (as in the UK, Finland, Austria and Spain) due to weak enforcement and/or firms' reluctance to notify their agreements. Over time new forms of restrictive agreement emerged as important, later becoming totally banned as authorities lost patience with the private sector's continued use of such schemes. Until the arrival of a strong common European competition policy national competition policies were also less a matter of anti-trust ideology and more a matter of pragmatic problem solving. For example, the quest for economic advancement required balancing different interests and consideration of multiple policy goals (growth, price moderation, a peaceful labour market, social policy goals etc.). As in the case of Austria, the first legislation was written as a compromise between conservatives and social democrats in an extremely sensitive political situation in 1951. Balancing sensitive political considerations marked the cartel law in Austria for decades (Hoffmann, 1969). Such balancing and multiple goals also explains why the transition to less tolerant legislation often occurred in small increments; there were multiple goals to consider simultaneously. In 1953 Timberg observed

> .... the national legislation in this field [in Europe] differs in broadness of legal scope, detail of administrative articulation, extent of economic activity covered, intensiveness of enforcement, and animating public policy objectives. These differences are only partially due to the diverse economic circumstances and organic and legal institutions ... They depend largely on the balance (or lack of it) which individual countries have drawn between two 'liberal' principles –freedom of trade and competition on the one hand, and freedom of contract and association on the other. (Timberg, 1953, p. 445).

Our examination of the various economic, legal, and development factors potentially influencing the cartel registers, would appear to be consistent with his observations. To this we would add the importance of policy path dependence in explaining the different policy journeys in each country.

Conclusions

Our conclusions, based on the evidence presented in the cartel register policies of 13 OECD countries, is that each followed different paths to a common, supra-nationally imposed end; the outright prohibition of serious cartel conduct. Our results also show national variations in the timing, extent and transitions in both the pace and scope of legislation that established and expanded the registers of anti-competitive business practices in these countries. Tables 4a and 4b also reflect the rise of these registers, which were originally restricted to selected countries in the 1950s, and which then expanded rapidly in the 1960s before declining in use though the 1970s and 1980s. Originally the legislation was designed to register, and in some countries, through public pressure or administrative action curb anti-competitive behaviour. By the 1990s most had been superseded by other forms of legislation that were far less tolerant and which explicitly prohibited or, in some jurisdictions, criminalised anti-competitive behaviour among firms

Our work highlights variations in the 'starting points' for such legislation in each country, Some began with comparatively tolerant and open attitudes to cartel-like behaviour; others were less tolerant, but not prepared to aggressively prohibit such activities. In all cases the technique of establishing a register served the administrative purpose of formalising government-business regulations in this field of private sector activity and signalled governments' attitudes to anti-competitive arrangements. As these attitudes hardened, and businesses appeared little affected by the registration process, so the legislation changed in response to the particular national priorities.

This case study of one critical intersection between government and business and their gradual transition, also suggests that the VoC categories are too statistically oriented to explain such gradual shifts and they fail to reflect the dynamic evolution of government-business relations. The VoC focus on institutional complementarities, can however provide some insight into the transition from tolerant to intolerant attitudes. As mentioned, policies in different countries were often a result of balancing a number of interests, and a range of policy goals other than competition in the market. This reinforces the point that competition legislation is always one component in a larger institutional, political and legislative framework – or regime – and to understand individual features, needs to be studied in context.

We further conclude from this evidence that the simple narrative that many European anti-cartel policies were the result of post WWII 'Americanisation' overlooks the multiple policy variants and important nuances that occurred over 50 years. While there was US influence, especially within the EU where there were direct contacts, how this influenced individual member countries or countries outside of the EC is complex and needs to be studied in detail. As we observe, it was not uncommon that a jurisdiction modelled its approach on policies drawn from a neighbouring country and/or a large European nation. Influence from other jurisdiction was diffused via several steps and 'filters'.

In many countries, the establishment of registers and the stepwise changes to legislation on anti-competitive agreements began as part of a process of 'watching and waiting'. For many years, the optimum approach to anti-competitive behaviour was to learn and observe. Moreover, some industries and lobby groups were able to stall the development towards a tighter legislation, which also slowed change towards more non-tolerant practices. In several of these countries, cartels and restrictive trade agreements were occasionally even considered beneficial, not only for the firms themselves, but also for the economy and other actors in the market, by preventing fluctuations. To change such attitudes was a slow process. Only over time, as attitudes hardened, and an international consensus about the primacy of competitive markets emerged, did the processes of registration and regulation become harsher. Depending on a country's previous experience with competition, the political and economic situation of the individual country, and its particular attitude to the importance of regulation to foster growth or development, or counter inflationary pressures, a country might move more or less quickly to stricter measures against cartels. By the mid-1990s, the importance of coordinating large trading blocs and the push for more globalised trade saw the individual differences between national regulatory systems give way almost entirely to the force of international standardisation and the outlawing of serous cartel conduct. The internal transition of government-business relations under the weight of such forces, however, was neither simple, smooth nor necessarily inevitable.

Notes

1. Corporate governance; inter-firm relations; work organisation; industrial relations; product market; labour–wage nexus; financial systems; education and skill creation; welfare and social protection; Rougier and Combarnous (2017, p. 71).
2. For example, circular reasoning could result from 'finding' clusters existed because other institutional mechanisms could be present; and 'finding' coordinating mechanisms that produced clusters.
3. Especially as the 1918 Webb–Pomerene Act allowed US firms to form cartels if they traded internationally.
4. These were the views of the Inter Parliamentary Union IPU of 1930 and 1931.
5. Our analysis is restricted to only one form of competition policy legislation.
6. On average, the LME countries maintained their registers for only 60 percent as long as the CME group of nations.
7. The OECD has a long record of tracking the competition legislation in member countries and (more recently) elsewhere. The organisation also adapted an active policy to promote policies and legislative reforms that improved competition and decreased barriers to trade. It has published regular reports and surveys of the regulation of restrictive business practices, which have been useful also in our research.
8. The original version is based on over 70 questions sent to the competition authorities in 49 jurisdictions in 2013. With a coverage of 100 percent, the responses were recorded on a six-point scale in four separate categories and analysed using cluster analysis and correlation to detect similarities between jurisdictions. The scale and coverage of our approach is reduced by the availability of historical data and our reliance on written evidence.
9. These values are clearly arbitrary. As our interest lies in assessing change and comparing the relative path of each country's register policies, the focus is on relative rather than total scores.
10. Our approach also follows the spirit of Thorelli (1959). He based his analyses on five dimensions: i) stated policy objections, ii) aims regarding interaction of firms, iii) approaches or strategies to implement the objectives of the legislation, iv) scope of the legislation (i.e. the type of agreements in focus) and finally, v) enforcement. Thorelli also emphasised the 'sliding scale of friendliness' in European legislations.
11. As our focus is to compare national registers in different time periods and across decades, the somewhat arbitrary and subjective values given to the components of each dimension are arguably less important than adopting a consistent and comprehensive scale over time. Changing the weights given to a particular component will clearly impact on the aggregate scores in particular cases, but the overall conclusions as to the rise and fall of the registers, and which countries adopted more or less comprehensive registers recording restrictive business practices remain relatively unchanged.
12. This approach is similar in concept to others, for example, Nicholson (2007) who introduced an Antitrust Law Index to compare legislation since 2000 and Kaufmann, Kraay, & Mastruzzi (2010), who used more sophisticated methods to create governance indicators for over 200 countries since 1996.
13. Assessing a country's full transition from accommodating (or tolerating) cartels to one which banned them entirely would require identifying and measuring a wide range of legislation that existed under a range of policies including: competition policy; anti-merger policy; foreign ownership policy; consumer protection or trade practices policy etc. Such a study is beyond the scope of this project.

14. Note the difference between legislative 'activity' and what occurred in the economy. In Britain, for example, Broadberry & Crafts (2001) find only a quarter of manufacturing in the 1950s was free of price fixing; their price-cost margins were almost double those of West Germany (Crafts & Mills, 2005); and around 60 per cent were in collusive agreements, something which was negatively correlated with productivity (Broadberry & Crafts, 1996). We are grateful to an anonymous referee for these references. Anti-trust policy in the UK was not, however, really effective until the passing of the 1956 Restrictive Practices Act (Broadberry & Crafts, 1996, p. 77).

Disclosure statement

No potential conflict of interest was reported by the authors.

References

Ahlquist, J. S., & Breunig, C. (2009). *Country clustering in comparative political economy* (MPIfG Discussion Paper 09/5). Cologne: Max Plank Institut fur Gesellschaftsforschurung (Max Plank Institute for the Study of Societies).

Alemani, E., Klein, C., Koske, I., Vitale, C., & Wanner, I. (2013). *New indicators of competition law and policy in 2013 for OECD and Non-OECD countries* (OECD Economics Department Working Paper No 1104, 96). OECD. Paris. Retrieved from www.oecd.org/eco/Workingpapers

Bhattacharjea, A. (2012). India's new antitrust regime: The first two years of enforcement. *The Antitrust Bulletin*, *57*(3), 449–483.

Bertilorenzi, M. (2016). Legitimising cartels: The joint roles of the League of Nations and of the International Chamber of Commerce. In S. Fellman & M. Shanahan (Eds.), *Regulating competition. Cartel registers in the twentieth-century world* (pp. 30–47). Oxon: Routledge.

Borrel, J. (1998). Spanish competition policy: A case of government's response to domestically perceived problems. *The Antitrust Bulletin*, *43*(2), 445–466.

Broadberry, S., & Crafts, N. F. R. (1996). British economic policy and industrial performance in the early post-war period. *Business History*, *38*(4), 65–91. doi:10.1080/00076799600000135

Broadberry, S., & Crafts, N. F. R. (2001). Competition and innovation in 1950s Britain. *Business History*, *43*(1), 97–118. doi:10.1080/713999207

Collinge, J. (1969). *The law relating to the control of competition, restrictive trade practices and monopolies in New Zealand*. Wellington: Sweet and Maxwell.

Crafts, N., & Mills, T. C. (2005). TFP growth in Britain and German manufacturing, 1950-1996. *The Economic Journal*, *115*(505), 649–670.

Djelic, M. L. (2002). Does Europe mean Americanization? The case for competition. *Competition & Change*, *6*(3), 233–250. doi:10.1080/10245290215046

Edwards, C. D. (1967). *Control of cartels and monopolies: An international comparison*. New York, NY: Oceana Publications.

Fellman, S., & Shanahan, M. (Eds.) (2016). *Regulating competition. Cartel registers in the twentieth-century world*. Oxon: Routledge.

Fellman, S., & Shanahan, M. P. (2018). Sectorial influence on competition legislation: Evidence from the cartel registers, 1920–2000, *Business History Review* 92(4) 633–660. doi:10.1017/S0007680518001058

Glaeser, E. L., La Porta, R., Lopez-de-Silanes, F., & Shleifer, A. (2004). Do institutions cause growth? *Journal of Economic Growth*, *9*(3), 271–303. doi:10.1023/B:JOEG.0000038933.16398.ed

Hall, R. A. & Soskice, D. (Eds.) (2001). *Varieties of capitalism. The institutional foundations of comparative advantage*. Oxford: Oxford University Press.

Hanke, B., Rhodes, M., & Thatcher M. (Eds.) (2008). *Beyond varieties of capitalism. Conflict, contradictions and complementarities in the European economy*. Oxford: Oxford University Press.

Harding, C., & Joshua, J. (2010). *Regulating cartels in Europe. A study of legal control of corporate delinquency* (2nd ed.). Oxford: Oxford University Press.

Hirsch, J. (1926). *National and international monopolies from the point of view and labour, the consuming public and rationalisation, Preparatory Committee for the International Economic Conference*. Geneva: League of Nations.

Hoffmann, G. (1969). Austrian cartel law: Principles and background, the foreign antitrust. *Antitrust Bulletin*, *14*(1), 249–270.

Howell, C. (2003). 'Review: Varieties of Capitalism: And Then There Was One?' *Comparative Politics*, *36*(1), 103–124.

Hunter, A. (1961). Restrictive practices and monopolies in Australia. *Economic Record*, *37*(77), 25–49. doi:10.1111/j.1475-4932.1961.tb01353.x

Hunter, A. (1963). Restrictions of competition in New Zealand. *Economic Record*, *39*(86), 131–141. doi:10.1111/j.1475-4932.1963.tb01467.x

Jackson, G., & Deeg, R. (2006). *How many varieties of capitalism? Comparing the comparative institutional analyses of capitalist diversity* (MPIfG Discussion Paper No. 06/2). Cologne: Max Plank Institut fur Gesellschaftsforschurung (Max Plank Institute for the Study of Societies).

Jaffe, J. (1967). Cartel control in Israel. *Antitrust Bulletin*, *12*(3), 931–948.

Kaufmann, D., Kraay, A., & Mastruzzi, M. (2010). *The Worldwide Governance Indicators: Methodology and Analytical Issues* (Policy Research Working Paper; no. WPS 5430). The World Bank. © World Bank. Development Research Group. https://openknowledge.worldbank.org/handle/10986/3913 License: CC BY 3.0 IGO.

Kestenbaum, L. (1973). Israel's restrictive trade practices law: Antitrust misadventures in a small developing country. *Israel Law Review*, *8*(3), 411–465. doi:10.1017/S0021223700004283

League of Nations Geneva. (1927). International Economic Conference: Resolutions Adopted by the Assembly, September. 24. A. 117. II (B).

Lee, C. (2007). Model competition laws. In R. Fabella, P. Cook, & C. Lee (Eds.), *Competitive advantage and competition policy in developing countries* (pp. 29–53). Cheltenham: Edward Elgar.

Leucht, B. (2009). Transatlantic policy networks in the creation of the first European anti-trust law. Mediating between American anti-trust and German ordo-liberalism. In W. Kaiser, B. Leucht, & M. Rasmussen (Eds.), *The history of European Union: The origin of trans- and supranational polity, 1950–72* (pp. 56–73). Abingdon: Routledge.

Leucht, B., & Marquis, M. (2013). American influences on EEC competition law: Two paths, how much dependence? In K. K. Patel & H. Schweitzer (Eds.), *The historical foundations of EU competition law*. (pp. 125–161). Oxford: Oxford University Press.

McGowan, L. (2010). *The antitrust revolution in Europe: Exploring the European Commission's cartel policy*. Cheltenham: Edward Elgar.

Nicholson, M. W. (2007). Quantifying antitrust regimes. *Erasmus Law and Economics Review*, *3*(1), 41–62.

North, D. C. (1990). *Institutions, institutional change and economic performance*. New York, NY: Cambridge University Press.

OECD. (1964). *Restrictive business practices: Comparative summary of legislations in Europe and North America*. Paris: OECD.

OECD. (1967–1975). *Guide to legislation on restrictive business practices*. Paris: OECD.

OECD. (1971). *Restrictive business practices. Comparative summary of legislations in Europe and North America*. Paris: OECD.

OECD. (1978a). *Comparative summary of legislation on restrictive business practices*. Paris: OECD.

OECD. (1978b). *Restrictive business practices: Comparative summary of legislations in Europe and North America*. Paris: OECD.

OECD. (1987). *Competition policy in OECD countries 1989–90*. Paris: OECD.

OECD. (1991). *Competition policy in OECD countries 1989–90*. Paris: OECD.

OECD. (1993). *Competition policy in OECD countries 1990–1991*. Paris: OECD.

OECD. (1995). *Competition policy in OECD countries 1992–1993*. Paris: OECD.

OECD. (1997). *Competition policy in OECD countries 1993–1994*. Paris: OECD.

OECD. (1998). Recommendation of the council concerning effective action against hard core cartels, C/M(98)7/PROV, March, OECD, Paris.

OECD. (2007). *Competition policy in OECD countries 2005-06*. Paris: OECD.

Ohata, T., & Kurosawa, T. (2016). Policy transfer and its limits: Authorised cartels in twentieth-century Japan. In S. Fellman & M. Shanahan (Eds.), *Regulating competition. Cartel registers in the twentieth-century world* (pp. 169–190). Oxon: Routledge.

Rampilla, N. R. (1989). A developing judicial perspective to India's monopolies and Restrictive Trade Practices Act of 1969. *The Antitrust Bulletin*, *34*(3), 655–682.

Rougier, E. & Combarnous, F. (Eds.) (2017). *The diversity of emerging capitalism in developing countries. Globalization, institutional convergence and experimentation*. Switzerland: Palgrave Macmillan.

Schneider, M. R., & Paunescu, M. (2012). Changing varieties of capitalism and revealed comparative advantages from 1990 to 2005: A test of the Hall and Soskice claims. *Socio-Economic Review*, *10*(4), 731–753. doi:10.1093/ser/mwr038

Schröter, H. G. (2005). *Americanization of the European economy. A compact survey of American economic influence in Europe since the 1880s*. Dordrecht: Springer.

Schröter, H. G. (2010). Loser in power-plays? Small states and international cartelisation. *The Journal of European Economic History*, *39*(3), 527–555.

Segreto, L., & Wubs, B. (2014). Resistance of the defeated: German and Italian big business and the American antitrust policy, 1945-1957. *Enterprise & Society*, *15*(92), 307–336. doi:10.1093/es/khu001

Shanahan, M. (2012). *History, measurement and varieties of capitalism*. XVIth World Economic History Congress, Stellenbosch, 9–13 July.

Thorelli, H. B. (1959). Antitrust in Europe: National policies after 1945. *The University of Chicago Law Review*, *26*(2), 222–236. doi:10.2307/1598181

Timberg, S. (1953). Restrictive business practices: Comparative legislation and the problems that lie ahead. *The American Journal of Comparative Law*, *2*(4), 445–473. doi:10.2307/838096

Appendix 1. Register indicator values

The allocation of numerical weights to each dimension of our indicator is an arbitrary process, the main purpose of which is to create a relative ranking of the registers. In the table below, we provide the range of possible values for each dimension, and a brief justification for these. The values are aggregated to create the final values for each country's policies in each decade.

Indicator	Scale/points	Justification and explanation
Duration of register		
Years in existence	0–10	Split into years existing each decade.
Scope of the Register		
Number of sectors covered in economy	0–6	Ideally a percentage figure, given data limitations, score 1 for each of: Manufacturing; Merchandise services (wholesale and retail trade); Agriculture; Transportation; Building and Construction; Other.
Were all restrictive agreements included or were there exemptions?	0–3	As the proportion of restrictive agreements actually covered is unknown, we estimate scores from 1-3. The value 3= no exemptions; 2= few exemptions, 1= several or many exemptions
Local firms with international partners included?	0–1	Score 1 if local firms with international partners were required to register.
Foreign owned firms	0–1	Score 1 if foreign owned firms were required to register
Activities included in register		
Horizontal agreements	0–1	1 if register included horizontal agreements
Vertical agreements	0–1	1 if register included vertical agreements
Resale price maintenance	0–1	1 if register included resale price maintenance
Dominant firm	0–1	1 if register included dominant firm
Refusal to sell	0–1	1 if register included refusal to sell
Merger and acquisition	0–1	1 if mergers included in register
Exclusive dealing	0–1	1 if register included exclusive dealing
Register transparency		
Public or private	0–1	1 if a public (open) register
Vigour of enforcement	0–1	1 if vigorously enforced, (plus 1 if legal action used to enforce regulations).

Notes: Adapted from Alemani et al. (2013).

Shaping the rules of the game: Spanish capitalism and the publishing industry under dictatorship (1939–1975)

Maria Fernandez-Moya and Nuria Puig

ABSTRACT
This article examines the development of Spanish capitalism under Franco's dictatorship (1939–1975) through the interaction between two major actors: the book publishing industry, a fast growing and internationally minded sector, and the Spanish Government. We argue that Spanish publishers, by defending their interests and redefining their strategies in an extremely restrictive and vulnerable environment, strengthened their coordinating capacities while shaping Spain's economic institutions. The main conclusion of this empirical study is that engaged and/or legitimacy seeking actors can effectively contribute to change the rules of the economic game. We contend that this ability of entrepreneurial actors to shape the rules over time needs to be better integrated into the VOC theoretical framework.

Institutions have recently regained a central role in the social sciences. Why are some institutions good for economic growth and social welfare and others not? Why do some countries endow themselves with adequate institutions while others are apparently unable to do so? The temptation to classify countries according to the quality of their institutions is as old as industrial capitalism itself. Nevertheless, at the beginning of the 21st century, political scientists Peter Hall and David Soskice proposed a theoretical framework, the comparative institutional advantage, to identify and analyze the different types of capitalism prevalent in the most advanced economies of the world (Hall and Soskice, 2001). The varieties of capitalism (VoC) approach, initially limited to liberal market economies (LMEs) and coordinated market economies (CMEs), has been a source of inspiration for the social sciences to this day.

This article seeks to advance in that direction using the tools of business history and borrowing many ideas from the *Business History Review* 'Varieties of Capitalism' Roundtable. This paper examines the role of private firms in the institutional design of capitalist systems from a historical and institutional perspective. We explore how the rules of the game changed in Spain and the role played by two actors: entrepreneurs and Government. The interest of the former to grow and gain new markets and of the latter to survive and obtain international recognition would lead them to support each other and coordinate their interests/efforts, thereby contributing to changing the rules of Spanish capitalism. Our research covers the decades 1940s, 1950s, and 1960s, 1970s, i.e. the Franco dictatorship. The complete industrialization of the country, with the development of Spanish capitalism, took place during our observation period. We argue that the relevance of the observation period for the Spanish economy, and the changing context through the different phases of the Franco regime, make Spain a perfect laboratory to analyse how institutional changes materialize, and what actors and dynamics influence the process.

The article focuses on one illustrative case study: the experience of the publishing industry during the Franco period. The evolution of the book publishing industry enables us to follow the track of the Spanish variety of capitalism at a crucial stage for the modernization of the country. A relevant industry since the early twentieth century, publishing grew spectacularly in the national and international markets between 1950 and 1975 and has ranked among the top ten worldwide ever since. How and why do these two actors interact? To what extent did their coordination capacities transform the institutional arrangements inherited or imposed by the political objectives of Franco's regime and international isolation?

The editors of this volume affirm that the development of the varieties of capitalism is the result of the complex interaction between Government and entrepreneurs over time and in different contexts. We want to verify this by analyzing the Spanish publishing sector on a solid empirical basis that allows us to identify the interests and strategies of both actors, and evaluate their impact on the economic performance of the firms and Spain's political economy. Our intention here has been to avoid the merely formal or legal analysis of institutions, or the interpretation of these as entities isolated from society. For this reason, part of our effort in this research has been dedicated to reconstructing the interest groups that existed within the industry and their relationships with the public administration, in the hope of contributing to the debate regarding the influence of these groups on decision-making and, ultimately, on economic development (see, for example, McCraw, 1997; Fellman et al., 2008). In this way, the article will allow us to make a twofold contribution to this Special Issue: an empirically sound understanding of the active role of entrepreneurs and firms in the shaping of national business systems through stable coalitions, and a historically informed analysis of the specific impact of such coalitions on the evolution of the industry.

Our research is based on four governmental archives (General Administration Archive, Ministry of Finance, Bank of Spain, and Spanish Book National Institute), and five corporate archives (Gustavo Gili, Salvat, Espasa Calpe, Urquijo Bank Archive, and Industrial Credit Bank). We have also examined the periodical publications *El Libro Español* (1958 to 1975), *Anuario Financiero y de Sociedades Anónimas*, the census of the book publishing industry and the register of publishing companies. To improve our understanding of the interaction between business and Government and the dynamics of informal networks, we have relied on personal interviews, autobiographies and memoirs.

Table 1. Investment per capita in books, 1966–1971 (in pesetas).

Year	Investment per capita in books
1966	386.97
1967	444.93
1968	553.46
1969	655.86
1970	800.36
1971	1,046.50

Source: Cedán Pazos (1972).

Table 2. Fiscal write-offs for exportation, publishing sector (in pesetas).

Year	Amount of write-off
1963	61,354,438
1964	82,283,577
1965	86,444,958
1966	96,248,261
1967	95,641,523
1968	266,358,057
1969	335,866,630
1970	354,881,128

Source: Cedán Pazos (1972, p. 214).

The paper is organized as follows. The first section is a brief overview of previous literature on Spanish capitalism. The second section presents the institutional context, the Spanish political and economic situation during the Franco regime. The next three- sections show the central part of the research: the presentation of the actors (entrepreneurs and government), and the relation between them. The following sections present the new legal and fiscal framework, and the impact on the publishing industry. The final section explain our main conclusions.

Spanish capitalism in historical perspective

Before the formalization of the debate about VoC by Hall and Soskice in 2001, its main hypothesis and underlying ideas already constituted a central topic in business history literature (Wilkins, 2010). A defining moment was the publication of Alfred D. Chandler's book, *Scale and Scope*, in 1990. The book encouraged scholars from all over the world to test the advances of US-style managerial capitalism in their research countries (Chandler, 1990). The Spanish case was addressed by Albert Carreras, Xavier Tafunell and Eugenio Torres, who determined that until the 1980s the Chandlerian model had made little progress in Spain. They argued that the persistence of small family businesses and the ubiquity of the State made it difficult to develop economies of scale and the multidivisional firm (Carreras & Tafunell, 1997; Carreras et al., 1997). Spanish business historians then turned their attention to explain the persistence of family capitalism and trust-based relationships, noting that large family firms and entrepreneurial families, in fact, have led the modernization and internationalization of the Spanish firm between the 1970s and 2008 (Fernández Pérez & Puig, 2007; Puig & Fernández, 2008).

In Spain, however, attention to the (mostly negative) peculiarities of indigenous capitalism rose long before Chandler´s works. A generation of economists and sociologists as prolific as influential took care of it since the nineteen sixties. The economists Juan Velarde and Enrique Fuentes Quintana, among many others, pointed out that a strong presence of the State and the resulting extreme regulation that hindered competition, had consolidated in the Spanish institutional framework, notwithstanding the frequent turns in the country's economic policy since the beginning of the industrialization (Velarde, 2009; Fuentes Quintana, 2009). At the same time, the Spanish born sociologist at Yale University Juan Linz and his numerous disciples put the focus on Spanish corporatism, more specifically on the ability or tendency of governments and businessmen to coordinate their interests during the years of accelerated industrial growth (1960–1975)

Table 3. Comparison of percentages of BCI loans granted to each sector in relation to the percentage of their participation in the general industrial production in 1962, 1966 and 1969.

INDUSTRY	1962	1966	1969
Extractive	0.63	2.76	3.05
Food and beverages	0.39	0.23	0.36
Textiles	1.33	0.35	0.43
Footwear	–	0.21	0.85
Wood, Cork and Furniture	0.65	0.5	0.41
Paper, Publishing and Printing	*1.16*	*1.23*	*1.69*
Non-metallic Minerals	3.28	2.01	0.89
Mechanical Metals	1.16	2.31	2.05

Source: Tortella and Jiménez (1986, p. 147).
Note: A figure higher than the unit indicates that the BCI loaned to this sector a proportion higher than its weight in the industrial output. If the figure is lower than the unit, loans were proportionately lower than the sector's weight.

and the democratic transition (1975–1982). These researchers were struck by the ability of the State, in Spain and in Southern Europe in general, to reach lasting agreements with employers and workers, as well as the formation or transformation of often parapublic associations (Linz, 1983).

A later generation of political scientists influenced by Hall and Soskice's research have applied the VoC paradigm to the Spanish case, focusing on the institutional adaptation to the market economy, to the European Union and to globalization. The most explicit analysis was conducted by Sebastián Royo (Royo, 2002, 2007). This author is interested in the development of coordination capacities in the field of industrial relations, a process that depends on the organization, interests and strategies of the Administration, employers and unions. Institutions would be therefore designed and redesigned through a dynamic process influenced by the environment as much as by the social actors. Certain exogenous shocks and historical circumstances, argues this political scientist, can exert a lot of pressure on the actors, accelerating change. Our article falls in this debate. It makes use of the VoC specific framework, proposed by Hall and Soskice, to understand institutional changes during the Franco regime. We also consider Royo's works on Spanish capitalism, and his exhortation to study 'the logic of the social actors' strategies' (Royo, 2007, p. 61). By doing so, our study focuses on the interaction between publishers and Government, and its probable impact on Spanish capitalism.

Spain's institutional context

The final victory of the nationalist military in the Spanish Civil War (1936–1939) would lead to almost four decades of dictatorship. The previous literature has divided Franco's dictatorship into two periods. The first covers the years between 1939 and 1959, when Spain –isolated in the international context– was still constrained by autarkic economic policies. During this period, the new regime tried to guide the economy with a set of anti-market policies that resulted in high inflation rates, the development of black markets and a substantial reduction of international trade. The turning point would come in November of 1950, when the United Nations and the United States began to dialogue with Franco. The support of the US administration for Spain was a key factor in breaking down international isolation and building economic confidence within the country, thus helping to perpetuate Franco's power (Calvo-González, 2007). From 1950 onwards, the Government would change its economic strategy,

Table 4. Leading publishing countries, 1937–1973 *Number of book titles.*

	1937–39	1940–44	1945–49	1950	1955	1960	1965	1970	1973
United States	10,873	9,452	8,851	11,022	12,589	15,012	54,378	79,530	83,724
Soviet Union	43,348	45,800		43,100	54,732	76,064	76,101	78,899	80,196
Germany, Federal Republic	25,400			14,094	16,660	21,103	25,994	45,369	48,034
Japan	30,732			13,009	21,653	23,682	24,203	31,249	35,857
Great Britain	16,087	7,874	12,585	17,072	19,962	23,783	26,314	33,441	35,177
France	8,124	6,379	10,670	9,993	11,793	11,872	17,138	22,935	27,186
Spain		**4,892**	**3,689**	**3,633**	**4,812**	**6,085**	**17,342**	**19,717**	**23,608**
India	24,000	18,740		18,769	18,559	10,741	13,094	14,145	14,064
Netherlands	6,207	3,566	6,177	6,537	7,353	7,893	10,193	11,159	11,640
Poland			4,602	5,218	7,199	7,305	8,509	10,038	10,744

Source: Division of statistics on culture and communication, office of statistics, UNESCO.

introducing successive pro-market changes, relaxing its control over the economy and loosening its extreme interventionist policies. As the coercive power of the State decreased, economic recovery began.

The second period began in 1959 (Townson, 2007). The adoption of the Stabilization and Liberalization Plan (Plan de Estabilización y Liberalización) signalled a new phase in Spanish economic development. A new Government of technocrats elaborated the plan, which included important liberalization measures and a conventional stabilization programme to control inflation and public spending, as well as promote market liberalization and international market integration. The practical aspect took primacy over the ideological and the State took a step back from its original postulates. The 1960s would be a decade of intensive economic growth and the country's complete industrialization. During these years, Spain was experiencing its own 'golden age', in line with the considerable economic growth taking place in other capitalist countries (Martín Aceña & Martínez Ruiz, 2007).

The nation's industrial policy would have to wait until this second, post-1959, phase. The tools designed by the Franco Government to accelerate industrialization were known as the Development Plans. Three such plans were implemented: the first from 1964 to 1967; the second from 1969 to 1971; and the third from 1972 to 1975. They established incentive programmes for industrial investment, priority sectors, poles of growth, export subsidies and a series of other measures to stimulate business. In imitation of the central planning designed by De Gaulle in France, Spain's Development Plans were quadrennial and contained a series of targets or projected milestones that, although not of obligatory compliance for private companies, were indeed compulsory for public entities. Industry thus grew at a greater speed than other sectors and spearheaded the structural transformation of the economy. This institutional context, at first autarkic, then liberalizing, but always tinged with interventionism, would condition the dynamics of the country's business fabric (De la Torre, 2005; Fernández Pérez, 2006; Torres Villanueva, 2003; Valdaliso, 2007).

During the 1960s, Spain underwent a sound social and economic transformation led by a new generation of brilliant engineers and recently graduated economists usually referred to as 'the technocrats'. Inspired and supported by international institutions such as IMF and OECE, these professionals used their newly reached positions of power within the post-1959 Spanish Government to challenge the economic ideas that had been hegemonic during the two previous decades (Caballero Miguez, 2008). Without questioning the political structure of Franco's regime, the technocrats implemented more rational and free-market policies that revealed their permeability to the business community and paved the way for

Table 5. Ranking of Spanish publishers, 1975.

Company	Type	Ownership	% Exports	Affiliates	Catalogue	**Average workers in Spain 1974–1975**	**Average Turnover in thousand pesetas 1974–1975**
Planeta	Newborn firm	Family firm	40%	Mexico, Colombia and Argentina	Literature, best-sellers and encyclopaedias	700	1,235
Salvat Editores	Historical firm	Family firm	60%	Mexico, Buenos Aires, Caracas, Rio de Janeiro and Bogotá; France, Switzerland, Great Britain, Germany and Belgium	Encyclopaedias, large format, fascicles	282	1,115
Bruguera	Newborn firm	Family firm	50%	Mexico, Buenos Aires, Bogotá, Rio de Janeiro	Paperbacks, children's books, magazines and comics for children and young people	1,175	974
Editorial Labor	Historical firm	Family firm	50%	Mexico, Buenos Aires, Caracas, Bogotá, Rio de Janeiro, Quito and Lisbon	Technical books, large format, encyclopaedias	200	710
Plaza y Janés	Newborn firm	Family firm	50%	Mexico, Buenos Aires and Montevideo	Literature, Best-sellers	315	610
Espasa Calpe	Historical firm	Listed company	40%	Mexico and Argentina	Encyclopaedias, large format, literature	427	522
Aguilar	Historical firm	Family firm	50%	Mexico, Buenos Aires, Montevideo and Santiago de Chile	Literature, Best-sellers	505	518
Editorial Ramón Sopena	Historical firm	Family firm	50%	Buenos Aires, Mexico	Encyclopaedias	805	512
Seix Barral	Newborn firm	Family firm	60%	Mexico, Caracas, Bogotá, Quito, Lima, Santiago de Chile and Buenos Aires	Literature		
Santillana	Newborn firm	Family firm	40%	Buenos Aires, Mexico, Chile	Textbooks		

Source: Annual Accounts of Seix Barral, Santillana, Editorial Labor, Aguilar, Editorial Labor; *Anuario Financiero y de Sociedades Anónimas* 1950, 1955, 1960, 1965, 1970 and 1975; Fomento de Producción . Urquijo Bank Archive, Gustavo Gili, Salvat, Espasa Calpe Archives. Newborn is a company founded during Franco regime. Historical firm is a company founded before the Spanish Civil War of 1936.

administrative reform and economic growth. This new environment favoured the rise of a reformist faction within the regime that would play a crucial role in the Spanish democratic transition (1975–1982) (Palomares, 2007).

The actors (I): the entrepreneurs

The Spanish publishing sector was not born during the Franco era. From the late 19th century through the early 20th century, Spain had boasted an important book industry, with a strong presence in Latin America (Larraz Elorriaga, 2007; Martínez Rus, 2008). It was in that period that Spanish publishers, restricted by a limited national market, had decided to begin exporting their books. In the principal destination for Spain's publishing output, Argentina, market share for Spanish publishers in the imported book market was 41% in the period 1911–1914 and 47% in the period between 1915 and 1919 (General Administration Archive, Foreign Affairs, Boxes 447 and 463). Market shares for Spanish publishers were also high in Cuba (48%), Peru (30%), Panama (8%), Chile (19%) and Nicaragua (10%) (Martínez Rus, 2002).

Spanish companies did not receive any governmental support to assist them in this pioneering internationalization process. Moreover, Spanish trade associations would develop later than those in other European countries such as France, Germany or Great Britain. The Official Chambers of the Book, in Barcelona and Madrid, were created in 1918 and 1922, respectively (Sánchez García et al., 2004). Their performance was uneven, but the Catalonian Chamber of the Book was exceptionally active in terms of internationalization. For our study, however, it is important to note that these business associations would set the tone for Spanish associationism within the publishing sector, constituting an important legacy from this earlier phase and a determinant for understanding the behavior of the industry during our own period of study.

In the 1920s, the average for Spanish book exportation of 39% of total production (Gili, 1944). For companies such as Salvat and Gustavo Gili, this rose to over 50% (Gustavo Gili and Salvat Archives). One-off or on-demand exportation evolved over time into a firm process of internationalization in the 1920s and 30 s, with title adaptation and foreign direct investment. Unfortunately, the Spanish Civil War would put an end to this promising phenomenon. The war and post-war period were catastrophic for the publishing sector, as the country's disastrous economic situation, together with restrictions of production due to shortages of energy and raw materials, combined to plunge the industry into a profound crisis. If, during the war, Spanish publishing exports had totalled 39% of production, by the mid-1940s this had fallen to less than 10%, while the number of publishers even capable of exporting had decreased as well (Fernández Moya, 2012).

Added to the problems common to other industries within the Spanish business panorama, the publishing sector would suffer a more singular problem: the exile of a great many publishing professionals and intellectuals. Indeed, many of the prime movers of the sector's pre-war transformation would be forced into self-exile for their connections with the Republican cause (Larraz Elorriaga, 2009; 2010). In business terms, this exile had two negative consequences for the Spanish publishing sector. First, it was in effect 'orphaned' by the disappearance of many of its most important figures and entities. Second, the publishing sectors of Mexico and Argentina, countries in which many Spanish exiles settled, were consequently strengthened (De Diego, 2006). The new companies that arose on the other side of the

Atlantic would become the main competitors of Spain's publishing houses in the middle decades of the 20th century.

The evolution of the publishing sector, in terms of company size and capitalization, paralleled that of the general Spanish economic context. However, the available documentary sources, according to their nature and objective, offer only disparate quantitative data regarding the development of the Spanish publishing sector in the Franco era. In 1945, the *Anuario financiero y de sociedades anónimas* recorded a total of 142 companies for the entire graphic arts sector (Anuario financiero y de sociedades anónimas, 1945/46, 296). The economic recovery of the 1950s is reflected in an increase in the number of *sociedades anónimas* (limited liability companies) registered, which in 1960 already comprised 303 companies (Anuario financiero y de sociedades anónimas, 1960/61, XLVII). The developmentalism of the 1960s is also reflected in the figures presented in the *Anuario*. In 1965, 406 *sociedades anónimas* were registered for the graphic arts sector (Anuario financiero y de sociedades anónimas, 1965/66, XLVII). In 1970, this would reach 506 and, at the end of the Franco era (1975), 611 (Anuario financiero y de sociedades anónimas, 1975/76, XXIV).

The second documentary source, the census of the publishing sector, shows much higher figures. In 1945, the census listed a total of 290 publishers, forming a category independent from the rest of the graphic arts and press sector (Martínez Martín, 2015b, 234). In the 1950s, the number of publishers in Spain fluctuated between 550 and 600 companies (Martínez Martín, 2015b, 253). A third source, the Register of Publishing Companies, within the Spanish Book National Institute (INLE, by its acronym in Spanish), bears witness to the sector's dynamism in the later years of the Francoist era. From 1966 to 1975, a total of 1,920 companies would apply for inscription in the Register (Martínez Martín, 2015c, 275). All of the documentary sources reveal a clear tendency: this was toward growth, beginning in the1950s and becoming notably heightened in the 1960s. However, the disparity of these figures indicates that the publishing sector was still comprised mostly of small-sized businesses, some of only intermittent activity and publishing a meagre number of titles annually. The legal status of *sociedad anónima* was reserved for the sector's more prominent publishers, understood as being those with the largest sales volumes.

From these sectoral statistics, we are able to distinguish three types of companies. The first were the historical market leaders, for their size and revenue, which had been founded in the early 20th century and had gained experience and knowledge in both domestic and foreign markets. This was the case of companies like Espasa Calpe, Aguilar, Gustavo Gili, Sopena, Labor and Salvat. The second were new publishers that, although still young and small in size, had been born with the ambition to scale the ranks of the domestic publishing sector and developed aggressive growth strategies to do so. Some of these remain in operation today, such as Planeta (founded in 1949 and currently the eighth largest publisher in the world), Taurus (1954), Plaza y Janés (1959), Anaya (1959), Seix Barral (1954), Santillana (1960), Alfaguara (1964), Alianza (1966), Anagrama (1969) and Tusquets (1969). The third group was comprised of smaller, lesser known companies, created sometimes by an individual entrepreneur. Operating with low capital, their activity was circumscribed to a specific line of publishing in which they specialized, a strategy which enabled them to survive in the market. Barcelona and Madrid continued to be the two great poles of the industry, with 44% of publishers having their headquarters in Madrid and 30% in Barcelona.

Our research reveals that Spanish book publishers were fully integrated into the international industry through their active participation in international associations. Spanish publishers also began to attend international fairs. Statistics for the 1962 Frankfurt Fair (the most important world publishing event) show that of the publishers in attendance, 171 were Spanish, 81 German, 68 French, 39 American, 28 Swiss, 23 Dutch, 6 Mexican and 6 Argentinian (General Administration Archive, Culture Section, Box 73-000475, Report 'España pierde su mercado en América Latina', Sept. 1962). The 14th annual International Publishers Conference was held in Barcelona in 1962. Santiago Salvat Espasa, company owner and a leading figure in the Catalonian publishing industry of this period, served as president of the International Publishers Association from 1962 to 1966 (Fernández Moya, 2010).

On the supply side, the number of companies and their productive capacity increased. The technical modernization of the graphic arts sector, beginning in 1950, would bring about the latter development. As for demand, the advances that were then taking place in educational level and purchasing power must be noted. Illiteracy rates dropped considerably; in 1940, 23% of the Spanish population was illiterate, a figure that would fall to 14.2% in 1950, 11.2% in 1960 and 8.5% in 1970. The rise in scholarization in the 1960s was greatly marked at the secondary and higher educational levels, with the number of secondary school students growing by 159% and that of university students by 142% (Martínez Martín, 2015c, 278). Growth rate in GDP in the 1940s was 1.37%, rising to 5.43% from 1950 to 1958 and reaching 6.92% in the period between 1958 and 1974 (Prados de la Escosura, 2003,133 and 151) This increase would occur in parallel to increased consumption and investment in books. This is shown by the data in the following table:

As for financing, the publishing sector was comprised mainly of family-run companies or individual entrepreneurs who had created their enterprises with minimal resources of their own. Business people and companies in other sectors had no interest in publishing, either as investors or as managers.

The actors (II): the government

For the entire duration of the Franco regime, the State would play a central role in driving the publishing sector forward. Political institutions that were involved in some way in the production and sale of books included: the National Paper, Press and Graphic Arts Union, the Council of Spanish Culture, the Ministry of Foreign Affairs, the Ministry of National Education and the Vice-Secretariat of Popular Education and Propaganda Services. To provide an outlet for publications aligned with the regime, the Editora Nacional (National Publishing House) was created in 1941. This publicly owned entity was charged with combining commercial criteria with objectives of propaganda (General Administration Archive, Culture Section, Boxes 66-20615 and 66-20349). However, the greatest tutelary exponent of the Franco Government in this area would be the Spanish Book National Institute (INLE, by its acronym in Spanish).

The INLE was an entity modelled on the Republican Spanish Book Institute, and classed as an autonomous body depending on the Ministry of the Interior's Sub-Secretariat of Press and Propaganda. The Institute arose from the Ministerial Order of 23 May, 1939, as the 'central body of consultation and management for all issues relative to the production and distribution of Spanish books'. As such, the INLE exercised the functions of: managing the domestic and foreign policies of the Spanish book; promoting propaganda through competitions, festivals, fairs, expositions and contests; organizing Spain's representation in international assemblies and conferences related to books; proposing and drafting norms designed to combat illicit competition; publishing a bibliographical bulletin of Spanish-language books; and editing the General Catalogue of the Spanish and Latin American Book Industry (Cedán Pazos, 1969, pp. 43–44). That is to say, the INLE was given the functions which before the Civil War had been carried out by the official Book Chambers of Madrid and Barcelona before the Civil War.

After its victory in the Civil War, the new State had first to decide what kind of publishing sector it would allow to exist. In theory, the Government could have either opted for a production monopoly and control the final product in this way, or allow private enterprise and exercise control over its output. As for the type of books published, its dilemma in the postwar period was whether the *blue book*, which exalted the values of the State and propagated its message, should be the only one authorized, or whether the *commercial boo*k should also be permitted (Martínez Martín, 2015a, 33). We have no documentary record of the existence of any open debate on the possibility of channelling publishing output through a monopoly, something which would have been difficult in any case. This was the idea, however, which underpinned the formation of the Editora Nacional in 1941, as practicality took precedence over ideals (García Naharro, 2015). It is true that in the postwar period, the Spanish publishing sector found itself in dire straits, but it carried with it a considerable historical legacy that would aid its speedy recovery. Companies like Salvat, Gustavo Gili and Espasa Calpe were the heavyweights of the publishing industry; the State, unable to ignore this reality, chose to respect the actions of the private publishing sector, while marking its legal limits and supervising its production.

The most visible aspect of the Franco Government's control was censorship. In the year 1939, an iron-fisted censorship board was established within the Nationalist administration. The so-called 'Serrano Suñer' law brought into being a system of censor approval under which all published works had to be reviewed before they were released onto the market (Ruiz Bautista, 2015). Publishers were required to send their publication plans semi-annually to this board for Government approval. Changes in Spanish society and in the power structure of the regime itself would lead to the modification of this legislation in 1966. In that year, a new Press Law went into effect, under the authority of Information Minister Manuel Fraga. The law did away with the previously compulsory censor approval program, at the same time that it heightened state supervision of the publishers themselves. Police files of their biographical details were registered with the INLE, together with the rest of their companies' documentary data. It is important to note that the objective of the new legislation was not to make censorship more flexible or permissive, but rather to better manage a massive bureaucracy that, given the rise in supply and demand, had become a problem for the public administration. The words of Manuel Fraga, who said that the State 'must either channel these changes, or be overwhelmed by them', reflect this desire to adapt to the new reality (Menchero de los Ríos, 2015, p. 69). As with other controlling procedures, censorship was not exercised in a rigorous or systematic way, but rather discretionally (Ruiz Bautista, 2008).

Relations between entrepreneurs and the government

Franco's Government limited freedom of movement for entrepreneurs, instead channelling this officially through the 'Vertical Unions'. In general terms, this system granted very little freedom of operation to the few existing business organizations, thereby reducing their capacity for dealing with the abuses of the State at the same time that State power was increasing (Cabrera & Del Rey, 2011).

Of course, in the case of the publishing sector, the creation of the INLE implied the dissolution of the Book Chambers of Barcelona and Madrid (founded in 1918 and 1922, respectively). However, the publishers soon realized the necessity, or convenience, of dialoguing with the Regime. To do this, the sector needed to be well-structured and cohesive. The historical chain of events that took place before the Civil War, the legacy of the period addressed in the first section, may explain the early creation of a common front to defend the sector's interests: the National Assembly of Authors, Publishers and Booksellers, founded in 1944.

How was collective action in the sector structured? Its operations were carried out, on the margin of the official orders, by mixing legal activities with illegal ones. The sector's geographical concentration in Madrid and Barcelona would facilitate the process of coordination. Meetings held within the sector but outside the associations stipulated by law, for example, were a frequent but illegal practice. The testimony of Francisco Pérez González, the co-founder of Santillana and a frequent interlocutor with the administration, describes the situation like this:

> Here (Madrid), we didn't have a collective feeling as a trade like there was in Barcelona. And I learned many things; I also learned that this legal-illegal system worked, because at the same time that Santiago Salvat (leading publisher) was going to official trade group meetings, there were those meetings going on where decisions were made that they would later apply and I would pass on to Ernesto Antón and to Ignacio Caballero (attendees of the Madrid meetings) (Fundación Germán Sánchez Ruipérez, 2006, p. 78).

The Barcelona meetings were held, for example, in the offices of Salvat. In Madrid, the premises used for such meetings were the offices of *Selecciones del Reader's Digest* or Espasa Calpe. That is to say, the meetings, however clandestine they might have been, were held in the headquarters of leading publishers who were not markedly anti-Francoist. Indeed, the directors of the various official organisms, including the INLE, knew about and tolerated these type of gatherings.

The actions of the publishers as a pressure group became patent in the revision of the INLE, an entity that had hitherto resisted reform. Initially, the INLE depended on the Vice-Secretariat of Popular Education (Secretariat-General of the Movement). In this first phase, ideology had prevailed over economic considerations. The first president, Julián Pemartín, would justify the Government's actions with bombastic rhetoric. In his understanding, the Institute, unlike the former Chambers, should not support the publishers' commercial activities, but instead redeem the book from its purely commercial character (Rodrigo Echalecu, 2015, p. 100). This orientation and philosophy was maintained in the years that followed, despite the modification of the public body that supervised the INLE. In 1945, the Institute found itself under the authority of the Directorate General of Propaganda, within the Ministry of National Education. In 1951, with the creation of the Ministry of Information and, the INLE became dependent on the Directorate General of Information.

In 1957, with the arrival of the technocrats to political power, a deeper reform of the Institute's internal structure took place, aimed at adapting it to the sector's new reality and needs. Joining the INLE's administrative board were various technicians from the public administration, along with influential politicians such as Laureano López Rodó, at that time technical secretary-general of the Presidency, and later to become both a minister and chief officer of the Government's industrial policy.

The reform of 1957 was a turning point in the relations between the publishers and the administration. Initially, the new managers tried to control and guide the workings of the Institute without the consent of the publishers. The publishers, on the other hand, were eager to take an active role in the political and economic transformation of Spain that was then under way. Acting collectively, they sought to approach the highest officials of the Ministries of Information and Tourism and of Trade (Escolar Sobrino, 1999, pp. 231–235). The publishers had the support of the Secretary-General of the INLE, Eduardo Nolla, who was described as an 'intelligent Galician and heterodox Falangist, whose general sympathies were inclined toward solving the publishers' problems' (Escolar Sobrino, 1999, p. 231). Finally, at a meeting in El Escorial, they drafted a document in which they formulated their goals and suggested a series of measures favouring the book and the publishing industry. This document was received and supported by Laureano López Rodó, General Manager of the INLE and, as we have already mentioned, a key representative of the new economic policy (Comín & Vallejo, 2009, pp. 140–141). Through his mediation, the Franco Government accepted the demands of the publishers, who then came to form part of both the board of directors, and the general delegated commission of the INLE, the entity's most powerful governmental bodies. This was the first step taken by the publishers toward shaping the institutional framework from within.

After the reform of 1957, the INLE became an official institution with a mixed character, aimed at serving individuals as well as the State. Highly skilled technical personnel were added to the top management of the INLE, including Foreign Trade and Customs officials, as well as private publishers, to help solve the sector's most pressing problems. Archival data supports this affirmation of the dual role played by the INLE. The publishers used the Institute to deal with sectoral issues –and, consequently, to influence Government decisions– and to participate in the application and execution of measures and policies favourable to the industry. Time-honoured Spanish publishers, such as Joaquín Sopena, Victor Seix, Francisco Bruguera and the Salvat brothers, sat on the board of the INLE and its delegated commission and participated in all of its debates. Their participation was wide-ranging and would affect the handling of the issues which most concerned them.

The Institute was clearly a channel through which they could transmit their complaints and requests to the top officials of the Franco Government's political hierarchy. In the records of the board of directors, it can be clearly seen that these executives proposed measures, participated in the execution of Governmental plans and designed cultural, business and diplomatic initiatives. There were a great number of interactions with the Ministry of Trade, to communicate problems in bilateral trade dealings with some countries and overcome obstacles to the exportation of books, and with the Ministry of Finance to reduce or modify the criteria for some of the taxes levied on publishers. (Bank of Spain Archive, Spanish Institute of Foreign Currency, Box 226, INLE, Agreements 1/64 and 2/64 Board of directors INLE). They tried as well to interfere in the slow and cumbersome system of exportation and currencies, even going beyond the authority of the entity responsible for this, the Spanish Institute of Foreign Currency (IEME, by its acronym in Spanish) (Bank of Spain Archive, Spanish Institute of Foreign Currency, Box 227, INLE General Notes, October 1963, Exports of books).

The publishers, then, had a presence at all levels, and not only on the board of directors. They appointed commissions for various tasks, from organizing expositions to handling tax payments (Bank of Spain Archive, Spanish Institute of Foreign Currency, Boxes 224, 226 and 227). The opening of the INLE's office in Costa Rica, the Institute's only foreign delegation, was proposed the publishers themselves, specifically Santiago Salvat, the owner and director of the company with the highest sales volume and with five delegations in Latin America (Bank of Spain Archive, Spanish Institute of Foreign Currency, Box 224, Minutes of a Meeting of the Board of Directors, January, 14th, 1966). The proposal for the restructuring of the INLE itself (a reorganization of the services it provided and the restructuring of its legal regime) was the work of a group formed by the director and secretary of the INLE, the academic José Mª Desantes and publishers Hipólito Escolar and Victor Seix (Bank of Spain Archive, Spanish Institute of Foreign Currency, Box 227, INLE, Minutes of a Meeting of the Board of Directors, May 17th, 1963, Agreement 44/63). The debate centred on the manner of reorganization and the consequences of this for the balance of public administration vs. private sector. These are only a few examples of the quite significant involvement of private publishers in the INLE and their influence on sectoral policy.

This second phase of Government support confirms that State policy regarding book publishing was not a closed plan, in accordance with a preconceived idea and a consistent ideological base. On the contrary, it was a response to the context, a pragmatic attempt to balance the interests of the regime, the currents or groups of power within it and the demands of the publishing companies. The Franco Government, then, must not be understood as a monolith of homogeneous thinking that was isolated from the country's business fabric.

The new legal and fiscal framework

This inclusion into the State organism that controlled the Government's policy on books was one of the two aspects in which collective action came to the fore in the publishers' dealings with the State. The other was the change that was occurring in the legal and fiscal framework. This began to be felt as early as 1946; that is to say, during the period of autarky. The early association of publishers in the National Assembly of Authors, Publishers and Booksellers (1944) was instrumental in the creation of the Book Protection Law of 1946. This law was drafted according to the ideas of the publishers themselves. In particular, many of its measures had been presented in a book published by Gustavo Gili in 1944. However, the law was eventually blocked by bureaucratic obstacles. Although the State was willing to respond to the demands of the publishers, the administration did not know how to put these measures into practice. The confusing regulations of the 1946 law and its application by the entities charged with enforcing it would in the end annul its theoretical benefits (Bank of Spain Archive, Spanish Institute of Foreign Currency, INLE Boxes 244 & 227).

At the beginning of the 1960s, the Law of 1946 had still barely been applied, due to its various bureaucratic entanglements, and the publishers found themselves without a legal framework to protect them. At that same time, however, they would see an opportunity in the change that was then taking place in the Government's economic policy, aimed at the country's complete industrialization. From within the INLE, the leading publishers in Madrid and in Catalonia demanded a reform of the Book Protection Law of 1946 and requested that this be included in the Franco Government's new plans. The called-for reforms were articulated through various instruments of economic policy. Two laws in particular had a central role in this process: the Industries of Preferential Interest Law of 2 December 1963; and the

Development Plans (the first arising from Law 194/1963, on 28 December). In reality, the plans represented a step backward in the liberal trend marked by the Stabilization Plan, as they involved strong Government intervention. It was the State that would direct the country's investment and production.

The publishing industry was declared as being of preferential interest in December 1963 (Industrial Credit Bank, BBVA Historical Archive, Archive Credit concession policies). Articles 16ª and 17ª of Law 1964/1963 of 28 December, by which the Social Development Plan for the period 1964–1967 was created, classified the publishing industry as a prioritary sector for the concession of official credit. The terms under which such assistance had to be given were developed by the Ministry de Finance on 23 July 1964, and by the Ministry of Information and Tourism on 26 November, 1964. After granting this priority classification, however, the Government did not create a new law for the publishing sector. A series of decrees published between the years 1963 and 1971 would for all purposes annul the law of 1946, which nevertheless remained officially in effect (General Administration Archive, Culture Section, Box 73-000475). These were a collection of norms intended to solve the problems of the earlier period regarding the importation of paper, tax exemption for utilities, tax write-offs for exports, the facilitation of financing and reforms in export insurance policies. There is no doubt that the Spanish administration was reacting to pressure from the publishers by establishing norms aimed at facilitating the transformation of the entire Spanish publishing sector.

One of the most beneficial measures for the industry was that of giving tax write-offs for exported products. It consisted of the Tax Office returning all or part of the indirect taxes levied on publishers in the processes of production and sale of exported books. The INLE worked together with the Directorate General of Customs to effect these write-offs for its members. The amounts received by publishers exporting under the licences granted by INLE membership are shown in the following table:

The growth in these figures beginning in 1968 was due to the application of another new measure. The Legislative Decree of 30 November, 1967 established that the tax write-off for

Table 6. Interests, strategies, instruments and institutional outcome of Government-publishers interaction under Franco's dictatorship.

	Autarchic Period (1939–1957)	Developmental Period (1957–1975)
Government	Seeks ideological control and protectionist framework through: Spanish Book National Institute (INLE) 1939 Censorship 1939 Editora Nacional 1941 Book Protection Law 1946	Seeks domestic and international legitimation and more efficient management of rising publishing activity and book demand through: Technocratic shift 1957 Preferential Interest Law 1963 Press Law 1966 Tax and financial incentives decree 1967
Publishers	Seek to keep domestic and international markets and pre-war trade guilds, engaging in new institutions and limiting the damage of new regulatory framework.	Seek to maximize impact of domestic technocratic shift and worldwide publishing boom influencing regulatory framework.
Institutional Outcome	Book publishing becomes tightly regulated and ideologically controlled but private firms and pre-war trade guilds survive and historical leaders retain some influence in new regulatory bodies (but fail to fully shape 1946 Law).	Leading historical and new book publishers increase their formal and informal influence in INLE and new legal framework, which provides extensive tax and financial incentives to private publishing firms. Dramatic domestic and international growth of Spanish book publishing.

Source: Authors' own elaboration.

exported books would be 9% of the total value exported, plus an additional 2% for pertaining to an industry included in the Development Plans.

The principal advantage derived from the sector's being declared prioritary or preferential was the ease with which credit could be obtained on advantageous terms, Law 2/1962 on the Bases for the Ordering of Credit and Banking. This preferential financing is made evident in two specific figures: exportation credit; and prioritary credit. The central component in this peculiar banking system was the Industrial Credit Bank (BCI, by its acronym in Spanish). From the BCI, the publishing sector would receive substantial loans with favourable terms, even disproportionate to its weight in the country's total industrial output, as can be observed in the table below:

The publishers embraced this form of financing *en masse*. For example, in the liabilities of Seix Barral from 1966 to 1968, exportation loans accounted for 8% to 12% of the company's total liabilities. The accounts of Santillana S.A. showed export loans of 4 million pesetas, 4% of total liabilities, with the amounts still rising. From 1968 to 1975, the company's export loans would represent between 5% and 8% of its total liabilities and an average of 17% of current liabilities (Urquijo Bank Archive, Juan March Foundation, Annual Accounts Barral Editores Annual Accounts 1974 and 1976, Editorial Labor Annual Account 1970, Santillana Annual Accounts 1967–1977, and Seix Barral Annual Accounts 1966–1968).

Effects on business performance

What effect did these measures have on the economic evolution of the publishing sector? They were very positive, especially with regard to internationalization. The graph below traces the evolution of book exports in this period (Figure 1).

The graph enables us to distinguish four periods. The first stage began in 1940 and continued until 1950, and was characterized by very low export figures, as it reflects the harshest years of the post-war period. The second was the decade of the 1950s, when the historical Spanish publishers, those which already had experience in internationalization before the Civil War, resumed their foreign business dealings. The third period ran from 1960 to 1965 and was a time of higher export figures, thanks to the change in the general political and

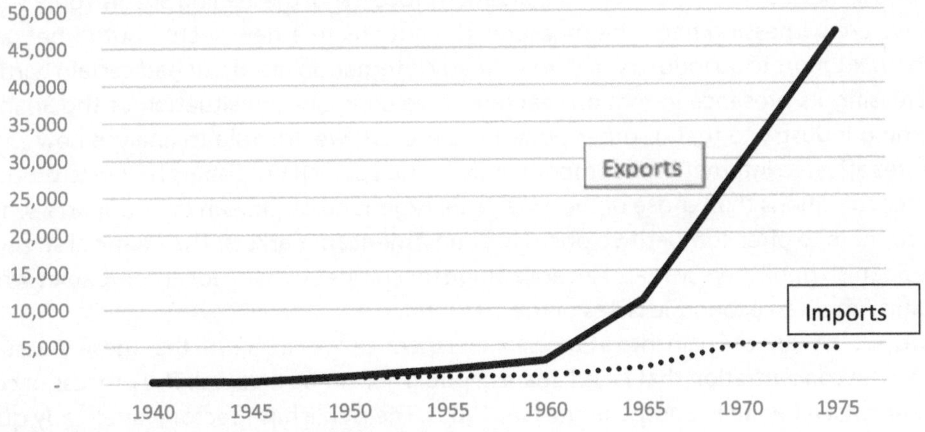

Figure 1. Exportation of books (1940–1975) (in kilogrammes).
Source: Anuario Estadístico del Comercio Exterior de España, Ministry of Finance Archive.

legal framework. The Stabilization Plan of 1959 not only stabilized and liberalized, but stimulated export activity as well. Within the new framework, the publishers would design individual strategies that, generally speaking, proved to be highly profitable. In 1962, Spain was already the principal provider of the Latin American book sector. Indeed, in that year its exports to Latin America were double that of the second biggest provider, the United States (*El Libro Español*, Jan. 1965, pp. 38–39) However, Spanish publishers also encountered barriers that would slow this foreign growth. One principal problem was that their Mexican and Argentine competitors, companies often founded by exiled Spanish Republicans, were distributing their catalogues throughout the entirety of Latin America. Other barriers included production difficulties from the use of obsolete technology, the high cost of transport (a serious obstacle to international shipping), the difficult and expensive acquisition of quality paper and problems in obtaining credit in a sector which demanded a heavy initial investment but offered a very slow return (Fernández Moya, 2009).

A great many of these problems would be solved by the Government's measures of support for the industry. The fourth period, then, begins with the implementation of these measures in 1963–64. It is clear that the new institutional framework provided strong incentives for internationalization. More than this, the design of the new measures would mark the business strategies of these companies, encouraging exportation rather than other forms of internationalization, such as direct investment with production in the country of destination or the concession of licences for publishing abroad. To maximize fiscal benefits (loans and tax write-offs for exportation), printing had to be done on national soil, which also generated a beneficial carry-over effect for the graphic arts sector. As a result, Spanish publishing exports would skyrocket after the mid-1960s.

In contrast to the official Government statistics, we present below figures from UNESCO regarding publishing output. In the lower table, it can be seen that the great change that was in store for the publishing sector would have to wait until the 1960s. It was then that Spain would take its position among the elite of the international sector.

The main Spanish publishers, both the historical leaders and those of more recent creation but intent on growth, would use these measures to renovate their facilities and to either increase or initiate their expansion into foreign markets. The measures also enabled them to effectively balance their finances, with easy access to credit and subsidies for exportation. The table below shows data on the internationalization processes of the leading Spanish publishers.

As we are witnessing here, the measures did not create a new sector, but rather gave economic support to an industry that was already internationalized but had certain barriers to increasing its presence in foreign markets. If we compare the situation of the Spanish publishing industry to that of other publishing sectors, we are able to analyse how these measures affected international competitiveness. The Spanish publishers began to produce in better conditions than those of their Mexican, Argentine or Chilean counterparts, which allowed them to offer competitive prices in Latin American markets. The financial strength of the Spanish publishers was also an advantage for competing with local companies when the Latin American economic crises of the 1970s hit.

If we put the case of Spain into a European perspective, we can affirm that these measures allowed the concentration that faced Spanish publishers to be delayed. The process of concentration itself began in Europe in the late 1960s. The publishing sector was already quite mature, with low growth rates and limited profit margins that demanded an increase in sales volume. The formation of large publishing groups permitted companies to exploit synergies and economies of scale where possible. In 1968, in Germany, nineteen publishers were doing business of 5 to 50 million DM, while fifty-six others had turnovers of 50,000 to 500,000 DM (Fernández Moya, 2012). In the mid-1960s, the turnover of nineteen French companies represented 54.2 percent of the total sector total in that country, while that of 192 small publishing houses was barely 7.3 percent (*El Libro Español*, Mar. 1975, pp. 103–104). In Spain, the process of concentration would not begin until the mid-1980s. Meanwhile, in the 1960s and 70 s, the measures taken would provide the publishers with sufficient financial support, and it would thus be unnecessary to pursue efficiency through mergers and acquisitions or the creation of economies of scale in order to reduce costs.

Conclusions

The purpose of this article was to examine the development of Spanish capitalism under Franco's dictatorship (1939–1975) through the interaction between two major players: the book publishing industry, a fast growing and internationally minded industry, and the Spanish Government. Based on extensive empirical data, we argue that Spanish book publishers, by defending their interests and redefining their strategies strengthened their coordinating capacities on two levels: within the publishing industry and with the many governmental bodies that regulated their business activity. Ultimately, these capacities contributed to shape Spain's economic policy and institutions in a crucial period for the modernization of Spain.

The findings of this study are summarized in Table 6. The basic idea of the theory of varieties of capitalism argues that a certain institutional framework, by establishing the rules of the game, encouraged cooperative behavior among companies, in case the of CMEs, or prevent it, in the case of LMEs (Hall and Soskice, 2001). In our case study, a predatory State limited autonomy of movement for entrepreneurs, reducing their capacity to react against its abuses. Cooperative behaviors were theoretically hindered by an official framework which offer one single channel: 'Vertical Unions', and conceded very little freedom to the existing business organizations. Notwithstanding, over and above the official framework, the entrepreneurs found ways to cooperate and defend their interest, thanks to informal networks and corporatist practices. Under the leadership from historical firms, publishers transformed the existing trade associations into coalition tools. New entrants soon joined this proactive group.

It is important to note that Franco's Government did not develop a defined, coherent and structured book publishing policy. Despite the strong ideological dimension of the post-war institutions, this article shows that Spain's book policy was dictated by the evolving interests and strategies of Government and entrepreneurs, and the imperatives of economic growth and national and international legitimacy. This bidirectional process was necessarily pragmatic. The coordination capacities developed throughout the process by private publishers and public administrators ended up transforming the institutional arrangements of Spanish capitalism. In sort, this is not a typical case study of lobbies. It was a dictatorial Government in the middle of an institutional change, which dialogued with the entrepreneurs, and invited them to participate in the process. They were active players in the elaboration of the new measures and even in their implementation, from their leading positions in the institutions. Publishing was not the only industry subsidized by the State, many sectors were financially supported to foster a rapid industrialization of the country. This is how the regime managed the transformation of Spain from an agrarian to an industrial economy during our observation period.

What does this article add to the VoC debate? First, the research findings explained here are consistent with previous literature about Spanish VoC. Preceding works, mostly focused on Spanish economic development during the democracy (1975–2018), demonstrated that Spanish capitalism is based on coordination, coalitions, and corporatism (Royo, 2002, 2007). Our paper shows that, even in a dictatorship, during a period of liberalization (after 1959), when the international context and Spanish openness increased convergence with liberal models, informal networks and corporatist bargaining, two typical non- market mechanisms, coordinated economic activity.

Second, the Spanish experience related in these pages challenges the classic interpretation in several aspects. We have attempted to reveal that the institutional fabric of national economic and social models can change over time, even in authoritarian regimes with highly intervened markets. The VoC debate was born as an ahistorical theoretical debate, nonetheless the question of why and how change takes place requires detailed historical analysis. In this sense, the Spanish case is extremely relevant because it allows us to study a deep institutional change within that same dictatorial regime. Our historical analysis illustrates that the State is a dynamic entity with significant adaptation and coordination capacities. The research reveals that institutional change is not always the consequence of an exogenous shock, but the result of a more complex process. What dynamics and actors played a role in this transformation? Our study states that firms and entrepreneurs, whose role is undervalued in the proposal of Hall and Soskice (2001), are active and pragmatic actors capable of and motivated to modify the existing rules of the game through stable industrial coalitions as well as through ad-hoc coordination with governmental institutions. We have made the point that the theory of institutional determinism is insufficient to understand institutional change. Institutional evolution and adaptation seem to be the result of the actions of different actors with particular incentives and interests.

Disclosure statement

No potential conflict of interest was reported by the author(s).

References

Caballero Miguez, G. (2008). El cambio institucional de la economía española del franquismo a la democracia. Un análisis histórico institucional. *Política y Gobierno, 15*(2), 353–401.

Cabrera, M., & Del Rey, F. (2011). *El poder de los empresarios. Política y economía en la España contemporánea 1875-2010.* RBA.

Calvo-González, O. (2007). American military interests and economic confidence in Spain under the Franco dictatorship. *The Journal of Economic History, 67*(3), 740–767.

Carreras, A., & Tafunell, X. (1997). Spain: "Big Manufacturing Firms Between State and Market, 1917–1990. In A. D., Jr., Chandler, F. Amatori, and T. Hikino (Eds.), *Big business and the wealth of nations* (pp. 277–304). Cambridge University Press.

Carreras, A., Tafunell, X., & Torres, E. (1997). Against integration. The rise and decline of spanish state-owned firms and the decline and rise of multinationals, 1939–1990. In OlssonU. (Ed.), *Business and European integration since 1800. regional, national and international perspectives* (pp. 31–49). University of Göteborg Press.

Cedán Pazos, F. (1972). *Edición y comercio del libro español (1900–1972).* Editora Nacional.

Cedán Pazos, F. (1969). XXX Aniversario del Instituto Nacional del Libro Español. *Información Comercial Española. Revista de Economía, 431*, 43–52.

Chandler, A. D. (1990). *Scale and scope: The dynamics of industrial capitalism.* Harvard University Press.

Comín, F., & Vallejo, R. (2009). Los Programas de Inversiones Públicas (1964–1976): ¿El instrumento presupuestario al servicio de los Planes de Desarrollo? In J. De la Torre & M. García Zúñiga (Eds.), *Entre el Mercado y el Estado. Los planes de desarrollo durante el franquismo* (pp. 89–146). Sección de Publicaciones de la Universidad Pública de Navarra.

De Diego, J. L. (2006). La época de oro de la industria editorial. In J.L. De Diego (Ed.), *Editoriales y políticas editoriales en Argentina, 1880–2000* (pp. 91–121). Fondo de Cultura Económica.

De la Torre, J. (2005). Instituciones, empresarios y mercado: la industrialización de Navarra bajo el franquismo. *Revista de Historial Industrial, 27*, 121–161.

Escolar Sobrino, H. (1999). *Gente del libro: autores, editores y bibliotecarios 1939–1999.* Gredos.

Fellman, S., Iversen, M., Sjögren, H., & Thue, L. (2008). *Creating nordic capitalism: The development of a competitive periphery.* Palgrave.

Fernández Moya, M. (2012). Creating knowledge networks: Spanish multinational publishers in Mexico. *Business History Review, 86*(1), 69–98.

Fernández Moya, M. (2010). A family-owned publishing multinational: the Salvat company (1869-1988). *Business History, 52*(3), 453–470. https://doi.org/10.1080/00076791003721969

Fernández Moya, M. (2009). Multinacionales del castellano. La internacionalización del sector editorial español. *Revista de Historia Industrial, 40*, 23–50.

Fernández Pérez, P., & Puiq, N. (2007). Bonsais in a wild forest? A historical interpretation of the longevity of Spanish large family firms. *Revista de Historia Económica. Revista de Historia Económica / Journal of Iberian and Latin American Economic History, 25*(3), 459–498. https://doi.org/10.1017/S0212610900000203

Fernández Pérez, P. (2006). Empresas familiares y acuerdos cooperativos en el metal español: El caso de las industrias del alambre de hierro y acero (1880–1974). *Investigaciones de Historia Económica, 2*(4), 51–76.

Fuentes Quintana, E. (2009). *Lecciones de economía española.* Marcial Pons.

Fundación Germán Sánchez Ruipérez. (2006). *Conversaciones con editores en primera persona.* Papeles de la Fundación Germán Sánchez Ruipérez.

García Naharro, F. (2015). Las publicaciones oficiales. Editora Nacional. In J. A. Martínez Martín (Ed.), *Historia de la Edición en España (1939–1975)* (pp. 209–232). Marcial Pons.

Gili, G. (1944). *Bosquejo de una política del libro.* Impresora Hispano Americana.

Hall, P. A., & Soskice, D. (2001). *Varieties of capitalism: The institutional foundations of comparative advantage.* Oxford University Press.

Larraz Elorriaga, F. (2010). *Una historia transatlántica del libro: relaciones editoriales entre España y América Latina (1936–1950).* Trea.

Larraz Elorriaga, F. (2009). *El monopolio de la palabra: el exilio intelectual en la España franquista.* Biblioteca Nueva.

Larraz Elorriaga, F. (2007). Los editores españoles ante los mercados de lectura americanos (1900–1939). *Cuadernos Americanos: Nueva Epoca, 119*(1), 131–150.

Linz, J. (1983). A Century of Politics and Interests in Spain. In S. Berger (Ed.), *Organizing interests in Western Europe: Pluralism, corporatism, and the transformation of politics* (pp. 367–415). Cambridge University Press.

McCraw, Thomas K. (Ed.). (1997). *Creating modern capitalism: How entrepreneurs, companies, and countries triumphed in three industrial revolutions*. Harvard University. https://doi.org/10.1086/ahr/104.4.1271

Martín Aceña, P., & Martínez Ruiz, E. (2007). The golden age of Spanish capitalism: Economic growth without political freedom. In N. Townson (Ed.), *Spain transformed the late Franco dictatorship, 1959–75* (pp. 30–46). Palgrave Macmillan.

Martínez Martín, J. A. (2015a). Editar en tiempos de dictadura. La política del libro y las condiciones del campo editorial. In J. A. Martínez Martín (Ed.), *Historia de la Edición en España (1939–1975)* (pp. 27–42). Marcial Pons.

Martínez Martín, J. A. (2015b). La autarquía editorial. Los años cuarenta y cincuenta. In J. A. Martínez Martín (Ed.), *Historia de la Edición en España (1939–1975)* (pp. 233–272). Marcial Pons.

Martínez Martín, J. A. (2015c). El capitalismo de la edición moderno. Las empresas editoriales: negocios, política y cultura. Los años sesenta. In J. A. Martínez Martín (Ed.), *Historia de la Edición en España (1939–1975)* (pp. 273–328). Marcial Pons.

Martínez Rus, A. (2002). La industria editorial española ante los mercados americanos del libro 1892–1936. *Hispania, 62*(212), 1021–1058. https://doi.org/10.3989/hispania.2002.v62.i212.248

Martínez Rus, A. (2008). Exportando cultura: las estrategias transatlánticas de los editores españoles, 1892–1936. *Revista de la Historia de la Economía y de la Empresa 2*, 183–204.

Menchero de los Ríos, C. (2015). La modernización de la censura: la ley de 1966 y su aplicación. In J. A. Martínez Martín (Ed.), *Historia de la Edición en España (1939–1975)* (pp. 67–96). Marcial Pons.

Palomares, C. (2007). New Political Mentalities in the Tardofranquismo. In N. Townson (Ed.) *Spain transformed. The late Franco dictatorship, 1959–75* (pp. 118–139). Palgrave Macmillan.

Prados de la Escosura, L. (2003). *El progreso económico de España (1850- 2000)*. Fundación BBVA.

Puig, N., & Fernández, P. (2008). La gran empresa familiar española en el siglo XX: claves de su profesionalización. *Revista de la Historia de la Economía y la Empresa, 2*, 93–122.

Sánchez García, R., Martínez Rus, A., & Martín, M. (2004). *Jesús A. Los patronos del libro: Las asociaciones corporativas de editores y libreros*. Ediciones Trea.

Rodrigo Echalecu, A. M. (2015). Los organismos del libro y el corporativismo editorial. El Instituto Nacional del Libro Español. In J. A. Martínez Martín (Ed.), *Historia de la Edición en España (1939–1975)* (pp. 97–120). Marcial Pons.

Royo, S. (2007). Varieties of capitalism in Spain: Business and the politics of coordination. *European Journal of Industrial Relations, 13*(1), 47–65. https://doi.org/10.1177/0959680107073967

Royo, S. (2002). *A new century of corporatism? Corporatism in Southern Europe*. Praeger Publishers.

Ruiz Bautista, E. (2015). La censura editorial. Depuraciones de libros y bibliotecas. In J. A. Martínez Martín (Ed.), *Historia de la edición en España (1939–1975)* (pp. 43–65). Marcial Pons.

Ruiz Bautista, E. (2008). *Tiempo de censura: la represión editorial durante el franquismo*. Ediciones Trea.

Torres Villanueva, E. (2003). Comportamientos empresariales en una economía intervenida: España, 1936–1957. In G. Sánchez and J. Tascón (Eds.), *Los empresarios de Franco. Política y economía en España, 1936–1957* (pp. 199–224). Crítica.

Tortella, G., & Jiménez, J. C. (1986). *Historia del Banco de Crédito Industrial*. Alianza.

Townson, Nigel (Ed.). (2007). *Spain Transformed. The Late Franco Dictatorship, 1959–75*. Palgrave Macmillan.

Valdaliso, J. M. (2007). Spanish shipping firms in twentieth century: Between the Internationalisation of the market and the nationalism of the state. *International Journal of Maritime History, 19*(2), 21–42. https://doi.org/10.1177/084387140701900203

Velarde, J. (2009). *Cien años de economía española*. Encuentro.

Wilkins, M. (2010). Multinational Enterprises and the Varieties of capitalism. *Business History Review, 84*(4), 638–45. https://doi.org/10.1017/S0007680500080569

'No mutiny will be allowed': business, the tax system and the Greek version of Mediterranean capitalism during dictatorship, 1967–1974

Zoi Pittaki

ABSTRACT
This article analyses the interaction between the system of taxation and business in Greece during the crucial period of the military dictatorship (1967-1974) in order to throw light on the Greek version of Mediterranean capitalism that developed in the post-Second World War framework and how it affected business doing in the country. It will be shown that through this type of capitalism clientelism and 'shadow' or informal economic transactions ended up being prevalent features of the current Greek economic reality.

Introduction

At around 2am in the morning of 21 April 1967, tanks rolled onto the streets of Athens. A group of middle rank military officers comprised of four colonels and one brigadier, had overthrown the government and arrested the Prime Minister, the leaders of the opposition as well as members of the leadership of the Armed Forces (Tsounakos, 1999, p. 12). The dictators presented their movement as a way out of the country's political deadlock created 'because of the responsible political forces' inability to reach a consensus' (The trial of the junta, 1981, pp. 05:58–06:37) but also as a means to avert the 'communist danger' (Tsounakos, 1999, p.14).

It seems that there were many reasons that led to the dictatorship which included the intensification of political unrest in 1965 that led to the fall of the Centre Union government and the fact that the Crown[1] 'intervened in any aspect of the Greek political reality' not hesitating, according to Markezinis (2011, p. 56), even to bribe politicians in order to support the first 'apostate' government in July 1965. Another cause was probably the strength of the role of the army after the winning of elections by General Alexandros Papagos in 1952 and the establishment of paramilitary groups within it (Stebilis, 2014).

The dismantling of democracy and the imposition of a military dictatorship regime that ruled the country for seven consecutive years (Efstathiades, 2000) was a key period in Greek history, being marked not only by the socio-political upheaval that followed the abolition of democracy, but also the Turkish invasion in Cyprus. An additional consequence of the dictatorship that marked the political and economic history of modern Greece was the rapid deterioration of the quality of public administration. As will be shown in the next pages, this deterioration also affected negatively the functioning of the tax system, relations between tax authorities and taxpayers but also the type and character of capitalism that developed in the country.

In more detail, during the time examined in this article, Greece was a country with a large agrarian sector, liberal arrangements with regards to labour relations, but also a state intervening into the market process. This is to a large extent true for the current economic model of the country as well. Hall and Soskice call this variant of capitalism, which combines characteristics from Liberal Market Economies (LMEs) and Coordinated Market Economies (CMEs) a Mediterranean one (Hall and Soskice 2001, p. 21). This classification of capitalism is found in South and South-Eastern European countries like Greece, Spain, Italy and Cyprus, where economic transactions take place within a framework that combines laissez-faire and coordinated market arrangements (Epaminonda, 2016, pp. 322–3). There have been many studies on countries with 'hybrid' economic systems, that is, systems that combine characteristics of both Liberal and Coordinated Market economies and do not represent the main Varieties of Capitalism countries. The capitalist systems of such countries have been characterised (arguably rather simplistically) as 'combinations of regulated product markets, regulated (or 'rigid') labour markets, bank-based finance, and weak education systems (Amable in Meardi (2012), p. 58). In most of such cases, market coordination is done through institutions. For the case of Greece, an institution that, as will be shown here, had a significant impact on economic transactions and relations between business and the government, was the system of taxation.

By exploring how the system of taxation shaped the variety of capitalism that developed in Greece, this article falls within the broader category of studies that explore the European South from a Varieties of Capitalism perspective. Regini's work was one of the first examples of this kind of literature. Focusing on the Italian system of production, he suggested that the 'flexible specialization' strategy used in the various industrial districts of Italy was the most successful one due to a combination of weak regulations and 'unstable voluntaristic' institutions (Regini, 1997, p. 105). There have also been approaches where countries representing the 'hybrid capitalism' sphere have been explored in terms of whether institutional changes lead to convergence or divergence with the LME and CME paradigms, a notion known as the 'dual convergence hypothesis' that was analysed by Hay (2004), among others. This was the approach also followed by Kornelakis (2011), who comparatively examined Italy and Greece with Germany and Britain by focusing on the institutional domains of industrial relations and finance/corporate governance. Kornelakis' research suggested that no convergence existed and that different institutions changed in different directions since 'industrial relations are becoming more coordinated and corporate governance/finance more liberal' (p. 49). Following a different approach, Royo (2007) focused on Spain as a representative of the Mediterranean variety of capitalism and suggested that if the Spanish political system allowed the economic one to adopt more 'coordinated economy' features, this would promote positive institutional change that would support the competitiveness of Spanish firms. More recently, Vallejo-Pena and Giachi (2018) examined Spain, Greece, Italy and Portugal as representatives of the Mediterranean variety of capitalism and compared them from a sociological perspective with the rest of Europe, focusing on labour productivity and work schedules. Among their findings was that policies introducing the European employment policy stimulus of 'flexicurity' in the work schedules seemed to be associated with higher levels of productivity in the European South. The present article contributes to the VoC literature by focusing exclusively on the case of Greece and exploring how the system of taxation created difficulties for business and shaped the kind of capitalism that developed in the country.

In more detail, during the period under consideration, the Greek system of taxation was burdened with a series of weaknesses. The disruption in the system's structures, which already existed prior to the dictatorship but got deeper during the seven years that it lasted for, was expressed through problems such as corruption,[2] bureaucratic rigidities of the tax procedures and complexity of legislation. All this caused a lot of difficulties for business but also ended up promoting unproductive forms of entrepreneurship, such as tax evasion. It should be noted here that corruption has been an endemic problem in the modern Greek state, affecting it even from its establishment in the late nineteenth century.[3]

During the seven years of dictatorship, apart from imposing severe fines against tax law offences and ardently declaring its willingness to modernise the public sector and eradicate corruption from it, the junta established a regime that was anything but modern and non-corrupt. In this way, it solidified and consolidated long-standing perceptions about the illegitimacy of the tax system and by an extension, the illegitimacy of the whole state apparatus.

This article will analyse the interaction between the system of taxation and business in Greece during the crucial period of the military dictatorship in order to throw light on the version of Mediterranean capitalism that developed in the country in the post-Second World War framework. It will be shown that through this type of capitalism clientelism[4] and 'shadow' or informal economic transactions ended up being prevalent features of the current Greek economic reality.[5] The theoretical framework within which the present analysis will develop will be that of historical institutionalism, a sub-category of new institutionalism that emerged in the 1960s and 1970s and which considers institutions such as the system of taxation as 'the legacy of concrete historical processes' (Thelen, 1999, p. 382). Following a historical institutionalist approach, this article will view the Greek tax system as an outcome of past events but will also will take into consideration the interactions between various agents relating to it (predominantly, between the representatives of the state, the members of tax administration and entrepreneurs/taxpayers).

Economy and industry during the dictatorship

According to Veremis, the group of people that subverted democracy and imposed a dictatorial regime in 1967 Greece did not have a 'politically comprehensible ideology or sensible views about the form of the regime or the nature of their choices' (Veremis 1999, p. 15). However, the views they expressed with regards to the economic policies that they would follow probably seemed pretty clear, as they pronounced their eagerness to establish a state that would be smaller (Kazakos, 2001, p. 268), less regulated (Psalidopoulos, 2014, p. 249) and more 'open' to entrepreneurship (Kazakos, 2001, p. 268). Indeed, in the Bank of Greece Governor's Annual Report for 1967 presenting the basic principles of the five-year economic plan for 1968-1972 it was noted that 'private business initiative is considered to be the basic pillar of the process of economic development, evolving within a framework of free competition, having profit as its main motivation...The role of the State and other...public bodies...shall be strictly limited to offering services of economic and social infrastructure in order to assist private business activities' (Bank of Greece, 1968, p. 24).

Further on this issue, Pesmazoglou wrote that the dictators considered entrepreneurs' support to be necessary for the establishment of the regime, and, for this reason, their stance towards the latters' requests and propositions was one of a 'relaxed laissez faire' (in Kazakos, 2001, pp. 268-9). By this it was meant that the economic policies followed adhered to some (hence the use of the word 'relaxed') liberal principles, as the regime 'was more open to entrepreneurship and attributed less importance to the role of the state aside of its traditional functions (defence, public order, infrastructure)' (Ibid., p. 268). However, this was obviously an 'asymmetric' laissez faire (Kazakos, 2001, p. 269). It functioned in a non-democratic framework which, through the imprisonment of thousands, made it impossible for large parts of the Greek society to actively participate in the economy.

With regards to the general characteristics of the economy, after a temporary recession in 1967 (manifested through a reduction in the GDP growth rate), the first years of the coup saw a rapid increase of growth since 'the governments of the dictatorship attempted from the outset to give a new impetus to the economy and to secure their legitimacy or, simply, [the people's] tolerance' (ibid., p. 268).

There was also an increase in the number of incentives for investment mainly for building construction and tourism (Kazakos, 2001, p. 268.), the two major factors of economic expansion during this period (ibid., p. 271). In addition, the number of loans given to enterprises increased (Karakousis, 1999, p. 24). Indeed, in contrast to the strict credit policies of the 1950s (Psalidopoulos, 2014, p. 227), during the dictatorship it became much easier to obtain a loan. Psalidopoulos notes that for the first time, 'the Bank of Greece prepaid [commercial] banks' medium-term loans for investment in industry, construction, tourism and shipping' (ibid., p. 250). Low-interest rate credit was also provided to wheat trade firms and companies undertaking public works. More generally, the procedures required for the provision of loans to commercial enterprises were simplified. Furthermore, liquidity assistance was provided to commercial banks and there was a reduction in the discount rate of the Bank of Greece (ibid). The dictatorship's governments also made attempts to attract investors from abroad (Kazakos, 2001, p. 268.) Their efforts were not without success, as the amount of foreign investment capital in 1972 was double that of 1966.[6]

Also, it was during the dictatorship that the industrial sector's share of the country's national product reached its highest percentage (28% for the years 1970–1974) (Mitchell, 2007, p. 1038). Actually, according to an official announcement of the government on the basis of OECD data, for the twelve-month period February 1971–January 1972, Greece's rate of increase of industrial production was the highest amongst all OECD member-states. (Bulletin of the Federation of Greek Industrialists (FGI), 1972a).

However, it is important to note that in many cases, as far as the exercise of economic policy is concerned, the dictatorship was more successful in producing highly populist statements rather than in implementing plans that would actually benefit the economy. For example, in November 1968, the regime concluded an agreement with Aristotle Onassis, regarding 'the functioning of the State oil refineries and the establishment and exploitation of a third refinery'. The USD 400 million investment[7] was the largest Greece had seen up to that point, most conveniently serving the dictators' propaganda that the 'Revolution', as they called their regime, created a sense of stability that persuaded 'Greek capital throughout the world and the Greek spirit of entrepreneurship to come back to the...motherland in order to actively contribute to the realisation of Greece's leap of rapid economic development' (Bulletin of the Chamber of Commerce & Industry of Athens, 1968). In truth, what happened was that at some point, Onassis withdrew his interest and the functioning of the refinery was offered with favourable terms to the Niarchos Group. The Group assumed the obligation to 'make various other investments as a compensation for the advantages [it had been given]' (Psalidopoulos, 2014, p. 47). Yet, it was 'extraordinarily late' in fulfilling such obligations, and it actually never did so. More to the point, after the fall of dictatorship the state bought the refinery back from the Niarchos Group for USD 12 million, and it released the Group 'from its other contractual obligations' (ibid).

In the same vein, as Psalidopoulos mentions, according to the Bank of Greece the growth in building construction, (the sector which saw the most 'explosive' growth during the junta) 'could not be considered a favourable factor in the long run, because it [would result] in an unbalanced structuring of production factors' (Psalidopoulos, 2014, p. 272). Recent literature has supported this view; for example, it has been noted that construction 'excessively absorbed entrepreneurial capacity and sources...at the expense of other activities. Even more so, when the crisis of 1973 emerged, manufacturing also entered a period of stagnation (ibid., p. 288).

Generally, in the 1967–1970 period there was an excessive amount of loan funds channeled to already existing enterprises, something that 'not only reduced the funds available for new productive activities and investments, but also slowed down, according to [the Governor of the Bank of Greece], the transition from family enterprises to...joint stock companies, which offer a wider and more stable basis for the development of entrepreneurial activity' (Psalidopoulos, 2014, p. 257). In this framework, in the midst of the economic downturn in 1974 and a few months before the fall of dictatorship, the president of the Federation of Greek Industrialists (FGI), Ioannis Mitsos, referred to the inconsistency characterising the policies the regime undertook for the development of industry. Such policies, noted Mitsos, 'add to the already existing uncertainty because of the international developments, breed entrepreneurial reluctance, make investment planning...difficult, [and] impede export efforts...' (Panselina & Mavroeidi, 2007, p. 424).

The deterioration of the economic environment can be indicated by the fact that, in spite of the significant growth of the period,[8] the rate of increase of investment in manufacturing industry throughout dictatorship (1967–1974), although less volatile, was lower than previous years and significantly lower than 1964 and 1965.[9]

Problems with credit probably contributed to the worsening of the economic environment. Indeed, in spite of the fact that, as noted above, the number of loans given to enterprises increased significantly during the dictatorship, the FGI still complained about the difficulty of securing a loan. This difficulty had to do, among others, with the level of collateral required as well as with the 'obsolete' criteria on the basis of which loan funds were given, i.e. the time-consuming procedures required for the provision of such loan funds (Bulletin of the FGI, 1972b).

Many other factors could be examined too; for instance, according to Kazakos, although, in broad terms, the dictatorship followed liberal economic policies, many supporters of the regime envisioned models of development of a socialist type, in which, for example, business initiatives would be undertaken not by business people but by the army (2001, p. 275). An additional difficulty, which in fact comprises part of the main locus of interest of this article, is that the modernisation in the system of public administration and the broader state apparatus that the junta fervently declared from the first day of the dictatorship did not materialise. The present analysis suggests that this was the case by focusing on the system of tax administration.

Generally, the matter of modernisation is a contested subject in the literature exploring the impact that the junta had on Greece's state mechanisms but also on the Greek socio-political and economic reality. For example, Samarinis (2017), examining modernisation from the perspective of the transformation of the urban landscape, suggested that during the junta years Greece did indeed experience substantial transformation since building activities saw an explosive growth and the natural environment changed significantly. Similarly, Kalyvas noted that the country went through a process of social modernisation during the dictatorship, since, among other things, patterns of consumption and recreation started resembling those followed in Western European countries (2017). However, other than that, it seems that there is a consensus in the literature that many of the declarations of the junta about the modernisation of the state apparatus per se and the relevant necessary reforms in the public administration never became a reality (see for example Poulantzas, 1976, p. 121 and Zolotas,1975, p. 8.) As Bermeo notes, the Greek dictatorship did not have the bureaucratic-authoritarian character of Latin-American dictatorships, which had clearly defined aspirations for the modernisation of the state mechanism. In the case of Greece, the coup 'was more personalist and less dominated by a technocratic bureaucracy' (Bermeo, 1995, p. 443). This was not only due to the power and influence that the leaders of the dictatorship had but also because '[t]he vast majority of the nation's technocrats would have nothing to do with the regime' (ibid). The modernisation of the state apparatus that the dictatorship seemed to espouse did not materialise: 'The regime's rhetoric was laced with populist themes, but...the themes were meaningless in terms of concrete policies' (ibid., p. 445). However, the literature does not offer specific examples of how modernisation failed to materialise in the various sectors of the state mechanism and how this affected business. As will be shown in the following pages, the present article does this by focusing on the system of tax administration.

The tax system: further deterioration in spite of the declarations

The period of dictatorship saw particularly significant tax incentives for the promotion of industrial development, however the system was suffering from a series of weaknesses. In spite of their declarations, the members of the coup did very little to modernise and improve the tax administration structures and reduce corruption. On the contrary, and as will be shown in the next pages, this period witnessed a dismantling of the tax services because of the dismissals of civil servants that were not on good terms with the regime.

In more detail, a few months after the imposition of the coup, the Deputy Minister of Economics Spyridon Lizardos, representing a government that declared its willingness to 'combat tax evasion in any possible way' (Bulletin of the Chamber of Commerce & Industry of Athens, 1967a), announced a new compulsory tax law (185/1967 (ibid, 1967b)). The law set the procedures of criminal prosecution against those who were accused of having broken 'paragraph 4 of the 5th article of the Tax Code and article 3 of the legislative order 3848/1958', by affecting the validity of accounting books. In more detail, the law, entitled 'On the imposition of penal sanctions against tax law offenders' stated that owners or managers of Greek companies and managers or representatives of foreign companies based in Greece being accused of such acts would be called before emergency military courts. Chief accounting officers of companies and 'any third person who in any way contributes to acts or omissions that constitute [the accounting books] inaccurate' would also face emergency military courts. The same applied for 'civil servants and any third person... [committing] crimes having to do with bribing' (ibid., 1967a).

More significantly, according to Lizardos, the penal and administrative sanctions that the law provided for the types of offences mentioned above, such as imprisonment, imposition of large fines and loan-granting bans, were 'severe and economically devastating' (ibid). For the cases of bribes, it was stated that 'any civil servant belonging to the Ministry of Economics, demanding or accepting gifts or other inappropriate benefits, or [demanding or accepting] the promise [of such gifts or other inappropriate benefits] in order for him to perform or omit a specific act relating to...tax matters, in the future or presently, will be punished with one year imprisonment' (ibid., 1967b).

The regime also used strong language to condemn the instances of corrupt tax officers (and civil servants in general), employing a discourse comprised of a mixture of patriotic rhetoric, advice, warnings, and veiled threats. For example, a few months after the imposition of the coup, in a congress of tax officers organised in the Athens College of Commerce,[10] the regime's Minister of Economics Adamantios Androutsopoulos stressed in his speech that it was true that, 'maybe unfairly so, when the Greeks hear about civil servants having no integrity, they think of tax officers...We have to convince Greek taxpayers that this is not the case. Most important, we have to convince so ourselves (Makedonia, 1967).' Acknowledging that lately there had been cases in which 'worthless civil servants fell short of their mission and of the Greek people's expectations', Androutsopoulos addressed tax officers with the following words:

> I would like you to do your job bearing in mind...the presumption that you are honest, that you have integrity and that you do all you can to perform your duties in the best possible way. Take initiatives. Being scared and avoiding responsibilities will not be forgiven...[r]egardless of your beliefs about...relations with the state, if any of you...do not have the moral strength to courageously perform your duties as civil servants...if [you] do not want to remain on board the ship, you can state so. [Because], when in the middle of the sea, no mutiny will be allowed (ibid, p. 7)

The reality though is that despite the discourse that the junta put forward, the malaises of the tax system did not disappear. Chronic problems that existed since long before the dictatorship kept on burdening it. There were various critiques about that, coming also from the representatives of business organisations. For example, in the 31 May 1972 issue of the *Bulletin of the FGI* there was a critique about taxes in favour of third parties. Such taxes were imposed on transactions and funded professional groups, lobbies or organisations with great negotiating power 'of a political, economic or trade-union nature' (Glykou, 2009, p. 177). It is no surprise that the existence of such taxes increased the perceived unfairness and illegitimacy of the tax system. In the *Bulletin of the FGI* it was noted that 'the state's advice and requests to industry regarding the [reduction] of production costs to competitive levels could have practical value if they were accompanied by...measures that would eliminate a series of...charges that have nothing to do with production', meaning the 'various taxes in favour of third parties', a reality of the past that was 'unacceptable' (Bulletin of the FGI, 20, 238, 31.05.1972, pp. 3–4).

Moreover, in the 29 February 1972 issue of the *Bulletin of the FGI*, industrialists complained about the low level of depreciation rates. Specifically, it was stressed that for the first year of the 'life' of every piece of mechanical equipment, the maximum depreciation rate in Greece was 8%,[11] in comparison to 40% in France, 20% in Germany, 35% in Italy, 30% in Sweden [and] 60% in Britain...' (ibid., 20, 232, 29.02.1972, p. 2.) Low depreciation rates delayed the renewal of mechanical equipment, reducing thus the effectiveness of various relevant incentives that the state had introduced. For the FGI, the state policies on this matter indicated 'confusion and inconsistency', because, 'on the one hand the State implores industry to modernise its mechanical equipment and on the other prevents it from doing so by limiting depreciation rates to 8%, considering perhaps that in this way it will have more revenue from taxation in the short run, without realising what itself and the whole economy lose in the long run because of the technological backwardness in production...'. 'It is...very dangerous', continued the article, 'to treat industry as a kind of an experimental animal for development, [t]o try to compromise the State's need for revenues with industry's modernisation' (ibid., 20, 231, 15.02.1972, pp. 1–2).

References to the problematic role of the tax authorities also increased in this period, coming mostly from tax experts but also tax officers themselves. There were also references in the press regarding cases of corruption. One such involved the arrest of a tax officer after having been accused of extortion by a taxpayer in June 1972. The regime's representatives commented on the incident using the type of discourse they were familiar with; specifically, the Deputy Prime Minister of the government Stylianos Pattakos declared, among others, that 'delays...cause, on the one hand, the...citizen's dissatisfaction and on the other...force him to form an unworthy transaction with vicious and opportunist intermediaries or with disloyal civil servants, in order to achieve the speeding-up of the procedures... (Ta Nea, 1972).

A significant amount of critique expressed by the Greek business community during the time also had to do with the problem of bureaucracy. For example, in November 1971 the business magazine *Viomichaniki Epitheorissis* referred to the 'Herculean task of exterminating the lernaean hydra of bureaucracy', as it characterised 'the new "campaign" of the Government for the lifting of the purposeless, complex...procedures...which make it impossible for the state mechanisms to function properly, undermine the efforts for progress in our country and prevent the improvement of the relations between citizens and the State' (p. 11).

Similar points were made by the FGI too, which through its Bulletin noted that, among others, bureaucratic incompetence adversely impacted upon economic development: '[T]he mistakes of the public administration', it was noted, 'burden the whole of the national economy, having usually immensely inhibitive effects on economic progress (Bulletin of the FGI, 1972c).

There were also references about the lack of uniform criteria and principles governing the audits, the complexity and frequency of change of the various tax laws, but also the tax officers' training needs. As for their arbitrariness, it was very often associated with the way the tax laws had been constructed (Sellas, 1972, pp. 957–8). For example, in a speech that was published in the *Tax Review* in December 1972, Stephanos Sellas, a tax official, noted that, although in the past twenty years the tax services had seen important improvements, there were not any specific regulations governing the way tax audits should be conducted. The available laws contained the provisions that should be implemented in the audits, but they did not include any information about how the audits should be carried out. There only existed the Code of the Status of Civil Servants (Law 1811/1951) which referred, in general terms and among others, to the civil servants' responsibilities and rights, containing also general guidelines about the rules and official orders governing the conduct of civil servants belonging to the Ministry of Economics. In spite of its generality, 'it would have been desirable', noted Sellas, 'that every tax auditor had a clearer view of such texts when taking an oath [in order to assume his duties], and that every tax officer had a copy of [the Code]...I urge you all...to study this [Code]' (ibid.)

In the same year, in a commentary about, among others, the compulsory law 185/1967 against tax law offences analysed above, Theodoros Staikos, a tax expert, noted that the law was 'a sword of Damocles' that 'unexpectedly criminalised the country's economic life, being introduced without the prior...establishment of modern Economic Laws, and being based mostly on the excessive formalism [and] improvisation of the Tax Code' (Staikos, 1972, pp. 81–2). Criticising also the Tax Code and characterising it as an 'experimentation...against [the] [n] ational [e]conomy, being subject to constant modifications', Staikos noted that due to the complexity of the various provisions of the Code, tax payers' accounting books were usually found to be inaccurate. Owing to this, tax payers would have to face 'a) the imposition of a fine, b) the arbitrary assessment of gross revenue for multiple fiscal years with the use of the maximum net profit rate and without taking into consideration business expenses, and c) a criminal prosecution' (ibid., p. 82). 'The phrase "you will either compromise or I will audit [your books]", continued Staikos, 'should stop being heard and we should, at last...introduce in our country too the modern accounting and audit systems that apply in the healthy economies of the EEC countries.' Staikos noted that in such systems, accounting and auditing principles were based on scientific methods and offered the ability to conduct audits on an individualised but also secure basis (ibid., p. 83).

The law 185/1967 was criticized also by the business community in the *Bulletin of the FGI*, again with regards to the lack of uniformity in auditing rules. Here, it was noted that, according to a tax expert, 'having three tax officers separately auditing the accounting books of a large company and making the same assessment for the level of its [taxable] income, would be a random coincidence, under the current tax regime (1970, p.1).' It was also recorded that tax experts agreed that the lack of accounting control mechanisms, the lack of any certain criteria that would allow the distinction between tax evasion and tax avoidance but also the arbitrary penalisation of certain acts made the law unacceptable. It was clear, the article continued, 'that the prosecution in penal courts as "offenders against the law" of large numbers of companies that are perfectly reputable and have an excellent tax-paying record' was a result of provisions that were not well thought-of. Overall, the article stressed that the law needed to change, because some parts of it were 'clear disincentives for private entrepreneurial initiative.'

It should also be noted that in spite of its severity, with the exception of the first years of its implementation, the law did not seem particularly effective in terms of increasing tax revenues. This is indicated by the fact that after 1969 there was no clear positive trend in the ratio Tax Revenues/GDP (ibid., pp. 13; 86–7). More broadly, in the Bank of Greece Governor's annual reports for 1972, 1973 and 1974 there were no references on any reduction of tax evasion or improvement of the function of the tax services, as was the case in the reports for previous years, such as for example 1968, 1969 and 1971.[12]

Indeed, it seems that there was not any improvement in the function of the tax services throughout the seven years of dictatorship. On the contrary, during the coup the problems in the broader public sector grew much larger, something that undoubtedly adversely affected the tax services too. The case of George Langrod, the professor and OECD consultant that visited Greece in 1963 in order to offer advice for the re-organisation of the public services is indicative of this reality. According to Argyriades (2010), certain obstacles existed which prevented promotion of research in administration. Argyriades, Langrod and others, were part of a group that attempted to overcome such obstacles, their cooperation however was discontinued because of the dictatorship. (ibid, pp. 3-4.) The coup was also the reason why, according to Argyriades, the 'ambitious' ideas for the creation of a School of Public Administration following 'more or less' the model of the National School of Administration (ENA) in France did not materialise at that point (ibid., p. 2).[13]

Generally, as Zolotas noted in 1975, the dictatorship left public organisations and the broader public administration in a state of 'generalised disruption' (p. 8). With regards to the system of tax administration, apart from all the other issues, the dictatorship also led to the demise of the Central Service of the Ministry of Economics, a structure of the system of taxation that operated relatively satisfactorily up to this point, in comparison to what followed next. According to Charalampos Nikolakopoulos, the former president of the trade union of tax officers, the Central Service 'had the executive role of administration and legislating. That is, it was focused on the administrative issues of the tax services throughout the country (transfers of officers, payroll, etc.) and on creating tax legislation such as the VAT, taxes according to the Code of Accounting Books and Records, etc.' (interview excerpt). Ioannis Photopoulos, who served as an executive of the Service during the period 1965-1981, noted:

> When I entered the Central Service in 1965, the procedure followed was this one: there was a need of...ten people for permanent posts in the Service. First, the responsible inspectors recommended the thirty best employees from the peripheral services of the ministry. They were highly knowledgeable, had executive capacities, spoke foreign languages, etc. Out of those thirty people, who would be seconded to the ministry for two years, the ten best would be chosen. Those ten best would be transferred to the Central Service of the ministry, with increased responsibilities but also higher wages. Within those two years, a thorough evaluation of the candidates' operational capabilities took place. At the end of this strictly supervised procedure, reports of operational capacity were produced. Those of the thirty who were not finally chosen..., went back to the peripheral services they had come from, with absolutely no negative reference or suspicion with regards to their capabilities and competences in their role as employees of the ministry. In other words, this Central Service, in which I was privileged to be chosen to work, functioned perfectly. We had a great library, and generally, we were offered all the necessary means in order to faultlessly implement the decisions of the various governments, without however being subjected to any influences from them (interview excerpt).

The Service was essentially dismantled after 1967, as the junta regime 'dismissed a large number of capable employees for political reasons' (ibid). From this point onwards, noted Photopoulos, the members of the Service came directly from the peripheral tax offices, lacking the necessary training and executive capabilities. The argument that tax officers did not receive the necessary training was supported also by a retired tax officer that was interviewed for the purposes of this research, who joined the Ministry of Economics in January 1974, a few months before the fall of the dictatorship: 'We had no training. I was given a post in a department and the director used to tell me what to do. If your manager wanted you to learn, you would learn. If not, he kept the knowledge to himself and you were asked to do all the dull work (interview excerpt).'

Adding to this point, in an article originally written in 1995, Photopoulos noted that the dismantling of the Central Service of the Ministry of Economics by the dictatorial government 'was a severe blow to the creation of executives of high scientific standards; its results became obvious several years later, with the decline in the quality of the tax bills that were proposed in the Parliament and of the interpretative statements issued [by the Ministry of Economics] in cases of controversial [tax] matters.' (2010, p. 896). Confirming Photopoulos' point in a more general sense, Kazakos noted that the people the junta appointed as executives in the various ministries were 'distinctively uneducated' (2001, pp. 269–70). This point is supported also by Bermeo, since 'the junta had trouble recruiting ministers who were even remotely presentable.' Ministries were sometimes 'offered to five or six people before finding a taker' (1995, p. 443).

Indeed, in order to understand how the generalised disruption of the public services (part of which were the tax services too) manifested itself during dictatorship, one has to examine what measures the junta undertook in order to achieve the modernisation of the civil service it had been proclaiming since 1967. In the same manner, one needs to examine whether the dictators' fervent condemnations of corruption had any real impact on the public services. In such terms, it should be noted that the junta indeed dismissed a large number of civil servants, but no reliable information has been found about whether such dismissals were on grounds of corruption or incompetency. On the contrary, there has been a considerable amount of material suggesting that the modernisation the regime had declared failed. This is because, in spite of the regime's rhetoric for the need to eradicate corruption, reorganise and clean up the public sector, the dismissals of civil servants were made not on the basis of their integrity and professional capabilities, but, as Photopoulos noted, on the basis of whether or not they were loyal to the regime.

For example, on 26 April 1967, five days after the imposition of the dictatorship, the junta announced a plan for the 'reorganization of government administration' (Schwab & Frangos, 1970, p. 24), with Stylianos Pattakos, the Minister of Internal Affairs, declaring that '[n]epotism, corruption and demagoguery must be purged from the government' (ibid., pp. 24–5). In the same manner, on 3 May 'the abolition of bureaucracy' was announced, (ibid., p. 25) with the cabinet deciding 'the obligation of all civil servants to defend their actions on application by citizens, within 3 days for simple cases and 7 days for more complicated affairs', and also stressing that '[i]ntervention by [third] parties, influence peddlers and contact men in government is prohibited' (ibid.). Schwab and Frangos noted that the regime also drafted three decrees '[providing] for the termination of the term in office of 'all special advisers and senior officials of state organizations…as well as for the abolition of certain provisions which are opposed to the common sentiment of justice and morality' (ibid.).

However, according to Gallant, '[most of the dictators'] domestic initiatives were aimed at removing anyone whose loyalty to the regime was suspect…' (Gallant, 2001, p. 199.) Indeed, in the text of the three decrees the regime produced it was stated that '[c]ivil servants…are formally dismissed…if their disloyalty is established; the provisions of the constitution concerning irremovability [of civil servants] and all those protecting labor agreements are suspended in the cases referred to' (Schwab & Frangos, 1970, p. 25). Those accused of disloyalty would be the ones found to have and/or promote 'Communist or anti-national ideas', or those who had 'any form of contact or relations with the holders of these opinions' (ibid). For the verification of loyalty, the decrees stated that 'all…civil servants…must submit to the responsible minister…a written declaration of their loyalty…' (ibid., p. 27).

According to a documentary focusing on the period and characterising the regime's declared principles of meritocracy as 'only imaginary', (I Michani tou Chronou, n.d., 23:20–24:18) the dictatorship dismissed hundreds of thousands of civil servants that were not 'approved of,' (ibid) giving their posts to people who were friendly to the regime (ibid., 25:00–25:08). For example, a large number of teachers who were considered to be 'dangerous' were fired and replaced by retired teachers. Younger teachers were hired only with a 'certificate of social ideals' (ibid., 12:25–12:40).[14] Also, it has been noted that, in order to better control the public sector, the dictators usually appointed retired military officers in key positions in it, giving them the title of the 'Commissioner of the Administration' (I Michani tou Chronou, n.d., 44:23–44:42).

The fact that no actual modernisation of the civil service took place was something even followers of the regime admitted. For example, in November 1967, only seven months after the imposition of the coup, Savvas Konstantopoulos, the publisher of the newspaper *Free World* that supported the dictatorial regime, admitted, in a letter he sent to Konstantinos Karamanlis, that the 'revolution' had failed in achieving its goal to 'resolve some permanent… problems in order to… make a step of progress and normalise public life' (The Konstantinos G. Karamanlis Archive, pp. 49–50). Amongst the reasons for such failure, wrote Konstantopoulos, was that almost none of those in the government had political skills and none was willing to use the services of competent technocrats: 'Part of the military officers proclaimed that people which [in the past] had some public role should not get involved in the revolution. Thus, they turned to those who were incompetent or inexperienced' (ibid., p. 50). The 'revolution's' failure, continued Konstantopoulos, was also due to the fact that there was often a complete lack of any serious organisation: 'Solemnly taken decisions were recalled. Laws that had been published at the Government's Gazette were withdrawn. Measures that had been already communicated, changed from one moment to the next'. In such a state, continued Konstantopoulos, 'the Government does not move forward; it is like a car stuck in the mud. No progress has been made in the education and the administration, although it has been seven months since the 21st of April. No revolutionary measures and no profound changes [have been implemented]' (ibid.).

In the same vein, Yannopoulos, writing in 1972, noted that '[t]he lack of any political programme and the low quality of the junta's collaborators are evidence enough that the regime cannot claim to lead the country towards modernization' (p. 173).

Also, it was proven over time that the regime's anti-corruption rhetoric was mostly a facade. Even its supporters acknowledged that political 'nefariousness' had re-emerged, taking often the form of self-promotion but also personal favours and spoils towards friends and relatives (The Konstantinos G. Karamanlis Archive, p. 50). Indeed, in the documentary mentioned above it was stressed that 'the junta was denouncing clientelism, yet it did spoils all the time. Whatever one needed, e.g. an export license, etc., he had to turn to the military officers' (I Michani tou Chronou, n.d., 08:56-09:37). Moreover, in spite of the fact that the regime proclaimed its willingness to enforce a sound and honest administration system, the wage of the Prime Minister more than doubled and that of Ministers and Deputy Ministers increased from DRS 22,400 to DRS 35,000.[15] Members of the government also took advantage of their position in order to benefit friends or members of their families (I Michani tou Chronou, n.d., 22:20–22:50). For example, relatives or friends of the dictators were given governmental posts (ibid.,34:12–34:29); Papadopoulos, the leader of the coup up to November 1973, appointed his brothers to high-ranking positions in the public sector (ibid.,

22:20–22:50) and public works of many million drachmas were awarded to relatives of the vice-president of the Cabinet and Minister of Internal Affairs Stylianos Pattakos, the same person who, in 1967, declared that corruption and nepotism should be 'purged'.

It has also been argued that those who were close to the regime were able to receive very generous business loans ((ibid., 40:20–40:40.)[16] Indicative of this was the case of Pavlos Totomis, president of the Hellenic Industrial Development Bank (ETVA). He had also served as a Minister of Public Order of the junta and was accused of illegally providing loans during that period. According to the press of the period, more than DRS 1.5 billion were squandered from ETVA. After the fall of the regime, Totomis was sentenced to more than four years imprisonment (ibid., 40:46–41:44).

Conclusion

The developments that unfolded during the coup showed that 'the junta failed to 'purify' political life, [gradually becoming] a regime with long term aspirations and of a 'corrupted' nature similar to its predecessors' (Dimitras, 1987, p. 66). It becomes clear that during the seven-year period of dictatorship in Greece the situation in the system of tax administration deteriorated, creating obstacles and discouraging business initiative, in spite of the regime's fervent declarations about the importance of promoting indigenous entrepreneurship. Moreover, corruption solidified its position as an endemic problem of the Greek economic reality, becoming in this way an integral part of Greek capitalism. The junta dismantled democracy and inflicted a 'severe [and] long-lasting blow… [to] the democratic procedures which, in the peoples' conscience, legalise political decisions' (Karkagiannis, 2012). Indeed, in spite of espousing the creation of a 'purer' and more modern and efficient state, the junta actually established a regime in which inefficiency and corruption in the public sector increased. In this way, not only the tax system, but also the whole state apparatus became even more illegitimate than before. This point, and also the fact that there were not any significant improvements in the functioning of the tax system post-1980s (Tatsos, 2001, p.287), say a lot about why, in the first ever study examining Greeks' perceptions about corruption in 1996, 67% of the respondents agreed with the statement that 'the State is corrupt' (ibid., pp. 247–9). This latter point suggests that tax evasion can be seen as an indication of the taxpayers' doubt about the legitimacy of taxes and, by an extension, the legitimacy of the state that imposed such taxes. Ultimately, it can be seen an expression of doubt about the authority of the Greek state itself. Apart from being a factor of uncertainty discouraging investment, taxation has also been an issue about which the lack of trust between the state and civil society in Greece has been expressed in its most direct manner, affecting in this way the character of Mediterranean capitalism that developed in the country. As this article has shown, the role that dictatorship played in this regard was of crucial importance.

Notes

1. During and prior to the period analysed here Greece's political system was a constitutional monarchy.
2. For the present analysis, corruption occurs when there is an abuse of public office for private gain or, as Rose-Ackerman notes, when 'officials use their positions of public trust for private gain' (1996, p. 365).

3. Corruption affected the political system and spread to the whole body of the public administration. See, indicatively, Mouzelis about corruption in the pre-dictatorship years (1996, pp. 71-2) or Meynaud about the clientelistic relations and spoils that have been burdening the political system since the 19th century (2002, pp. 47-8).
4. The depiction of clientelism here follows the perspective of Rose-Ackerman and Palifka, who note that '...clientelistic systems develop where favours and payoffs are exchanged that undermine the transparency and effectiveness of public and private institutions' (2016, p. 251).
5. For an analysis of the varieties of capitalism and informal economies in the south-eastern European economic context see, among others, Williams, Kedir, Fethi and Nadin, 2012.
6. The reference here is to the level of imported investment capital per year (Kazakos, 2001, p. 271).
7. This is according to the press of the time.
8. With the exception of 1974.
9. See *Long-term Statistical Series of the Greek Economy,* 1992, p. 27.
10. Known today as the Athens University of Economics and Business.
11. This rate applied in the zones A and B, that is in Athens, Piraeus and the wider region of Attica.
12. In the reports for 1968 and 1969 the increase in tax revenues was attributed to the increase of the national income and the measures against tax evasion that contributed to the better capture of the tax base. Also, in the report for 1971 it was noted that the better capture of the tax base due to the 'further improvement of the function of the tax services' might had contributed to such an increase in tax revenues for that year (Bank of Greece, 1972, pp. 83-4).
13. This school, called The National Centre for Public Administration and Local Government, was finally established in 1983 (see Argyriades, 2010, p. 3 and National Centre for Public Administration and Local Government (http://www.ekdd.gr/ekdda/index.php/en/2012-06-29-09-59-33).
14. Certificates of social ideals were 'public certificates which were issued by a competent authority (the army or the police) and attested that the citizens [who had them] were not, themselves or other members of their family, communists, or even friendly to communist ideals' (Karafillis, 2008).
15. This was done through compulsory law 5/1967 - see 'Iospress', *Τα ξεχασμένα σκάνδαλα της 'Εθνοσωτηρίου [The forgotten scandals of the 'Nation-saving' revolution]* (http://www.iospress.gr/ios2010/ios20100725.htm).
16. 'The Dictatorship's fascism and spoils', 40:20-40:40.

Acknowledgment

I would like to thank Niall Mackenzie for his useful comments and feedback during the preparation of this article.

Disclosure statement

No potential conflict of interest was reported by the authors.

References

Ackerman, S. R. (1996). Democracy and 'grand' corruption. *International Social Science Journal, 48*(3), 365–380.

Ackerman, S. R., & Palifka, B. J. (2016). *Corruption and government – Causes, consequences, and reform*. Cambridge University Press.

Argyriades, D. (2010). Ηθική και Διακυβέρνηση στο Σφαιρικό Χώρο: Πώς θα Αντιμετωπίσωμε τις Πολλαπλές Προκλήσεις της Εποχής μας [Ethics and governance from a comprehensive perspective: How we will face the multiple challenges of our times], Panteion University of Political and

Social Sciences, Centre of Governance and Sustainable Development. [Retrieved from http://www.dee.gr/mediaupload/publications/20100618_ithiki_kai_diakibernisi.pdf].

Bank of Greece. (1968). *Bank of Greece Governor's Annual Report for 1967*. Athens: Bank of Greece.

Bank of Greece. (1972). *Bank of Greece Governor's Annual Report for 1971*. Athens: Bank of Greece.

Bermeo, N. (1995). Classification and Consolidation: Some Lessons from the Greek Dictatorship. *Political Science Quarterly*, *110*(3), 435–452. (Autumn, 1995). https://doi.org/10.2307/2152573

Bulletin of the Chamber of Commerce and Industry of Athens. (1967a). August-September, p. 457.

Bulletin of the Chamber of Commerce and Industry of Athens. (1967b). November-December p. 646.

Bulletin of the Chamber of Commerce and Industry of Athens. (1968). November, pp. 703–729.

Bulletin of the Federation of Greek Industrialists (FGI). (1970). 15 August, 17, 195, p. 1.

Bulletin of the Federation of Greek Industrialists (FGI). (1972a). 31 May, 20, 238, Annex, p. 33.

Bulletin of the Federation of Greek Industrialists (FGI). (1972b). 21, 243, p. 4.

Bulletin of the Federation of Greek Industrialists (FGI). (1972c). 15 June, 20, 239, p. 3.

Dimitras, P. E. (1987). Changes in public attitudes. In K. Featherstone and D. K. Katsioudas (Eds.), *Political change in Greece before and after the colonels*. London: Croom Helm.

Efstathiades, S. (2000). Τα παρασκήνια ενός πραξικοπήματος το οποίο άνοιξε τον δρόμο για τη δημοκρατία μέσω μιας… δικτατορίας [The backstage of a coup that paved the road for democracy through a… dictatorship], *To Vima*. [Retrieved from http://www.tovima.gr/politics/article/?aid=124233].

Epaminonda, E. (2016). A hybrid model of Mediterranean capitalism with British influences: the case of Cyprus. *Management & Organizatinal History*, *11*(3):2016.

Gallant, T. G. (2001). *Modern Greece*. London: Arnold.

Glykou, I. (2009). *State and Tax Policy, an historical and theoretical approach and the case of Greece*. Athens: Sakoullas, in Greek.

Hall, P. A., & David, S. (2001). *Varieties of Capitalism: The Institutional Foundations of Comparative Advantage*. Oxford: Oxford University Press.

Hay, C. (2004). Common trajectories, variable paces, divergent outcomes? Models of European Capitalism under conditions of complex interdependence. *Review of International Political Economy*, *11*(2), 231–236. https://doi.org/10.1080/0969229042000167279б

Michani Tou Chronou, I. [The Time Machine] (Producer) (n.d). *The Dictatorship's fascism and spoils*. [Documentary]. Greece: NERIT. https://www.youtube.com/watch?v=x0lVB0-Cl8s.

Karafillis, A. (2008). Πιστοποιητικά κοινωνικών φρονημάτων: Μια κλασική περίπτωση κοινωνικής δικαιοσύνης ή αδικίας κατά την επιλογή των υποψηφίων σπουδαστών στις Παιδαγωγικές Ακαδημίες [Certificates of social ideals: A case of social justice or injustice in the selection of candidate students for the Pedagogical Academies']. In *5ο Επιστημονικό Συνέδριο Ιστορίας Εκπαίδευσης με θέμα: «Εκπαίδευση και Κοινωνική Δικαιοσύνη» [5th Congress of History of Education on 'Education and Social Justice]* Congress conducted in Patras, Greece. [Retrieved from http://eriande.elemedu.upatras.gr/?section=985&language=el&page706=1&itemid706=1113]

Karakousis, A. (1999). Μία ταραχώδης δεκαετία [A tumultuous decade], in *Η Ελλάδα τον 20ό αιώνα, 1970-1980* [*Greece in the* 20th century, *1970-1980*], I Kathimerini – Epta Imeres. Athens: I Kathimerini.

Karkagiannis, A. (2012). Τί άφησε πίσω της η χούντα του 67 [What did the junta of '67 left behind], *I Kathimerini*. [Retrieved from http://www.kathimerini.gr/456126/article/epikairothta/ellada/ti-afhse-pisw-ths-h-xoynta-toy-67]

Kazakos, P. (2001). *Μεταξύ Κράτους και Αγοράς* [*Between state and market*]. Patakis.

Kornelakis, A. (2011). Dual Convergence or Hybridization? Institutional Change in Italy and Greece from the Varieties of Capitalism Perspective. *CEU Political Science Journal*, *6*(1), 47–82.

Long-term Statistical Series of the Greek Economy. (1992). Athens: Bank of Greece.

Makedonia (1967). There need to be corrections and modifications in the fiscal mechanisms and individual responsibility of the taxpayers; The Minister and the Deputy Minister of Economics spoke in a congress of tax officers. 19 August, p. 7.

Markezinis, V. (2011). *Greece of Crises, A personal essay*. Athens: Livanis.

Meardi, G. (2012). Mediterranean Capitalism' under EU Pressure: Labour Market Reforms in Spain and Italy, 2010–2012. *Warsaw Forum of Economic Sociology*, *3:1*(5).

Meynaud, J. (2002). *Political Forces in Greece*, vol. I. trans. by P. Merlopoulos (Athens: Savvalas, [The source used here is a Greek translation, the original work's title was *Les forces politiques en Grèce*].

Mitchell, B. R. (2007). *International historical statistics: Europe 1750-2005*. New York: Palgrave Macmilan.

Mouzelis, N. (1996, April). Capitalism and Dictatorship in Post-war Greece. New Left Review, I, (March, 57–80.

Panselina, G. M., & Mavroeidi, M. (2007). Σύνδεσμος Ελληνικών Βιομηχανιών. 1907–2007. In *Ένας Αιώνας στην υπηρεσία της επιχειρηματικής ιδέας [The Federation of Greek Industrialists, 1907-2007. A century in the service of the idea of entrepreneurship]*. Athens: Economia Publishing.

Poulantzas, N. (1976). *The crisis of the dictatorships*. London: NLB.

Photopoulos, I. (2010). Η Διοίκηση του Ελληνικού Φορολογικού Συστήματος ['The Administration of the Greek Tax System]. *Enterprise*, reprint, issue 63, pp. 893–907.

Psalidopoulos, M. (2014). *Η Ιστορία της Τράπεζας της Ελλάδος, 1928–2008 [History of the Bank of Greece, 1928-2008]*. Athens: The Bank of Greece.

Regini, M. (1997). Social institutions and production structure: The Italian variety of capitalism in the 1980s. In Colin Crouch and Wolfgang Streeck (Eds.), *Political economy of modern capitalism*. London: Sage.

Royo, S. (2007). Varieties of capitalism in Spain: Business and the politics of coordination. *European Journal of Industrial Relations*, *13*(1), 47–65. https://doi.org/10.1177/0959680107073967

Samarinis, P. (2017). Urban politics, planning, and public discourses on the city during the Greek Dictatorship (1967–1974): Continuities and ruptures in postwar modernization. *Journal of Modern Greek Studies*, *35*(2), 397–424. https://doi.org/10.1353/mgs.2017.0025

Schwab, P., & Frangos, G. D. (1970). *Greece under the junta*. New York: Facts on File.

Sellas, S. M. (1972). Προβλήματα κοινωνικής ψυχολογίας κατά τη διάρκεια των φορολογικών ελέγχων [Problems relating to social psychology during tax audits] *The Tax Review*, December 1972.

Staikos, T. (1972). Το πρόβλημα των φορολογικών ελέγχων [The Problem of Tax Audits], *The Tax Review*, February 1972.

Stebilis, D. (2014). (21 April, 1967). The ending of a chronic political crisis and the beginning of a dark period', History – Theoretical Texts, Documents of the revolutionary movement. http://istori-ka-ntokoumenta.blogspot.co.uk/2013/06/21-1967.html, in Greek.

Ta Nea. (1972). The tax officer has been brought before the interrogator. 22 June, 12.

Tatsos, N. (2001). *Παραοικονομία και Φοροδιαφυγή στην Ελλάδα [Shadow economy and tax evasion in Greece]*. Athens: Papazisi.

Thelen, K. (1999). Historical institutionalism in comparative politics. *Annual Review of Political Science*, *2*(1), 369–404. https://doi.org/10.1146/annurev.polisci.2.1.369

The Konstantinos G. Karamanlis' Foundation, Konstantinos G. Karamanlis Archive, Vol. 07, *A Period of Ordeal, 1963-1974* (Period B', 21.4.1967-24.7.1974), 1974.

The trial of the junta (1981). *[Documentary]*. Greece: NERIT.

Tsounakos, O. (1999). Η δικτατορία της 21ης Απριλίου 1967 [The coup of 21 April 1967]. In *Η Ελλάδα τον 20ό αιώνα, 1970-1980 [Greece in the 20th century, 1965-1970]*, I Kathimerini – Epta Imeres (special issue). I Kathimerini.

Vallejo-Pena, A., & Giachi, S. (2018). The Mediterranean variety of capitalism, flexibility of work schedules, and labour productivity in Southern Europe. *REGION*, *5*(3), 21–38. https://doi.org/10.18335/region.v5i3.204

Veremis, T. (1999). Αυτοσχέδιες Ιδεολογίες. [Impromptu ideologies]. In *Η Ελλάδα τον 20ό αιώνα, 1970–1980 [Greece in the 20th century, 1965-1970]*, I Kathimerini – Epta Imeres (special issue). Athens: I Kathimerini.

Williams, C., Kedir, A., Fethi, M., & Nadin, S. (2012). Evaluating 'Varieties of Capitalism' by the Extent and Nature of the Informal Economy: The Case of South-Eastern Europe. *South-Eastern Europe Journal of Economics*, *2*(2012).

Yannopoulos, G. (1972). The state of the opposition forces since the military coup. In R. Clogg and G. Yannopoulos (Eds.), *Greece under military rule*. London: Secker & Warburg.

Zolotas, X. (1975). *Our Economic Problem – A TV discussion*. Athens: The Bank of Greece – Surveys and Talks Archive.

State intervention in East Asia's varieties of capitalism: A case study of the electric power industry in China and Japan, 1882–1951

Chenxiao Xia

ABSTRACT
This article studies the history of state intervention in East Asia's varieties of capitalism through a case study of the electric power industry. The reasons for state intervention in China and Japan, their similarities and differences, and their relative importance are described and analysed. The origin and evolution of the different national models of state–business relations in the two countries are influenced by domestic factors such as national defence and internal unification, as well as external circumstances such as colonialism, occupation, and war.

Introduction

In a series of studies, Millward considered the similarities and differences in state intervention across western Europe, Russia, and the United States (Millward, 2005, 2006, 2008, 2011, 2015, 2017). The relative importance of the economic, military, political, and social factors in the regulation and deregulation of utilities was analysed and contextualised (Clifton, Lanthier, & Schröter, 2011). Following this approach, Eriksson provided a case study of the Swedish national grid, highlighting policies concerning agriculture and cohesion (Eriksson, 2015). The primary purpose of this article is to extend the geographical scope of the recent studies conducted into business–state relations by presenting a comparative case study of China and Japan's electric power industries. The history of electrification in the two countries has been studied in the western world (For English literatures see Kikkawa (2006, 2012). For standard works in Japanese see Watari (1996), Kikkawa (1995, 2004), and Umemoto (2000). For Chinese literature see Yang (2013), Wang (1991a,b, 1992, 1997, 1999). For Japanese works on China see Kanamaru (1993) and Tashima (2008)). The key questions are: what were the reasons for state intervention in China and Japan, what was their relative importance, and in what context?

Another goal of the article is to contribute to the discussion on varieties of capitalism using a historical approach by comparing the different national models of state intervention. Business–state relations are one of the integral components of capitalist societies (Hancké, 2007). Regarding East Asia, scholars have recently begun to recognise China's development model, which is not based on either a liberal market economy or a coordinated market economy (CME), but rather on state capitalism (Bremmer, 2010). The terminology is still debatable,[1] but one wonders from a historian's point of view what the origin of the Chinese model was. The dominance of state-owned enterprises was thought to have been copied from Stalinist Russia after 1949, but Bian argued using the case of the steel and iron industry that the formation of China's state enterprise system was a reaction to the systematic crisis triggered by the Sino-Japanese War (1937–1945) (Bian, 2002, 2007). This article develops Bian's argument by extending case studies to the electric power sector. Moreover, from a comparative perspective, one finds a story of convergence and divergence between China and Japan. Exemplified by the nationalisation of electricity, the Japanese economy experienced control and planning by the state during the Second World War (Pauer, 1999). However, most wartime business–state relations, including nationalisation, were dismantled in the post-war reforms and the Japanese business system evolved towards a CME (Hall & Soskice, 2001; Streeck & Yamamura, 2005). The comparison gives rise to the question: what was the origin of East Asia's varieties of capitalism and to what extent did the state matter to their evolution?

In the following, this article first presents a comparative overview and then explores the history of state intervention in electricity in three chronologically organised sections. In each section, the comparative history will be recounted, followed by a brief interim analysis of the relative importance of the variables. A summary discussion is given in the 'Conclusion' section. The primary source comes from the government records at the Academia Sinica Institute of Modern History (ASIMH) and the Japan Centre for Asian Historical Records (JACAR).

China and Japan's electricity industry: an overview

Tables 1–3 provide a bird's-eye view of China and Japan's electricity industry. Table 1 provides comparative data on the number of installed capacities of electric utilities in China and Japan. Since reliable data regarding China before 1931 is not available, Table 1 includes data from 1932 to 1951.[2] Owing to the complicated geopolitical context in China, the data from this country is divided into regions controlled by the Nationalist government (1927–1949), Japanese-controlled Manchuria, and Japanese-annexed Taiwan before China was again unified as a nation-state in 1945. Data from Taiwan (controlled by the Nationalist regime which fled there) after the Chinese Civil War (1947–1949) is also provided. Tables 2 and 3 present the largest electric utilities in each country, their ownership, and geographical spread.

China's installed capacity increased continuously from 1932 to 1951, except for the five years after the outbreak of the Sino-Japanese War. Private ownership was dominant in the regions controlled by the Nationalist government, but colonial government-owned enterprises accounted for the majority of power production in Japanese-controlled Manchuria and Taiwan (see Tables 1 and 2). So, the whole of China witnessed a balance between private and government ownership before the war. The coexistence of the Nationalist government and the colonial governments in Shanghai, Manchuria, and Taiwan complicated China's political structure and accentuated her semi-colonial geopolitical issues. Foreigners, according to the1842 Treaty of Nanjing, the first of the unequal treaties, were immune to all Chinese laws. Based on these extraterritorial privileges, some colonial enclaves were created in China, the most

Table 1. Statistics on China and Japan's electricity industry, 1932–1951.

	Installed power capacity (MW)						Number of enterprises			
	China					Japan	China		Japan	
	Nationalist regions (PRC after 1949)									
Year	Private and government-owned	Government-owned	Manchuria	Taiwan	China total	Japan total	Private and government-owned	Government-owned	Private and government-owned	Government-owned
1903	–				–	30			123	1
1907	–				–	74			114	2
1917	–				–	653			546	27
1927	–				–	3032			628	54
1932	479	55	264	48	846	4306	463	19	816	114
1933	496	56	271	48	871	4520	458	21	818	120
1934	542	38	388	149	1117	4739	460	28	803	121
1935	585	18	395	149	1147	5137	456	32	787	122
1936	631	28	410	147	1216	5794	460	35	767	121
1937	51	0	483	190	749	6183	85	12	730	120
1938	35	2	573	188	798	6620	63	17	662	121
1939	40	9	725	224	998	7249	71	24	601	114
1940	41	11	806	224	1082	7881	75	29	539	118
1941	44	11	1055	251	1361	8190	67	24	486	114
1942	50	13	1269	267	1599	8447	66	26		–
1943	64	17	1512	308	1901	8611	87	41		–
1944	70	21	1777	321	2189	8721	94	36		–
1945	74	24		105	203	8465	97	38		–
1946	1281	948			1281	8507	175	100		–
1947	1455	1138			1455	8548	291	133		–
1948	–				–	8824				–
1949	1849	1337		258	2107	8709				–
1950	1866	1378		262	2128	8746				–
1951	1883	1580	–	288	2171	8941	–	–	–	–

Sources: Japan's data is based on Kikkawa, *Nihon denryokugyo*, 107 and Kurihara, *Denryoky*, 16–18; both are further based on the yearbook of Japan's Ministry of Communications. Nationalist regional data of China regarding capacity and number of enterprises is based on Zhu, *Shinianlai*, j14, j24–25. Manchuria's data from 1932 to 1937 is based on Academia Historica, Ref. 008-011103-00008–006, 'dong bei dian ye gai guang', Chen Cheng Records and is consistent with data from the Japanese side in Manshudengyo (1937), *Manshuniokeru denki kyokyujigyo gaisetsu*, 12–13. Manchuria's data from 1938 to 1944 is based on Noshima, *Manshudengyoshi*, 781. Taiwan's data is based on Taiwanyinhang jingjiyanjiushi (1952), *Taiwan zhi dian li wen ti*, 204–207 and the pre-war part is consistent with the Taiwan Governor-General's statistical yearbooks. People's Republic of China (PRC)'s data from 1949 to 1951 is based on Ajia, *Chugoku*, 13. Note: (1) 1 MW = 1000 kW. (2) 1946 and 1947's Nationalist regional data includes Manchuria and Taiwan. 1949–1951's PRC data does not include Taiwan. (3) In 1947 the Communists controlled a capacity of about 210 MW in Manchuria. This is not included in the table.

Table 2. The 10 largest electricity enterprises in China ranked by installed capacity, their ownership, and geographical spread 1919–1934.

	1919			1927			1934		
Rank	Enterprise name	Capacity (kW)	Categories	Enterprise name	Capacity (MW)	Categories	Enterprise name	Capacity (MW)	Categories
1	SMC Electricity Bureau	19,600	Colonial, G, U	SMC Electricity Bureau	121	Colonial, G, U	Manchuria Electric Power	388	J+Colonial, G, R
2	South Manchuria Railway	6516	J+Colonial, G, R	South Manchuria Railway	19	J+Colonial, G, R	Shanghai Power	183	American, P, U
3	Peking Chinese Electric Light	2881	Chinese, P, U	Taiwan Electric Power	17	J+Colonial, G, R	Taiwan Electric Power	145	J+Colonial, G, R
4	Hong Kong Electric Light	2600	British, P, U	Hong Kong Electric Light	15	British, P, U	Hongkong Electric	39	British, P, U
5	Kowloon China Electric Light & Power	2510	British, P, U	Hankou Jiji Electric Light	15	Chinese, P, U	Compagnie Francaise de Tramways et d'Eclairage Electrique Shanghai	26	French, P, U
6	Canton Electric	2400	Chinese, P, U	South Manchuria Electric	12	J, G, R	Canton Electric	24	Chinese, G, U
7	Electric Tramway and Lighting Tiensin	2250	Belgian, P, U	Compagnie Francaise de Tramways et d'Eclairage Electrique Shanghai	12	French, P, U	Electric Tramway and Lighting of Tientsin	21	Belgian, P, U
8	Qingdao Electricity Bureau	1752	J, G, U	Peking Chinese Electric Light	10	Chinese, P, U	Zhabei Electric & Water Supply	20	Chinese, P, U
9	East China Railway	1573	Russian, P, R	Fengtian Electric Light	9	Chinese, G, U	Hangzhou Electric	20	Chinese, P, U
10	Compagnie Francaise de Tramways et d'Eclairage Electrique Shanghai	1500	French, P, U	Canton Electric	7	Chinese, G, U	Peking Chinese Electric Light	20	Chinese, P, U
–	Hankou Jiji Electric Light	1500	Chinese, P, U	–		–			–
–	Fuzhou Electric Light	1500	Chinese, P, U	–	–	–	–	–	–

Note: G = government ownership, P = private ownership, U = urban utility, R = regional utility, Colonial = colonial government ownership.
Sources: compiled by the author based on Toadobunkai, *Shinanenkan daiyonkai*, 1102–1108 for the year 1920; Toadobunkai, *Shinhenshinanenkan*, 971–980 for the year 1927; ASIMH Ref. 23-25-00-017-02, 'zhong guo min ying dian qi shi ye zhi zu zhi', National Constructions Commission and JACAR C13032478300, 'chuka minkoku niokeru denkijigyo', Japan Ministry of Defence for 1934.

Table 3. The 10 largest electricity enterprises in Japan ranked by installed capacity, their ownership, and geographical spread 1895–1933.

	1895			1914			1933		
Rank	Enterprise name	Number of bulbs	Categories	Enterprise name	Capacity (MW)	Categories	Enterprise name	Capacity (MW)	Categories
1	Tokyo Electric Light	31,711	J, P, U	Tokyo Electric Light	109	J, P, R	Tokyo Electric Light	1011	J, P, R
2	Osaka Electric Light	21,371	J, P, U	Inawashiro Hydropower	73	J, P, R	Daido Electric Power	587	J, P, R
3	Kyoto Electric Light	10,214	J, P, U	Kinugawa Hydropower	70	J, P, R	Nippon Electric Power	448	J, P, R
4	Nagoya Electric Light	9443	J, P, U	Osaka Electric Light	43	J, P, U	Ujikawa Electric Power	358	J, P, R
5	Yokohama Electric Light	9275	J, P, U	Tokyo Municipal Government	32	J, G, U	Toho Electric Power	315	J, P, R
6	Kobe Electric Light	5745	J, P, U	Ujikawa Electric Power	27	J, P, R	Kyushu Hydropower	190	J, P, R
7	Shinagawa Electric Light	2955	J, P, U	Fuji Gas Spinning	25	J, P, R	Toshin Electric	155	J, P, R
8	Sendai Electric Light	2072	J, P, U	Katsuragawa Electric Power	24	J, P, R	Osaka Municipal Government	135	J, G, U
9	Hiroshima Electric Light	1544	J, P, U	Shinanogawa Electric	14	J, P, R	Yasaku Hydropower	135	J, P, R
10	Fukagawa Electric Light	1453	J, P, U	Kobe Electric	14	J, P, U	Kyoto Electric Light	128	J, P, R

Note: G = government ownership, P = private ownership, U = urban utility, R = regional utility.
Sources: compiled by the author based on Kurihara, *Denryoku*, 35 for the year 1895; Teishinsho denkikyoku, *Denkijigyo yoran dainanakai*, 16–121 for 1915; Teishinsho denkikyoku, *Denkijigyo yoran dainijuyonkai*, 11–78 for 1934.

representative being the Shanghai International Settlement (Jackson, 2018, pp. 15–17). Both national and municipal governments in Nationalist regions were involved in creating government-owned utilities, but the colonial governments owned the largest utilities. After the Sino-Japanese War, the colonial governments were abolished and there was a significant increase in government ownership, first in Nationalist China, and then in Communist China.

Japan possesses a more advanced electricity industry. Japan's installed capacity increased continuously from 1903 to 1951 except for a few years after the end of the Sino-Japanese War. Furthermore, Japan enjoyed a much higher level of electrification. Compared with China's per capita electricity production of 8.1 kW in 1936, Japan's stood at 397.7 kW. Even after the Second World War, Japan's per capita production was still 60 times that of China's (Ajia keizaikenkyujo, 1974, p. 8). Japan was dominated by private ownership, and the national government did not create state-owned enterprises until 1936. The majority of government ownership was carried out by villages, municipalities, and prefectural governments (Kikkawa, 2004, p. 107). There was no foreign direct investment in Japan (Hausman, Hertner, & Wilkins, 2008, p. 32).

The brief overview above shows that despite the development gap there were at least three major differences across the country. First, although multiple layers of government were involved in the ownership of utilities, China's situation was complicated due to ownership by colonial governments. Second, before the outbreak of the Sino-Japanese War in 1937, the governments of China and Japan both chose arm's-length regulation, but in Manchuria and Taiwan 'state' ownership dominated. Third, there was a lot of foreign direct investment in China but none in Japan. All three points indicate the impact of geopolitical issues such as treaty system, colonialism, and invasion on how national governments approach ownership, regulation, and foreign investment. So, while examining both domestic and external issues, the discussion below will highlight the geopolitical context in the evolution of business–government relations.

Between colonialism and nationalism, 1882–1927

China's electrification started in 1882 when Shanghai Electric, a British firm, received a franchise from Shanghai Municipal Council (SMC) (Yang, 2013, p. 91). Shanghai Electric was allowed to construct an arc light system in the Shanghai International Settlement, and the SMC regulated its tariffs and claimed an annual royalty. In 1893, the SMC municipalised Shanghai Electric on the grounds that electricity was a municipal matter in most British cities. The franchise between Shanghai Electric and the SMC signalled the earliest municipal regulation in China's electrification. The 1893 municipal takeover created China's earliest government-owned electric utility, albeit by a colonial government.[3] In the 1880s–1990s, a few electric utilities appeared in colonial enclaves such as Shanghai, Hong Kong, and Kowloon and were regulated by the colonial governments. Chinese-owned utilities did not appear until after 1904 (Wang, 1991b, pp. 473–475).

Compared with China, Japan prevented the influence of colonialism and witnessed a more advanced electricity industry. Tokyo Electric Light, the first Japanese electric utility, was launched in 1883 and 53 electric utilities had been set up by 1900 (Kikkawa, 2004, p. 27). The Meiji government prohibited foreign ownership of Japanese land, mines, and corporate stocks and banned foreigners from entering the mainland as a reaction to the unequal treaty system which had been copied from China and used in Japan by western nations (Gordon, 2014, p. 49). After year-long diplomatic negotiations, Japan abolished foreigners' extraterritorial privileges in 1899 (Kawashima & Ryuji, 2007, pp. 42–50). However, it was not nationalism but stark technological education and lively capital markets that underpinned Japan's electrification. The Tokyo Imperial Engineering College was launched by the Meiji government in 1873. The Institute of Electrical Engineers of Japan, a professional engineering society, was founded in 1888. On the contrary, China did not have an electrical engineering department until 1908 and the Chinese Society for Electrical Engineering was launched in 1934; in both cases, there was a delay of 40 years. Likewise, the Tokyo Stock Exchange was established in 1878 and by the 1890s utility stocks were a popular investment target. But in semi-colonial China, the Shanghai Share Broker's Association (founded in 1891) mainly traded in the shares of foreign-registered companies and, in doing so, prohibited the Chinese from trading (Goetzmann, Ukhov, & Zhu, 2007, p. 273).

As the case of SMC shows, western municipal regulation models were introduced in China as soon as electrification started. But the effects were limited. Chinese-owned utilities normally received concessions from the government at central or provincial level rather than from the municipal government (Wang, 1991b, p. 459). A report made by the Nationalist government in 1936 recognised that only a few private electric enterprises had concluded a franchise agreement with a municipal government.[4]

Municipal regulation was, however, adopted by Japanese cities. In 1903, the City of Osaka went into negotiations with the Osaka Electric Light Company (OEL) over the formation of a municipal franchise. Before that OEL, as well as other urban utilities, received business licences from the central government. Osaka's initiative provoked disagreements among businessmen, senators, lawyers, and scholars. OEL and the Japan Electric Association (the trade association of Japan's electric enterprises) denounced the idea of municipal franchises (Tokyo shiseichousakai, 1928, pp. 11–12). But eventually OEL conceded, and the franchise which established the model for Japanese municipal regulation was concluded in 1906 (Yamada, 2013). Other big cities followed suit: Nagoya in 1908, Tokyo in 1912, and Kobe in 1914. By 1919, 12 Japanese municipalities had agreed franchises with privately owned utilities (Tokyo shiseichousakai, 1928, pp. 15–16). In most cases, municipal governments retained the right to purchase the contracted enterprises and claimed an annual royalty from their profits. For the municipal governments, there was an important fiscal incentive as electricity was one of the most profitable industries. The margin percentage of the Japanese electricity industry was 17.8% in 1911–1915, 16.6% in 1916–1920, 14% in 1921–1925, 15.8% in 1926–1930, and 12.4% in 1931–1935 (Minami, 1965, p. 89). The Japanese term for a municipal franchise, *hoshokeiyaku*, literally means a contract involving compensation.

Nevertheless, the spread of municipal franchises in Japan was preceded by regulation from the national government. The Ministry of Communications centralised the authority to grant licences in 1891, and a ministerial ordinance was declared in 1896 which gave supervisory guidelines. However, as the ordinance was concerned primarily with electrical safety matters, it was accompanied by municipal franchises for issues such as tariffs, supply conditions, etc. The electricity industry's demand for a nationwide regulatory law grew as hydropower and high-tension transmission were developing at a rapid pace in the 1900s. In response, the National Diet of Japan passed the Electric Utility Law in 1911. Since the majority of senators were of the opinion that electricity should be a free market, the law did not affect either the monopolistic status of the utilities or the government's regulations on tariffs. In this respect, the natural monopolies, the high level of sunk costs, and the network economies of electricity were neglected by the Japanese lawmakers. Since the 1910s, tariff wars have frequently been fought in Japan's electric lighting and power market.[5]

The coexistence of national and municipal regulations caused friction in the political system. In 1919, the National Diet passed the Road Law, which declared that the property rights of public roads would be transferred to the national government (Shirakizawa, 2010). Consequently OEL, proclaiming that municipal franchises were illegal according to the Road Law, raised its tariff without permission from the City of Osaka. The rivalry launched a new debate in Japan about the validity of municipal franchises, and some leading jurists even took OEL's side. Eventually Osaka settled the dispute by purchasing OEL.[6] Throughout the 1920s, municipal franchises continued to be forced, but their legitimacy became a contentious issue (Tokyodento kabushikikaisha, 1936, p. 109).

Compared with Japan, regulation in China, where the electricity industry was still in its infancy, was indefinite and fragmented. The revolution of 1911 brought an end to the Qing dynasty but the new central state, the Peking government, had been weakened through regionalism and warlords (Hsü 2000).[7] The Peking government, nevertheless, promulgated China's earliest electricity regulatory law in 1918. The law was primarily concerned with the conditions necessary to secure a licence and mentioned neither service quality nor tariff regulation.[8] Although the national government was vested with the authority to issue franchises and settle disputes, practical matters were handled in a disparate fashion by provincial and municipal-level governments.[9]

Despite regionalism, the Chinese government at all levels shared a common policy aimed at excluding foreign capital. In 1905–1907, the national government rejected a British–Chinese joint venture registered in Britain to sell electricity beyond the boundary of the foreign settlement area of Peking.[10] In 1909, the Hunan provincial government asked the national government to grant a monopolistic franchise to some Chinese businessmen when a business plan led by foreigners was uncovered.[11] The earliest government-owned electricity enterprises were launched under the auspices of this xenophobic policy. The Guangdong provincial government purchased a British-owned utility in 1909 and reorganised it along the lines of a government–private joint venture (Wang, 1999).[12]

China's xenophobic policy, however, was only partially successful. Thanks to the policy, the geographical spread of foreign-owned utilities was limited to a handful of settlements, leaseholds, and annexations where foreigners were not subject to Chinese jurisdiction (Table 2). But about 73% of China's installed capacity in 1925 was from foreign-owned utilities (Ajia keizaikenkyujo, 1974, 3).[13] Direct foreign investment was forbidden in regions under Chinese jurisdiction, but it did exist in colonial enclaves; and there, colonial governments implemented their own systems of regulation.

China's policy towards the use of foreign capital can be understood as part of wider national security issues in a semi-colonial geopolitical setting. For example, the railroad, which also involved a high sunk cost, building networks, and negotiating rights of way, involved similar issues to electricity. Virtually all the major rail firms operating in China before the twentieth century were registered in Europe and some of them were administered and policed by foreign officials who benefited from extraterritoriality. This approach thereby opened the way for colonial expansion (Goetzmann et al., 2007, pp. 286, 293–294). In this regard, China's anti-foreign policy as regards the electricity industry can be justified as the protective reaction of a weak nation-state surrounded by colonialism and foreigners' extra-territorial rights. Despite this, joint Chinese–foreign business was permitted in exceptional cases. Siemens, for example, launched a power plant in Changzhou near Shanghai and constructed a 33 kV power transportation system, which was at that point the highest voltage in China (Kirchberg, 2010, p. 287).[14] Furthermore, the Japanese were allowed to launch a joint electricity enterprise in Qingdao.[15]

The origin of government intervention in the formative years of China's and Japan's electrification can be understood through a combination of defensive, economic, and political arguments. Against the backdrop of common geopolitical issues characterised by the unequal treaties with western countries, both countries adopted exclusion policies early on. But as Meiji Japan rose to be a major power in the 1900s, the focus of government intervention switched from issues of defending national interests to the creation of municipal regulations and the conciliation of regulations at national and municipal levels. However, national defence still dominated China's policies because of the delayed nation-state building process and the unstable political order.

Internal unification, 1928–1937

In 1919, the Kuomintang created an independent government in Guangdong Province, the Nationalist government, which launched the northern expedition and toppled the Peking government in 1927.[16] The decade leading up to the outbreak of the Sino-Japanese War was a golden age for Chinese industries, including electricity. Colonialism was still an inevitable part of China's electrification. In 1936, 68% of the installed capacity of Nationalist regions was from colonial government-owned and foreign-owned utilities even though their total number was only 10 (Ajia keizaikenkyujo, 1974, p. 3). But the unification of China by the Nationalist regime in 1928 increased the pace of change.

The new regime regarded the elimination of extraterritoriality and the centralisation of regulation as integral parts of its state-building agenda. As a first step, the National Construction Commission (NCC) was launched in 1928 to promote, plan, and supervise China's industrial and engineering development, including electrification. The Public Utility Regulation Law was promulgated in 1929 to provide basic guidelines for the regulation of utilities. Since this law did not cover government-owned enterprises, the Electric Utility Law was passed a year later.[17] The two laws jointly clarified the division of authority between different layers of government, stipulated the conditions for a licence, and defined the legal obligations of electric utilities. Clause 11 of the Public Utility Regulation Law is significant as, in principle, it prohibited both foreign capital and debt. Meanwhile, the NCC recognised the unification of industrial standards as an imperative task. In 1928, 69% of Chinese utilities had a frequency standard of 50 cycles, the rest being mostly 60 cycles.[18] Although most utilities remained part of isolated municipal plants, the NCC, learning lessons from Britain and Japan, concluded that a unified standard would lead to an interconnected system in the future.[19] In 1931, the NCC set the national frequency standard to 50 cycles. Three years later, 83% of China's generating capacity was in 50 cycles.[20] Meanwhile, the voltage standard was unified to 200 V for residential and 380 V for industrial purposes.

Aside from regulation, the Nationalist regime's state-owned enterprise policy can be seen through the nationalisation and reprivatisation of the Qishuyen Electric Works and the Capital Electric Works. They were the earliest and, until 1936, the only electric utilities owned by the central government. Before being nationalised both were on the brink of bankruptcy. An integral target of the nationalisation by the NCC was to overhaul them into a model plant for Chinese-owned utilities.[21] The annual output of the Capital plant grew nearly 400% and its revenue tripled in seven years. The Qishuyen plant had an excellent annual load factor of 58%.[22] A 60 km-long 60 kV line, then the highest voltage transmission system in China, was under construction by the Capital plant in 1936. To promote electrification, the two plants charged residential customers a low price for electric meters and rented motors to small industrial users. Qishuyen was the first Chinese plant to provide a large-scale electrified irrigation service, and many privately owned electric utilities followed suit to extend lines to rural areas. Moreover, available data indicates that the margin rate of the two state-owned plants was among the highest in China (Wang, 1992, pp. 50–51).[23] However, they were sold to the privately owned Yangzi Electric Company in June 1937 – just one month before the unanticipated outbreak of war.[24] In that month, the NCC retained only a minor interest in a power plant in Xi'an.

Despite the creation of a centralised regulation framework, the growth of China's electricity industry was dominated by private business. Overall, in the decade from1928, at least 13 electric utilities were nationalised by the national and local governments, but nine of them were privatised again.[25] A report made by the NCC in 1936 admitted that the development of government-owned utilities was still in its infancy and most of the provincially and municipally owned plants fell below the standard of modern utilities.[26] In that year, 95.6% of China's power-generating capacity originated from privately owned plants. The data did not include Japanese-controlled regions, but suffice to say that state capitalism was not pursued by the Nationalist regime.

However, 'state' intervention in Japanese-controlled Manchuria and Taiwan marked China's earliest record of state capitalism. After the Mukden Incident of 1931, Japan occupied Manchuria and launched the puppet state Manchoukuo. Manchuria Electric Power (MEP) was created in 1934, as an essential part of Japan's design to develop Manchuria into a hub for the anticipated total war against Russia (Hori, 1988, pp. 15–17). MEP was nominally owned by the Manchoukuo 'state', but 56% of the workforce was Japanese (Noshima, 1976, p. 98). The majority of autonomous power plants were confiscated by MEP and a 220 kV transmission line stretching over a distance of 300 miles was constructed to integrate the regional grid (US Navy, 1945, p. 95). By monopolising and integrating Manchuria's electricity production, transmission, and distribution, MEP grew to become China's largest electric utility ranked by installed capacity (388 MW as of 1934). In Taiwan, the monopolistic 'state'-owned enterprise Taiwan Electric Power was launched in 1919 by the Japanese government to develop the island's hydropower. Its capacity, ranked third in China, reached 145 MW in 1934 (Kitanami, 2003, pp. 19–24).

Despite the creation of state ownership in the colonies, Japan was still dominated by private business. However, structural changes in business–government relations started to happen in the 1930s. Following many rounds of vicious tariff competition, the Japanese electricity industry was not making a profit by the end of the 1920s; and because of the reliance on market forces, both the government and the business communities underestimated the necessity to unify industrial standards. In 1931, 99.9% of west Japan had a frequency standard of 60 cycles and 86.9% of east Japan had 50 cycles (Teishinsho denkikyoku gijutsuka, 1931, p. 371). Nationalisation was an issue raised by some political parties in the National Diet of Japan as a potential way of reforming the status quo, but the only compromise that the government and the private utilities could agree upon was the creation of a self-regulation cartel under state supervision (Kikkawa, 1995, pp. 181–182). In 1932 a cartel, the Electric Power League, was created by the five largest Japanese utilities (Kikkawa, 1995, p. 189). In the same year, the National Diet passed the Revised Electric Utility Law, which banned the overlapping of supply areas and subjected tariffs to approval by the Ministry of Communications. However, the unification of cycles was suspended because of the enormous estimated cost.

Meanwhile, a centralised and unified regulation structure was created. As the municipal franchises reached 20-year maturity in Nagoya, Kumamoto, and Hakodate cities, the municipal government was preparing for takeover (Umemoto, 2000, pp. 243–249). Moreover, Gunma, Chiba, Shizuoka, Aomori, Nagano, Iwate, and Shimane's prefectural governments planned to create a prefectural-owned electricity enterprise so as to relieve their deteriorating fiscal situation. But in 1934 the Ministry of Communications issued an administrative ordinance which prohibited all lower layers of government from launching electric utilities without ministerial approval (Kikkawa, 2004, pp. 154–155). The city of Hakodate brought a case to the Supreme Court in vain (Sakamoto, 1936). The national government's veto on prefectural and municipal ownership prevented the Japanese electricity system from falling into Balkanisation. By denouncing takeover based on franchise contracts, this move also symbolised the nullification of intervention from lower layers of governments. The regulation system was unified.

In the decade from 1928 to 1937, the electricity industry in both China and Japan was dominated by private ownership with arm's-length regulation from the state. It should be noted that Manchuria and Taiwan were colonial enclaves in China where the 'state' was restructuring the industry through the creation and expansion of state-owned enterprises. State intervention in China and Japan in that decade was common in what Millward labelled 'internal unification' (Millward, 2015, p. 241). Japan's national government unified the structure of regulation by invalidating municipal franchises and stopping new government ownership at a local level. China's Nationalist regime also established a strong form of supervision by the state, but the friction between national and local governments was intangible partly because of the relatively undeveloped urbanisation and the formation of a new centralised nation-state.

War and its legacies, 1937–1951

The sudden outbreak of the Sino-Japanese War on 7 July 1937 split China in two, Free China and the territories occupied by Japan. By the end of 1937, Free China's capacity to generate power had plummeted by 91%. The territories occupied by Japan were estimated to possess 85% of China's pre-war capacity by 1939.[27]

The NCC was dissolved in 1938 and its authority was transferred to the National Resources Commission (NRC). Owing to the Japanese occupation of coastal ports, the import of foreign machineries to Free China became impossible except by land transport via Southeast Asia, and even these routes were cut off by Japan in 1940 (Hatano, Ryoichi, Takashi, Junichiro, & Shin, 2018, pp. 108, 112). Industrial production relied on the inadequate machineries transferred to the mountainous hinterland. The NRC was launched in 1932 to plan and build defence-related industries, including power plants. However, by the outbreak of war most of these projects still existed only on paper (Zhang & Zhu, 2007, pp. 93–94). Nevertheless, despite the invasion and west China's weak industrial base, the NRC took the lead in the transfer, recovery, operation, and expansion of the mining, heavy-chemical, and electric power industries. The NRC's share in Free China's electricity output stood at 7.7% in 1939 but had increased to 33.5% by 1944 (Zheng, Cheng, & Zhang, 1991, p. 114). Military-related industries consumed up to nearly 80% of the electricity produced by the NRC (Zheng et al., 1991, p. 84). The share of government-owned enterprises in the capital asset of Chinese industries stood at only 11% in 1935, but by 1944 nearly 70% of the total paid-up capital in Free China was government-owned, of which the NRC claimed three-quarters (Kirby, 1990, p. 128; Zhang & Zhu, 2007, p. 103). However, calculated in terms of industrial production, the share of private enterprises stood at about 60–80% from 1939 to 1944 (Zhang & Zhu, 2007, p. 215–216). Overall, except for banking and mining, Free China's industries continued to be dominated by private ownership, in sharp contrast to Japan's policies in the occupied territories.

The Japanese government's premise was that basic industries including railways, shipping, mining, steel, and electricity in occupied China should be subject to 'state' control.[28] This was achieved through the creation of state-owned Japanese holding companies that supervised the reorganisation of Chinese industries. In 1938, the National Diet of Japan passed laws that launched the North China Development Company and the Central China Development Company. In 1939, North China Electric Power (NCEP) was launched jointly by North China

Development and a puppet regional government. Based on the Manchurian model, NCEP had monopolised north China's electricity industry by the end of 1942.[29] NCEP undertook the reconstruction and operation of power facilities for defensive industries and made long-term plans for system expansion and hydroelectricity development.[30] A 70 kV transmission line at a total length of 98 km, the highest voltage ever in north China's history, was under construction by March 1944.[31] NCEP's counterpart in central China's occupied regions, Central China Electric Power & Water Supply, was created by Central China Development Company in 1938 and reorganised the electric power sector in similar ways.[32] The American-owned Shanghai Power Company was expropriated after the attack on Pearl Harbour.[33]

During the war, state-led reorganisation of the electric power sector was implemented in Japan as well. The nationalisation of electricity was raised as an imperative national project by the fascist-minded military and bureaucrats who took political power in 1936. Despite stubborn resistance from the business communities, the wartime National Diet promulgated the Electric Power State Control Law in 1938. A privately owned but state-controlled enterprise, the Japan Power Generation and Transmission Company (Nippatsu), was launched in the same year. The acquisition of Nippatsu and its integration with the whole of Japan's power production and transmission facilities was a gradual process from 1939 to 1942. During this period, power distribution enterprises all over the country were coerced to integrate into nine state-controlled regional firms (Kikkawa, 2004, pp. 187–188). In the process of this integration, all the local government-owned electricity enterprises were forced by the national government to be dissolved. In this regard, the wartime state control may be understood as an extension of the internal unification in the pre-war decade. Moreover, from 1939 to 1942 tariffs across the country were unified, indicative of the social arguments behind nationalisation (Kurihara, 1962, pp. 348–351). Nevertheless, due to the lack of resources during the war, the Japanese government fell short of some economic targets such as cycle unification and national interconnection (Kurihara, 1962, pp. 332–335).

As an interim synopsis, wartime state intervention was justified by war-related issues in both countries. Free China, deprived of coastal industrial bases, was forced to expand state holdings in basic industries. The occupied Chinese territories were subject to 'state'-led restructuring which culminated in the rise of monopolistic state-owned enterprises. Japan's case was more complex in that nationalisation was a mix of military, social, economic, and political considerations. Free China became the only part of East Asia whose electricity industry was still dominated by private ownership after Japan had nationalised its electricity. For China as a whole, the war was the first time that state capitalism had dominated the electricity industry.

The Allied Powers' victory over Japan in 1945 changed the circumstances. Nationalist China returned to the formerly occupied territories, anticipating the expropriation of Japanese-owned industries. The NRC supervised the takeover process. The general premise was that the government should return the Japanese assets to their pre-war Chinese proprietors upon valid proof, otherwise they would be nationalised.[34] This premise naturally implied the confiscation of Japanese multinationals launched before the war. Thus, industries in Manchuria and Taiwan were transferred to the NRC's holdings. Although the Russian military usurped 60–70% of Manchuria's power production capacity,[35] the share of government ownership in China's electric power sector ballooned ridiculously after the confiscation: the generation capacity of government ownership increased from 24 to 948 MW from 1945 to 1946 (Tan, 1948, pp. J24–25). In north and mid-China, the NRC implemented the takeover policy selectively to the advantage of state ownership. The majority of the Central China Electric Power and Water Supply's assets was returned to private ownership as these were heavily damaged during the war.[36] Thus, the Yangzi Electric Company reclaimed the Qishuyen and Capital plants.[37] However, the main bulk of the NCEP was reorganised into NRC's holdings (Zheng et al., 1991, pp. 162–163). The grid systems constructed by Japan in Manchuria, Taiwan, and north China were inherited and repaired (Zheng et al., 1991, pp. 170–174). Overall, most of the monopolistic, vertically, and horizontally integrated regional utilities created by state-owned Japanese multinationals during the war were inherited by the Nationalist regime. Many of the pre-war privately owned utilities usurped by Japan during the war were never restored. By 1947, 78.6% of China's installed capacity belonged to state-owned enterprises. Thanks to the nationalisation accompanying the confiscation of Japanese assets, state capitalism was not only inherited, but also strengthened.

The Chinese Civil War broke out in 1947 and, with the fall of the Nationalist regime, NRC's industrial holdings were put in the hands of the communist regime. As the majority of NRC's engineers refused to flee with the Nationalist regime to Taiwan, Communist China already possessed the expertise of state-owned enterprise management by the time of its inauguration in 1949 (Cheng, 2005, pp. 45–64). The country's oldest utility, the Shanghai Power Company, was first returned to American investors by the NRC and then confiscated by the communist regime after the United States launched an embargo against mainland China (Tashima, 2008, pp. 93–95). Privately owned utilities in the whole country would be subject to state control in the 1950s.

Japan was reduced to an occupied state ruled by the American-controlled Supreme Commander for the Allied Powers (SCAP). In the beginning, it was anticipated that the Japanese economy would be de-industrialised, with the war-related machineries transferred to China as reparation. But upon the communist victory in China's civil war and the onset of the Cold War, the United States switched its occupation policy. Instead, a democratisation of the Japanese economy in the form of breaking up the excessive concentration of diversified, oligopolistic family-owned business groups (*zaibatsu*) was initiated by the SCAP in 1947. Nippatsu and the nine regional distribution utilities were on the list of excessively concentrated firms. From 1947 to 1951, numerous proposals regarding the reorganisation of the electricity industry were submitted to the SCAP on behalf of the business community, political parties, labour organisations, local governments, and special committees. Most of the proposals supported the continuation of state ownership (Kikkawa, 2006, pp. 211–212). In particular, industrial customers feared the return of cross-regional tariff inequality, and local governments requested the return of confiscated government-owned enterprises. The proposal that the SCAP eventually accepted was the one submitted by the revered businessman Matsunaga Yasuzaemon, who proposed the creation of nine privately owned regional monopolistic firms that could integrate production, transmission, and distribution under ministerial regulation. However, the National Diet of Japan vetoed the plan (Kurihara, 1962, pp. 385–386). So the SCAP bypassed the legislative process, wielded its ultra-government authority, and granted the Matsunaga plan with the full force of the law (Kurihara, 1962, p. 386). With the regulatory authority vested in the Ministry of International Trade and Industry, Nippatsu and the distribution utilities were dissolved and nine regional utilities were launched in 1951. In the same year, the Treaty of Peace with Japan was signed in San Francisco and Japan regained her sovereignty.

The years from 1945 to 1951 witnessed a divergence regarding the national models of business–state relations. As this article has shown, the Chinese government kept an arm's-length regulation until the outbreak of the war, but even the wartime expansion of state-owned enterprises did not lead to their domination in the electric power industry. Instead, it was Japan that patronised the mass 'nationalisation' of Chinese industries in the colonies and the occupied territories. The direct trigger for the rise of state capitalism in China was therefore Japanese policies. And it was after the confiscation of Japanese assets in the post-war years that state capitalism dominated China's electric power industry for the first time in history – similar was true for many other basic industries. In this respect, the rise of state capitalism in China may be understood as an extension of national defence and efforts to build the nation-state against the backdrop of war, invasion, and colonisation. By contrast, in Japan the American occupation authority implemented the reprivatisation of electricity as part of the dissolution of economic concentration. Political factors also played an important role in the reorganisation, not only in the SCAP's indifference to parliamentary vetoes, but also in the perpetuation of the elimination of local government ownership and regulation. The reshuffling of business–government relations was due to an external influence which might never have been implemented without foreign occupation. This statement may be applied to the rise of state capitalism in China as well.

Conclusion

This comparative study of the electric power industry in China and Japan has shown that the reasons for state intervention changed over time, as did their relative importance. Utility regulation in both countries began with the blockage of foreign capital in the interests of national defence. The policy continued as China struggled to build a nation-state. But the rapid rise of Meiji Japan as a major power altered the geopolitical surroundings, and the domestic political structure then emerged as the next issue. Against the backdrop of municipal franchises and local government ownership, the central state's unification of the regulation framework was a continuous motif over the following decades. Internal unification also became a dominant factor in Nationalist China's utility regulation, but more as a part of nation-state building than as a solution to the tensions in the domestic political structure. Until the outbreak of the Sino-Japanese War, government ownership was modest in both countries except the Japanese colonial enclaves in China.

As a result of the war, national defence again emerged as the major determinant for state intervention. The state capitalistic style of government intervention in Manchuria and Taiwan was implemented in the Japanese home islands and introduced to the occupied Chinese territories. In Free China, state ownership has been increasing as a response to the circumstances of war, but it was the nationalisation of Japanese assets after the war that finally consolidated state capitalism in the whole country. The legacies of Japanese-led state capitalism were inherited first by the Nationalist government and then by the communist regime. Thus, Japan's war-related policies were the direct and unplanned origin of the rise of state capitalism in China. By contrast, the Japanese electric power sector was reprivatised but the reorganisation neglected local government ownership and may be viewed as an extension of the pre-war internal unification. On the other hand, the reprivatisation, even though based on domestic drafting, might never have been implemented without the external ultra-authority of the SCAP. Therefore, in the case of the electric power sector, the post-war business–state relations in China and Japan had transnational origins. External influences related to geopolitical issues such as colonialism, occupation, and war were pivotal in the evolution of East Asia's varieties of capitalism.

Notes

1. For an epistemological history of state capitalism see Ambrosius (1981).
2. China's national government did not begin to publish annual statistical reports on electricity production until 1932. And the Chinese government recognised that even the reported annual data could not be registered accurately because many small plants did not keep a production record. See ASIMH Ref. 23-25-00-017-01, p. 271. The Japanese Ministry of Communications has been publishing an annual statistical yearbook on the electricity industry since 1903. The data was believed to be highly reliable.
3. As Jackson (2018, p. 16) noted, Shanghai 'was colonial, in the sense that it was based on rule by foreign settlers.' The SMC's board was multinational in its composition, but excluded Chinese nationalities until 1928. There were Britons, Germans, and Americans on the board from 1873 to 1914. Japanese and Russian nationalities were included after the First World War. For details see Jackson (2016 , pp. 45–46).
4. ASIMH, Ref. 23-25-00-017-02, p. 76, "shi jie dong li hui yi," National Constructions Commission.
5. For rate wars in Japan see Kikkawa (2004, pp. 83–85).
6. For details of the rivalry see Umemoto (2000, pp. 64–68).
7. Hsü, *The Rise of Modern China*, 482.
8. ASIMH Ref. 23-25-00-017-01, p. 90, "shi jie dong li hui yi," National Constructions Commission.
9. ASIMH Ref. 23-25-00-017-01, p. 101, "shi jie dong li hui yi," National Constructions Commission.
10. ASIMH Ref. 02-02-008-01-004, p. 4, "bei jing yao hua dian deng gong si," China Ministry of Foreign Affairs.
11. ASIMH Ref. 02-02-008-01-012, p. 12, "yang shang ni zai chang sha," China Ministry of Foreign Affairs; AS Ref. 02-02-008-01-013, p. 13, "hua shang cheng wen," China Ministry of Foreign Affairs.
12. It was fully reprivatised a decade later, but in 1932 the Guangzhou municipal government took it over again.
13. Annual data in 1932–1951 on foreign direct investment in China is not available despite some sporadic information.
14. The Siemens interest in electricity supply was divested in 1927. In 1928 that utility was nationalised, forming the basis of the Qishuyen Electric Works.
15. JACAR Ref. B04011203300, p. 28, "kyooku dento koshi," 25 December 1922, Japan Ministry of Foreign Affairs.
16. Hsü, *The Rise of Modern China*, 514–553.
17. ASIMH Ref. 23-25-00-017-01, pp. 92–96, "shi jie dong li hui yi," National Constructions Commission.
18. ASIMH Ref. 23-25-00-003-01, p. 59, "dian ya ji zhou lü," National Constructions Commission. In electrical engineering, frequency is the number of cycles per second in an alternating current; in other words, it is the rate at which current changes direction per second. It is measured in hertz.
19. ASIMH Ref. 23-25-00-003-01, p. 49, "dian ya ji zhou lü," National Constructions Commission.
20. ASIMH Ref. 23-25-00-017-02, p. 52, "shi jie dong li hui yi," National Constructions Commission.
21. ASIMH Ref. 23-25-00-017-01, p. 315, "shi jie dong li hui yi," National Constructions Commission.
22. ASIMH Ref. 23-25-00-017-02, p. 79, "shi jie dong li hui yi," National Constructions Commission.
23. There is sporadic margin statistics on some utilities in the 1930s, but collective yearly margin data on China's electricity industry, like Japan's, is not available.
24. ASIMH Ref. 23-04-023-01, p. 41, "zhong guo jian she yin gong si," National Constructions Commission.
25. Calculated by the author based on Wang (1997), adding the Qishuyen and the Capital works.

26. ASIMH Ref. 23-25-00-017-01, p. 316, "shi jie dong li hui yi," National Constructions Commission.
27. JACAR Ref. C12121848500, p. 775, "shina niokeru denkijigyo no gaiyo," Japan Ministry of Defence.
28. JACAR Ref. B02030552400, p. 305, "kahoku sangyokoshi seiritsu yokoan", 31 May 1945, Japan Ministry of Foreign Affairs.
29. JACAR Ref. C04123740400, p. 794, "kahoku denki jigyo togo yoryo no ken," Japan Ministry of Defence.
30. JACAR Ref. C12122019900, p. 2055, "hokushi denkijigyo kondankai," Japan Ministry of Defence.
31. JACAR Ref. B06050421800, pp. 270–271, "kahoku denryoku kofun yugen koshi," Japan Ministry of Foreign Affairs.
32. JACAR Ref. B02130137100, pp. 26–30, "chushina shinko kabushikikaisha," Japan Ministry of Foreign Affairs.
33. JACAR Ref. B0806126100, p. 20, "zoushi oyobi kessan kankei," Japan Ministry of Foreign Affairs.
34. ASIMH Ref. 24-04-058-01, p. 194, "jie shou di wei dian li shi ye," National Resources Commission.
35. ASIMH Ref. 18-22-01-035-02, p. 8, "dong bei ri qiao," China Ministry of Economic Affairs.
36. ASIMH Ref. 24-04-058-01, pp. 29–43, "jie shou di wei dian li shi ye," National Resources Commission.
37. ASIMH Ref. 18-23-01-72-16-022, p. 13, "yang zi dian qi you xian gong si," China Ministry of Economic Affairs.

Disclosure statement

No potential conflict of interest was reported by the author.

References

Ajia keizaikenkyujo. (1974). *Chugoku no denryoku sekitan boseki seishikogyo*. Tokyo: Ajia keizaikenkyujo.

Ambrosius, G. (1981). *Zur Geschichte des Begriffs und der Theorie des Staatskapitalismus und des staatsmonopolistischen Kapitalismus*. Tubingen: Mohr.

Bian, M. L. (2007). How crisis shapes change: New perspectives on China's political economy during the Sino-Japanese War, 1937–1945. *History Compass, 5/4*, 1091–1110. doi:10.1111/j.1478-0542.2007.00443.x

Bian, M. L. (2002). The Sino-Japanese War and the formation of the state enterprise system in China: A case study of the Dadukou Iron and Steel Works, 1938–1945. *Enterprise and Society, 3-1*, 80–123. doi:10.1093/es/3.1.80

Bremmer, I. (2010). *The end of the free market: Who wins the war between states and corporations*. New York: Portfolio.

Cheng, L. (2005). The industrial activities of the National Resources Commission and their legacies in Communist China. *American Journal of Chinese Studies, 12-1*, 45–64.

Clifton, J., Lanthier, P., & Schröter, H. (2011). Regulating and deregulating the public utilities 1830–2010. *Business History, 53*(5), 659–672. doi:10.1080/00076791.2011.599592

Electric Power Division. (1945). *United States Strategic Bombing Survey: The Electric Power Industry of Japan*. Washington: US Navy.

Eriksson, M. (2015). Beyond industrial policy. State intervention in the Swedish electricity supply industry, 1936–1946. *Business History, 57*(6), 903–918. doi:10.1080/00076791.2014.986107

Goetzmann, W., Ukhov, A. D., & Zhu, N. (2007). China and the world financial markets, 1870–1939: Modern lessons from historical globalization. *The Economic History Review, 60*(2), 267–312. doi:10.1111/j.1468-0289.2007.00376.x

Gordon, A. (2014). *A modern history of Japan*. Oxford: Oxford University Press.

Hall, P. A., & Soskice, D. (2001). *Varieties of capitalism: The institutional foundations of comparative advantage*. Oxford: Oxford University Press.

Hancké, B. (2007). *Beyond varieties of capitalism: Conflict, contradictions, and complementarities in the European economy*. Oxford: Oxford University Press.

Hatano, S., Ryoichi, T., Takashi, M., Junichiro, S., & Shin, K. (2018). *Nicchusenso*. Tokyo: Shinchosha.

Hausman, W. J., Hertner, P., & Wilkins, M. (2008). *Global electrification: Multinational enterprise and international finance in the history of light and power, 1878–2007*. Cambridge, MA: Cambridge University Press.

Hori, K. (1988). Manshukoku niokeru denryokugyo to tosei seisaku. *Rekishigakukenkyu, 564*, 13–30.

Hsü, I. (2000). *The rise of modern China*. New York: Oxford University Press.

Jackson, I. (2016). Who run the treaty ports. In R. Bickers & I. Jackson (Eds.), *Treaty ports in modern China* (pp. 43–60). London: Routledge.

Jackson, I. (2018). *Shaping modern Shanghai: Colonialism in China's global city*. Cambridge: Cambridge University Press.

Kanamaru, Y. (1993). Chugoku minzokukogyo no ogonjiki to denryokusangyo. *Ajiakenkyu, 39*(4), 29–84.

Kawashima, M., & Ryuji, H. (2007). *Higashiajia kokusai seijishi*. Nagoya: Nagoya daigaku shuppankai.

Kirby, W. (1990). Continuity and change in modern China: Economic planning on the Mainland and on Taiwan, 1943-1958. *The Australian Journal of Chinese Affairs, 24*, 121–141. doi:10.2307/2158891

Kirchberg, D. (2010). *Analyse der internationalen Unternehmenstätigkeit des Hauses Siemens in Ostasien vor dem Zweiten Weltkrieg* (PhD dissertation). Nuremberg: Friedrich-Alexander-Universität Erlangen-Nürnberg.

Kikkawa, T. (1995). *Nihondenryokugyo no hatten to Matsunaga Yasuzaemon*. Nagoya: Nagoya daigaku shuppan kai.

Kikkawa, T. (2004). *Nihondenryokugyo hatten no dainamizumu*. Nagoya: Nagoya daigaku shuppan kai.

Kikkawa, T. (2006). The role of Matsunaga Yasuzaemon in the development of Japan's electric power industry. *Social Science Japan Journal, 9*(2), 203–219. doi:10.1093/ssjj/jyl032

Kikkawa, T. (2012). The history of Japan's electric power industry before World War II. *Hitotsubashi Journal of Commerce and Management, 46*(1), 1–16.

Kitanami, M. (2003). *Koshinkoku no keizaihatten to denryokujigyo*. Kyoto: Akihiro.

Kurihara, T. (1962). *Denryoku*. Tokyo: Koujunsha.

Manshudengyo (1937). *Manshuniokeru denki kyokyujigyo gaisetsu*. Xinjing: Manshudengyo.

Millward, R. (2005). *Private and public enterprise in Europe: Energy, telecommunications and transport, 1830-1990*. Cambridge: Cambridge University Press.

Millward, R. (2006). Business and government in electricity network integration in western Europe, c.1900–1950. *Business History, 48*(4), 479–500. doi:10.1080/00076790600808617

Millward, R. (2008). Business and the state. In G. Jones & J. Zeitlin (Eds.), *Oxford handbook of business history* (pp. 529–557). Oxford: Oxford University Press.

Millward, R. (2011). Geo-politics versus market structure interventions in Europe's infrastructure industries c. 1830–1939. *Business History, 53*(5), 673–687. doi:10.1080/00076791.2011.599595

Millward, R. (2015). *The state and business in the major powers: An economic history 1815–1939*. Abingdon: Routledge.

Millward, R. (2017). Business institutions and the state. In J. F. Wilson, S. Toms, A. de Jong, & E. Buchnea (Eds.), *The Routledge companion to business history* (pp. 274–299). London: Routledge.

Minami, R. (1965). *Tetsudo to denryoku*. Tokyo: Toyokeizaishinposha.

Noshima, I. (1976). *Manshudengyoshi*. Tokyo: Manshudengyokai.

Pauer, E. (1999). *Japan's war economy*. London: Routledge.

Sakamoto, M. (1936). *Hoshokeiyaku ni kitaisuru denkijigyobaishukosho no keika*. Hakotade: Hakotadeshi.

Shirakizawa, R. (2010). Senzenki niokeru chiho jichitai to denki jigyo. *Nihon Rekishi, 751*, 74–90.

Streeck, W., & Yamamura, K. (2005). *The origins of nonliberal capitalism: Germany and Japan in comparison*. Ithaca, NY: Cornell University Press.

Taiwanyinhang jingjiyanjiushi (1952). *Taiwan zhi dian li wen ti*. Taipei: Taiwanyinhang.

Tan, X. (1948). *Shinianlai zhi zhongguojingji*. Shanghai: Zhonghuashuju.

Tashima, H. (2008). *Gendaichugoku no denryokusangyo*. Kyoto: Showado.

Teishinsho denkikyoku. (1915). *Denkijigyo yoran dainanakai*. Tokyo: Teishinsho.
Teishinsho denkikyoku. (1934). *Denkijigyo yoran dainijuyonkai*. Tokyo: Teishinsho.
Teishinsho denkikyoku gijutsuka, "denki juyo narabini hatsudenryoku tokei," *Denigakkai Zasshi 51*, (1931 July): 357–381.
Toadobunkai chosahensanbu. (1920). *Shinanenkan daiyonkai*. Tokyo: Dobunkai.
Toadobunkai chosahensanbu. (1927). *Shinhenshinanenkan*. Tokyo: Dobunkai.
Tokyo shiseichousakai (1928). *Denki jigyo hosho keiyaku*. Tokyo: Tokyoshi.
Tokyodento kabushikikaisha. (1936). *Tokyodento kabushikikaisha kaigyo gojunen shi*. Tokyo: Tokyodento.
Umemoto, T. (2000). *Senzen nihonshihonshugi to denryoku*. Tokyo: Hassakusha.
Wang, S. (1991a). Shoudu dianchang de chenzhang. *Jindaishiyanjiusuo Jikan, 20*, 293–334.
Wang, S. (1991b). Zhongguo zaoqide dianqishiye, 1882–1928. In *Academia Sinica Institute of Modern History edit, Zhongguo xiandaihua lunwenji*. Taipei: Institute of Modern History, Academia Sinica.
Wang, S. (1992). Jiangsu wujin qishuyen dianchang de jingying. *Jindaishiyanjiusuo Jikan, 21*, 1–51.
Wang, S. (1997). Guomin zhengfu jieguan minying dianchang de zhengce yu shijian. *Jindaishiyanjiusuo Jikan, 28*, 89–132.
Wang, S. (1999). Zhengfu jieguan qianhou de guangzhou dianli gongsi. *Zhongyang Yanjiuyuan Jindaishiyanjiusuo Jikan, 31*, 89–132.
Watari, T. (1996). *Senzenki waga kuni no denryoku dokusentai*. Kyoto: Akihiro.
US Navy. (1945). *Electric power division of the United States Strategic Bombing Survey*. The Electric Power Industry of Japan.
Yamada, H. (2013). *Shiei koeikijigyo to toshi keiei no rekishi*. Suida: Osaka daigaku shuppankai.
Yang, Y. (2013). Gongbuju zhudaoxia jindai shanghai dianlihaiming chanye de fazhan, 1882-1893. *Zhongyang Yanjiuyuan Jindaishiyanjiusuo Jikan, 81*, 53–98.
Zhang, Z., & Zhu, T. (2007). *Nanjing guominzhengfu shiqi de guoyouqiye*. Shanghai: Shehuikexue chubanshe.
Zheng, Y., Cheng, L., & Zhang, C. (1991). *Jiuzhongguo de ziyuanweiyuanhui 1932-1949 shishiyupingjia*. Shanghai: Shanghai shehuikexue chubanshe.

OPEN ACCESS

From state-owned smokestacks to post-industrial dreams: The Finnish government in business, 1970–2010

Pasi Nevalainen and Ville Yliaska

ABSTRACT

While state-owned enterprises (SOEs) used to be considered obsolete tools for governmental intervention in the economy, in recent years governmental intervention in the business sector has re-emerged as a topic of debate. However, scholarship on the changes in and the modernisation of the SOE model is limited. In this article, we examine how the Finnish state's ownership policy adapted to the requirements of economic globalisation between the 1970s and the 2010s. We show that the attitude towards globalisation was pragmatic and aimed at safeguarding the competitiveness of domestic companies. The state-owned company system was gradually adapted to meet new needs, losing most of its original industrial policy significance. SOEs had to be made competitive and profitable, but company-specific targets depended on the ownership criteria associated with the companies. At the same time, the government paid more attention to supporting research and development in the private sector.

Introduction

In December 2016, the Finnish government established a new state-owned enterprise (SOE), Valtion Kehitysyhtiö (Vake), whose objective was 'to get the capital invested in state-owned enterprises to circulate more efficiently'.[1] The idea behind Vake was to form a state-owned fund (EUR 2.4 billion in the beginning) using the stocks of other SOEs in order to invest in new businesses. The establishment of this new state-owned company symbolises the change in the Finnish state's policy that developed between the 1970s to the 2010s and shows that although government ownership is far from obsolete, its basis and implementation have changed. Attention has shifted from traditional 'smokestack industries' to encouraging innovation and investments in high technology.

Over the last 40 years, the economic policies of Western countries have shifted from coordination towards market liberalisation. The most important common denominators during this period were the decline of direct state ownership and the opening up of state

This is an Open Access article distributed under the terms of the Creative Commons Attribution License (http://creativecommons.org/licenses/by/4.0/), which permits unrestricted use, distribution, and reproduction in any medium, provided the original work is properly cited.

monopolies (e.g. Millward, 2011; Parker, 1999; Toninelli, 2000). However, economic globalisation did not, as scholars noted in the early 2010s, lead to the complete disappearance of state-owned companies or government interventions (Christiansen, 2011; OECD, 2017). On the contrary, there have been several examples of politics and political interests being connected to both state-owned and private businesses (Musacchio et al., 2015). Over the past decade, international phenomena, such as the concentration of economic growth in Asia, the economic crises in Europe and the current pandemic, have further highlighted the importance of government-business interventions (Lazzarini & Musacchio, 2020; Megginson, 2017). However, the majority of recent academic research on SOEs deals with emerging economies, especially China (Bruton et al., 2015; Grøgaard et al., 2019; Grosman et al., 2016; Megginson, 2017).

The Western SOE model has converged with the private enterprise (Colli & Nevalainen, 2020; Musacchio & Lazzarini, 2018). This development is far from unambiguous. Although most countries are part of the global economic system, the importance of state ownership is hardly the same across the globe. According to the Varieties of Capitalism discussion, international influences lead to different outcomes in national contexts. Understanding change – for example, how the 'old' SOE model was transformed into the 'new' one (see Colli & Nevalainen, 2020, p. 301) – requires further empirical research.

Finland is a Nordic country where SOEs have historically played a significant role in the industrialisation policy and where the role of SOEs has been strongly developed since the late 1970s. In this article, we investigate the following major phenomena in the reorganisation of Finland's state-ownership and industrial policies between the 1970s and the 2010s:

First, *what were the various influences on state institutions and did these influences affect the state-ownership model?* Second, we will examine *the extent to which external influences led to the convergence of national SOE systems in Europe*. Third, we will look at *the extent to which new state interventions, such as innovation policies, emerged to replace 'old-school' industrial policies*. Through our historical analysis, we will review how the state-ownership policy has adapted to global phenomena in a small country, such as Finland.

Analysing the turning points in ownership policy reveals how the underlying economic logic changed. Following Fellman (2008), we divided the research period into three phases (Table 1) and added three perspectives (external influences, the state and SOEs) through which to examine the changes in the SOE model. Although a specific 'mental turnabout' is apparent during the 1970s in the aftermath of the oil crisis, the most profound reforms only took place in the late 1980s and especially in the 1990s, when the European-integration process became an increasingly important factor that accelerated the course of events.

In the public debate, policy changes are typically presented as necessary solutions to an acute crisis or structural problem. In Finland, crisis management efforts focused on political consensus, specifically regarding the problem of the profit squeeze and the necessary structural changes. As the roots of the economic crisis of the 1970s could be found at the structural level, the proposed reforms were designed to have far-reaching effects. Everything was under reconsideration and negotiation: taxes, SOEs' management, the public sector, state finances and the power balance between the administrative sectors. Our main argument is that the efforts of the different parties shared the desire to restructure the country so that it could face the post-industrial era.

In our analysis, the interaction between international phenomena and the domestic context is key (Figure 1). We propose that external factors, such as the end of the post-war

Table 1. Periodisation.

	Economic globalisation	The Finnish state administration	State-owned enterprises
State-led growth (1956–1981): inwardly closed, highly coordinated market economy	The Cold War – an era of SOEs and national monopolies	A bureaucratic administrator-state became a Nordic welfare state	100% state ownership, mainly domestic operations, participation in international trade
Liberalisation (1982–1993): the speculative bubble and the delayed structural crisis; the third interlude	Liberalisation – the initial stages of European economic integration	New public management-style reform, political transition towards a more market-friendly orientation, beginning of corporate-governance development	Development of business organisations, rapid growth of foreign subsidiaries, first partial privatisations, exposition of former monopolies and national champions to competition
Towards an inwardly and outwardly open coordinated market economy (1993–2008)	European Economic Area – industrial jobs are increasingly moved to low-cost countries	New public management-thinking is an established norm, further and wider reforms	State as a minority owner, some state-owned multinationals, privatisations, some agencies incorporated, public–private partnership

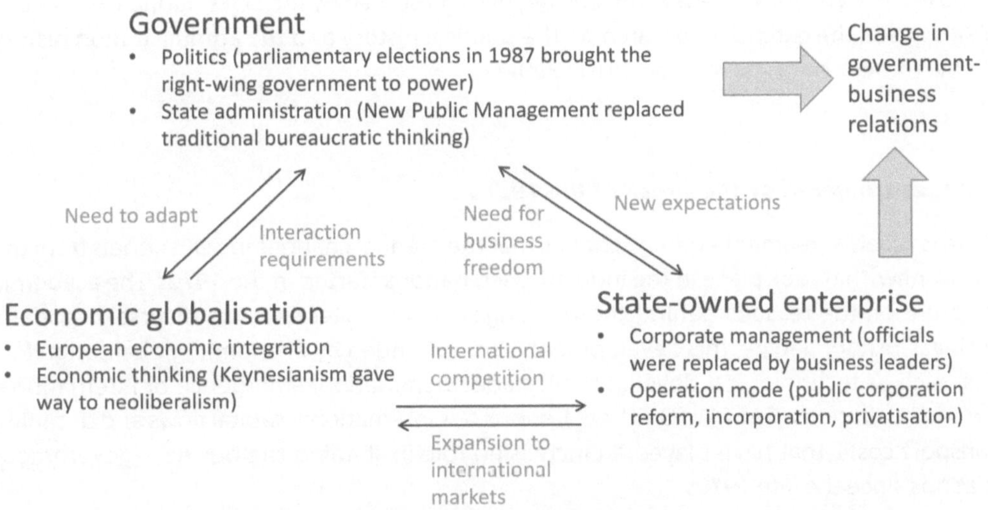

Figure 1. The impact of international influences on the domestic context.

economic boom in the 1970s[2] and the growth in international trade, influenced the national context, leading to changes in domestic politics and institutions and changing the government-business relations. By looking at the interaction between the external (international) and the domestic factors, we seek to find the most important mechanisms for policy change. The major external impact, labelled as 'economic globalisation', includes a variety of structural and ideological elements. The government refers to both political decision-making and state administration. SOEs can be seen either from the perspective of active management or as organisational structures under state administration.

First, we are interested in the formation of *ownership policy* or *ownership steering*, the laws, institutions, practices and regulations that determined how SOEs were run (e.g. Megginson & Netter, 2001, p. 377).[3] Using these various instruments, the state could effectively define

SOEs' goals and structures and engage in industrial policies via ownership. In Finland, these principles and structures were formed not only via political decision-making but also via the work of government civil servants. The interaction between government and SOEs was not one-way; rather, state-owned companies also had their own means of influencing the government.

Second, we are interested in the formation of the new innovation or industrial policies that favoured public investment in private companies. We are interested in the extent to which such policies can be connected with a change in state-ownership policy.

To investigate the government's industrial policy, we systematically reviewed key public documents: policy decisions, committee reports and working-group reports. A particularly important source was the government's decision in principle on the ownership policy, which were typically made once during the term of government and which outlined the main objectives and policies of ownership policy. The issues that were noted in government guidelines were generally prepared in advance in committees and work groups, whose memos are publicly available. In addition to these documents, we have used archival resources (other memos and protocols of interest groups) to further understand the flow of events and the underlying reasons for the changes. These same sources, especially the working documents found in the archives, also reveal the perspectives presented by the SOEs during the process. We also used the extensive research on the political history and the administration history of government-business relationship in Finland.

Changes triggered by the shock of the 1970s

There is broad agreement among scholars that the gradual changes in SOE models from the 'old' to 'new' that took place in the industrialised nations started in the 1970s. The academic literature on the reasons behind these changes is now extensive and diverse. In today's business-history debate, this development is compounded by economic-globalisation factors, such as technological development, trade liberalisation, emergence of international law and institutions (GATT, WTO, EU, etc.), enormous international capital flows and declining transport costs, that have played an increasing role in shaping the business-government relations since the late 1970s.

Chronologically, the starting point was the oil crisis and the subsequent economic crisis, which broke economic predictability and performance (Rodger, 2011, p. 256). The generally accepted view was that there was a need for new policies to replace the collapsing Bretton Woods system and to reverse the onset of stagflation. Another explanation for the change was the structural shift in the economy. During the crisis, economists note that profits were being squeezed in many of the OECD countries. Investments were low compared to the previous decades (e.g. McCracken, 1977). The stagflation and the profit squeeze put pressure on the collaboration between the social-democratic governments and the labour unions in several countries. Past coordinated-stabilisation policies (for capital, labour and the state) fell apart (Scharpf, 1991). The common response to these issues was to deregulate and increase competition.

However, these explanations are inadequate because the chronology does not include both the culture and the ideas that played a part in process earlier than the structural changes became apparent. The post-war system seemed stable and predictable and created a productive environment for individualism. The post-modern era moved away from the concepts of national consensus, managed markets and citizen responsibility, replacing them with individual interest *á la* public choice theory, flexible and instantly acting markets and diverse conceptions of identities (gender, racial, etc.) (Rodger, 2011).

All these factors had an impact on the grounds for state ownership. The golden age of traditional SOEs (from the 1950s to the 1970s) was strongly linked to the construction of an industrialised society. The gradual change from the golden age to the neoliberal/globalisation era started in the late 1970s. At the same time, the economic structures shifted towards the technology of the third industrial revolution (e.g. Schön, 2013, p. 48). In Europe, the pro-market reforms together with the potential of new technology were expected to lead to a convergence of market and business structures (Parker, 1999; Thatcher, 2004, 2007). In this context, SOEs began to look like relics, mainly hindering and distorting the free market economy (e.g. Clifton et al., 2006). In the early 2000s, it seemed like SOEs were disappearing altogether, at least in the Western countries (Toninelli, 2000).

Although this development was true in some cases, it is also apparent that the answer to the crisis of the 1970s varied from country to country and that institutional and political structures created local path dependencies (Hancké, 2009). Moreover, while state ownership and control are interrelated, state ownership does not automatically mean that an SOE would operate in a particular way because the impact of state ownership depends on the local institutional context (Cuervo-Cazurra et al., 2014, p. 924).

In the 2010s, scholars discovered that Western SOEs had not disappeared but, instead, had transformed, as was the case with Vake. In addition, we should not forget that many of the activities previously carried out by the state agencies have been incorporated into SOEs (Clifton et al., 2011; Grossi et al., 2015). The new coming of the SOE was not a return to the past (see Cuervo-Cazurra et al., 2019). States were still involved in businesses, but the state's full ownership had changed to minority ownership and to different forms of partnership with private investors. In addition, SOEs operated in different industries than before, and in the globalising world, several state-owned companies became multinationals (Christiansen, 2011; Colli & Nevalainen, 2020; Cuervo-Cazurra et al., 2014; Musacchio & Lazzarini, 2014; Musacchio et al., 2015). Multinational state-owned companies did not come exclusively from China and other developing countries. The World Investment Report of 2017 found nearly 1,500 state-owned multinational enterprises, of which 420 were from Europe (UNCTAD, 2017).

The scholarly perception of government intervention in business has expanded. Government influence in business is not limited to state-owned activities as states also use different means to support private enterprises. However, SOEs still have a special role in the economy. As Megginson and Netter (2001) noted, although governments can intervene in *any* firm, regardless of ownership, 'the government's transaction costs of intervening in production arrangements and other decisions of the firm are greater when firms are privately owned' (p. 330).

State-owned enterprises as a 20th-century solution

The Finnish SOE system consisted of multiple layers that had been built over time and, by the 1970s, formed a rather fragmented structure. The oldest layer consisted of state business agencies, such as the post office (established in 1638), the telegraph (1855) and the railway

(1862), which, in the 20th century, were developed into national service institutions. Although the latter were also considered to be 'business agencies'[4] to some extent, they were not, until the 1990s, defined as SOEs in the full sense of the term.

In the decades following Finland's independence (1917), the growth of the state-owned company sector was related to the industrialisation of a newly independent and economically backward nation. The first SOE is often considered to be the forestry company W. Gutzeit Co, which the Finnish state bought from a Norwegian owner in 1918. Afterwards, state ownership expanded into basic industry and infrastructure. Initially, each SOE had a clear objective, such as prospecting for an abundant ore reserve, building a large hydropower plant to support electrification or producing fertilisers to improve inefficient agriculture (e.g. Kuisma, 2016). In the early 1930s, some of these organisations were transformed, as a result of a political compromise, into state-owned limited companies (Puumalainen, 1976).

During the interbellum, the existence of specific industries was considered by the government to be a sign of a respectable nation state, yet these industries were not thought to be able to exist and evolve without government investments (e.g. Kuisma, 2016). According to Fellman (2008, p. 160), 'The motivation behind the foundation of state-owned companies was not outspokenly ideological, in the sense that state ownership was preferred to private capital, but primarily pragmatic'. Due to Finland lagging behind in terms of economic development and the very complicated foreign policy situation, SOEs were clearly involved in the process of 'catching up'. This meant a state-promoted industrialisation policy.

> State-owned companies have a special role in the implementation of industrial policy. As the owner, the government can influence the decision-making in these companies. (Industrial Committee's Report 1975:47, p. 205)

After the Second World War, SOEs slowly changed in the context of rationalisation and centralisation. The most obvious example is the state-owned war-material industry, which was forced to direct its production towards the civilian market. The state-owned metal industry group Valmet was formed from the military engineering workshops that began to apply their expertise by building tractors and paper-machine rolls (e.g. Björklund, 1990). After the war, the Valmet's main tasks were to employ workers, to produce commodities to pay the war reparations to the Soviet Union and to act as a 'spare valve' for trade with the Soviet Union (Sahari, 2018). Through growth and acquisitions, SOEs expanded into new businesses, thus expanding the entire SOE sector. During the decades following the war, the existence of SOEs was justified by the argument that they were needed in order to invest in projects where private capital was insufficient. The Economic Planning Agency concentrated largely on regional policy and on the industrialisation of the periphery (Committee Report, 1954:4; Paavilainen, 1963).

In a sense, during the Cold War, Finland truly was a mixed economy. All at the same time, Finland traded with the Soviet Union and developed trade relations with countries in the socialist trade block (SEV) while integrating into the West (through the EFTA Agreement in 1961 and the EEC in 1973). In this context, Finland experienced rapid industrialisation and strong economic growth (Hjerppe, 1988, 1990). From the 1960s onwards, Finland began to develop into a Nordic welfare state. Confidence in social and economic planning peaked in the 1970s. Different planning systems were implemented within the state administration, and the number of central agencies in the government increased.

The large and still expanding role of the state began to become a problem. In the mid-1970s, the working group on SOEs' objectives[5] noted that the expansion of SOEs and, in particular, their extension to new products and industries, which no longer had anything to do with the state's original ownership interest, was causing conflicts and uncertainty. From the SOE's point of view, the biggest problem was to balance the politicians' will and the company's own objectives.

The Finnish SOE system was much more decentralised than in Italy or Sweden. In the government hierarchy, the companies were placed under the supervision of various ministries and were quite independent in their daily activities. The link between SOEs and political decision-making was, in practice, based on nominations. The CEO appointments of important SOEs required the approval of the President of the Republic (Kuisma, 1997, p. 466). The companies were overseen by supervisory boards[6] to which politicians and civil servants were appointed. In practice, political control took place in various forms, often employing informal routes, such as through personal contacts. Political interference was especially evident in big projects (e.g. Kuisma, 1997). The contradiction between political guidance and the company's own interests could be seen, for example, in the fact that companies often had to locate their new production facilities to 'development areas' – that is, regions suffering from unemployment and depopulation.

Decentralised ownership control was an obstacle to the kind of coordination that the politicians in power would have preferred to practice (e.g. Industrial Committee's Report 1975:47, p. 201). For example, it was difficult to concentrate SOEs' resources for major projects. The alternative option in the 1970s was to centralise ownership management into a holding company.[7] However, the proposal did not receive sufficient support, especially from the managers of SOEs, who were accustomed to their fairly independent positions.

Adhering to the wave of international liberalism

The criticism of the welfare state increased during the recession of the 1970s. The recession took place in Finland in a slightly different manner than in the other nations that suffered from stagflation. Finland's high inflation (17% in 1975) was seen as a problem in the mid-1970s, but unemployment (at less than 2% in 1975) had not yet become a problem, thanks to the demand from the Soviet Union. Instead of unemployment, Finland suffered from a trade deficit. With the help of the IMF, the situation was stabilised, and by 1977 inflation was only at 7 per cent; however, unemployment was rising. In the 1975 deal with the IMF, Finland promised to keep domestic debt in check and to stop the growth of the public sector (Kuusterä & Tarkka, 2012, pp. 405–420).

The weakened state of public finances during the recession concretely affected the work of the state administration. A few years later, a person involved in planning the state administration recalled the situation as follows:

> By 1975, the situation had changed completely: the policy-making had been paralyzed, the economic situation threatened the development of the welfare sector, the plans made by the

> government planning systems lost their meaning, and the centralization of central government and technocratization became the subject of increasing public criticism. (Heiskanen, 1977, pp. 8–9)

The general conclusion was that the decades of exceptionally fast economic growth had ended. Expressions like 'The crisis of the welfare state', 'Eurosclerosis' and the 'English/Swedish/Finnish disease' became part of the discussion (Holkeri, 1977, pp. 71–73; Pierson, 1998, p. 148; Smolander, 2000, pp. 274–279, 289–293). At the same time, private businesses and some politicians became more vocal in considering the state's increased role in society as a threat. High taxation, regulation and SOEs were supposedly the factors that limited private entrepreneurship. The business community wanted to restore the value of private entrepreneurship, improve the country's international competitiveness, focus development more clearly towards the Western model and reduce the share of the public sector in the economy (Tarkka, 2002; Wuokko, 2016).

At the same time, the old industrialisation policy experienced spectacular losses: symbolically, the most important event was the television-tube manufacturer Valco (1976–1979/1980) in a consortium with Japanese and Finnish private companies. The original purpose of Valco was related to the Social Democratic Party's (SDP) industrial policy project meant to support the development of the country's electronics industry. The project was a contradictory combination of traditional objectives, such as the protectionist goal of replacing imports with domestic production, and new objectives, such as opening a new export industry in cooperation with a multinational Japanese partner and a domestic private television-set producer. Within the private industry, the project aroused loud resistance and fears of socialisation (e.g. Marttila, 2016, p. 304).

The project proved to be an economic and political disaster. In addition to the fact that the factory did not reach its production targets, some high-ranking politicians were involved in a related corruption scandal. In the public sphere, the company, drifting into financial difficulties in the autumn of 1979, was considered a failure of the SDP's economic policy and had a dire impact on the general perception of the state's ability to conduct business (e.g. Kuisma & Seppänen, 2015). Ten years later, the Valco case was considered to be a turning point in state-ownership policy and was the last Finnish SOE established to develop industrialisation (Working Group, 1989, p. 17).

After the 1970s, the Finland's economic policy experienced a turnabout known as the 'consensus'. The turnabout occurred without the country's political leadership being changed (e.g. Tarkka, 2002),[8] with the recession providing the immediate reason. A symbolically important event was the convention held in 1977 to tackle growing unemployment. At the convention, the biggest political party, the SDP, declared itself to be a party with a new political programme, in which the leading role was given to private instead of state-owned businesses. 'The operational environment' of private firms was put on the pedestal, and the success of private businesses was now seen as being of 'shared interest' for the nation. The biggest issue in the programme was that the SDP publicly abandoned the objective of socialism. This abandonment, which might have been a tactical move, became firmly established in the ranks of the party during the 1980s (Outinen, 2015, pp. 317–319). Other aspects of the SDP's new programme have been labelled as supply-side economics – for example, the measures to stop inflation and the refusal to devalue the currency and take on more public debt (Hämäläinen, 1993, p. 151).

While Prime Minister Margaret Thatcher, for example, actively searched for confrontation with the left wing and the unions, in Finland a *Blairian* consensus was on the table from the beginning. Even though political battles existed, they were less fierce than during the previous decades. Wide support for several key issues was achieved by major political parties. One of the major issues was to transition from an industrial society to a post-industrial one, but this time, the transition was to go ahead without the previously conventional form of state ownership.

Faith in high technology

Experts in the 1970s widely agreed that the economic crisis brought about by the 1970s recession heralded a structural shift from an industrial society to a post-industrial world. This conclusion was an important notion for many politicians and led to the revision of economic policy, with a new emphasis on public research and development (R&D) and venture capital. It also led to the reconsideration of the bureaucratic model of administration and the size and responsibilities of the public sector. All resources and all capital in the SOEs as well as all public resources in general were required in order to implement the change from the industrial to the post-industrial society.

Unemployment figures pointed to a structural change. There was a record number of 170,000 unemployed people in 1977. Recession hit the traditional industries, not just agriculture. The number of industrial workers dropped from 404,033 in 1972 to 388,322 in 1978.[9] This de-industrialisation trend continued over the next decade. By the end of the 1980s, the number of industrial workers had dropped below 250,000 (Koivuniemi, 2018, p. 225). In Norway, too, the Labour Party changed its economic policy when the number of industrial workers fell (Christensen, 2018, p. 145).

Before the 1980s, Finnish businesses developed their technology very cautiously. Most of the companies copied technology from foreign companies and adjusted it to their own uses (Aunesluoma, 2011, p. 289). Finnish technology and R&D policy were concentrated mainly within the public higher education sector (Jalava, 2011). After the recession, the university system was seen as inadequate at keeping Finland on a par with international competition. Although the new structural policy was developed within the framework of 'economic recovery', the concept did not refer to Keynesianism.[10] It was defined as (a) having tight budgetary limits to stop the growth of the public sector, (b) impeding public indebtedness, (c) stopping currency devaluations, (d) minimising inflation and (e) establishing the groundwork for new branches of industry (Sorsa, 1977).

Kalevi Sorsa's *recovery government* (May 1977–May 1979) made it clear that its aim was to help the private industry; consequently, the government had to make a few exceptions to the *debt* rule. Public debt was permissible (1) to finance investments in the export industry, (2) to develop industries that would replace the import industry, (3) to increase the equity capital of SOEs and (4) to finance the energy policy.[11] The investment policy was paramount.[12]

For the most part, these investments were supposed to go to the electronics/technology industry to help Finland adapt to the post-industrial world. For example, the leader of the SDP and the prime minister of four governments, Kalevi Sorsa, said in a 1979 television interview that the recession was an overproduction crisis. He referred to Kondratiev's waves and argued that capitalism was at a crossroads and no salvation could be found in 'bureaucratic planning'. A cycle of growth could only be restarted by developing new industrial branches. According to Sorsa, the electronics industry was the most promising bet, but it 'had not happened yet'.[13] The Valco project was a state-owned effort to steer the industrial base towards electronics, but because it had failed so spectacularly, the publicly funded private route was the only possibility (e.g. Skurnik, 2005, pp. 199–200). Nokia, which had strongly opposed the government electronics industry projects, bought the state-owned telephone-network equipment producer Televa in 1981 (Häikiö, 2001b).

The theoretical foundations of de-industrialisation were an established fact in the public sphere. From the end of the 1960s onwards, public intellectuals, futurologists and technology researchers in the West and in the East started to sketch ideas about the next structural change and the role of technological development. Two major trends were present in most of the predictions: information technology and biotechnology.[14]

The OECD also interpreted the recession as a structural change. In 1975, the OECD organised a conference on computers and telecommunications that interpreted the crisis as a crisis of overproduction. 'Computers and telecommunications will become major new infrastructure, which will give birth to new branches of industry. Car industry and other old branches of industry have been saturated and it is urgent to find new areas of growth' (Pietarinen et al., 1975, pp. 11–12; also, OECD, 1979a, 1979b, 1979c; Mattelart, 2003, pp. 64, 111–113). According to the predictions, the public sector had an important task. Bell (1974, p. 250) observed that the US federal government supplied most of the funds for R&D, while industry, universities and non-profit organisations performed the work. Because the state had a role in allocating resources, a post-industrial society would 'involve *more* politics than ever before' (Bell, 1974, p. 263).

According to Finland's Ministry of Finance, a new electronic service infrastructure was developing: 'To exploit these opportunities and their economic growth potential in the interest of the public, major investments will be needed. The commitment of such requires careful planning and allocation of national resources' (Pietarinen et al., 1975, Appendix 1, p. 12). The Industry Committee (1975) also drew attention to the importance of technology. The general objectives – to expand production, increase the degree of processing and use labour more efficiently – emphasised the importance of technology as a force for development:

> The development of technology through research and development – to achieve the best possible results for the whole economy – will be one of the most important areas of industrial policy in the future. (Industrial Committee's Report 1975:47, p. 21)

In 1977, the OECD published the McCracken Report. According to the report, the recession was caused by a decline in profitability, which, in turn, was caused by the lack of fear of unemployment, the growth of the public sector and wages being raised by the labour unions. The report suggested that the public sector should be downsized via marketisation, user fees and privatisation. But, most importantly, the public sector should take a bigger role in R&D investments (McCracken, 1977).

The investment percentage of the gross domestic product (GDP) in R&D became an important yardstick. This yardstick was alluring because R&D was easy to measure. Politicians could set clear quantifiable targets and hope for the best. In the words of the OECD, by investing 3 per cent of the GDP in R&D, the United States became 'a symbol for other countries which now regard this as a target to be reached' (Bell, 1974, p. 250). In Europe, France made strong commitments to the techno-optimism, and the role of the state was significant from the beginning in the new industrial policy. The most famous example is the report by Nora and Minc (1978/1980), which proposed a new national communication infrastructure based on computers (Minitel) and a long-term strategy to computerise both the private and public sectors.

These futurologist predictions were well known in Finland (Allardt, 1969; Kullberg, 1996, p. 16; Larna, 1969; Pöyry, 1983; Tarkka, 1988, p. 237). Civil servants participated in the OECD meetings, and the structural change was debated at the Ministry of Finance, which was responsible for the restructuring of the state administration. According to the expert findings at the time, international competition would involve not only companies but nations as well (through public investments in private companies).[15] Finland resorted to the old national narrative of 'catching up': there was an urgent perceived need to invest more in R&D. Some of the future forecasts were downright alarming – for example, the prediction that computers and electronic communications would replace paper was considered a direct threat to Finland, whose largest export sector was the forestry industry.[16]

In 1979, the Finnish government set up a committee on technology. The committee's prediction was that the structural change triggered by the advancement of technology would kill the old industries, making it important to increase investments in R&D 'to prevent Finland from falling behind in technologic and economic development'. According to committee's findings, R&D was important in two regards: it could both enhance productivity and create new branches of industry. The committee predicted that telecommunications would be the most rapidly advancing line of business. Data/video transfer, 'tele post', electronic banking and electronic newspapers could be a reality as early as the 1980s. At the same time, the introduction of new technologies was considered to require deregulation measures that would free up private entrepreneurship (Committee Report, 1980, pp. 1–3, 12–17, 26–28).[17]

In the late 1970s, Finland's R&D to GDP ratio was only 1.08, and the technology committee hoped it would be 2 by the end of the 1980s. In addition, the committee recommended tax cuts for corporate R&D investments. The main idea was that public investments in R&D would also encourage private companies to invest in R&D. Moreover, the committee proposed that a new technology division should be established in the Ministry of Trade and Industry (Committee Report, 1980).[18] Private Finnish companies supported the idea and hoped for public investments in R&D and education.[19] The new innovation policy led to the creation of the Development Centre of Innovation and Technology (Tekes) in 1983, which worked as an R&D financier to private and public companies and universities according to the guidelines set by the Ministry of Trade and Industry (Tiitta, 2007).

From consensus to a wave of reforms

The will to develop the public sector and public corporations was enhanced by the international management trend that swept over Finland in the 1980s. Later, in the 1990s, this trend was called New Public Management (NPM), referring to the market-oriented administrative doctrines that were adopted in the majority of OECD countries during the 1980s and 1990s. In the NPM reforms, governments privatised public companies and introduced market-type mechanisms into the public sector (Hood, 1991; Pollitt & Bouckaert, 2000, p. 159).[20]

In Finland, structural reforms began with 'business agencies', which 'represented the oldest layer of the state's business', as already described by a government organisation committee in 1957.[21] In 1981, the government launched the first committee to examine better ways of organising these agencies. The committee's starting point was existential: why did these agencies exist, what was the 'common good' by which these agencies were justified and were there still grounds for their existence (Committee Report, 1983a)? Because these organisations combined features of the government, public utilities and business, the committee decided to develop said organisations into a new specific type of organisation that would combine the best aspects of a government agency and a limited company (Committee Report, 1985).

The preparation phase for the Finnish 'public corporation reform' lasted almost the whole decade. During this period, some traditional institutions, such as the post office, telecommunications and the railway as well as several smaller agencies, were converted into organisations resembling the old British 'Morrison's' (1933) model during the 1989–1995 period, which gave agencies more independence in business (Ahonen, 1987; Nevalainen, 2014).

The managers of public corporations were cautiously optimistic regarding some aspects of the public corporation reform, but overall, feelings were mixed. Others, usually the younger-generation managers, were more enthusiastic about the reforms, but all agreed that the existing rules unnecessarily restricted their working environment (Committee Report, 1983b, pp. 85–95).[22] The managers had long complained that different bureaucratic rigidities related to state administration were limiting the companies' opportunities in unreasonable ways. The managers especially wanted to have more autonomy, which the separation from the state budget offered. However, some doubted that autonomy would lose its relevance due to the new auditing systems.[23]

The public corporation reform proved to be an intermediate step, or a training phase, for full corporatisation and, finally, privatisation. Although developments along this direction were believed to continue, the pace of development was surprising to most reformers (Nevalainen, 2014, p. 272). As the reforms of the 1990s were considered successful, the government wanted to continue and go further, especially in the administrative sector of the Ministry of Transport. The most important of these reforms culminated in the incorporation and privatisation of the public telecommunications company PTL telecommunications, which gradually lost its partial monopoly (1987–1994) and was turned into a 'public corporation' (1990), incorporated (1994) and partly privatised (1998), by which time it had already turned into a state-owned multinational enterprise Sonera (Nevalainen, 2017). In the early 2000s, the state ownership of the company was gradually decreased. The government decided to use the proceeds from these sales to secure R&D expenditure and industrial investments.[24]

The government policy was to boost the service sector through competition. In Finland, the share of private businesses, especially in the service sector, was small compared to the OECD average, as many public services were publicly owned. At the same time, as the international trade in services grew (especially in sectors that had just been liberalised), Finland's service exports were also clearly lower than the EU average. Structures that favoured public service production, such as taxation, were considered problematic by the dominant public discourse. One of the factors preventing the emergence of an efficient service market was the financial resources required for R&D.[25]

The extension of the business logic to public-sector organisations was an important factor that further accelerated the ongoing change in SOE system. In the 1980s, several Finnish SOEs established subsidiaries abroad.[26] This was related to the new business opportunities, but also to perceived pressure on the domestic market. For example, in telecommunications, international operators were aggressively increasing their operations. According to the management of the Finnish state telecommunications company, the company was forced to react, which is why it started its first international businesses for 'defensive reasons'. The management felt that it had to take over important markets in neighbouring areas to prevent international competitors from gaining a foothold or a favourable position to penetrate the Finnish market. As the company expanded into international business, its own operating logic changed to the operating logic of a multinational company, and the company's management began to demand further reforms from the government (Cheung et al., 2020).

From the state administration's point of view, the SOE expansion abroad was initially a financial issue. As SOEs needed more capital for investments, the pressure to list SOEs on the stock exchange grew (Ranki, 2012). A working group set up by the Ministry of Trade and Industry concluded in 1991 that the original industrial policy objective was no longer significant for any of the SOEs under the Ministry.[27] Therefore, there was no reason to maintain significant state shareholding in these companies. Responsible ministries also decided that as the success of SOEs required compliance with business principles, these companies could no longer be used as tools for economic policy unless they were compensated (e.g. Junka, 2010, p. 5).[28]

Previously, state ownership was generally perceived as permanent, but since the late 1980s, the thinking changed (Working Group, 1989). Listing public companies on the stock market was still a politically sensitive issue.[29] In its formulation of the new managerial guidelines, the stated that the government retained its control over listed companies. Also, Prime Minister Holkeri underlined that listing some SOEs (in 1988 and 1989) was not about privatising them but about giving them an opportunity to gain risk financing from the private capital market. According to Junka 2010, p. 35 this meant that the primary purpose was not to privatise SOEs but to ensure their capital maintenance and to broaden their ownership base to promote the expansion of the so-called people's capitalism.[30] Despite the fact that there was a public debate on privatisation in the late 1980s, a large-scale privatisation trend began only after the recession of the early 1990s, and the trend was strongest in the late 1990s and early 2000s, in line with European trends (e.g. Clifton et al., 2006).

By the late 1980s, public opinion had turned from suspicion of profit-seeking companies to sympathy for private entrepreneurship. According to Millward (2011), the fairly widespread suspicion of private entrepreneurship was largely due to the recession of the 1930s. The fact that this distrust had died down by the 1980s also helped the Finns to see new ways of regulating the market. For the Finns, Margaret Thatcher and Ronald Reagan represented neoliberalism in its extreme form, from which even the big businesses and right-wing parties detached themselves in the 1980s and early 1990s (e.g. Vares, 2017, p. 315). However, the objectives of Prime Minister Holkeri's right-wing government (1987–1991) – deregulation, economic liberalisation and a reduction of the public sector – aligned Finland with the international neoliberal trend (Wuokko, 2016, pp. 256, 260; Yliaska, 2014, pp. 35, 187, 240). For example, in telecommunications, the Finnish market opened rapidly in European terms (e.g. Graack & Elixman, 1999).

In Finland, the 'necessary solutions' were much more subdued than in the Anglo-Saxon countries. During the fierce privatisation of the late 1990s, the Working Group (1999, p. 3) noted that there was no reason to sell the state's property solely as a matter of principle or for short-term interests. However, the Finnish case reinforces the views according to which the phenomena of incorporation, privatisation and deregulation, together with the emergence of international competition, strengthened one another in the domestic context (see Thatcher, 2004). Next, we will discuss how the internationalisation of the market affected the state's ownership policy.

The 'faceless owner' looks for an identity

The 1980s was clearly an era of reconsidering the state as an entrepreneurial model. In the public debate of the early 1980s, state-owned companies were often depicted as loss-making. The reason was not only the Valco disaster but also the revealed losses of other SOEs, especially Valmet. In the public debate, political guidance and the associated 'ownerless money' were seen as the main reasons for the poor success of state-owned companies.

Previously, SOEs were sometimes allowed to operate at a loss if the overall social impact of an SOE's activity was assessed as positive; however, in 1983, the Finnish government issued its resolution that SOEs had to be profitable, at least at a mature stage in their life cycle. As Junka (2010, p. 5) summarised, it was considered that 'the industrial base and infrastructure of the national economy had already been built and that meeting the self-sufficiency needs of the national economy no longer required state entrepreneurship'. From then onwards, increasing attention was paid to SOEs' corporate governance.

The biggest perceived problem was that state ownership was 'faceless'. This refers to the vagueness of ownership steering and liability relationships. In particular, no one seemed to know who eventually decided who represented the 'state' at the annual general meeting and how the 'state' should be represented in the SOE's administration (Working Group, 1989).

These questions regarding the disconnect between 'the agent' and 'the principle' (the agency dilemma) were at the core of the NPM reforms (Lynn, 2006). In short, the principle-agent problem states that different interests and asymmetric information make it difficult for the principle to ensure that the agent acts in the best interests of the principle (Berle & Means, 1932). According to organisational theory, some kind of control is necessary to prevent the factory floor and/or corporate management (depending on the point of view) from acting according to its own preferences (Jensen, 1998). In the public sector, this problem was seen as more profound than in the private sector because even the roles of the different actors were undefined (facelessness). The aim was to create administrational structures (result targets and market signals) to ensure that the agents worked according to the principle. The concern over the agency dilemma in the public sector in the 1990s was inspired by public choice theory, which emphasised the self-interests of civil servants and had made an international breakthrough in the 1980s (Barzelay, 2001).

At the beginning of the 1990s, most Finnish SOEs were still having difficulties or were earning less profit than their private competitors. The Working Group by the Ministry of Trade and Industry recommended increasing private ownership. In the case of industrial companies, privatisation was even seen as a means for facilitating the restructuring of the entire industry.[31] However, significant privatisation efforts did not take place due to the deep economic recession (1990–1993).

During the following years, the ownership issue was investigated with a particular emphasis on SOEs' internationalisation. Corporate structures were to be adjusted to become consistent with 'international practices and standards'. As noted by the working group (1995), 'Instead of a specific knowledge of social interests, it is becoming increasingly important to have a coherent understanding of international business and related risks' (pp. 16–17). The discussion focused on the form and composition of the company's highest decision-making body (e.g. Kaisanlahti, 2001). Traditionally, the supreme institution in the company was the supervisory board, in which the state administration was represented by MPs and senior officials:

> Supervisory boards are internationally a rather unknown type of corporate governance. They are mainly used in Nordic and German-speaking Europe. (...) In Anglo-Saxon countries, the supervisory boards are not used. As the SOEs' ownership base will be expanded, especially when foreign investors become business owners, the supervisory boards together with state ownership become a problem for credibility. (...) From a management point of view, the value in using supervisory boards is not high. (Working Group, 1995, p. 24)

Also, in the public debate, these governing bodies had begun to be seen not so much as instruments of political control and coordination between government-owned companies but as reward-posts for politicians.[32] Such structures had begun to emerge as evidence mounted regarding the unprofessional management of and vague decision-making in SOEs.

In the coming years, the supervisory boards were not unambiguously removed; rather, the question became linked to the state's ownership interest in the SOEs. The companies were divided into groups according to the reasons of state ownership, and this classification influenced the development of the corporate governance structure in line with the private business model.[33] Changes in owner policy were justified by changed circumstances. Liberalisation in the 1980s and the accession to the European Union in 1995 were the turning points that resulted in the destruction of the old structures, practices and perpetual organisations (e.g. Kuisma, 2004, p. 11).

The Working Group on State-Ownership Policy (1999, pp. 3–5) summarised the developments of the 1990s, stating that the government was focused on the following goals:

1. to ensure that the companies had enough capital;
2. to ensure the conditions of operation and the conditions for internationalisation;
3. to develop the ownership structure of SOEs so that companies could develop steadily and create jobs;
4. to use the proceeds from the sales of company assets in a way that would strengthen the national economy; and
5. to raise the value of state ownership through incorporations and other streamlining measures.

Generally, these development goals align well with the general scholarly findings (e.g. Megginson & Netter, 2001). It is worth noticing, however, that many of these arguments emphasised the development of the SOEs' competitiveness. SOEs wanted to be put at the same level as private companies, which meant removing both obligations and privileges. In principle, the business had to be profitable, and SOEs had to be guaranteed the same opportunities as private companies. In the 2000s, the practices of SOEs had to coincide with the rules of the Helsinki Stock Exchange.[34]

For politicians, SOEs were often dangerous. At the beginning of the 21st century, ownership policy was marked by the discussion on failures and blame. The partial privatisation of the telecommunications company Sonera in November 1998 led to a disagreement between the CEO of the company and the minister responsible for state ownership, a heated public debate and ultimately to a government announcement and the creation of privatisation rules (Working Group, 1999). Only a few years later, in 2002, the state minority-owned Sonera made major investment mistakes for third-generation mobile-network licences across Europe, finding itself on the brink of bankruptcy. The public debate focused on whether the state, as the largest shareholder, should have prevented such high-risk foreign ventures. The follow-up discussion revealed that corporate governance practices were still much more fragmented than had been thought.[35]

The 2004 government decision on ownership policy emphasised the *effective* separation of SOEs' ownership and regulation within the state administration. This separation happened because there was, first, a debate on the centralisation of the ownership function and, second, a need to be clear about the state owner's interest in each company. In 2007, The State Shareholding and Ownership Act (1368/2007) further specified the division of labour between the government and the parliament. This act was seen as an instrument in the final separation of the ownership function from regulatory and policy responsibilities.[36] Marked-based SOEs were transferred to the new corporate-governance unit set up under the Prime Minister's Office (in total, 11 listed and 26 unlisted companies). Special-assignment companies, whose ownership was not based on investor interests, were left to the branch ministries. Such companies included, for example, the public broadcasting company Yleisradio and the alcohol monopoly Alko. In October 2008, the government transferred some non-strategic minority holdings to the state-owned company Solidium's portfolio.[37] The idea was that government holdings with investor interests would be placed outside the reach of political decision-making. However, in September 2016, Solidium was declared to be 'a Finnish anchor owner'.[38]

In 2016, the government once again adopted a more active stance on ownership policy, the real impact of which has yet to be assessed. The government platform again saw SOEs and their balance sheets as tools to actively reform society.[39] According to Prime Minister Juha Sipilä, 'The use of capital must be intensified, and the current ownership must be activated. This is to be done by putting the equity balance to work'.[40] The development company Vake was founded not only to sell state property but also to use the sales revenue to finance new businesses.[41] In addition to previous ownership interests (profit-seeking, strategic, and natural monopolies and special assignments), the new potential interests were *creating new businesses* and *defending Finnish ownership*,[42] criteria reminiscent of the 20th century SOEs.

SOEs and their corporate governance structures have changed to meet the needs of the times. However, in the public debate, even former state-owned companies are associated with specific social expectations. Over the 1990s, the state abandoned many of the major industrial companies that originally had a clear reason for existence but had become ordinary businesses without a direct link to government interests. While in the 1980s, SOEs were discussed from a resource perspective, since the 1990s, the debate has been dominated by management-related themes. The most discussed topic in the 2000s was management incentive systems, along with the occasional references to the special social responsibility of state-owned companies – for example, in 2015, SOEs' aggressive tax planning was debated in the Finnish public sphere.

According to Tuovinen-Thuesen et al. (2019), during the 2007–2016 period, the goal of ownership policy was to develop the SOEs' operations and shareholder value. According to them, the state succeeded. Although the share of state-owned companies decreased in employment (from 6.5% to 3.1%) and GDP (from 8.5% to 3.5%), there were no other noticeable differences in the companies' profitability and income compared to private companies.

Between 1980 and 2008, the state received a total of EUR 16 billion of net revenue from privatisations, while the position of state-owned companies in the economy declined markedly. However, if we look at the change in the value of the share capital from the early 1970s to the end of the 2000s, we find that equity capital started to grow rapidly in the early 1990s. At the same time, the ownership focus shifted from manufacturing to other sectors, such as finance, transport and energy. The annual dividend income received by the state also increased. As early as the beginning of the 1990s, dividend income rose to EUR 100 million, rising further to over EUR 800 million in 2000. In 2007, dividend income was already over EUR 1.6 billion. Half of the dividends came from SOEs' subsidiaries and associates (Junka, 2010, p. 16).[43]

Today, the number of stated-owned companies compared to 50 years ago has increased, especially through incorporations. New companies have also been set up for tasks that would have previously been handled within the agency organisation.[44] Indeed, whereas formerly SOEs were often large industrial conglomerates, today many SOEs are smaller and more specialised. In the 2010s, the Finnish state also held a small number of very large multinational companies, such as the power company Fortum and the fuel company Neste, with the grounds for ownership being linked to strategic interests. Despite this justification, Fortum was able to sell its electricity grid to international investors in 2013.

Also, when it comes to strategically important companies, the state has increasingly become a minority owner. The ownership amount that suffices to meet the 'strategic need' has fallen. Traditionally, the state-owned holding limits (the minimum level of state ownership in a company) were 100 or 50.1 per cent, depending on the company's strategic weight, and a new limit of 33.4 per cent was introduced in 2016. The justification for this was that by reducing government ownership in specific companies, 'better opportunities are available to exploit the company balance sheet to create new growth and develop the company'.[45] Such proportion of shares was considered enough to allow the state to exercise its veto if, for example, the company's articles of association needed to be amended.

Next, we argue that the Finnish state continues to pursue its industrial policy by promoting the development of its preferred industries – for example, through its R&D policy.

Government investment in innovation policy

The decisions to reform the state administration using NPM doctrines were based on the analyses of structural changes and were made in the context of the changing economic base. In 1979, the SDP leader Sorsa clarified his thoughts on the development of the state administration and its connection to the investments in the private sector: 'To make room for these measures [finance investments in the private sector], we have to stop the growth of the public sector. (…) Tight budget policy must be directed especially to administration'.[46] In Sorsa's view, the salvaged resources were to be reallocated to the private industry (R&D).

Although the SDP publicly referenced only the public administration, the discussed reforms were clearly intended for the public sector as a whole.

The new policy regarding investments in R&D was in harmony with the predominant ideas in the OECD. The question of ongoing structural change was debated in the Technical Cooperation Committee (TECO), which was responsible for the administrative initiatives. One aspect of the discussions in the TECO meetings during the 1970s was the question of how to deal with the ongoing shift to the post-industrial era and how civil servants could manage the change.[47] TECO regarded the growth of the public sector as a hazard to the efficient allocation of resources and to the functioning of democracy.[48] The instruments that TECO recommended were privatisation, market-type mechanisms and resource allocation by centralising the power over public resources.[49] The new policy mix included public investments in R&D and, at the same time, demanded measures to decrease the size of the public sector, which were difficult to undertake without better control over public resources.

In Finland, the most disputed administrative reform was related to *decentralisation*, which was popular from the 1960s to the early 1980s and was understood as a way of strengthening local democracy.[50] However, the problem with the new industrial policy was that it required centralising the power over public resources. To start with, cutting the expenditures of the municipalities in the existing system was difficult because the municipalities were guaranteed to receive back a percentage of their expenditure from the state government (Harisalo et al., 1992, pp. 67–68).[51] Eventually, the dispute led to political battles regarding the meaning of the concept of 'decentralisation'. The new state subsidy law, which put the power over resources firmly in the hands of the state (and the Ministry of Finance) and offered the municipalities a lump sum instead of a percentage of expenditures, was put into effect in 1993 (Law 688/1992). The impetus behind the reform was the severe recession Finland faced in 1991.

At the height of this crisis of the recession, unemployment rose to almost 20 per cent (from less than 6% in the 1980s). The new crisis brought back the old answers: the government, led by the Agrarian-Centre Party, wanted to give priority to public R&D and venture capital (Ministry of Finance, 1992, pp. 69–72). The conclusion was that Finland had not done enough to adapt to the post-industrial era during the 1980s and was paying the price for this indolence. The government stated that a state-subsidy reform was to be part of the austerity measures, though, at the same time, the government was ready to provide public investment for the R&D sector and for venture capital. Only through pain (cuts in welfare services) would there be gain.[52]

One aspect of centralising the power over public resources by shifting from the municipalities to the central government was the need to cut the public resources allocated to welfare services, for which the municipalities were responsible, in order to form the basis for the new industrial policy. In 1993, state subsidies formed 46 per cent of the municipalities' revenues, yet in 2002 this share was down to only 13 per cent. In total, during the 1990s the state cut the budget by a total of 57 billion marks (approximately 18 billion euros, 10% of the GNP) (Tiihonen, 2000, pp. 4, 60–64, 80).

The only parts of the budget that were not cut had to do with public R&D and public venture capital (Figure 2). The fastest growth occurred in the late 1990s (Luhtala, 2010). For example, the resources of the Development Centre of Innovation and Technology (Tekes) grew rapidly (Lemola, 2002, p. 482; also, Reinboth, 1995, p. 4). According to Prime Minister

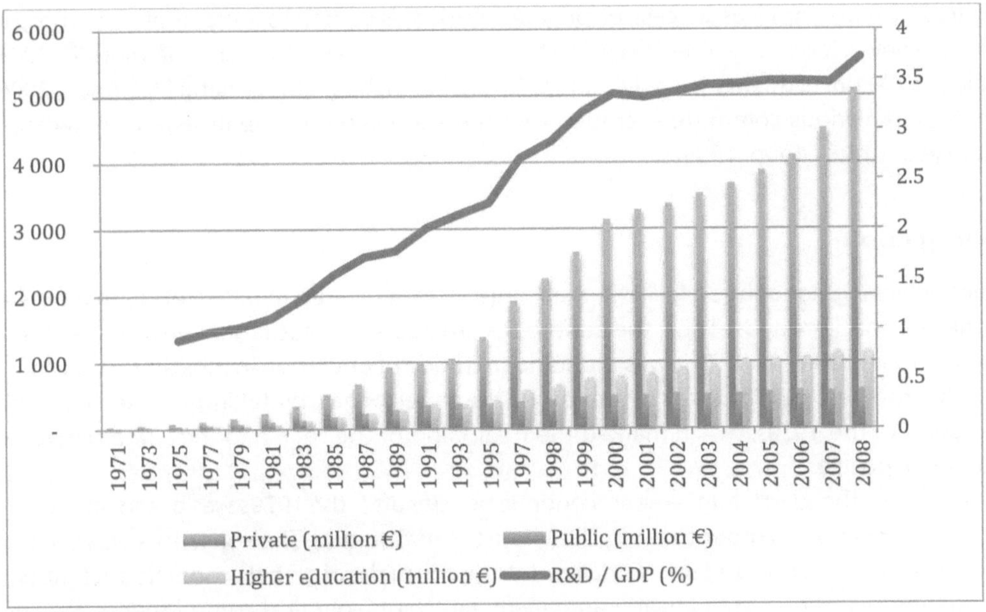

Figure 2. Investments in research and development in Finland, 1971–2008.
Source: Statistics Finland: Research and development and Government R&D funding in the state budget. Retrieved from https://www.stat.fi/til/ttt_en.html [23.9.2020].

Esko Aho, Finland needed serious rethinking and 'neo-industrialisation'.[53] The government set the objective of increasing R&D investment to 2.7 per cent of the GDP, which meant an annual increase in R&D expenditures of 7–9 per cent.[54] Any money extracted from privatisations was supposed to go to new investments rather than public services (Working Group, 1993).

During the 1990s the economists stated that there was a strong link between healthy domestic financial markets on the one hand and economic growth and innovation on the other (Vartia & Ylä-Anttila, 2005, p. 236). Also, Michael Porter's (1990) idea about a local 'cluster' of producers and users was an important aspect of the Finnish model, according to which 'nations' and not just individual companies competed in the international market (Kantola, 2010, pp. 110–113).

The lack of high-risk capital was one of the recurring economic themes in the intra-party debates of 1980s (Koivisto, 1993).[55] In order to start its public venture capital investments, the government passed a new law in 1991, which ordered the Finnish Innovation Fund (SITRA, established in 1967) to focus on high-risk investments. SITRA's funds consisted of the capital (400 million marks/95 million euros) it had acquired since the 1970s and of the Nokia stocks (100 million marks/24 million euros), which the government donated to SITRA in 1992. The state had received these shares as payment when it sold Televa to Nokia in 1981. The value of the donated shares increased 40-fold in a few years. As a result, 70 per cent of the venture capital investments in the early 1990s came from public sources. The government also founded other organisations to channel high-risk public investments, including the Finnish Industrial Investment, Finnvera and the Finnish Industrial Bail Fund (Särkikoski, 2007, pp. 246–254, 273–279, 290–294, 301).

We are not suggesting that R&D was solely a public affair. Instead, the original idea was to influence private companies so that they would start investing in R&D. As illustrated in

Figure 2, this attempt was successful: private companies started to invest more and more in R&D. However, it is impossible to say whether they would have done so regardless. In 2008, Finland's R&D investments were second (3.5% of GDP) in the global ranking (Pelkonen, 2008, pp. 60–61). Various committees argued that the state should have invested significantly more (e.g. TIKAS Group, 1995).[56]

Conclusion

Since achieving nationhood in 1917, the Finnish state acquired many assets with different ownership backgrounds. Thus, the state both created the institutional environment and acted on the market itself. This was the standard mode of operation in most industrial countries for the best part of the 20th century. This paper began by taking up the economic recession of the 1970s, which marked the beginning of the search for new alternatives in economic policies.

In Finland, the search for the new economic policies after the 1970s was based on seeking political consensus in order to avoid Thatcherist confrontation. The consensus was built on the assumption that Finland was a small country in the midst of global economic fluctuations, a situation that required political pragmatism without ideological commitments. Second, the consensus aimed to steer the nation through the ongoing structural change. The recession was widely interpreted as a structural change, whereby the overproduction of the industrial sector was forcing nations to adapt to the coming post-industrial age. According to the dominant interpretation at the time, the best option was to invest in new technology, such as electronics, computers and telematics. This required a new kind of state intervention and open-mindedness towards market competition.

The result was that, in Finland, the stance on public ownership moved slightly to the right in the political spectrum, but state intervention was not completely abandoned. The steering power of the state was reformed to be subtler. The chain of events we have analysed here had two effects. First, the SOE ownership policy was gradually reformed in favour of greater SOE autonomy from the government to enable facing the opening global markets. Corporate structures were to be adjusted to be consistent with international practices and standards. It was believed that it was important to have a coherent understanding of international business and the related risks. Second, public resources were allocated from the traditional welfare state towards post-industrial nation building with the help of new public-management doctrines. In this process, public resources were invested in venture capital and public R&D to encourage the private sector to increase its investment in innovation. Finland may not be a completely exceptional case, but its peripheral identity resulted in a peculiar situation due to the pressure of global markets.

Consensus politics with political compromises bypassed and downplayed possible resistance. Elsewhere, for example in the UK or New Zealand, straightforward privatisations engendered protest movements, which hindered the reforms. In Finland, small steps in implementing the reforms made the resistance more difficult.

Even though the Finnish case was built on consensus politics, the neoliberal wave had its effects. The antagonism towards state ownership came from several sources. First, the ownership structure of state-owned companies was openly criticised and, for many, the ownership in itself was problematic. Second, in 1979 the state project to establish an electronics corporation had just failed spectacularly, and in this context, the public support for private companies was the only way to move forward with the post-industrial structural change. Still, the system remained relatively stable as long as the market structure remained protective. The defensive position towards state intervention came from the national-historical narrative of a small nation in the periphery without capital. Public investments in innovation policy were interpreted as inevitable because big international investors did not have enough information about such a small peripheral country, leading to a shortage of investments, especially in high-risk cases. Market forces seemed to malfunction in this regard. A lack of capital became a persistent theme in national politics, a theme that was still evident in the case of establishing the state-owned high-risk investment agency Vake in 2016.

A particularly important factor was that since the 1980s, when it was directly stated that corporate governance had to comply with international business standards, this effectively referred to the introduction of Anglo-Saxon structures. By the 1990s, 'international standards and practices' were self-evident as development guidelines. Extending the companies' ownership base and attracting foreign investors was considered important. For this reason, it was often said that companies must follow certain models in order to be a credible investment targets in the eyes of international investors. The reforms were also aimed at improving the efficiency and effectiveness in achieving the commercial and/or non-commercial targets and improving the transparency and accountability of SOEs.

Ideological or intellectual forces also affected the reforms as state ownership was, in many cases, seen as an unnecessary barrier to the business environment, with efficiency ensuring competition. The institutional frameworks of international agreements also pushed Finland in the direction where competition barriers were no longer acceptable. The state almost abandoned its role as the owner, choosing, instead, to focus on regulating the market. When the state did continue to own SOEs, ownership was differentiated from regulation.

Private companies were active lobbyists for R&D and high-risk capital investments. For example, in the 1980s, Nokia stated many times that Finnish companies were unable to access enough high-risk capital and that companies needed more well-educated employees and more resources for R&D (Häikiö, 2001b, pp. 161, 176–178). Private companies also benefitted from public investments (OECD, 2009, pp. 86). It is safe to conclude that Nokia, which became a global leader in the mobile phone markets in the 1990s, was one of the success stories of Finland's innovation policy, even though the company later experienced serious problems after failing in the smartphone market. It is no wonder that in the Finnish discussion, the overall results of public investment in R&D have been the subject of a furious public debate. At the same time, it is hard to establish an unequivocal relation between R&D investments and profit-earning capacity, to individualise effective causes and to rule out alternative scenarios (Berghall et al., 2006, pp. 28–34).

The Finnish case shows how strongly the international influence was transmitted to the national context. Although Finnish corporate governance and corporate structures had their own characteristics, Finnish SOEs followed Western principles and recommendations. In many cases, the state abandoned the ownership of SOEs. In the cases where state ownership was maintained, the state's ability to pursue policies using the SOEs was weakened. However, the old SOE policies are still visible from time to time. New ways of influencing business can also include other routes than the (re-)regulation that emerged when old public monopolies were opened up in the 1980s and 1990s. In this article, we have dealt with innovation policy. Future research should also consider other means by which governments support domestic industries. We know, for example, that government agencies may have favoured domestic production in their purchasing policies in the 1970s and 1980s, giving domestic industry room to develop (e.g. Industrial Committee's Report 1975:47, p. 105; Ministry of Finance, 1993, p. 27). However, the extent or significance of such support has not yet been analysed.

Notes

1. Prime Minister's Office. (29.12.2015). *Valtion kehitysyhtiö Vake Oy:n toimintaohje.* Retrieved from https://valtioneuvosto.fi/documents/10616/1266558/Toimiohje+Valtion+kehitysyhtio+Vake+Oy.pdf/91664156-a8f2-4bb7-8e1c-f1f8a9bb0cfb/Toimiohje+Valtion+kehitysyhtio+Vake+Oy.pdf.pdf
2. Rapid economic growth took place from the late 1940s to the 1970s. This period has various names depending on the country: *Les Trente Glorieuses* (France), *Wirtschafthswunder* (West-Germany, Austria), *Il Miracolo Economico* (Italy), etc.
3. For more on *ownership policy*, *ownership steering* and *corporate governance* in the Finnish context, see the Finnish National Audit Office (2013, p. 17).
4. 'Liikelaitos' in Finnish.
5. Ministry of Trade and Industry. (17.6.1974). Memo. (valtionyhtiöt 1955–1977, HC2). FNA.
6. 'Hallintoneuvosto' in Finnish.
7. Ministry of Trade and Industry. (17.6.1974). Memo. (valtionyhtiöt 1955–1977, HC2). FNA.
8. Two parties, the Social Democratic Party and the Agrarian-Centre Party, dominated Finnish politics in the 1970s.
9. In a population of 4.7 million. Statistics Finland, Industrial Statistics XVIII (1972–1978).
10. The term 'recovery' ('elvytys') appeared in the Finnish economic discussions the 1930s, meaning that the state would rely on loan money to use public resources to tackle the recession (Heikkinen, 2009).
11. The government programme for *Sorsa II*: *Talous- ja työllisyyspolitiikka* [Economic and employment policy]; see also the memo of the Social Democratic Party Council of 24.11.1977, pp. 40–45. The Labour Archive, Helsinki.
12. Teemu Hiltunen's speech (12.10.1977). The Archive of the Ministry of Finance, Budget Department (Uaa:1). FNA.
13. Kalevi Sorsa in a television interview (28.8.1979). The Finnish Business and Policy Forum Archive (EVA) (file 86). FNA.
14. Regarding the history of the information age and the post-industrial society, see, e.g., Webster (1995, pp. 11, 30–32), Rothwell and Zegveld (1981, p. 15), Bell (1974), Toffler (1970) and Johnson (1971).
15. Teemu Hiltunen's speech (12.10.1977). The Archive of the Ministry of Finance, Budget Department (Uaa:1). FNA.
16. EVA meeting memo, Appendix C (25.10.1979); EVA meeting memo, Appendix A (31.5.1979). The Finnish Business and Policy Forum Archive (File 5). FNA.
17. This was already noticed in the mid-1970s. In the words of the Ministry of Finance, 'The application of computer/telecommunications and related systems (for instance, video-technology, cable TV), would create a new working-tool for the service sector of an economy. This comprises educational, legal, medical and other professions and a wide range of public services such as post and newspaper delivery, law enforcement and public health services now often the subject of public concern' (Pietarinen et al., 1975, Appendix 1, p. 12).
18. Also 'Teknologiakomitea vaatii 1980-luvulta: tutkimus kaksinkertaiseksi' [newspaper article] (16.12.1980). *Helsingin Sanomat.*
19. Newspaper articles: Kairamo, K. (29.9.1981). 'Elektroniikkatuotannolla on teollisuudessa keskeinen rooli'. *Helsingin Sanomat* (21.5.1982). 'Yrityksiin 55 000 tutkijaa lisää tällä vuosikymmenellä'. *Helsingin Sanomat.*

20. The specific tools used in the NPM reforms varied from country to country, including, for example, management by objectives, quality management with benchmarking, decentralisation, outsourcing, separating the purchaser and provider, etc.
21. Valtionhallinnon uudistamiskomitea. (28.3.1975). *Memo*. Committee archive. FNA.
22. Hjerppe, R. (1982). Liikelaitos valtion organisaatiomuotona. *Hallinto, 1982*(9–10), 14–24.
23. E.g. Archive of the Public Corporation Committee (1983–1985). *Statements by public corporations*. (Files 2, 5 & 9). Archive of the Council of the State, Helsinki.
24. The shares were sold several times in the following years. Government's decision in principle, 26.5.2000.
25. Ministry of Trade and Industry handouts 8/1998: 'Yksityisten palvelujen kehittäminen'. (KTM, Ucd:6). FNA.
26. Archive of the Industrial Department of the Ministry of Trade and Industry. (1970–1987). *State-owned enterprises* (Hc:4). FNA.
27. Workgroup (22.8.1991). *Valtionyhtiöiden yksityistämistyöryhmän raportti* [report]. (Ucc:34). FNA.
28. This principle was written in, e.g., Government's decision in principle, 23.6.1994.
29. The Social Democrats did not want to restrict the activities of state-owned companies and opposed the privatisation demands made by the bourgeois parties (Marttila, 2016, p. 127).
30. Citizens were encouraged to participate in the stock market. Also Workgroup (22.8.1991). Valtionyhtiöiden yksityistämistyöryhmän raportti [report]. (Ucc:34). FNA, pp. 8, 15.
31. Workgroup (22.8.1991). *Valtionyhtiöiden yksityistämistyöryhmän raportti* [report]. (Ucc: 34). FNA.
32. E.g. Hilkka Kunnas (10.7.1981). 'Kaikki omistavat – kukaan ei vastaa: Mikä se on?' *Suomen Kuvalehti* (28/1981). Retrieved from digi.kansalliskirjasto.fi
33. These ownership interests were industrialisation, social causes and profit-seeking. Ownership was influenced by the extent to which the company had a strategic interest (e.g. Working Group, 1989).
34. Government's decision in principle, 23.6.1994; Decision of the Cabinet Committee on Economic Policy, 17.4.2004.
35. Minister Pekkarinen's foreword in Government Ownership Steering Department (2002).
36. Government Ownership Steering Department (2007, 2008).
37. These were Kemira (chemicals), Metso (engineering works), Outokumpu (mining), Rautaruukki (steel), Sampo (banking), Sponda (real estates), Stora Enso (forest industry) and TeliaSonera (telecommunications).
38. Government's Ownership Steering Department (2016, p. 9).
39. E.g. Cabinet Committee on Economic Policy, 12.5.2016; Government's decision in principle 13.5.2016.
40. Government Ownership Steering Department (2015).
41. Government Ownership Steering Department (2016, p. 4).
42. Tuovinen-Thuesen et al., 2019; The policy of the Cabinet Committee on Economic Policy 12.5.2016.
43. In 2017, the SOEs paid EUR 1 845 million in dividends: Solidium EUR 585 million, special task companies 146 million, unlisted SOEs 444 million and listed SOEs 670 million. Retrieved from https://vnk.fi/en/ownership-changes-and-revenue (14 September 2020).
44. Between 1950 and 1980, there were 20–25 state-owned companies, in the 1980s and 1990s the number rose to over 30 and at the beginning of 2010, the total number of state-owned companies was 57. The numbers are based on the government's annual financial reports, 1917–2010.
45. Government Ownership Steering Department (2015, 2016, p. 4).
46. Social Democratic Party council meeting 9.3.1977, p. 14. The Labour Archive, Helsinki; see also the Government programme for the recovery government, *Economic and employment policy*.
47. OECD/TECO, 22. Oct. 1976 TECO (76)12, *Technical Cooperation Committee (TECO) proposed joint activity in the field of public management*. (Hd20). FNA. See also OECD/TECO, Paris, 27 Jun. 1980 C(80)115, *Programme of Work of the Organisation for 1981: General lines of the secretary-general's's proposals*. Archive of the Ministry of Finance (Hd22). FNA.

48. OECD/TECO, Paris, Mar. 1979, CT/PUMA/500, *Cooperative action programme. Joint activity on public management improvement. Seminar for controlling public expenditure*, Archive of the Ministry of Finance (Hd22). FNA.
49. OECD/TECO, Paris, 15 Apr. 1980, TECO(80)7, *Technical Cooperation Committee. Outline of the Cooperative Action Programme for 1981*, Archive of the Ministry of Finance (Hd22), FNA; OECD/TECO, Paris, 25 Aug. 1980, CT/PUMA(80)1, *Co-operation Programme. Steering Committee of the Joint Activity on Public Management Improvement*, 2–3, Archive of the Ministry of Finance (Hd22), FNA; OECD/TECO, 15.4.1980, TECO(80)7 *Technical Cooperation Committee. Outline of the Cooperative Action Programme for 1981*. Archive of the Ministry of Finance (Hd22), FNA; OECD/TECO, 25.8.1980, CT/PUMA(80)1 *Cooperative Programme, Steering Committee of the joint activity on public management improvement*, p. 2–3. Archive of the Ministry of Finance (Hd22). FNA; OECD/TECO,6.3.1979 *Cooperative Action Programme. Joint activity on public management: policies and institutions. Synthesis report on the symposium managing change in the public administration*. Archive of the Ministry of Finance (Hd21). FNA.
50. Committee Report (1978:22, pp. 3–10); Committee Report (1981:54, pp. 1–2); Committee Report (1982:22, pp. 1–6) and Committee Report (1983:3, pp. 1–3).
51. The most critical part was that the funds the state gave to the municipalities were paid according to the calculated percentage of their actual expenditure. This hindered any attempt to cut the expenditures in the core functions of the welfare state, which the municipalities were in charge of.
52. Newspaper article. (21.8.1992) 'Hallitus kehuu 5,8 miljardin lisäsäästöjä ja lupaa kansalle 'Kipua ja särkyä'' [The government praises 5.8 billion cuts and promises 'pain and aches' for the people]. *Helsingin Sanomat*.
53. Esko Aho (6.10.1993) 'Holhousvaltiosta yhteisvastuun ja yrittäjyyden yhteiskuntaa' [From tutelary state to a society of entrepreneurship and joint responsibility]. (Dc 1987–1995). Archive of the Agrarian-Centre Party, Helsinki.
54. Workgroup (16.8.1991). Memo: Teollisuuden rakenteen kehittäminen [Developing industrial structure]. (Ucc:34). FNA.
55. See Workgroup on industrial policy. (22.10.1982). *Meeting of the Social Democratic Party Council, Appendix 443*. (Ca 94). The Labour Archive, Helsinki.
56. In the 2010s, R&D investment fell to less than 3% of the GDP.

Acknowledgements

This article responds to *Business History*'s call for submissions for a special issue on the government-business relations. We would like to thank our colleagues who provided useful feedback at the development workshop in Sterling, June 2018. We also thank the editors of *Business History* and our anonymous reviewers.

Disclosure statement

No potential conflict of interest was reported by the authors.

ORCID

Pasi Nevalainen http://orcid.org/https://doi.org/0000-0003-1172-9537

References

Official government publications

Committee Report. (1954). *Valtakunnansuunnittelukomitean mietintö* [State planning] (1954:4). VAPK.
Committee Report. (1975). *Teollisuustoimikunta 1975: n mietintö* [Industrial structure] (1975:47). VAPK.
Committee Report. (1978). *Valtion keskushallintokomitean osamietintö* [Central administration] (1978). VAPK.
Committee Report. (1980). *Teknologiakomitean mietintö* [Technology] (1980:55). VAPK.
Committee Report. (1981). *Osallistumistoimikunnan mietintö* [Participation of Citizens] (1981:54). VAPK.
Committee Report. (1982). *Lähidemokratiatoimikunnan mietintö* [Local democracy] (1982:22). VAPK.
Committee Report. (1983a). *Kuntien itsehallintokomitean mietintö* [Autonomy of municipalities] (1983:3). VAPK.
Committee Report. (1983b). *Valtion liikelaitostyöryhmän mietintö* [Public corporations] (1982:64). VAPK.
Committee Report. (1985). *Liikelaitoskomitean mietintö*. [Public corporations] (1985:2). VAPK.
Government Ownership Steering Department. (2002). *Annual Report of the Ownership Steering Department in the Prime Minister's Office*. Retrieved from https://vnk.fi/en/government-ownership-steering/ownership-policy/data-bank [accessed 11.1.2016]
Government Ownership Steering Department. (2007). *Annual Report of the Ownership Steering Department in the Prime Minister's Office*. Retrieved from https://vnk.fi/en/government-ownership-steering/ownership-policy/data-bank [accessed 11.1.2016]
Government Ownership Steering Department. (2008). *Annual Report of the Ownership Steering Department in the Prime Minister's Office*. Retrieved from https://vnk.fi/en/government-ownership-steering/ownership-policy/data-bank [accessed 11.1.2016]
Government Ownership Steering Department. (2015). *Annual Report of the Ownership Steering Department in the Prime Minister's Office*. Retrieved from https://vnk.fi/en/government-ownership-steering/ownership-policy/data-bank [accessed 23.8.2017]
Government Ownership Steering Department. (2016). *Annual Report of the Ownership Steering Department in the Prime Minister's Office*. Retrieved from https://vnk.fi/en/government-ownership-steering/ownership-policy/data-bank [accessed 23.8.2017]
Government Ownership Steering Department. (2006–2017). *Annual Report of the Ownership Steering Department in the Prime Minister's Office*. Retrieved from https://vnk.fi/omistajaohjaus/aineistopankki
Kaisanlahti, T. (2001). *Valtion omistajaohjaus: Perusta ja välineet [Government ownership steering: Basis and tools]*. Ministry of Trade and Industry.
Ministry of Finance. (1992). *Näkymät ja talouspolitiikan linja vuoteen 1996*. [Economic policy outlook]. Ministry of Finance.
Ministry of Finance. (1993). *Kansallinen teollisuusstrategia [National industrial strategy for Finland]*. Ministry of Finance.
National Audit Office. (2013). *Hyvä hallintomalli valtion erityistehtävää hoitavissa yhtiöissä ja niiden omistajaohjauksessa. [A good governance model in state-owned companies and their corporate governance]*. Report 2013:7. Edita.
Paavilainen, V. (1963). *National planning in Finland*. Valtakunnansuunnittelutoimiston julkaisusarja A: 14.3. VAPK.
Pietarinen, I., Sauna-Aho, J., & Takanen, I. (1975). *ATK-politiikka ja tietoliikennepolitiikka: Raportti OECD: n helmikuussa 1975 järjestämästä konferenssista "Computer/telecommunications policy" [Computers and data transfer: Report on OECD conference Computer/telecommunications]*. Ministry of Finance.
TIKAS Group. (1995). *Suomi tietoyhteiskunnaksi, kansalliset linjaukset: Tikas-ohjausryhmän loppuraportti [Finland's way to the information society: The national strategy]*. Ministry of Finance.

Working Group. (1989). *Valtionyhtiölainsäädäntötyöryhmän muistio*. Ministry of Trade and Industry.
Working Group. (1993). *Valtionyhtiötyöryhmä 1993:n mietintö*. Ministry of Trade and Industry.
Working Group. (1995). *Valtionyhtiötyöryhmä 1995:n loppuraportti*. Ministry of Trade and Industry.
Working Group. (1999). *Valtionyhtiöiden omistajapolitiikkaa selvittänyt työryhmä*. Ministry of Finance.

Literature

Ahonen, P. (1987). *Valtion liiketoiminta, hallinnon teoriat ja finanssihallinto: tutkimus valtion liiketoiminnan organisoinnista Suomessa, erityisesti välilliseen valtionhallintoon sijoittuvien organisaatiomuotojen kannalta*. [Public Enterprise, Administrative Theories, and Financial Administration in Finland] Åbo Akademis Förlag.

Allardt, E. (1969). *Suomalaisen yhteiskunnan tuleva kehitys ja yhteiskuntaelämän yleiset ongelmat* [The future of Finnish society and it's discontents]. In *Taloutemme tienviittoja [Road signs of our economy]* (pp. 60–78). Weilin + Göös.

Aunesluoma, J. (2011). *Vapaakaupan tiellä: Suomen kauppa- ja integraatiopolitiikka maailmansodista EU-aikaan [On a road to liberalisation: Trade and integration policy of Finland from the World Wars to the European Union]*. SKS.

Barzelay, M. (2001). *The New Public Management: Improving research and policy dialogue*. University of California Press.

Bell, D. (1974). *The coming of post-industrial society: A venture in social forecasting*. Heinemann.

Berghall, E., Junka, T., & Kiander, J. (2006). *T&K, tuottavuus ja taloudellinen kasvu. [R&D and economic growth]*. VATT.

Berle, A., & Means, G. (1932). *The modern corporation and private property*. Transaction Publisher.

Björklund, N. (1990). *Valmet: Asetehtaiden muuttaminen kansainväliseksi suuryhtiöksi [Valmet: Transforming the weapons factory into an international corporation]*. Gummerus.

Bruton, G., Peng, M., Ahlstrom, D., Stan, C., Xu, K. (2015). State-owned enterprises around the world as hybrid organizations. *The Academy of Management Perspectives, 29*(1), 92–114.

Cheung, Z., Aalto, E., & Nevalainen, P. (2020). Institutional logics and the internationalization of a state-owned enterprise: Evaluation of international venture opportunities by Telecom Finland 1987–1998. *Journal of World Business, 55*(6), 101140. https://doi.org/10.1016/j.jwb.2020.101140

Christensen, S. (2018). The capitalist state or the state as private owner. In A. Sasson (Ed.), *At the forefront, looking ahead: Research based answers to contemporary uncertainties of management.* (pp. 134–158). Universitetsforlaget.

Christiansen, H. (2011). *The size and composition of the SOE sector in OECD countries* (OECD Corporate Governance Working Papers No. 5). https://doi.org/10.1787/5kg54cwps0s3-en

Clifton, J., Comín, F., & Díaz Fuentes, D. (2006). Privatizing public enterprises in the European Union 1960–2002: Ideological, pragmatic, inevitable?*Journal of European Public Policy, 13*(5), 736–756.

Clifton, J., Lanthier, P., & Schröter, H. (2011). Regulating and deregulating the public utilities 1830–2010. *Business History, 53*(5), 659–672. https://doi.org/10.1080/00076791.2011.599592

Colli, A., & Nevalainen, P. (2020). State-owned enterprises. In T. da Silva Lopes, C. Lubinski, & H. Tworek (Eds.), *The Routledge companion to the makers of global business* (pp. 294–311). Routledge.

Cuervo-Cazurra, A., Gaur, A., & Singh, D. (2019). Pro-market institutions and global strategy: The pendulum of pro-market reforms and reversals. *Journal of International Business Studies, 50*(4), 598–632. https://doi.org/10.1057/s41267-019-00221-z

Cuervo-Cazurra, A., Inkpen, A., Musacchio, A., & Ramaswamy, K. (2014). Governments as owners: State-owned multinational companies. *Journal of International Business Studies, 45*(8), 919–942. https://doi.org/10.1057/jibs.2014.43

Fellman, S. (2008). Growth and investment: Finnish capitalism, 1850s–2005s. In S. Fellman, M. Jes Iversen, H. Sjögren, & L. Thue (Eds.), *Creating Nordic capitalism: The business history of a competitive periphery* (pp. 139–217). Palgrave Macmillan.

Graack, C., & Elixman, D. (1999). Deregulation, privatization and internationalization of European telecoms markets. In P. J. J. Welfens, G. Yarrow, R. Grinberg, & C. Graack (Eds.), *Towards competition in network industries* (pp. 79–113). Springer.

Grosman, A., Okhmatovskiy, I., & Wright, M. (2016). State control and corporate governance in transition economics: 25 years on from 1989. *Corporate Governance, 24*(3), 200–221. https://doi.org/10.1111/corg.12145

Grossi, G., Papenfuß, U., & Tremblay, M.-S. (2015). Corporate governance and accountability of state-owned enterprises: Relevance for science and society and interdisciplinary research perspectives. *International Journal of Public Sector Management, 28*(4/5), 274–285. https://doi.org/10.1108/IJPSM-09-2015-0166

Grøgaard, B., Rygh, A., & Benito, G. (2019). Bringing corporate governance into internationalization theory: State ownership and foreign entry strategies. *Journal of International Business Studies, 50*(8), 1310–1337. https://doi.org/10.1057/s41267-019-00237-5

Hancké, B. (Ed.) (2009). *Debating varieties of capitalism: A reader*. Oxford University Press.

Harisalo, R., Rajala, T., & Ståhlberg, K. (1992). *Kunnallispolitiikka [Local policy-making]*. VAPK-kustannus.

Heikkinen, S. (2009). Kuka keksi elvytyksen? [Who invented recovery?]. *Kielikello, 2009*(1). http://www.kielikello.fi/index.php?mid=2&pid=11&aid=1974

Heiskanen, I. (1977). *Julkinen, kollektiivinen ja markkinaperusteinen: Suomalaisen yhteiskunnan hallintajärjestelmien ja julkisen päätöksenteon ja hallinnon kehitys ja kehittäminen 1960– ja 1970–luvuilla. [History of Finnish administration, 1960s and 1970s]*. Academy of Finland.

Hjerppe, R. (1982). Liikelaitos valtion organisaatiomuotona. *Hallinto*, 1982(9–10), 14–24.

Hjerppe, R. (1988). *Suomen talous 1860–1985: Kasvu ja rakennemuutos [Economy of Finland 1980-1985: Economic growth and structural change]*. Bank of Finland.

Hjerppe, R. (1990). *Kasvun vuosisata [Century of growth]*. VAPK-kustannus.

Holkeri, H. (1977). *Itsenäisiä ajatuksia [Independent ideas]*. Kirjayhtymä.

Hood, C. (1991). A public management for all seasons. *Public Administration, 69*(1), 3–19. https://doi.org/10.1111/j.1467-9299.1991.tb00779.x

Häikiö, M. (2001a). *Nokia Oyj:n: Fuusio – Yhdistymisten kautta suomalaiseksi monialayritykseksi 1865–1982 [History of Nokia 1]* Helsinki: Edita.

Häikiö, M. (2001b). *Nokia Oyj:n: Suurkaupoilla eurooppalaiseksi elektroniikkayritykseksi 1983–1991 [History of Nokia 2]* Helsinki: Edita.

Hämäläinen, S. (1993). Mauno Koivisto ja Suomen Pankki [President and the Bank of Finland]. In K. Immonen (Ed.), *Pitkä linja: Mauno Koivisto. Valtiomies ja vaikuttaja* (pp. 109–161). Kirjayhtymä.

Jalava, M. (2011). *The University in the making of the welfare state*. Peter Lang.

Jensen, M. (1998). *Foundations of organizational strategy*. Harvard University Press.

Johnson, T. (1971). *Tietokoneiden aika [The computers in our lives]*. WSOY.

Junka, T. (2010). *Valtionyhtiöt 1975–2008 [State-owned companies 1975–2008]*. Valtion taloudellinen tutkimuskeskus.

Kantola, A. (2010). Kilpailukyky politiikan valtastrategiana [Competitiveness as a strategy in politics]. In J. Kaisto & M. Pyykkönen (Eds.), *Hallintavalta: Sosiaalisen, politiikan ja talouden kysymyksiä*. Gaudeamus.

Koivisto, T. (1993). *Aluepolitiikan uudistus on välttämätön [Regional policy]*. In P. Pakarinen & K. Varila (Eds.), Kansallinen sivistysliitto.

Koivuniemi, J. (2018). Tehtaiden Suomi ja deindustrialisaatio, 1900–2000 [Structural change 1900-2000]. In P. Haapala & J. Eloranta (Eds.), *Suomen rakennehistoria: Näkökulmia muutokseen ja jatkuvuuteen*. Vastapaino.

Kuisma, M. (1997). *Kylmä sota, kuuma öljy: Neste, Suomi ja kaksi Eurooppaa* [Cold War, Hot oil: Neste, Finland and Two Europe]. Helsinki: WSOY.

Kuisma, M. (2004). *Kahlittu raha, kansallinen kapitalismi: Kansallis-Osake-Pankki, 1940–1995 [Chained money, national capitalism: History of KOP-Bank]*. SKS.

Kuisma, M. (2016). *Valtion yhtiöt: nousu ja tuho [State's enterprises: Rise and fall]*. Siltala.

Kuisma, M., & Seppänen, P. (2015). *Suomen pahimmat bisnesmokat: tarinoita huippujohtamisesta. [Finnish worst business mistakes]*. Siltala.

Kuusterä, A., & Tarkka, J. (2012). *Suomen Pankki 200 vuotta: Parlamentin pankki* [History of Bank of Finland] (Vol. 2). Otava.

Larna, K. (1969). Tieto taloudellisen kasvun avaintekijänä 1970-luvulla [Importance of Information/knowledge in the economic growth]. In *Taloutemme tienviittoja [Road signs of our economy]* (pp. 107–120). Weilin+Göös.

Lazzarini, S., & Musacchio, A. (2020). Leviathan as a partial cure? Opportunities and pitfalls of using the state-owned apparatus to respond to the Covid-19 crisis. *Revista Brasileira de Administração Pública, 54*(4), 561–577.

Lemola, T. (2002). Tiede- ja teknologiapolitiikan muotoutuminen [Science and technology policy]. In P. Tommila (Ed.), *Suomen tieteen historia* (Vol. 4). WSOY.

Luhtala, T. (2010). Suomi ja Ruotsi panostavat eniten T&K-toimintaan [Finland and Sweden: Leaders in R&D]. *Tieto & Trendit, 2010*(6), 30–33.

Lynn, L., Jr. (2006). *Public mangement: Old and new*. Routledge.

Marttila, J. (2016). *Hillitty markkinatalous: Kokoomuksen ja SDP:n lähetyminen ja hallitusyhteistyö 1980-luvulla [The convergence of economic policies of the National Coalition Party and the Social Democratic Party in the 1980s]* [Doctoral dissertation]. University of Helsinki.

Mattelart, A. (2003). *Informaatioyhteiskunnan historia. [History of information society]*. Vastapaino.

McCracken, P. (1977). *Towards full employment and price stability a report to the OECD by a group of independent experts*. OECD.

Megginson, W. (2017). Privatization, state capitalism, and state ownership of business in the 21st century. *Foundations and Trends® in Finance, 11*(1-2), 1–153. https://doi.org/10.1561/0500000053

Megginson, W. L., & Netter, J. M. (2001). From state to market: A survey of empirical studies on privatization. *Journal of Economic Literature, 39*(2), 321–389. https://doi.org/10.1257/jel.39.2.321

Millward, R. (2011). Public enterprise in the modern western world: An historical analysis. *Annals of Public and Cooperative Economics, 82*(4), 375–398. https://doi.org/10.1111/j.1467-8292.2011.00447.x

Musacchio, A., & Lazzarini, S. (2014). *Reinventing state capitalism: Leviathans in business, Brazil and beyond*. Harvard University Press.

Musacchio, A., & Lazzarini, S. (2018). State-owned enterprises as multinationals: Theory and research directions. In A. Cuervo-Cazurra (Ed.), *State-owned multinationals: Governments in global business* (pp. 255–276). Palgrave Macmillan.

Musacchio, A., Lazzarini, S. G., & Aguilera, R. V. (2015). New varieties of state capitalism: Strategic and governance implications. *Academy of Management Perspectives, 29*(1), 115–131. https://doi.org/10.5465/amp.2013.0094

Nevalainen, P. (2014). *Virastosta liikeyritys: Posti- ja telelaitoksen muutosprosessi 1930–1994 [From State Department to Business Enterprise: The Finnish Post and Tele-communications Department and the process of change 1930–1994]* [Doctoral dissertation]. University of Jyväskylä.

Nevalainen, P. (2017). Facing the inevitable? The public telecom monopoly's way of coping with deregulation. *Business History, 59*(3), 362–381. https://doi.org/10.1080/00076791.2016.1197207

Nora, S., & Minc, A. (1978/1980). *The computerization of society: A report to the President of France*. The MIT Press.

OECD. (1979a). *Facing the future: Mastering the probable and managing the unpredictable*. OECD Publishing.

OECD. (1979b). *Science and technology in the new socio-economic context*. OECD Publishing.

OECD. (1979c). *Technology and the structural adaptation of industry*. OECD Publishing.

OECD. (2009). *Policy responses to the economic crisis: Investing in innovation for long-term growth*. OECD Publishing.

OECD. (2017). *The size and sectoral distribution of state-owned enterprises*. OECD Publishing.

Outinen, S. (2015). *Sosiaalidemokraattien tie talouden ohjailusta markkinareaktioiden ennakointiin: työllisyys sosialidemokraattien politiikassa Suomessa 1975–1998* [Social Democratic Party and the policy of employment] [Doctoral dissertation]. University of Helsinki.

Parker, D. (1999). Privatization in the European Union: A critical assessment of its development, rationale and consequences. *Economic and Industrial Democracy, 20*(1), 9–38. https://doi.org/10.1177/0143831X99201002

Pelkonen, A. (2008). *The Finnish competition state and entrepreneurial policies in the Helsinki region*. University of Helsinki.

Pierson, C. (1998). *Beyond the welfare state: The new political economy of welfare*. Polity Press.

Pollitt, C., & Bouckaert, G. (2000). *Public management reform: A comparative analysis*. Oxford University Press.

Porter, M. (1990). *The competitive advantage of nations*. Free Press.

Pöyry, J. (1983). Näivettääkö sähköinen viestintä paperiteollisuutemme? [Will electric media kill our paper industry?]. In J. Tarkka (Ed.), *Max Jakobson: Kansainvälinen suomalainen* (pp. 129–152). Otava.

Puumalainen, A. (1976). *Valtion teollinen yritystoiminta tuotantorakenteen täydentäjänä [State-owned industrial enterprise as a complement to the production structure]* [Doctoral dissertation]. University of Helsinki.

Ranki, R. (2012). *Niin siinä käy kun omistaa: Tarinaa valtionyhtiöistä [So it happens when you own: Stories about state-owned companies]*. Helsinki: Edita.

Reinboth, R. (1995). Valtionosuudet supistuvat ensi vuosituhannelle saakka. [Cut in the State Subsidies]. *Hallinto, 1995*(4), 3–4.

Rodger, D. T. (2011). *Age of fracture*. Belknap Press of Harvard University Press.

Rothwell, R., & Zegveld, W. (1981). *Industrial innovation and public policy: Preparing for the 1980s and the 1990s*. Frances Pinter.

Sahari, A. (2018). *Valtio ja suurteollisuuden synty: Laivanrakennusteollisuuden kehittyminen yhteiskunnallisissa teknopoliittisissa järjestelmissä Suomessa 1918–1954 [The state and the making of big industry: The development of shipbuilding industry within societal, technopolitical systems in Finland, 1918–1954]* [Doctoral dissertation]. University of Helsinki.

Särkikoski, T. (2007). *Sitra: Tulevaisuus tehtävänä [History of SITRA]*, 3–4.

Scharpf, F. W. (1991). *Crisis and choice in European social democracy*. Cornell University Press.

Schön, L. (2013). *Maailman taloushistoria: Teollinen aika [World economic history]*. Vastapaino.

Skurnik, S. (2005). *Suomalaisen talousmallin murros. Suljetusta sääntelytaloudesta kaksinapaiseen globaalitalouteen* [The transformation of the Finnish business system] [Doctoral dissertation]. Helsinki School of Economics.

Smolander, J. (2000). *Suomalainen oikeisto ja "kansankoti" [The right wing and the welfare state]*. Gummerus.

Sorsa, K. (1977). *Elvytyksen linjat: Talouspoliittinen konferenssi 5.-6.1977 [Recovery policy]*. VAPK.

Tarkka, J. (1988). Kahlitun rahan aika: Suomen rahoitusmarkkinoiden säännöstelyn vuosikymmenet [History of the Regulation of Financial markets in Finland]. In Honkapohja, S., & Suvanto, A. (Eds.), *Raha, inflaatio ja talouspolitiikka* [Money, Inflation and Economic Policy] (pp. 189–238). Helsinki: Valtion Painatuskeskus.

Tarkka, J. (2002). *Uhan alta unioniin: asennemuutos ja sen unilukkari Eva [History of EVA]*. Otava.

Thatcher, M. (2004). Varieties of capitalism in an internationalized world: Domestic institutional change in European telecommunications. *Comparative Political Studies, 37*(7), 751–780. https://doi.org/10.1177/0010414004266868

Thatcher, M. (2007). Reforming national regulatory institutions: The EU and cross national variety in European network industries. In B. H. Rhodes, B. Hancké, B. Hancke, M. Rhodes, & M. Thatcher (Eds.), *Beyond varieties of capitalism: Conflict, contradiction, and complementarities in the European economy* (pp. 147–172). Oxford University Press.

Tiihonen, S. (2000). *From uniform administration to governance and management of diversity: Reforming state functions and public management in Finland*. Ministry of Finance.

Tiitta, A. (2007). Tiede ja teknologiapolitiikka Suomessa 1970–2006 [Science & technology policy in Finland 1970-2006]. In V. Pernaa, & A. Tiitta (Eds.), *Sivistyksen ja tiedon Suomi: Suomen eduskunta 100 vuotta* (Vol. 9). Edita.

Toffler, A. (1970). *The Future Shock*. New York: Bantam Books.

Toninelli, P. A. (2000). The rise and fall of public enterprise: The framework. In: P. A. Toninelli (Ed.), *The rise and fall of state-owned enterprise in the western world* (pp. 3–24). Cambridge University Press.

Tuovinen-Thuesen, M., Pekkala, H., Sievänen, R., Karlsson, S., Ali-Yrkkö, J., Pajarinen, M., & Ahonen, P. (2019). *Valtion omistajaohjauksne arviointi*. Valtioneuvoston selvitys- ja tutkimustoimikunnan julkaisusarja, 54.

UNCTAD. (2017). *World Investment Report 2017: Investment and Digital Economy* (Geneva: United Nations). http://unctad.org/en/PublicationsLibrary/wir2017_en.pdf

Vares, V. (2017). *Korpivallukselta vallan kahvaan: Kansallisen Kokoomuspuolueen historia 1966–1987 [History of the National Coalition Party]*. Docendo.
Vartia, P., & Ylä-Anttila, P. (2005). *Kansantalous 2028. [Predictions for economic development]*. Taloustieto.
Webster, F. (1995). *Theories of information society*. Routledge.
Wuokko, M. (2016). *Markkinatalouden etujoukot: Elinkeinoelämän valtuuskunta, Teollisuuden keskusliitto ja liike-elämän poliittinen toiminta 1970- ja 1980-lukujen Suomessa* [Doctoral dissertation] [History of Think Thank of Big Business]. University of Helsinki.
Yliaska, V. (2014). *Tehokkuuden toiveuni: Uuden julkisjohtamisen historia Suomessa 1970-luvulta 1990-luvulle [Pipe dream of efficiency: New Public Management in Finland 1970–1990]* [Doctoral dissertation]. University of Helsinki.

OPEN ACCESS

National institutions, regional outcomes. The political economy of post-war Swedish regional policy

Martin Eriksson, Lena Andersson-Skog and Josefin Sabo

ABSTRACT
One debate within the varieties of capitalism approach deals with the significance of institutions below the national level. On the basis of a case study of the loan guarantee system, this article deals with the interaction between institutions and regional actors in Sweden during the formation of post-war regional development policy. We conclude that regional economic problems have been addressed through adaptation of national institutions. From an actor perspective, these results correspond with the revised VoC framework which emphasises that state institutions provide both a framework for business activities and a means for pursuing them.

Introduction

Since its breakthrough, the Varieties of Capitalism (VoC) literature has primarily had a national perspective as it has demonstrated that successful national political economies are composed of complementary institutional systems. These institutional systems can be broadly classified into two distinct types of market economy: liberal market economies (LMEs) and coordinated market economies (CMEs). In LMEs, resources in the political economy are allocated overwhelmingly through arms-length market exchange. In CMEs, market exchanges are supplemented at many critical points by processes of institutional coordination among stakeholders. Such institutional systems are considered to be path-dependent and create self-reinforcing feedback loops that push development in the respective political economies along familiar paths and make departures from traditional practices very difficult (Hall & Soskice, 2001; Hancké et al., 2007a; Herrigel & Zeitlin, 2010; Sluyterman, 2014).

One debate which has emerged out of the VoC literature is to which extent such national elements also structure production at the local or regional level and how this leaves room for regional diversities and specificities (Ebner, 2016). In this respect, the Nordic countries represent an interesting case. From the latter part of the 1930s, the Nordic countries developed strong features of a CME as defined in the VoC literature (Fellman et al., 2008). However, one traditional feature in the Nordic countries is that the intermediate level of government is weak as the unitary state and the municipal level have been favoured in the Nordic welfare

This is an Open Access article distributed under the terms of the Creative Commons Attribution License (http://creativecommons.org/licenses/by/4.0/), which permits unrestricted use, distribution, and reproduction in any medium, provided the original work is properly cited.

system (Torfing et al., 2015). Hörnström (2013, p. 427) notes that the political and administrative system in the Nordic countries is often described as an hourglass, with a wide base representing the strong municipalities, a wide top representing the strong state level and a narrow 'waist' in between that represents the relatively weak regional level. In this respect, institutional coordination primarily occurred on the national level and the local level as the state transferred power as a mean to carry out the goals of the welfare state (Sellers & Lidström, 2007, p. 610).

This description raises questions regarding the formation of regional support policies during the post-war period. As noted by Scott (2000, pp. 485–486), the long post-war boom in North America and Western Europe brought with it a great expansion of Fordist mass-production industry and the emergence of modern consumer society. However, these features were also accompanied by complex and deepening systems of spatial disparities. At the same time, Keynesian and welfare-statist policies were also expanding as a mean for the government to correct imbalances. Altogether, this meant that cities and regions throughout the developing world were changing and growing in ways which launched hitherto unknown questions onto the agendas of academics and policy-makers.

Given the weak intermediate level, one challenge which emerged was how institutions should be designed to target regional problems. This spatial approach to institutions is an issue which has been subject to considerable debate in the VoC literature. One elaboration of the VoC concept has suggested a 'regional varieties of capitalism' approach (cf. Ebner, 2016) This tradition builds strongly on economic geography and emphasises the importance of adding the subnational level into the analysis. It suggests that firms face several different layers of institutions and these may differ depending on firm size, sectors and geographical location (Allen, 2004; Peck & Theodore, 2007; Rafiqui, 2010).

From an historical perspective, one problem with this approach is that it is difficult to align with the general image of post-war regional policy as a top-down framework (cf. Bachtler & Yuill, 2001). Regional policy, then, would tend to structure regional actors and constrain their agency. This rather primitive view might however be qualified by the historical institutional approach originally put forth in the VoC concept by Hall and Soskice (2001). While this approach acknowledges the role of national institutions in a top-down perspective, it moves away from a view of such institutions purely as factors that constrain actors towards one that sees them also as resources. Any strategy adopted by a firm or other stakeholder is likely to be conditioned by a number of institutions, which simultaneously provides opportunities for particular types of action (Hall & Thelen, 2008).

Against this background, this article examines the emergence of the state loan guarantee system in Sweden as an analysis of the relation between regional actors and regional policy within a CME. In this respect, we will elucidate the emergence of the institutions within Swedish regional policy and how they interacted with regional stakeholders. Because the loan guarantee system was the first regional development programme, we have been able to follow this formation over a relatively long time period (1945–1959). These results will then be analysed in relation to other cases from our previous research on relations between regional interest groups and the state during important projects and processes within post-war Swedish regional economic history.

In this study, the main intermediate level we deal with is the county (*län*), which historically has been the basis for the regional analysis in Sweden. In each county, there is a county administrative board (*länsstyrelse*). This is a central government agency with responsibility for the general State administration at the county level and should not be confused with the directly elected county council (*landsting*), whose main task has been health and medical care.

The article builds on published as well as unpublished source material from three decision-making processes concerning the loan guarantee system. As Swedish political decision-making processes follow a number of fixed steps, the ambition has been to study the documentation from these steps sequentially. In this respect, the starting point for the research process has been the archives from the committees (*kommittéarkiv*) material in the Swedish National Archive (SNA). These archives contain all documentation produced during the work of the committees tasked with the development of the loan guarantee system and thereby includes substantial amounts of unpublished material. On the basis of this archive material, the published committee report (the *SOU*) has been studied in combination with the archive of the cabinet meeting documents (the *konseljakt*). The cabinet meeting documents, which also are deposited in the SNA, include all the documents, published or unpublished, that were used to prepare and draft the government bills related to the loan guarantee system. For our study, these sources have been particularly valuable to determine the relevance and impact of the committee work. As the cabinet meeting documents include material from regional actors (for instance chambers of commerce, artisanal organisations and regional business associations), which the government has asked to comment on the committee reports, we have been able to determine that the views of the committees were representative of those of the concerned regional actors since they have commented extensively on arguments and proposals. During the final research phase, parliamentary material such as the government bills and parliamentary records have been reviewed.

Small business funding and the regulation of the post-war financial system

In 1945, the Social Democratic government appointed a commission to deal with the expansion of the state's role in the financial system (SOU 1949:13, 1949). This brought the problems of small businesses in the credit market to the fore. Historians of state banking such as Carnevali (2005), Verdier (2000), and Godley and Ross (1996) have summarised why small firms have encountered problems with their funding and why government intervention became necessary to deal with the problem. One key explanation departs from the fact that a functioning credit market is dependent on specialised intermediaries who can allocate credit. As in any market, the crucial function of financial intermediaries is to be able to respond to information. The problem in the credit market is that important information is extremely costly to acquire and process. Acquiring and processing relevant information in the credit market may lead to high transaction costs for each credit. To deal with this issue, banks often choose to simplify their control of a presumptive borrower's creditworthiness by introducing formalised controls which are based on set criteria. Such criteria often include the contents of the business plan, the borrowers' expected rate of return and past performance. Often, small businesses have problems in complying with such fixed criteria. For instance, while small businesses often have securities, banks may on formal grounds consider them too diverse and scattered. Often, the need for credit is also based on forward-looking business plans which involves such changes in relation to the past that past performance is an ambiguous concept. Altogether, this means that small businesses tend to become disadvantaged in relation to other borrowers. They may therefore be denied loans or must pay a high interest rate as a risk premium.

The emerging interest in small business funding resulted in two main changes. Firstly, there was an ambition from both the government and the commercial banks to create a regulation standard for small business credits. After 10 years of preparation, the Banking Act of 1955 included strictly regulated provisions which allowed the commercial banks to offer short-term credits as well as unsecured debts (debts without underlying security) to small businesses (Larsson, 1998, p. 153–156; SOU 1949:13, 1949; SOU 1952:2, 1952).

Secondly, small business credit expanded as a policy domain. This process was based on a comprehensive discussion on the role of the small business sector in the economy as a whole. For instance, several government commissions acknowledged that the expansion of large industrial firms since the latter part of the Nineteenth Century had not resulted in a corresponding decline of the small businesses. On the contrary, both the number of employees and the level of production in such firms had expanded. The government recognised that small businesses were natural arenas for entrepreneurs, and that many Swedish firms had emerged out of such circumstances. Small business could be important drivers of industrial development and renewal. They were a counterweight to monopoly tendencies and thereby important for the free competition in the economy (SOU 1946:22, 1946, p. 7; SOU 1959:7, 1959, p. 35). Small businesses were also important actors in the economy as subcontractors to larger firms (SOU 1959:7, 1959, p. 36). However, the key argument was related to employment. Here, the government recognised the importance of small businesses for the livelihood of large parts of the population through some estimates. It was estimated that in 1940, there existed 125,000 small businesses which employed one million people (SOU 1946:40, 1946, p. 13).

Business-government relations in a planned economy scenario

In June of 1945, a commission on the future of the small business sector was appointed by Bertil Ohlin as minister of trade in the war-time coalition government. Ohlin at the time had been a Liberal MP since 1938 and leader of the Liberal party since 1944. Ohlin's intention had been for a government commission to make a general review of the policy areas of importance to promote small business (Ohlin, 1945).

In practice, however, the small business commission appears to have been increasingly dominated by the ideas of economic planning which were advocated by some influential Social Democrats. In 1944, the Commission for post-war economic planning was set up, chaired by economist Gunnar Myrdal, who later became minister of trade in the Social Democratic government which was appointed on July 31, 1945. Myrdal warned of a major post-war depression, and to counter this depression, the government had to intervene and shore up the economy. The trade-off was simple: either high unemployment or some form of planned economy. For Myrdal, this meant that various government interventions must be co-ordinated into uniform systems of government regulations in a planned economy (Magnusson, 2000, p. 201).

All artisans and small industrial firms in the country should be able to enjoy the advantages of state support. In this respect, the government favoured a decentralised loan system.

It wanted to create bodies with own responsibilities to make decisions on issues delegated to them. However, it was admitted that this was related to the fulfilment of a number of complex conditions. The credit agency needed to include experts on the technical, administrative and economic issues which small industrial firms were confronted with. At the same time, it was also necessary to include representatives with sufficient knowledge about local/regional firms and their markets. Nevertheless, the local body should also represent not only the interest of local business interest, but also the public interest of the area where it was located (SOU 1946:22, 1946, pp. 8–9).

This could be achieved by creating regional councils with corporatist representation which would be organised according a nationally conform manner. The government planned to create 13 regional councils which each would be allocated its own district (SOU 1946:22, 1946, pp. 24–25). Each such council should have equal representation with four members representing private interest and four members representing the public interest. Furthermore, the public interest would be represented by the chairperson, appointed by the government, one representative from the county board and two representatives from the county council. The private interest, in turn, would be represented by two members from the regional chamber of commerce and two members from the artisan and small industry association (SOU 1946:22, 1946, p. 26).

However, this proposal never was realised. This may largely be explained by the increased resistance towards economic planning from business interests (the so called *Planhushållningsmotståndet*) which emerged during the latter part of the 1940s (Appelqvist, 2014, p. 42–44). In this respect, Stenlås (1998) has described how an elite group among business leaders who mobilised support against the ideas of economic planning. This culminated with the 1948 general election, which the Social Democrats won after a campaign characterised by strong ideological differences regarding the Social Democratic position on economic planning and the public/private divide.

In practice, business rejected the idea of participating in semi-public or public bodies where their primary role would be to provide the state with information. As business refused to provide such information, it would be impossible to build any functional alliance between public and private in such bodies (Benner, 1997, p. 89). While the Myrdal Commission on post-war economic planning was dismantled in 1946, there is no doubt that its impact on small business policy was negative. When it continued its inquiry into the design of a small business credit system, the Ministry of Trade decided that it needed to search for other options (Government bill 1/1950, 1950 appendix 12, 1950, pp. 91–92).

During this process, two ensuing developments would influence the process. In the debate on the report, the Swedish Savings Banks Association (*Svenska sparbanksföreningen*) noted that one way of increasing the supply of credits to small businesses would be to introduce loan guarantees provided by the state (Svenska Sparbanksföreningen, 1954). In 1949, the Ministry of Trade presented an initial proposal for a loan guarantee system based on co-operation with the regional business associations. In this respect, the Minister of Trade also noted that any further development of a loan guarantee system would be connected to the spatial and industrial policies which were emerging. The government was developing a cohesion policy to counter regional imbalances, which meant that important institutions were being designed (Government bill 1/1950, 1950, appendix 12, p. 92).

The emergence of national institutions for social and economic cohesion

In 1942, the Agriculture Commission of 1942 (*1942 års jordbruksutredning*) was appointed to elaborate the future goals for Swedish agriculture. In its report, published in 1946, the Commission envisioned a restructuring of agriculture production by proposing that small unviable farms ought to be shut down or taken over by financially strong farming units. The ambition was to create a structure of farms large enough to fully provide an income for the farming household. The emphasis on production scale and technology would also enable and promote the shift of labour from a relatively less productive agricultural sector to a more productive industrial sector where labour resources could be used more efficiently. This meant that abundant labour was expected to leave the rural areas in favour of the industrialised parts of Sweden (Flygare & Isacson, 2011; Gulbrandsen, 1957, p. 182; SOU 1946:42, 1946, pp. 16–17).

The government had an ambition to control the migration patterns resulting from the new agricultural policy. In this respect, it wanted to limit the migration to the bigger cities as this would result in congestion effects, housing shortages and other bottlenecks. Instead, it was desirable if part of the abundant labour force settled in existing countryside agglomerations (*tätorter*) where the government would expand public services such as housing, health care and infrastructure (SOU 1946:40, 1946, pp. 32–33). In this respect, it is important to note that while the government during the 1950s wanted the population to migrate and disperse according to a certain pattern, it was reluctant to introduce direct measures and instruments to control the location of economic activity in this direction (Government bill 127/1952, pp. 14–15). In this respect, support to existing small businesses appear to have been viewed as a functional compromise as many such firms already were located in the countryside. If these firms could be modernised through investments, they could employ at least some of the abundant agricultural labour and become one foundation in the new settlement structure after the agricultural reform.

There were also other state measures which affected rural and countryside firms in this direction. Schön (2012, pp. 225–26) notes that small business had been able to benefit from the developments during the inter-war period such as the intensified electrification and use of motor vehicles. Through improved electricity and transport networks, smaller towns and entities could more easily compete as economies of scale in various sectors played a lesser role than previously. Access to the electricity grid and small motors allowed small businesses, particularly in the rural areas, as well as crafts and cottage industries, to mechanise to an unprecedented extent. Motor vehicles permitted a more flexible flow of input goods to production and finished goods to the market.

Related to the above, the Social Democrats also viewed small business from an industrial policy perspective. This was related to the fact that large businesses were governed by the so called 'solidaristic wage policy', defined as equal pay for equal work across firms and industries, regardless of productivity and profit developments. This was combined with an active labour market policy that could quickly move those who became unemployed, as a consequence of the solidaristic wage policy and the restrictive demand policy, towards new employment. The goal was to eliminate low-productivity firms and industries, and move labour into firms with high productivity, thus improving economic growth as well as paying a higher wage rate (Henrekson et al., 1996).

By contrast, the Social Democratic government noted that small business in general were less vulnerable to such effects which made them an important employment alternative in cases when firms or sectors were affected negatively by the solidaristic wage policy (Government bill 210/1954, 1954). This position was shared by the Labour Market Administration. If they were able to invest, small businesses would become even more stable in this respect. They would thereby function as one of the measures which would absorb the transformation waves in situations when local labour markets were affected by economic change (Arbetsmarknadsstyrelsen, 1954).

Industrial rationalisation in a small business context

Integrated into the cohesion policies was a notion of the relation between employment resilience on one hand and industrial competitiveness and business dynamics on the micro level on the other hand which the Social Democrats had developed since the 1930s. This work aimed at introducing regulations which could influence the structure of industry, industrial rationalisation as well as regional and industrial sector policies. As for rationalisation, it was concluded that even if such measures could lead to unemployment and related social problems, it was also an important means for increasing the competitiveness of industry. The political background to these policy initiatives was the introduction of a new foundation in economic policy: to maximise the utilisation of the economy's resources. Policies were oriented towards structuring the pre-dominantly private economy, influencing the composition of industries, the corporate sizes and the regional location patterns, thereby maximising the efficiency of private enterprise. In this respect, it was an efficient economic structure rather than private ownership in itself that was seen as the cause of unemployment and economic crises. The state should therefore be more active within an unchanged ownership structure of the economy (Benner, 1997, pp. 81–82).

Within the small business sector, a government commission noted in 1946 that small industrial businesses had a large potential for rationalisations. Several small industrial businesses had successfully introduced modern industrial organisation and working methods such as tempo work and piece rates. This had put their profitability in parity with large industrial businesses. However, the commission also noted that many owners and managers within small industrial businesses were reluctant to make this shift. Instead, they continued to rely on traditional artisanal skills and methods of their trades. Areas in need of such improvement were physical and material such as work planning, working methods, machinery, site conditions, and logistics. They also included areas such as accounting and sales and marketing (SOU 1946:40, 1946, pp. 41–42).

However, the primary area was related to mechanisation and the introduction of modern technology (cf. De Geer, 1978, p. 34). In this respect, workshop conditions were closely scrutinised by government experts. They noted that one key aspect of the rationalisation process was the modernisation, expansion and construction of workshops. Nevertheless, the workshops of many industrial firms did not meet modern technological standards, which prevented a rational configuration of their equipment. It was therefore considered necessary to rationalise workshop conditions (SOU 1946:40, 1946, pp. 51–53). During the 1950s, the government continued to emphasise the need for rationalisation measures within small business. In 1959, a government commission on small business finance noted that as technological progress had increased, the need for the necessary capital to make such investments had also increased (SOU 1959:7, 1959, p. 41).

Business-government relations in the 1954 loan guarantee system

In 1954, the loan guarantee system was finally introduced. The rationale behind the system was that loan guarantee recipients would expand their production by investing in machinery and buildings, and that this investment would increase local employment. To obtain a loan guarantee, the applicant would submit the loan guarantee application to the regional business association (*företagarförening*) in his or her home county. This business association would thereafter process the individual applications and make an initial assessment. If the application passed that stage, it was passed on to a state agency which made the final decision which once again involved the regional business association to which the state delegated to underwrite the loan. The successful applicant could then take out the loan in a profit-based commercial financial institution (usually their regular bank) and use it for the intended purpose (Government bill 210/1954, 1954).

After a transition period (1954–1956) when loan guarantee applications were handled by the Ministry of Trade, the government delegated this task to the Royal Board of Trade (*Kungliga Kommerskollegium*) in 1957. The Royal Board of Trade had been established in 1651 and would remain the main state agency for industrial policy until 1973. During the Twentieth Century, the Royal Board of Trade had administered several programmes aimed at promoting small business and handicrafts and was the nexus between overall government policy on one hand and individual traders and industrialists on the other hand (Gerentz, 1951, pp. 362–363).

In the preparation of the loan guarantee system, the importance of a thorough state control had been emphasised by the Ministry of Trade. The implementation of such control, however, was characterised by some ambiguities. There did not exist any plans to create a dedicated state agency for loan guarantees. Instead, it was assumed that existing agencies or ministries would deal with such issues. However, this would mean a delegation of decision-making power to the regional business associations. Even if the credit assessment by the regional business associations was assumed to be one efficient way of dealing with risk, it was assumed that loan guarantee applications would be assessed in tandem with the County Labour Board (*Länsarbetsnämnden*). As the County Labour Board was responsible for coordinating national policy and regional employment, it had a strong position in determining if applicants complied with the established goals within the labour market policy, especially since it exercised the location control of new investments (Widell et al., 1954, pp. 26–27).

These principles were later reiterated and clarified in discussions undertaken by the review commission for small business finance, which submitted its report in 1959. It emphasised that the loan guarantee system was an instrument for achieving goals related to national institutions such as labour market policy and/or cohesion policy. It was therefore vital that the system was organised in a way which created the best conditions for implementing such policies. Even if non-state actors such as the regional business associations were suitable for assessing loan applications, policy-related consequences and impact should always be in the foreground. Inevitable, this meant that the state must be given the ultimate discretion regarding loan decisions (Utredningen angående översyn av det statliga kreditstödet åt hantverk och industri, 1957a, 1957b).

This created a system where decisions were made hierarchically, and firms were monitored and coordinated by bureaucrats in order to provide a solution to the problem of information asymmetry generally associated with credit allocation. Bureaucratic coordination was designed to economise on communication expense and reduce uncertainty (Verdier, 2000, p. 291). However, the system also implied an interaction between actors on the national and regional level. Sjögren and Jungerhem (1996, p. 31) conclude that in Sweden the state has been able to create an information system for screening, monitoring and enforcing loan contracts by building up national and regional networks of organisations. Even if allocation of credit occurred in a hierarchical structure, it was still dependent on information from networks on the local and regional level (cf. Hull & Hjern, 1982).

National institutions and regional strategies – an analysis

One important feature of the Social Democrats' post-war economic policy was the recognition that structural transformation also could result in spatial social and economic imbalances. This would require additional policy measures beyond the general growth-enhancing efforts within macroeconomic policy. Foreman-Peck and Federico (1999) note that such industrial polices may consist of either measures in support of industries in decline ('helping the losers') or stimulating promising, emerging activities ('picking the winners'). In this respect, it is important to recognise that during the 1940s and 1950s, the Swedish Social Democrats did not consider compensatory measures towards 'losers' such as subsidies or grants to be a sustainable solution to uphold a policy of full employment. Instead, the government favoured an investment policy directed towards those firms who were willing to expand and take on more employment. Since investment in machinery and buildings generally means more employment opportunities in a Fordist production structure, the Social Democrats wanted to identify such firms as 'winners' in the economy.

In our examined case, we note that by linking allocation of credit to the government's intentions as they were manifested within the contemporary national institutions for spatial cohesion, the government created a framework with distinct incentives for firms who were willing to invest and thereby conform to the goals and ambitions of the government. Here, it may be argued that the investment policy for small businesses was based on the same foundation as the investment policy for big business as it was regulated within the corporate tax system (Eriksson, 2014). In this respect, Steinmo (2003, p. 214) describes capital formation during the post-war period as a bargain between the state on one hand and business on the other hand which meant that if businesses invested in places, times or activities that the government determined, taxes would be lower. If business owners chose to ignore those incentives, they would pay higher taxes. Applied to the loan guarantee system, this meant that firms which did not adjust to policy goals could be denied credits, despite having other positive characteristics (less suitable candidates who were deemed not competent enough or had similar deficiencies were of course also denied credits).

In a wider perspective, it might be argued that this way of approaching regional problems by linking goals within national institutions to the strategies and ambitions of regional actors became an institutionalised method within post-war regional policy. In the following, we will illustrate how one such pattern developed. During the post-war period, the economic and social situation in the four northernmost counties, the so-called *Norrland* region, became a target for regional policy. The basic problem was that in *Norrland*, a process of non-agrarian pull away of labour resulted in a large interregional migration in the decades following the Second World War. The opportunities of getting employment in the non-agrarian sector improved through a shortage of labour in the industrialised southern parts of Sweden, which resulted in a large-scale migration from the northern periphery (Bäcklund, 1988).

The state initially responded to this situation by appointing the so-called *Norrland* Commission which was in session during 1944–1949 (SOU 1949:1, 1949). The emergence of a specific regional policy towards Norrland led to a forceful political mobilisation from the regional political and social elite in northern Sweden. These elite consisted of three major groups. The first group consisted of ministers and members of parliament from the region. The second group comprised regional state officials such as governors and officials in regional administrative bodies such as the county councils. These two groups had their major arena in the political system. The local and regional industrialists and major owners of natural resources established the third group. It did not act in parliament, but rather through other lobby organisations and by coordinating-meetings by industrialists and politicians (Andersson-Skog, 2001).

Over time, the interaction between the state and these actors over the future of *Norrland* intensified and gave rise to a distinct pattern of business-government relations. The most important issues in the debate on Norrland was transport problems and the expansion of higher education (Sörlin, 1988). For the sake of focussing on business-government relations, we will not deal with the expansion of higher education in this article, although the interaction between the state and interest groups during decision-making processes in this field followed the same pattern as in the transport sector (cf. Carlbom, 1965).

The business-government relations during decision-making on infrastructure projects in *Norrland* has been subject to several in-depth monographs, for instance Pettersson (1999), Andersson (2004), and Eriksson (2009). These cases are all based on the same type of problem background. Because *Norrland* has abundant natural resources such as forests and iron ore, its economy has increasingly been dominated by firms in the heavy manufacturing sectors. But since it has a peripheral location in relation to the export markets, industrialists have formed regional interest groups together with political actors and demanded that the government should compensate for at least part of the transport cost.

However, the degree of success for such regional interest groups was crucially linked to how well they formulated their arguments in relation to national institutions. Here, Eriksson (2009), dealing with the shipping sector, and Andersson (2004), dealing with the railway sector, show how regional interest groups have acted in relation to a combination of institutions at different administrative levels. The specific policy directed towards a given transport sector and the sectoral bureaucracy have influenced actors' strategies during the initial stages of decision-making processes. The final outcomes of a decision-making process have thereafter ultimately depended on how strongly the arguments brought forward by regional interest groups have corresponded to the general aims of economic policy. It was first when the state and regional interest groups were able to interact within this multiple institutional environment that decision-making processes have ended in tangible outcomes.

Summary and conclusion

As Sweden developed into a CME, it became apparent that the contemporary spatial imbalances and problems were so serious that some type of public intervention would be necessary. However, the intermediate administrative level, which governed the territory where spatial problems were appearing, did not have the necessary capacity to deal with them. Instead, it became an issue for the national government. In practice, the loan guarantee system studied in this paper became the first programme where the national institutions for a regional development policy as they had been devised by the government were applied on a given set of actors. Against the perspective of the institutional debate within the VoC tradition, we want to clarify that one of our findings is that even if we label them 'national' institutions, they were designed for actors and problems on the regional level. In this respect, there are clear sub-national dimensions within what would appear as an aggregate, macro model. Furthermore, we also highlight that in-depth studies based on primary sources strongly indicate that these institutions became a foundation for business-government relations between the state and regional firms.

Although this perspective differs from the institutional discussion within the regional varieties of capitalism discussion, it might still be argued that this is one version of the 'nuanced analysis of temporality *and spatiality* of capitalist development' called for by Peck and Theodore (2007, p. 760). As such, it represents an alternative which goes beyond the dichotomy of 'regional' (sub-national) and 'national' institutions. In the Swedish national context, where the intermediate level is relatively weak, it might be argued that the state has been perceived as too strong. With the rise during the 1960s of a regional policy based on the 'polarization' approach (cf. Myrdal, 1957), firms and related actors in depressed regions have been framed as constrained not only by the market, but also by the state as the intervening actor through regional policy programmes.

This argument ties in closely with the debate on the role of the state within the VoC tradition (Hancké et al., 2007b). While we observe that a radical expansion of the state was part of the emergence of Sweden as a CME, this does not mean that the state, as highlighted by Skocpol (1985), should be treated as an autonomous actor. By contrast, what we have highlighted in this article is that the design of national institutions allowed for regional actors with relatively strong agency, which in practice was needed to implement government policy. As argued by Hancké et al. (2007b, p. 27–28) in some forms of capitalism, the state is a central actor in the sense that it provides both a framework for business activities and a means for pursuing them. An awareness of this duality may be therefore crucial to understand why regional interest groups (or similar regional actors), over time, have been successful or failed in their attempts to influence the state.

While we acknowledge that the empirical cases covered in this article occurred in the specific economic-historical context of the post-war period, we also note that the method for implementation of regional policies which emerged during this period might be useful to consider within contemporary cohesion policy. For instance, with the Barca report (Barca, 2009), which analysed options for future EU cohesion policies, the governance challenges related to cohesion policy was once again brought to the fore. In this respect, it might be argued that while there in many cases is useful to reconsider the dichotomy of top down/bottom up as appropriate governance ideals. It has been recognised that some regions might have problems and actor/firm constellations which may benefit from the type of hybrid approach of national/regional interaction which we have highlighted in this article (cf. OECD, 2013, p. 20). From a policy perspective, the debate on the spatial application of the original VoC approach might benefit to be extended beyond its relevance for successful clusters and agglomerations in high-income regions. Instead, it may be used in novel and explorative approaches to deal with complex issues in regions which hitherto have been difficult to resolve through traditional analyses within regional science.

Disclosure statement

No potential conflict of interest was reported by the authors.

Funding

This work was supported by Jan Wallanders och Tom Hedelius Stiftelse under Grant P17-0108.

References

Allen, M. (2004). The varieties of capitalism approach: Not enough variety?*Socio-Economic Review*, *2*(1), 87–108. https://doi.org/10.1093/soceco/2.1.87

Andersson-Skog, L. (2001). Compensating the periphery: Railway policy and regional interest groups in northern Sweden. In L. Magnusson & J. Ottosson (Eds.), *The state, regulation and the economy – An historical perspective* (pp. 126–147). Edward Elgar.

Andersson, F. (2004). *Mot framtiden på gamla spår? Regionala intressegrupper och beslutsprocesser kring kustjärnvägarna i Norrland under 1900-talet* [Doctoral dissertation]. Umeå University.

Appelqvist, Ö. (2014). *The political economy of Gunnar Myrdal: Transcending Dilemmas post-2008*. Routledge. Taylor & Francis online version. https://doi.org/10.4324/9781315866970

Arbetsmarknadsstyrelsen. (1954). Yttrande över PM med förslag till statlig kreditgarantigivning i syfte att främja utvecklingen inom hantverk och industri, Swedish National Archive (hereafter SNA), Ministry of Trade Archive, Cabinet Meeting Documents, April 2, 1954, item 30.

Bachtler, J., & Yuill, D. (2001). *Policies and strategies for regional development: A shift in paradigm* (Regional and Industrial Policy Research Paper Number 46). University of Strathclyde.

Barca, F. (2009). *An agenda for a reformed cohesion policy. A place-based approach to meeting European Union challenges and expectations*. Retrieved from the European Commission website https://ec.europa.eu/regional_policy/archive/policy/future/pdf/report_barca_v0306.pdf. Retrieved on March 15, 2019.

Benner, M. (1997). *The politics of growth. Economic regulation in Sweden 1930–1994*. Arkiv förlag.

Bäcklund, D. (1988). *I industrisamhällets utkant: Småbrukens omvandling i Lappmarken 1870–1970* [Doctoral dissertation]. Umeå University.

Carlbom, T. (1965). *Tillkomsten av Universitet i Umeå. En studie i kommunal aktivitet och statlig lokaliseringspolitik*. Uppsala University.

Carnevali, F. (2005). *Europe's advantage: Banks and small firms in Britain, France, Germany, and Italy since 1918*. Oxford University Press (E-book).

De Geer, H. (1978). *Rationaliseringsrörelsen i Sverige* (Effektivitetsidéer och socialt ansvar under mellankrigstiden) [Doctoral dissertation]. Stockholm University.

Ebner, A. (2016). Editorial: Exploring regional varieties of capitalism. *Regional Studies*, *50*(1), 3–6. https://doi.org/10.1080/00343404.2015.1039227

Eriksson, M. (2009). *Trafikpolitik och regional omvandling Beslutsprocesserna om isbrytningen längs Norrlandskusten 1940–1975* [Doctoral dissertation]. Umeå University.

Eriksson, M. (2014). Embedding big business. The political economy of the 1938 corporate tax reform in Sweden. *Enterprise & Society, 15*(2), 285–306. https://doi.org/10.1093/es/khu003

Fellman, S., Iversen, M. J., Sjögren, H. & Thue, L. (Eds.). (2008). *Creating Nordic capitalism. The business history of a competitive periphery*. Palgrave MacMillan.

Flygare, I. A., & Isacson, M. (2011). The tension between modernity and reality, 1945-2010. In J. Myrdal & M. Morell (Ed.), *The Agrarian history of Sweden. From 4000 BC to AD 2000* (pp. 214–256). Nordic Academic Press.

Foreman-Peck, J., & Federico, G. (1999). Industrial policies in Europe: Introduction. In J. Foreman-Peck & G. Federico (Eds.), *European industrial policy. The twentieth century experience* (pp. 1–17). Oxford University Press.

Gerentz, S. (1951). *Kommerskollegium och näringslivet*. Royal Board of Trade.

Gulbrandsen, O. (1957). *Strukturomvandlingen i jordbruket*. Industrins Utredningsinstitut.

Godley, A., & Ross, D. M. (1996). Introduction: Banks, networks and small firm finance. *Business History, 38*(3), 1–10. https://doi.org/10.1080/00076799600000091

Government bill 1/1950. (1950). https://www.riksdagen.se/sv/dokument-lagar/dokument/proposition/kungl-majts-propositiontill-riksdagen_EB301b1/html

Government bill 210/1954. (1954). https://www.riksdagen.se/sv/dokument-lagar/dokument/proposition/kungl-majts-proposition-nr-210_EF30210/html

Government bill 127/1952 (1952). https://www.riksdagen.se/sv/dokument-lagar/dokument/proposition/kungi-majts-proposition-nr-127_ED30127/html

Hall, P. A., & Soskice, D. (Eds.). (2001). *Varieties of capitalism. The institutional foundations of comparative advantage*. Oxford University Press.

Hall, P. A., & Thelen, K. (2008). Institutional change in varieties of capitalism. *Socio-Economic Review, 7*(1), 7–34. https://doi.org/10.1093/ser/mwn020

Hancké, B, Rhodes, M., & Thatcher, M. (Eds.). (2007a). *Beyond varieties of capitalism. Conflict, contradictions, and complementarities in the European Economy* [Oxford Scholarship Online version]. Oxford University Press. https://doi.org/10.1093/acprof:oso/9780199206483.001.0001

Hancké, B., Rhodes, M., & Thatcher, M. (2007b). Introduction: Beyond varieties of capitalism. In B. Hancké, M. Rhodes, & M. Thatcher (Eds.), *Beyond varieties of capitalism. Conflict, contradictions, and complementarities in the European economy*. [Oxford Scholarship Online version]. https://doi.org/10.1093/acprof:oso/9780199206483.001.0001

Henrekson, M., Jonung, L., & Stymne, J. (1996). Economic growth and the Swedish model. In N. Crafts & G. Toniolo (Eds.), *Economic growth in Europe since 1945* (pp. 240–280). Cambridge University Press.

Herrigel, G., & Zeitlin, J. (2010). Alternatives to varieties of capitalism. *Business History Review, 84*(4), 637–674. https://doi.org/10.1017/S0007680500001975

Hörnström, L. (2013). Strong regions within the Unitary State. The Nordic experience of regionalization. *Regional & Federal Studies, 23*, 4, 427–443.

Hull, C. J., & Hjern, B. (1982). Helping small firms grow. An implementation analysis of small firm assistance structures. *European Journal of Political Research, 10*(2), 187–198. https://doi.org/10.1111/j.1475-6765.1982.tb00017.x

Larsson, M. (1998). *Staten och kapitalet – det svenska finansiella systemet under 1900-talet*. SNS förlag.

Magnusson, L. (2000). *An economic history of Sweden*. Routledge.

Myrdal, G. (1957). *Economic theory and under-developed regions*. Gerald Duckworth.

OECD. (2013). *Innovation-driven growth in regions: The role of smart specialisation*. OECD.

Ohlin, B. (1945). Utdrag av protokollet över handelsärenden, hållet inför Hans Maj:t Konungen i statsrådet å Stockholms slott 15 juni 1945. SNA, YK 958, vol. 1.

Peck, J., & Theodore, N. (2007). Variegated capitalism. *Progress in Human Geography, 31*(6), 731–772. https://doi.org/10.1177/0309132507083505

Pettersson, T. (1999). *Att kompensera för avstånd? Transportstödet 1970-1995 - ideologi, ekonomi och stigberoende* [Doctoral dissertation]. Umeå University.

Rafiqui, P. S. (2010). Varieties of capitalism and local outcomes. A Swedish case study. *European Urban and Regional Studies, 17*(3), 309–329. https://doi.org/10.1177/0969776409350792

Schön, L. (2012). *An economic history of modern Sweden*. Routledge.

Scott, A. J. (2000). Economic geography: The great half-century. *Cambridge Journal of Economics, 24*(4), 483–504. https://doi.org/10.1093/cje/24.4.483

Sellers, J. M., & Lidström, A. (2007). Decentralization, local government, and the welfare state. *Governance, 20*(4), 609–632. https://doi.org/10.1111/j.1468-0491.2007.00374.x

Sjögren, H., & Jungerhem, S. (1996). Small firm financing in Sweden, 1960–95. *Business History, 38*(3), 27–47. https://doi.org/10.1080/00076799600000093

Skocpol, T. (1985). Bringing the state back in: Strategies of analysis in current research. In P. Evans, D. Reuschemeyer, & T. Skocpol (Eds.), *Bringing the state back in* (pp. 3–37). Cambridge University Press.

Sluyterman, K. (Ed.). (2014). *Varieties of capitalism and business history. The Dutch case*. Routledge.

Sörlin, S. (1988). *Framtidslandet: Debatten om Norrland och naturresurserna*. Royal Skyttean Society.

SOU 1946:22. (1946). *Betänkande med förslag till ordnande av kreditgivnings- och rådgivningsverksamhet för hantverk och småindustri samt bildande av företagsnämnder*. Isaac Marcus Boktryckeri-Aktiebolag.

SOU 1946:40. (1946). *Betänkande angående hantverkets och småindustrins befrämjande*. Isaac Marcus Boktryckeri-Aktiebolag.

SOU 1946:42. (1946). *Riktlinjer för den framtida jordbrukspolitiken*. Fritzes förlag.

SOU 1949:1. (1949). *Norrlandskommitténs principbetänkande del 1: Norrländska utvecklingslinjer*. Esselte AB.

SOU 1949:13. (1949). *1945 års Bankkommitté. Betänkande med förslag om inrättande av en statlig affärsbank*. K.L. Beckmanns Boktryckeri.

SOU 1952:2. (1952). *Förslag till lag om bankrörelse m.m. Avgivet av 1949 års Banklagssakkunniga*. Gummessons Boktryckeri.

SOU 1959:7. (1959). *Betänkande angående statligt kreditstöd till hantverk och småindustri m.m.* Emil Kihlströms Tryckeri Aktiebolag.

Steinmo, S. (2003). The evolution of policy ideas. Tax policy in the 20th century. *The British Journal of Politics and International Relations, 5*(2), 206–236. https://doi.org/10.1111/1467-856X.00104

Stenlås, N. (1998). *Den inre kretsen. Den svenska ekonomiska elitens inflytande över partipolitik och opinionsbildning 1940–1949*. Arkiv förlag.

Svenska Sparbanksföreningen. (1954). Remiss 9 mars 1954. SNA, Ministry of Trade Archive, Cabinet Meeting Documents, April 2, 1954, item 30.

Torfing, J., Lidström, A., & Røiseland, S. (2015). The Scandinavian regional model: Accounting for the shift from convergence to divergence. *Scandinavian Journal of Public Administration, 19*(4), 7–28.

Utredningen angående översyn av det statliga kreditstödet åt hantverk och industri. (1957a). Frågan om Lokal Eller Central Handläggning av Låneärendena, SNA, YK 1692, vol. 2.

Utredningen angående översyn av det statliga kreditstödet åt hantverk och industri. (1957b). Protokoll hållet vid sammanträde med utredningen angående översyn av det statliga kreditstödet åt hantverk och småindustri den 25 och 26 november 1957, SNA, YK 1692, vol. 1.

Verdier, D. (2000). The rise and fall of state banking in OECD countries. *Comparative Political Studies, 33*(3), 283–318. https://doi.org/10.1177/0010414000033003001

Widell, C. G., Algott, S., Johansson, B., & Frithiofson, K. (1954). *P.M. med förslag till statlig kreditgivning i syfte att främja utvecklingen inom hantverk och småindustri*. Ministry of Trade.

Only one way to raise capital? Colombian business groups and the dawn of internal markets

Beatriz Rodriguez-Satizabal

ABSTRACT

What was the relationship between the sources of capital and the creation of internal markets in business groups in Colombia? A detailed history of the evolution of ownership schemes and capital structure of the 25 largest Colombian business groups between 1950 and 1975 answers this question. The business history and varieties of capitalism literatures have identified this organisational structure as one of the key characteristics of Latin American business and economic development. Business groups in Colombia have been key players since the second half of the twentieth century, when they adopted a new organisational structure that allowed the internalisation of capital provided by new financial legislation promoted by the World Bank. Analysis of previously unknown historical evidence explains the capital structure of the group-affiliated firms. Examples of specific groups illustrate the analysis.

Introduction

Whilst the existence of business groups[1] in developing economies is not news to business historians of Latin America (Barbero & Puig, 2016), the literature on varieties of capitalism can be credited with bringing the region's business groups to the attention of a wider audience (e.g. Bull et al., 2014; Colpan & Hikino, 2018; Fernández & Lluch, 2015; Jones & Lluch, 2015; Llorca-Jana et al., 2019). What calls the attention in this literature is the recognition that many types of capitalism have coexisted and continue to coexist across countries and regions (Wilkins et al., 2010). It shows that whilst capitalism took on different forms, it evolved through the interaction between economic actors and the environment (e.g. Morck & Steier, 2005; Musacchio, 2009; Touwen, 2010). Following Hall and Soskice (2001, pp. 1–68), this article focuses on one part of this interaction: how institutions and organisations provide solutions for firms to develop and resolve coordination problems. Colombia – one of Latin America's six largest economies – provides the case study. The article studies 25 privately-owned business groups with 428 group-affiliated firms during 1950–1975. More specifically still, the article looks at the relationship between the sources of capital (promoted by changes in legislation) and the creation of internal capital markets (a key factor for the creation of the organisational structure) in Colombian business groups during the quest for financial reforms in the second half of the twentieth century.

Why so specific? To date, the way financial and real variables interact to form business groups in Colombia has not been the subject of academic study. This article is a first attempt to fill this gap. According to Schneider (2009) and Miller (2010), distinct characteristics of Latin American capitalism are the close relationship between the state and the business sector, and the proliferation of business groups, which resulted in a high concentration of ownership and so-called hierarchical market capitalism. To undertake entrepreneurial activities, including the creation of business groups, entrepreneurs need capital (Gerschenkron, 1962, 1966; Leff, 1978, 1979). Interestingly, the existing studies of Latin America recognise the existence of business groups and draw attention to the need to study their access to credit (e.g. Haber, 1989; Maurer, 2002; Triner, 2000). Musacchio (2009, p. 233) discusses the need to understand their 'capacity to buy or outperform their capital-starved competitors', which meant they 'ended-up dominating and controlling large portions of the internal market'. Moreover, the interconnections of the business elite with finance and the links between the financial and non-financial sectors have also been emphasised in the research on Latin America (e.g. Marichal, 2014; Marichal & Ludlow, 1986; Miller, 2010). Marichal and Ludlow (1986) discuss the links between the banking system and the elites, whilst Marichal (2014) argues for the need to explore the interlinkages between the development of finance and the evolution of business, whether as family firms, business groups, or state-owned enterprises.

Why the choice of Colombian business groups? Similar to other Latin American countries (e.g. Haber, 2002; Schneider, 2009), the Colombian business system evolved from standalone companies to diversified family business groups, multinational enterprises, and state-owned enterprises that were then privatised. However, both multinationals and state-owned enterprises played a much smaller role in Colombia than in other countries in the region (Miller, 2010). Business groups dominated for most of the second half of the twentieth century (Dávila, 2012a, 2012b), which creates a laboratory for understanding their proliferation. Recent studies have shown that features of Colombian corporate governance include high ownership concentration (Pombo & Gutiérrez, 2011) tied to the formation of business groups (e.g. Fernández, 1995; Gutiérrez et al., 2008), the evolving enforcement of legal protection for investors (Reyes, 2016), and underdeveloped equity markets (Caballero & Urrutia, 2006). Thus, how Colombia evolved from a loose aggregation of small firms to a large, complex, and highly concentrated corporate governance system merits further investigation.

As this article shows, it was during the period 1950–1975 when large firm owners – in both manufacturing and finance – consolidated the business group form as a large, highly diversified, often family-controlled organisation with hierarchical ownership structures. The beginning of the second half of the twentieth century was marked by the arrival of the first ever International Bank for Reconstruction (that is, the World Bank) survey mission to a developing economy, which promoted reforms that championed private sector activities in finance, construction, and manufacturing (Currie, 1950). During the following three decades, larger firms consolidated under commercial legislation, issued in 1951, that reinforced the public limited company (*sociedad anónima*), facilitating the formation of highly diversified portfolios.

Business groups were a response to what was the most important barrier to entry in Colombia for most of the twentieth century: access to finance, which was solved by the interactions within ownership networks, leading to the consolidation of privately-owned business groups. In this, Colombia was similar to the rest of Latin America. As Musacchio and Read (2007) have shown for the case of Brazil and Mexico, ownership networks played a crucial role during early industrialisation. Furthermore, Del Angel (2016) findings on Mexico show that ties between business groups and banks were more diverse than is commonly suggested. Similar to the case of Mexico, in Colombia financial intermediaries were initially owned by various non-financial business groups, but then came but then came to be owned by business groups specialised in finance by the end of the period. As Islas (2015) argues for the case of Chile, the groups adapted to changes in financial legislation to remain dominant even after the import-substituting industrialisation (ISI) period. Salvaj and Lluch (2012) and Salvaj and Couyoumdjian (2016) conclude that local group-affiliated firms and banks played a central role in the interlocking directorates in Chile by the end of the 1970s, but were more fragmented in Argentina. The case of Colombia shows an increasing number of business groups during the ISI years and a pattern comparable to the Chilean case.

From a theoretical perspective, the origins of the business groups may, then, reside in the entrepreneurial reaction to capital market imperfections (Khanna & Yafeh, 2007). Business groups could not have been prevalent in Colombia until the mid-twentieth century, when industrialisation reached a more advanced stage and more sources of capital were available. Even once diversification became more common, it seems that most entrepreneurs and firms found the capital to grow, in a similar manner to the largest countries in Latin America. Yet the capital provided was concentrated in a small group of entrepreneurs who formed this specific organisational structure and used new capital sources created by legislation to keep growing.

Moreover, Colombian groups show an increase in the use of their 'contact capabilities' (Guillén, 2000, 2010; Guillén & García-Canal, 2009; Kock & Guillén, 2014) to push their growth further. As a result of business and economic developments during the first wave of globalisation, from around 1870 to 1930, in the second half of the twentieth century the government acted as a rule setter, strongly promoting businesses and allowing the participation of the business elite in economic and political decision-making by naming them in ministries and as members of the board of directors in state-owned enterprises, financial institutions, and other bodies.

A look back at the economic and business history is thus needed. By analysing the 25 largest business groups, this article explains the capital structure of the group-affiliated firms through three key factors: access to finance, the cost of capital, and the firms' performance. It relies on data collected from the financial statements of the group-affiliated firms and secondary sources with descriptions of Colombian firms and groups. The 25 groups are the largest privately-owned business groups in Colombia between 1950 and 1975. Business groups were selected from Rodriguez-Satizabal (2020) dataset, which collates the financial statements and descriptive variables of Colombian business groups between 1949 and 1980. The selection is based on their size given by assets or total sales in 1975. A careful revision was made backwards to capture new and dissolved groups during the period. The analysis shows that organisational and institutional factors, specifically financial legislation, each explain part of the heterogeneity in the fate of the Colombian business groups during a period that begins with the promotion of modernisation by the World Bank's first developmental mission, continues with a weak ISI model, and ends with a banking crisis that was begun by one particular business group (Caballero & Urrutia, 2006), Grupo Grancolombiano, in 1982.

The article is structured as follows. The next section introduces the reader to the historical background in which business groups and financial reforms flourished. It focuses specifically on the financial reforms that established the instruments for the allocation of credit and determined the mechanisms available for accessing capital, thereby making the financial system more flexible. A preliminary assessment of the sources and uses of capital for the Colombian group-affiliated firms is the subject of the first part of section two. The next section attempts to explain the capital structure of the group-affiliated firms. The last section summarises the findings and conclusions.

Pre-1950: source limitations and new research

Similar to other Latin American economies, the number and size of business groups in Colombia increased greatly during the second half of the twentieth century. Due to the availability of information, the dataset compiled by Rodriguez-Satizabal (2020) only considers the groups' that were founded, prominent, consolidated, or dissolved from 1949 to 1980. It does not include business groups consolidated and dissolved before 1949 or state- or foreign-owned groups. The information collected in the dataset shows an increasing number of business groups consolidating after 1950, more specifically from the mid-1960s, with the highest peak after 1972. This confirms the rapid growth of the family firm from stand-alone to diversified business groups during the post-war decades.

The 25 business groups and 428 group-affiliated firms selected from Rodriguez-Satizabal (2020) refer to the numbers at the end of the period 1950–1980, whilst the actual number of groups and firms varied across the years. Only 4 of the 25 groups were consolidated before 1950 and prevailed during the following years. In the case of Colombia, there is still a need in the literature to identify business groups between 1870 and 1950, the period in which Argentina, Chile, Mexico, and Brazil had a great number of groups forming. Recent studies on the German immigrant founder of Bavaria (Molina, 2019) and Jewish immigrants in Bogotá (Martínez Ruiz, 2018) have identified groups formed in Colombia during the mentioned period. Moreover, since 2018 there is ongoing research on Antioquia and Valle del Cauca's business groups in the years before 1940. There were, then, groups before 1950, but there are questions about their long-term performance and persistence.

Historical background: business groups and financial reforms

By 1950, Colombia was characterised by strong regional economies with defined business elites (Dávila, 2003; Safford & Palacios, 2002). Each region held specific groups of entrepreneurs and firms, with a concentration of the main activities in the major urban centres (Bogotá, Barranquilla, Medellín, and Cali). Given high levels of geographical fragmentation and the great distances between the main ports and large population centres, Colombia faced serious challenges. Significant improvements in transportation were indispensable to overcome geography (Ramírez, 2007). Moreover, after 1954, the economic cycle was driven by coffee exports (Ocampo et al., 1987/2007), which had an effect on the purchasing power of coffee growers and the availability of imported intermediate goods and capital.

Between 1950 and 1975, the main element of the ISI model was to internalise the production of manufacturing and consumer goods, while promoting backward integration and investment in new technologies. The movement from an agricultural and rural economy to a semi-industrial and urban economy was the most obvious transformation of these years. The result was the emergence and consolidation of new economic activities, specifically manufacturing, construction, and financial services. During the period, GDP grew by 5.1 per cent annually, multiplying about six times. Compared to other countries in Latin America, Colombia did well from 1967 on (Bértola & Ocampo, 2012). The highest growth rate was 8.4 per cent in 1973 and the lowest was 1.9 per cent in 1953. The net result of economic and population growth was an increase in output per capita by 2.3 per cent annually, which was close to the Latin American average of 2.7 per cent, and resulted in total growth of about 130 per cent over the three decades.

The manufacturing sector was the engine of economic growth, but modern services also expanded rapidly (Bulmer-Thomas, 2014, chapter 9). The decrease of the agricultural sector from 40 per cent of GDP in 1940–1945 to 24 per cent by 1975–1980 meant new economic activities such as financial services, transport, telecommunications, and public utilities saw increasing roles. By the 1960s, the manufacturing sector was already contributing 20 per cent of GDP and it rose to 29 per cent in 1975, while modern services came to represent 45 per cent (BanRep, 1930–1982). There was an increase in the number of industrial plants as an average of 130 factories were founded per year (Echavarría & Villamizar, 2007, p. 179). As the private sector built large industrial plants and warehouses, the number of vehicles increased and the stock of housing and office buildings in the cities grew sharply. Construction then expanded, becoming a key sector of the economy.

According to Misas (1973, p. 13), the expansion was accompanied by 'high private investment, some foreign direct investment, large firms' diversification and concentration into *grupos económicos*'. However, in the 1950s, the government was not expecting these future results. As the Superintendente de Sociedades[2] pointed out in a quarterly report, 'the growing number of public limited companies shows that this type of company is the most precious instrument to push economic development. Improving their conditions will result in the investment of national savings in shares' (Mejía (1959, p. 250). Accordingly, the number of companies grew from 1,352 in 1950 to 3,800 in 1980.[3] However, the impact on business groups was paramount, since the group-affiliated firms grew larger and more firms were added to the organisational structure. As a result, from 21 companies affiliated to 4 business groups in 1950, the country ended the period with 428 of the largest companies affiliated to 25 business groups.

As shown in Table 1, the number of business groups increased during the period. The 1960s saw the greatest increase in the number of groups with nine new consolidations and the appearance of the first two financial business groups, Grupo Bolívar and Grupo Grancolombiano. Only one of the 25 groups, Grupo Empresarial Antioqueño, was not family-owned, with its ultimate owners a group of regional entrepreneurs. With the exception of four business groups in the financial sector, the majority of the groups' core business was in manufacturing. Familia Puyana, Cementos Samper, and Organización Corona had their main investments in building materials. Today four are still the largest groups in the Colombian economy: Grupo Empresarial Antioqueño, Organización Sarmiento Ángulo, Organizacíon Ardila Lulle, and Grupo Santo Domingo. As a result of the regional economies, business groups are distributed among the four main economic regions: 11 in Bogotá, 7 in Medellín, 5 in Cali, and 2 in Barranquilla.

Table 1. Privately-owned business groups in Colombia by decade, 1950–1979.

Decades	No.	Consolidated business group[1]	Dissolved business group[2]
Before 1950	1	**Grupo Empresarial Antioqueño**	
	2	Grupo Familia Puyana	
	3	Organización Carvajal	
	4	Organización Corona	
1950–1959	5	Cementos Samper (Manufacturas de Cemento)	
	6	Familia Gutt Haime	
	7	Grupo Mayaguez	
	8	**Grupo Santo Domingo**	
	9	Organización Chaid Neme Hermanos	
	10	Grupo Fabricato	
	11	Grupo Colombina	
1960–1969	12	Cadenalco	
	13	Grupo Bolivar	
	14	Grupo Espinosa	
	15	Grupo Grancolombiano	
	16	Grupo Gilinski	
	17	Grupo Inversiones Mundial (Grupo Orbis)	
	18	Grupo Sanford	
	19	Inversiones Manuelita	
	20	**Organización Ardila Lulle**	
1970–1979	21	Grupo Casa Toro	
	22	Grupo Colpatria	
	23	Grupo Superior	
	24	Grupo Inversiones TQ	Grupo Familia Puyana (1981)
	25	**Organización Sarmiento Angulo**	Grupo Grancolombiano (1982)

[1]Refers to the business groups constituted during the period. A group is constituted when three firms in two different sectors are owned and controlled by the same owner.
[2]Business groups liquidated during the period. Groups highlighted correspond to the current four largest business groups.
Source: Compiled by the author from Rodriguez-Satizabal (2020).

Only one business group, Grupo Espinosa, had its core business in coffee, even though the country's economic cycle continued to be driven by coffee exports (Junguito, 1997). However, it is important to mention that five groups' core businesses were founded between 1870 and 1930, which means the initial capital came from either coffee or trade. In terms of the economic cycle, the effects of external coffee price fluctuations were twofold. First, an increase in coffee prices meant that growers had increased purchasing power and there was a rise in government revenues and expenditures, leading to higher demand for manufactured goods. Conversely, a decrease in external coffee prices had an adverse effect on domestic demand. Second, there was an effect on the availability of imported intermediate goods and capital due to shortages of foreign exchange. Whereas phases of rising coffee prices meant greater availability, low prices produced shortage. Consequently, the economic cycle was affected and the industrialisation strategy changed accordingly. Decisive until the 1960s, it weakened from 1967, and by the end of the period further openness was required.

In this context, the business groups found the relationship with a financial intermediary an essential part of their expansion through investments in sectors beyond their core business. Between 1960 and 1975, diversification into unrelated industries increased, with a peak after 1972. All the groups expanded their business to more than two industries other than the core sector, with each developing a distinct specialty and becoming major players in their chosen industries. Organización Ardila Lülle, one of the four major groups, had investments in seven industries, covering a broad spectrum from agriculture to recreation and cultural services. Grupo Empresarial Antioqueño, Santo Domingo, Gutt, and Cadenalco had major investments in five industries. Three groups, Carvajal, Espinosa, and Sarmiento, invested in four industries; the last being the only group who turned their portfolio completely from construction companies to financial institutions. Of the remaining groups, four controlled firms among three industries (Colpatria, Grupo Grancolombiano, and Corona), and the others (Bolivar, Puyana, Mayaguez, Corona, and Espinosa) were active in only two industries.

Dynamism and evolution in financial activities broadly paralleled the course of economic change. The dominant view in the economic historiography of Colombia is that the country's financial system is small and lagged behind other economies because of the agrarian nature of the economy (Sánchez et al., 2007). Indeed, measured by the Demirguc-Kunt and Levine (1999, pp. 22–23) structure index, the Colombian financial system was still classified as bank-based and underdeveloped by the end of the century. In a group of 47 countries, Colombia is ranked among those at the lower middle level of development, as are most of the 11 Latin American countries studied. As shown in Figure 1, throughout the years 1950–1980, the financial system was bank-based. Measured as the relation between stock exchange transactions and banking credit, the increase in credit transactions was evident from 1951, only decreasing sharply in 1975.

Although the literature agrees on this classification, Caballero and Urrutia (2006, p. 35) argue that during the second half of the twentieth century financial deepening increased slightly, leading to improved provision of financial services with a wider choice of services for all levels of society. The financial reforms – specifically of the banking and capital markets – are an especially useful lens through which to view the changes in ownership structure in any country (La Porta et al., 1999). As Ocampo et al. (1987/2007) explain, industrialisation was the dominant process during the period and was accompanied by state intervention, especially in relation to trade policies, foreign transactions, and the financial system. Four major financial reforms were implemented, mainly as a result of the awareness created by

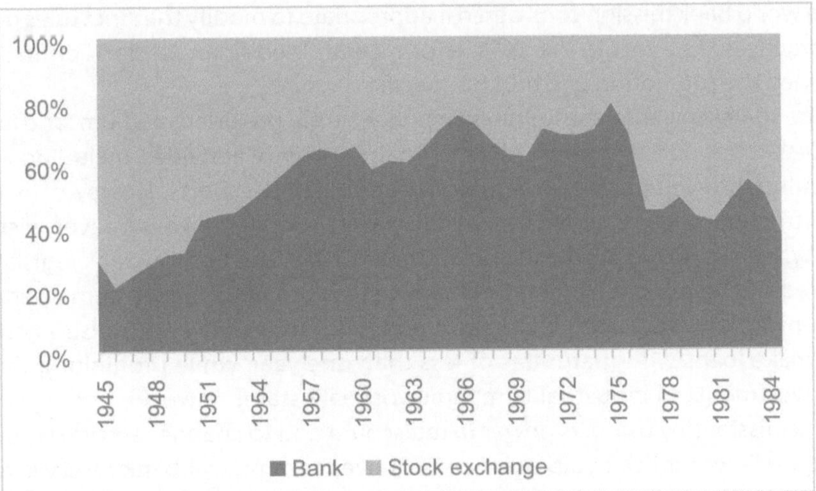

Figure 1. Financial system structure: Bank-based credit and stock exchange transactions, 1945–1985.

the World Bank mission on the need to provide sources of capital for entrepreneurs. After the reform of the Central Bank functions in 1951 to reduce credit rationing, the government allowed regional investment banks in 1959 and building societies in 1972. The aim was also to democratise ownership by increasing the number of shares owned by households; consequently, the government authorised the creation of investment funds in 1960.

At the beginning of the 1950s, then, investments requiring finance in amounts larger than could be raised by individuals and entrepreneurs within their personal networks were opportunities foregone. Currie (1950) identifies four aspects of the incipient Colombian financial system. First, the supply of short-term credit for commercial and industrial purposes was ample, yet there was great scarcity of short-term credit in agriculture. Second, funds for long-term investment in high-cost housing were available, but the supply of credit for middle- and low-cost housing was wholly insufficient. Third, while long-term funds were available in substantial amounts to establish companies with low projected profit margins, or to wealthy individuals who could reinvest their earnings, it was difficult for the outsider to secure capital from the market. Finally, the credit standing of the government, as reflected by the reluctance to hold public debt, was low.

In 1950, the government issued a law (Decreto 384) that increased the term from 150 days to 5 years for credit available for industrial purposes. According to Jaramillo (1955, p. 416), although it was not well received by the monetary authorities and represented a low percentage of the total loans, 'it was a required measure to increase the availability of capital'. The first reform of the Central Bank in 1951 spurred the greatest changes in the system during the period. Salazar (1996) maintains that, after years of active monetary and credit intervention, under the regulatory framework established by the Kemmerer Missions in 1923, there was a need for long-term financial reform. Caballero and Urrutia (2006) cite the inability to mobilise savings and channel them to more productive uses as driving the new legislation. Most of the debate was on the need to expand the Central Bank's regulation and allocation functions, the creation of new instruments of monetary regulation, and restrictions on private individuals in monetary and credit policy design. Credit supply measures were adopted and applied to provide for industrial sectors. Inspired by the belief that investment provides the seeds for industrial growth, which, in turn, fuels economic growth and prosperity, the World Bank mission considered it appropriate to modify the strict rules governing lending practices. As a result, the 1951 reform centralised financial decision-making and strengthened the promotion of credit for specific sectors.

From the 1940s onwards, the Colombian public sector provided medium- and long-term credit at less-than-market interest rates to finance priority activities, including industrial and agricultural development, urban infrastructure, and exports. However, in 1950 the financial structure of the Colombian capital market revealed a very uneven distribution of funds. When the World Bank mission arrived in 1949, the Central Bank legislation was still inspired by the principle of limiting bank lending to liquid short-term operations. In order to ensure an adequate volume of credit, bank rules only authorised commercial banks to make loans with maturities of less than one year, while prohibiting them from making investments in industrial companies or real estate. However, in the view of the World Bank mission, 'by using its power to rediscount and to change reserve requirements, the Banco de la República could exert control over commercial bank reserves and their lending capacity' (Currie, 1950, p. 295). This included rolling over loans to owners of the largest firms.

The World Bank mission considered the soundness of the banking system to depend on the maturity of the economy in general and not on the Central Bank. Therefore, the World Bank believed that in a healthy economy, long-term credits were needed and were quite compatible with a solid structure of bank assets, so the severe restrictions imposed by the law of 1923 did not have any merit as a means of automatic credit control and had gone beyond what was necessary to ensure bank liquidity, which resulted in a 'complete separation between commercial banking and capital formation' (Currie, 1950, p. 49) . Consequently, the mission considered it appropriate to reconsider 'the strict rules governing the lending practices of commercial banks' (Currie, 1950, p. 291) and suggested that the volume of credit should be controlled by the Central Bank, which would expand or restrict it as the economic situation demanded. To do so, the Central Bank could change the reserve requirements of commercial banks and provide a rediscounting facility. The Central Bank would thus continually adjust the ability of commercial banks to meet credit demand. In order to give the Central Bank the necessary freedom of action, the 1951 reform law established the bank as an autonomous entity.

All commercial banks were members of the Central Bank. Colombian banks provided an ample amount of funds to industry and trade, yet by law 'commercial banks may not grant loans of over one-year maturity and they may not invest in industrial enterprises or real estate except where such securities are offered as loan collateral' (Meisel, 1990, p. 455). Also, they were obliged to hold their required reserves, with 15 per cent as sight deposit and 5 per cent as term deposit, with the Central Bank. By using its power to rediscount and to change reserve requirements, the Central Bank could exert control over commercial bank reserves and their lending capacity. Lending by the Central Bank was aimed at providing commercial banks with additional reserve funds and at providing credit to the government.

With the reform of 1951, this panorama changed greatly. In this year, the first measures were undertaken to move the Central Bank towards assuming the role of credit supplier for the development of certain sectors of the economy. The government decided to direct the course of medium- and long-term credit towards productive activities (see Figure 2). Thus, commercial banks were authorised to grant credits with five-year maturity terms, exclusively destined for infrastructure development (electric plants and water provision), mining, agriculture, manufacture, and planned urbanisation – all sectors in which business groups expanded their activities. Commercial banks became embedded in business groups. Six banks (Banco Industrial Colombiano, Banco de Colombia, Banco Colpatria, Banco de Occidente, Banco Franco-Colombiano, and Banco Grancolombiano) were directly controlled by four groups. There were other banks controlled by several business groups or simply with directors from them.

After 1955, new instruments to channel private capital and long-term finance to manufacturing were developed (see Table 2). A development bank, the Instituto de Fomento Industrial (IFI), founded in 1940, became a strategic tool for the state's promotion of industrialisation; its objective was initially to advance risk capital to industrial investment projects. The role of the IFI in creating new manufacturing enterprises located in heavy industries was central during the 1950s and 1960s. The only other major financial intermediaries were the Caja Agraria, an official credit institution created in 1931 to provide credit to small-scale farmers that broadened to include the provision of credit to small industry and small-scale mining, as well as the Banco Central Hipotecario (BCH), an official bank created in 1932 to fulfil the full range of mortgage banking functions.

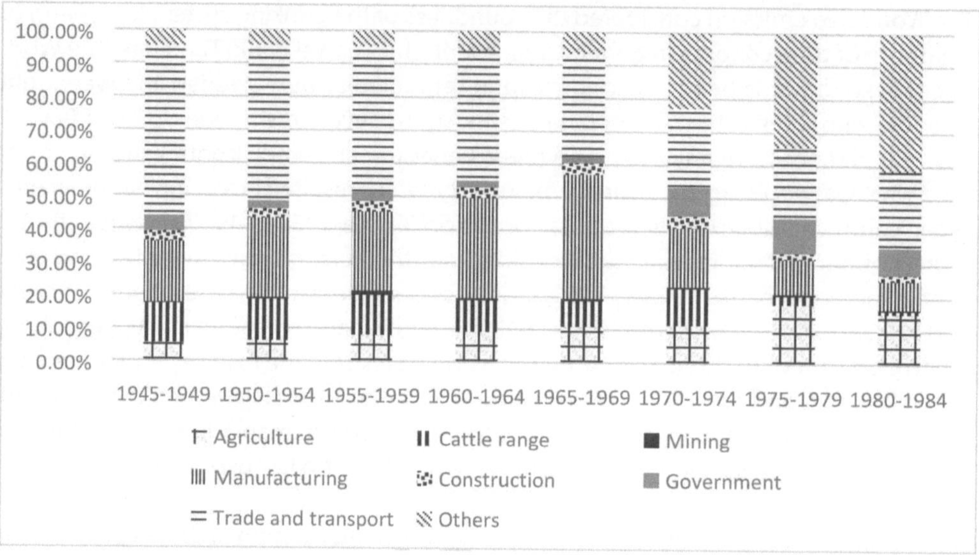

Figure 2. Credit by sector, 1945–1989.

Table 2. Characterisation of the Colombian financial system, 1945–1980[1].

	1945–1953	1954–1965	1966–1973	1974–1980
Commercial banks	13	17	25	24
Domestic	9	12	20	18
Foreign	4	5	5	6
Official banks	2	4	7	8
Regional investment banks			9	9
Building societies				12
Stock exchange	1	1	2	2

[1]The number of institutions corresponds to those at the beginning of each period.
Source: Compiled by the author based on Asobancaria (1990a); (Asobancaria, 1990b, 1990c, 1990d; BanRep, 1930–1982).

Investment banks (*corporaciones financieras*) were then created in 1959 to provide long-term credit for regional firms. Their main objective was to 'promote the creation, reorganisation, and transformation of firms (in the manufacturing, mining, and agricultural sectors), to participate in their capital or facilitate the participation of others, and to provide them credit' (Law 155 of 1959). By the end of the 1960s, there were 23 commercial banks, 9 investment banks, and two official credit institutions specialised in agriculture. Three of the investment banks were co-founded by business groups: Corporación Financiera del Norte, Corporación Financiera Colombiana, and Corporación Financiera del Valle. In the other six, ten groups had members on the board of directors.

Until the late 1960s, the financial system remained relatively simple and the functions of the different categories of credit institutions were clearly delineated. Apart from the specialised functions assigned to the two official banks, commercial banks were raising resources through checking and savings accounts and lending mainly through short-term operations, while the investment banks focussed their efforts primarily on the provision of medium- and long-term credit to regional productive sectors and to a limited extent participated in the share capital of productive enterprises.

In 1960, the government authorised the creation of investment funds. The developmental policy was reinforced during the 1960s by means of the creation of various financial funds associated with the Central Bank, such as the funds for agriculture and cattle, private investment, industry, export promotion, and urban development. Business groups founded on average two or three private investment funds to mobilise capital within the group. Through these investment funds, the groups created 'special purpose vehicles or entities',[4] with the purpose of accessing loans in specific industries and regions. The 25 business groups created 112 special purpose entities after 1968. The companies were registered for a year, but never performed any economic activity. Instead, the special purpose entity was commonly granted loans that were later distributed across the other group-affiliated firms through equity. Then, business groups created internal capital markets using the resources provided by the government.

It was not until 1967 that the system began to be gradually liberalised. A crawling peg was established in order to reduce the incentives for capital flight in anticipation of devaluation; as a result, the attractiveness of the financial sector increased. The government created export credit certificates, the Certificados de Abono Tributario, which had a free interest rate and for which a broad secondary market was rapidly developed. In the early 1970s, the interest rates on the publicly-held government debt and BCH certificates were raised.

The government created a system of building societies, the Corporaciones de Ahorro y Vivienda, in 1972, which finally moved the system towards liberalisation. These building societies grew under a system of savings created by Lauchlin Currie and his team of Colombian economists. The returns were equal to annual inflation plus a nominal interest rate. These resources were allocated to building houses with the objective of turning the country into a nation of homeowners, leading to an increase in the number of saving banks and a change in the structure of the building sector. During this period, the Central Bank also began to buy and sell securities itself as a mechanism to control the amount of money. Five building societies were founded by business groups: Davivienda, Colpatria, AV Villas, Conavi, Granahorrar, and Ahorramas.

As presented in Table 3, a result of the reforms was that 17 business groups diversified their position into financial services, including commercial banks, investment banks, investment funds, and insurance companies. By becoming shareholders in the financial sector, groups were able to diversify their sources of funding and identify investment opportunities through the board of directors. Moreover, five financial business groups consolidated after 1965.

The capital market was underdeveloped. As Currie (1950, p. 56) observed, 'people who wish to initiate new ventures must rely almost entirely on funds obtained through the retention of profits in their own businesses or through personal contact from friends (...) it is difficult to launch a new venture without direct personal access to capital (...) there is evident need for developing a more open capital market'. Although in the early 1920s the country witnessed a first wave of mergers and acquisitions via secondary equity offerings, the firms' share capital was negotiated among families or regional entrepreneurs without the need for a stock exchange (Álvarez, 2003, p. 225) – a pattern that continued during the second half of the twentieth century.

Table 3. Number of group-affiliated firms, non-financial and financial, 1955, 1965, 1975.

Consolidation decades	No.	Business Group	Non-Financial			Financial		
			1955	1965	1975	1955	1965	1975
Before 1950	1	Grupo Empresarial Antioqueño	13	17	27	3	4	6
	2	Grupo Familia Puyana	7	11	10	1	1	1
	3	Organización Carvajal	1	5	7	1	1	1
	4	Organización Corona	3	10	15	0	3	6
1950–1959	5	Cementos Samper	7	12	15	0	0	0
	6	Familia Gutt Haime	2	6	13	0	1	1
	7	Grupo Mayaguez	2	3	7	1	1	1
	8	Grupo Santo Domingo	6	27	46	1	4	6
	9	Organización Chaid Neme Hermanos	2	7	10	0	0	1
1960–1969	10	Cadenalco	1	9	10	0	3	3
	11	Grupo Fabricato	3	6	9	0	0	0
	12	Grupo Bolivar	0	1	4	3	5	9
	13	Grupo Espinosa	2	4	11	0	0	0
	14	Grupo Grancolombiano	0	1	4	0	6	9
	15	Grupo Gilinski	2	3	4	0	0	0
	16	Grupo Inversiones Mundial	1	2	9	0	1	2
	17	Grupo Sanford	1	5	4	0	0	0
	18	Inversiones Manuelita	1	4	4	0	0	1
	19	Organización Ardila Lulle	4	18	35	0	0	4
1970–1979	20	Grupo Colombina	1	2	4	0	0	0
	21	Grupo Casa Toro	0	0	3	0	0	2
	22	Grupo Colpatria	0	0	0	1	4	6
	23	Grupo Superior	0	1	2	0	0	0
	24	Grupo Inversiones TQ	0	2	4	0	0	1
	25	Organización Sarmiento Angulo	0	0	1	0	0	4
Total group-affiliated firms			**59**	**156**	**258**	**11**	**34**	**64**

Source: Compiled by the author from Rodriguez-Satizabal (2020).

Only Bogotá had a stock exchange from 1950 to 1961, when Medellín, the second industrial centre, opened another. The stock market was trading a small number of stocks and the value of these were low as a proportion of GDP – less than 3 per cent. The number of companies registered at the stock exchange increased from 85 in 1950 to almost 200 in the mid-1970s, although it was still less than 20 per cent of the active companies in the country (calculated from BanRep (1930–1982)). Concentration amongst a handful of large companies was high. For instance, between 1951 and 1961, Bavaria and Coltejer, both the largest companies of their business groups, accounted for two thirds of all the volume of stocks traded; and out of 17 bond emissions carried out, 13 corresponded to government securities and only 2 were industry issuances. The value of transactions nonetheless rose during the period, from 206.7 million pesos in 1950 to 4,878 million in 1974, mainly due to the creation of the second stock exchange (calculated from BanRep (1930–1982)). However, only a relatively small part of this expansion was for the issuance of new shares; the larger part was for the retention of earnings and the volume of transactions was highly concentrated in 6 firms in 1949, 17 firms in 1964, and 24 in 1978. The limited use of the stock exchange is partly explained by inflationary pressures that put investors off fixed-income securities, and more probably, by the return of economic normality and the preference for real estate investments in expanding cities and in land and farms in the countryside.

Sources and capital structure patterns

The rent-seeking capabilities hypothesis provides a motivation for the different choices firms make in financing their activities. After the reform of the Central Bank in 1951, a few industrialists started to benefit from credit allocation. According to Kalmanovitz and Avella (1998), both industrialists and agrarians (mainly the coffee growers) managed to advance their corporative interests by capturing the rents originating in the seigniorage of the Central Bank. In particular, it is possible that the policies had an effect on the private sector's investment financing and savings, as well as causing changes in ownership concentration. Different forms of finance present varying costs to the firm, affecting returns to investment and possibly the decision to invest at all. Firm capital structure may reveal insights into the costs of finance as well as potential financial constraints faced by individual firms and the economy as a whole.

Moreover, as Baccaro and Pontusson (2016) argue, the varieties of capitalism literature has emphasised institutional differences between countries, but not the dynamic relationship between economic agents and the government or their interaction with the financial system. As the literature on corporate governance claims, the underlying factors for the emergence of complex ownership structures, such as business groups, are related to the ways the individual firms finance their investments. In other words, it is possible that firms use debt instead of equity to finance their investments and consolidate (and later protect) their ownership and control structures, creating strong internal markets.

Overall, group-affiliated firms finance their activities in several ways, ranging from reinvestment to debt. As presented in Table 4, the primary methods of financing were mainly external. Debt funding, particularly credit from domestic banks, was the most important type of capital for the firms. As the use of credit increased in the 1960s, reinvestment decreased. Group-affiliated firms moved from relying on funds from family and friends, the main source of capital between 1920 and 1950, to more use of formal credit through commercial bank loans, upon which the interest rate declined from 1968 to 1974.

The increase in the demand for capital from other financial institutions is explained by the creation of the regional investment banks, which provided access to government funds for the development of the private sector. Owners and senior managers of the business groups were board members of the recently created regional investment funds, while the government provided the funds. As a result, Grupo Santo Domingo participated in Corporación Financiera del Norte, Grupo Empresarial Antioqueño in Corporación Financiera Nacional, Grupo Carvajal in Corporación Financiera del Valle. Three of the largest business groups, located in the main industrial regions, were thus promoting regional investment.

Table 4. Aggregated sources of capital in group-affiliated firms, 1950-1975.

Year	Internal sources	Reinvestment	Depreciation	External sources	Credit	Equity
1950	41.94%	28.39%	13.56%	58.05%	47.92%	10.13%
1955	36.14%	15.26%	20.88%	63.86%	−10.99%	74.85%
1960	44.55%	31.74%	12.81%	55.97%	31.18%	24.27%
1965	33.53%	21.47%	12.06%	66.47%	43.29%	23.18%
1970	28.84%	18.56%	10.28%	71.16%	40.19%	30.97%
1975	32.59%	23.01%	9.58%	67.41%	50.93%	16.48%

Source: Compiled by the author from statements of financial positions, specifically the information related to current assets and liabilities (capital and loans). The total corresponds to the sum of the group-affiliated firms in each year. In the years 1952 and 1958 not all the companies registered are included.

Later in the period when building societies where approved by law, the business groups moved towards investments in construction and the financial sector through the ownership of building societies. The financial groups previously listed increased their market share, creating an oligopoly over which the government had no regulation. Grupo Grancolombiano, Grupo Bolívar, Grupo Empresarial Antioqueño, and Grupo Colpatria owned building societies that promoted housing in the main cities.

Also, there was an increase in the use of equity by more than four times between 1959 and 1965. From the data collected on the total securities by issuer, the importance of group affiliation is notable. The value of the shares issued by corporations steadily increased, while bonds increased by only a small proportion and were mainly the ones issued by law. Therefore, it seems that the issuing of corporate equity was considered perhaps the most effective way to use savings for investment. This increased the cross investment between groups, since the largest listed group-affiliated firms invested in the shares of companies from the other groups, increasing cross-ownership. For example, Organización Ardila Lulle bought 51 per cent of the shares of Coltejer from Grupo Empresarial Antioqueño, to then sell them a percentage of Banco Industrial Antioqueño, redistributing the ownership and market power in two industries: textiles and commercial banking (Table 5).

It is noticeable that business groups derived a large share of their funds from sources external to the firm. As shown in Table 5, for all firms in the sample, external sources provided 73 per cent of total capital (loans provided 41 per cent and equity 32), while internal reinvestment provided just 27 per cent. While the number of group-affiliated firms listed on the stock exchange declined from 54 per cent of the total companies in the groups in 1950 to 28 per cent in 1980, in practical terms all these firms traded actively on a regular basis, becoming the major share traders. However, the share turnover by the end of the period only accounted for 8.5 per cent of the total funding. As a result, there was an increase in ownership concentration compared to 1950. In fact, business group agglomeration increased in the period 1965–1975 across all industries, with a peak in the years 1972–1975, when building societies were created.

Prolonging the partnership experience in mining, colonisation, and trade enterprises, the smallest firms merged, creating large firms per industry. The complexity and size obtained by the companies forced their owners to learn the management and production methods in vogue abroad. Although the textile, food, and beverage industries became the leaders of the Colombian economy, they kept experiencing short cycles of capital scarcity. This produced an important change in the ownership structure: businesses moved from partnerships to companies with limited liability, just to gain access to capital (Figure 3).

As presented in Figure 3, the uses of capital mainly related to the operation of the group-affiliated firms and in second place to investments in fixed capital. A noticeable feature in the use of funds is the high degree of financial investment (including equity investments and loans to other firms). Of these financial investments, more than 60 per cent were in the form of loans to other firms, and less than 10 per cent were equity investments in other firms affiliated with the same group. Looking at the largest 94 manufacturing firms extracted from the total of 428, they show a similar pattern: financial investments accounted for about half of total capital used during the 1960s and 1970s.

To sum up, the financial reforms during the period allowed business group leaders to strengthen their participation in the board of directors of the commercial banks by

Table 5. Sources of capital by business group, 1950–1975.

Business Groups (1)	Holding (2)	No. Firms	Equity (%)	Reinvestment (%)	Loans (%)
Grupo Empresarial Antioqueño	Cementos Argos	13	20.30	34.10	45.60
	Cía. Nacional de Chocolates	6	21.20	46.70	32.10
	Ind. de Alimentos Zenu	4	17.30	34.20	48.50
Grupo Familia Puyana		11	21.40	63.00	15.60
Cementos Samper		15	45.40	13.80	40.80
Organización Carvajal		8	29.40	64.00	6.60
Familia Gutt Haime		14	29.90	24.90	45.20
Grupo Mayaguez		8	36.00	64.00	0.00
Grupo Santo Domingo	Bavaria	23	48.00	29.50	22.50
	Avianca	5	19.40	17.30	63.30
	Colinsa	9	20.50	44.30	35.20
	Flia. Santo Domingo	13	17.30	50.10	32.60
Organización Chaid Neme Hermanos		11	30.50	34.50	35.00
Organización Corona		21	22.80	25.20	52.00
Cadenalco		13	31.70	30.20	38.10
Grupo Fabricato	Fabricato	9	35.20	31.80	33.00
	Tejicóndor	8	20.90	36.20	42.90
Grupo Espinosa		11	33.90	18.60	47.50
Grupo Gilinski		4	23.10	49.50	27.40
Inversiones Manuelita		5	33.10	44.50	22.40
Organización Ardila Lulle	Coltejer	6	15.60	25.70	58.70
	Postobon	20	43.00	36.00	21.00

[1]Only non-financial business groups and group-affiliated firms are presented here.
[2]By 1975 only four of the studied business groups were showing a pyramidal structure, in which the main company in a certain industry was holding the firms within the same industry. The number of business groups moving from Type 1 - Diversified horizontal to Type 2 – Pyramidal kept increasing after 1975.
Source: Compiled by the author from Rodriguez-Satizabal (2020).

increasing their shareholdings and become members of the board of directors of the newly created regional investment banks. Moreover, they became owners and majority shareholders of the building societies. This changed the allocation of credit. Business groups were able to increase their access to loans and captured the capital market, since the transactions on the stock exchanges were only performed by the largest group-affiliated firms.

Internal capital markets growth

The availability of new sources of capital promoted by the government during the period spurred the creation of internal capital markets, which allowed the allocation of capital among group-affiliated firms. Colombian business groups' structure, as in many other countries, is dynamic. Most of the business groups during the period remained as diversified horizontal groups. However, as mentioned before, they all affiliated with investment funds to manage the shareholding and control of the various group-affiliated firms. Moreover, groups reorganised their group-affiliated firms under one company, coordinating the others

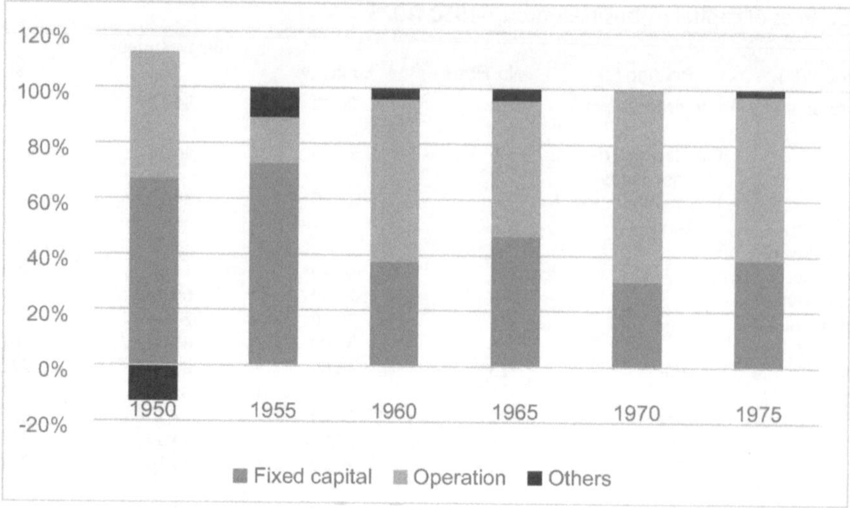

Figure 3. Uses of capital in group-affiliated firms.

through shareholding and directors. Only four non-financial and two financial groups presented the beginning of a pyramidal structure since the late 1960s. Grupo Empresarial Antioqueño, Grupo Santo Domingo, Grupo Fabricato, Organización Ardila Lulle, Grupo Grancolombiano, and Grupo Bolívar reorganised their group-affiliated firms under holdings by sector, thereby facilitating the access to loans and directing reinvestment. As a result, the structure became more hierarchical over the rest and cross shareholding between the largest firms was adopted.

The opening of new opportunities in the financial sector, the absence of intermediaries (as the business groups' leaders were part of the business elite), and the small concentrated capital market encouraged the strengthening of the business groups. Through the internal market, within groups and extended through crossholdings between groups after 1967, groups diversified into unrelated activities, overcoming financial constraints for some of their affiliates by using loans granted to either the core business or to the special purpose entities. However, group-affiliated firms became more dependent on internal sources of capital. Through this internal capital market, firms with the best performance were able to channel cash flow to liquidity-constrained affiliates in the network. Equity and reinvestment accounted on average for more than 61 per cent of the sources of funds between 1967 and 1975.

As a result of business groups' increasing investment in financial institutions, there was a change in the configuration of the board of directors. Business groups' leaders were increasingly members of the boards of the commercial banks, regional investment banks, and building societies. As shown in Table 6, the number of groups with at least one member on the board of directors of a financial institution increased from 7 in 1955 to 18 in 1975. Moreover, interlocking directorates became a common feature after the mid-1960s, when more than 50 per cent of the group-affiliated firms had common board members in both the financial and non-financial sectors. Most of the largest group-affiliated firms had at least two common members on the boards of directors across financial institutions. The fast growth of the ownership network was more evident between 1972 to 1978, when

Table 6. Business groups members of boards of directors of domestic commercial banks, regional investment banks, and building societies, 1950–1980.

	1955	1965	1975
Number of financial institutions	9	12	39
Average board members	5	8	14
Number of groups with at least one member on the board of directors of a financial institution	7	12	18
Group-affiliated firms with common board members	21	98	218
Group-affiliated firms common board members / Total group-affiliated firms (%)	30	51	67

Source: Compiled by the author from the Superintendencia Financiera's archives.

business groups increased cross-shareholding, mainly in traditional industries and banking.

Only in a few cases did business groups keep increasing debt with external sources, mainly in those firms highly indebted before 1965, with need of fixed capital or with losses for more than five years. Cementos Argos, Avianca, Tejicóndor, and Coltejer kept using external loans from commercial banks and the government. In the case of the first two companies, a cement producer and the largest airline, the increase in loans was a result of the buying out of smaller companies in their sector. The last two companies, both in the textile sector, were highly indebted as an attempt to save them from dissolution.

In general, groups in non-financial industries maintained the core business, usually the largest firm in the group, with debt at 22 per cent on average. In the cases of Grupo Santo Domingo (Bavaria), Organización Corona, Inversiones Manuelita, Organización Ardila Lulle (Postobón), Grupo Gillinski, and Familia Puyana the strategy was a way to stabilise the aggregate profits and increase the chances of the group gaining access to other sources of capital. Organización Carvajal and Grupo Mayaguez, both owned by business families from the early industrialisation process, maintained the lowest level of debt. For all cases, the growth of the internal capital market can be seen in the increase of group-affiliated firms from 70 to 428.

The increased affiliation to the group of 'special purpose entities' became a reality after the changes in the Code of Commerce in 1955. Under the legal figure of '*inversiones*' (investment funds), the business groups were able to affiliate companies to maximise the access to loans and avoid adding debt to the largest group-affiliated firm, which was the core business of the group. A total of 35 special purpose entities were affiliated to 16 business groups during the period, mainly between 1965 to 1975, when the number of special purpose entities increased from 18 to 35. In the cases of Grupo Santo Domingo, Organización Ardila Lulle, Grupo Grancolombiano, Cadenalco, and Grupo Inversiones Mundial, the largest group-affiliated firm was never in debt during the period. The special purpose entities of these groups were used to hedge the value of investments in diversified industries, such as building, textiles, food, cleaning products, and chemicals.

Through their internal capital markets, business groups diversified across related and unrelated industries to smoothen out capital flows, thereby capturing the financial institutions and overcoming any other constraints in the environment. The relationship between external sources and business groups became one of trust. For those financial intermediaries outside the business groups' networks, the existence of an internal capital market gave them the guarantee of expected returns. Moreover, it increased the cross-shareholding between business groups.

Final remarks

In the case of Colombia, business groups co-evolved with their institutional settings and national policies. The dominant business elite created before 1950 used the groups' organisational structure to capture both new financial intermediaries and capital markets. Although in this study only the changes in the financial legislation were considered, group-affiliated firms presented a pattern of sources and uses of capital that helped to develop stronger internal capital markets and, as a result, a highly diversified, strong organisational structure. It is commonly understood that internal capital markets played a significant role under market imperfections (Khanna & Yafeh, 2007). As this article shows, massive investments and new entries in alternative industries were supported by internal capital markets, which became stronger whilst the organisational structure was growing. More often, business groups invested their high profits from the core business (a cash sector) into growth sectors, following changes in the financial sector. Once the firms started to go public or increase their access to new credit, the internal capital markets started to play a role in reallocating funds that had been raised externally.

The policies promoted by the World Bank mission shaped the strategy of the business groups after their implementation. In practice, both reforms resulted in opportunities for business groups to enter the banking sector and consolidate their domestic position. The government acted, first, as a rule-maker to later increase the close links between the state and the business, through the formal membership of business group owners in the board of directors of the newly created financial institutions. Moreover, business groups changed their portfolio strategies by increasing their investments in banks and regional investment funds. As a result, groups looked to rapidly increase their domestic market shares and, even, buy shares from other groups across the country.

The business system was thus dominated by business groups with enough market power to diversify into every sector with credit available. The government settled into its role as rule-maker issuing laws that benefitted the largest companies, which grew faster from 1965 to 1974. Groups continued being the dominant actor in the Colombian economy and the government kept promoting the central role of entrepreneurs in the economic development of this so-called emerging country. The Colombian business groups had a growth pattern very similar to the Chilean and Mexican cases. The barrier to entry was mainly the restrictions on access to capital, the business networks grew during the ISI period, and there was a close relationship between non-financial and financial firms. However, in contrast to the Mexican case, only a few groups fully controlled a commercial bank.

The consolidation of business groups, followed by their investments in the financial institutions created by the new legislation in Colombia, are an example of how the interaction between institutions and organisations results in solutions for the expansion of the firm. Business groups allow flexibility to react to the changes in the financial legislation and to increase the firms' access to capital, creating a hierarchical capitalism, which is now seen as a characteristic of Latin America's business and economic development.

Notes

1. Business groups typically consist of a set of legally independent firms, operating in multiple (often unrelated) industries, which are bound together by persistent formal (for example,

equity) and informal (for example, family) ties. They are neither bound merely by short term strategic alliances nor legally consolidated into a single entity, but are owned, and often controlled, by the same owner(s) (whether individual, family, or regional entrepreneurs).

2. Superintendencia de Sociedades is the government agency responsible for inspecting and overseeing large public limited companies since 1931.
3. The number of companies refers to those registered as active in the Superintendencia de Sociedades.
4. This terminology is taken from the literature on the Enron case; it refers to limited partnerships or companies created to fulfill a temporary or specific purpose to fund or manage risks associated with specific assets.

Disclosure statement

No potential conflict of interest was reported by the author(s). This paper is based on Chapter 4 of the author's doctoral thesis at the School of Business and Management at Queen Mary University of London.

References

Álvarez, V. (2003). De las sociedades de negocios al Sindicato Antioqueño. Un camino centenario. In C. Dávila (Ed.), *Empresas y empresarios en la historia de Colombia, Siglos XIX-XX: una colección de estudios recientes.* (Vol. 1, pp. 213–246). Grupo Editorial Norma, Ediciones Uniandes - Facultad de Administración, Cepal.

Asobancaria. (1990a). *Series estadísticas del sistema financiero colombiano. Sistema bancario, 1924-1989 (Vol. 1).* Bogotá: Asociación Bancaria de Colombia.

Asobancaria. (1990b). *Series estadísticas del sistema financiero colombiano. Corporaciones financieras, 1965-1989 (Vol. 2).* Bogotá: Asociación Bancaria de Colombia.

Asobancaria. (1990c). *Series estadísticas del sistema financiero colombiano. Corporaciones de ahorro y vivienda, 1972-1989 (Vol. 3).* Bogotá: Asociación Bancaria de Colombia.

Asobancaria. (1990d). *Series estadísticas del sistema financiero colombiano. Almacenes generales de depósito, 1978-1989 (Vol. 4).* Bogotá: Asociación Bancaria de Colombia.

Baccaro, L., & Pontusson, J. (2016). Rethinking comparative political economy: The growth models perspective. *Politics & Society, 44*(2), 175–207. https://doi.org/10.1177/0032329216638053

BanRep. (1930–1982). *Revista del Banco de la República. Estadísticas.* Colombia: Banco de la República.

Barbero, M. I., & Puig, N. (2016). Business groups around the world: an introduction. *Business History, 58*(1), 6–29. https://doi.org/10.1080/00076791.2015.1051530

Bértola, L., & Ocampo, J. A. (2012). *The economic development of Latin America since independence.* Oxford University Press.

Bulmer-Thomas, V. (2014). *The economic history of Latin America since independence (3 ed.).* New York: Cambridge University Press.

Bull, B., Castellacci, F., & Kasahara, Y. (2014). *Business groups and transnational capitalism in Central America. Economic and political strategies.* (1st ed.). Palgrave Macmillan UK.

Caballero, C. E., & Urrutia, M. (2006). *Historia del sector financiero colombiano en el siglo XX: Ensayos sobre su desarrollo y sus crisis*. Grupo Editorial Norma.

Colpan, A. M., & Hikino, T. (Eds.). (2018). *Business groups in the West: Origins, evolution, and resilience*. Oxford University Press.

Currie, L. (1950). *The basis of a development program for Colombia*. International Bank for Reconstruction and Development.

Dávila, C. (2003). *Empresas y empresarios en la historia de Colombia, Siglos XIX-XX: Una colección de estudios recientes*. Grupo Editorial Norma, Ediciones Uniandes - Facultad de Administración, Cepal.

Dávila, C. (2012a). El empresariado colombiano (1850–2010) ¿microcosmos del empresariado latinoamericano? Una aproximación a sus características. *Apuntes Revista de Ciencias Sociales, 70*(Dossier en Empresas y Grupos Económicos), 29–68.

Dávila, C. (2012b). *Empresariado en Colombia: Perspectiva histórica y regional*. Universidad de los Andes, Facultad de Administración, Facultad de Ciencias Sociales.

Del Angel, G. A. (2016). The nexus between business groups and banks: Mexico, 1932–1982. *Business History, 58*(1), 111–128. https://doi.org/10.1080/00076791.2015.1044519

Demirguc-Kunt, A., & Levine, R. (1999). *Bank-based and market-based financial systems: Cross-country Comparisons*. World Bank.

Echavarría, J. J., & Villamizar, M. (2007). El Proceso Colombiano de Desindustrialización. In J. Robinson & M. Urrutia (Eds.), *Economía colombiana del siglo XX. Un análisis cuantitativo* (pp. 173–238). Bogotá: Banco de la República - Fondo de Cultura Económica de México.

Fernández, J. (1995). *Adquisición de empresas y grupos económicos*. Fiduciaria de Occidente, ANIF.

Fernández, P., & Lluch, A. (Eds.). (2015). *Familias empresarias y grandes empresas familiares en América Latina y España. Una visión de largo plazo*. Fundación BBVA.

Gerschenkron, A. (1962). *Economic backwardness in historical perspective: A book of essays*. Harvard University.

Gerschenkron, A. (1966). The modernization of entrepreneurship. In M. E. Weiner (Ed.), *Modernization: The dynamics of growth* (pp. 311–324). Basic Books.

Guillén, M. (2000). Business groups in emerging economies: A resource-based view. *Academy of Management Journal, 43*(3), 362–380. https://doi.org/10.5465/1556400

Guillén, M. (2010). Capability building in business groups. In A. M. Colpan, T. Hikino, & J. R. Lincoln (Eds.), *The Oxford handbook of business groups* (pp. 743–763). Oxford University Press.

Guillén, M., & García-Canal, E. (2009). The American model of the multinational firm and the "New" multinationals from emerging economies. *Academy of Management Perspectives, 23*(2), 23–35. https://doi.org/10.5465/amp.2009.39985538

Gutiérrez, L. H., Pombo, C., & Taborda, R. (2008). Ownership and control in Colombian corporations. *The Quarterly Review of Economics and Finance, 48*(1), 22–47. https://doi.org/10.1016/j.qref.2006.01.002

Haber, S. H. (1989). *Industry and underdevelopment: the industrialization of Mexico, 1980–1940*. Stanford University Press.

Haber, S. H. (2002). *Crony capitalism and economic growth in Latin America: theory and evidence*. Hoover Institution Press.

Hall, P. A., & Soskice, D. (2001). *Varieties of Capitalism. The institutional foundations of comparative advantage*. Oxford University Press.

Islas, G. (2015). Corporate governance and ownership in Chile, 1854–2012. In G. Jones & A. Lluch (Eds.), *The impact of globalization on Argentina and Chile* (pp. 45–76). Edward Elgar.

Jaramillo, H. (1955). Moneda fácil para fomento de la producción nacional. In BanRep (Ed.), *Revista del Banco de la República* (Vol. Abril, pp. 413–419). Colombia: Banco de la República.

Jones, G., & Lluch, A. (2015). *The impact of globalization on Argentina and Chile.* (G. Jones & A. Lluch, Eds.; 1st ed.). Elgar.

Junguito, R. (1997). *Economía Cafetera*. Fedesarrollo - Fondo Cultural Cafetero.

Kalmanovitz, S., & Avella, M. (1998). Barreras del desarrollo financiero: las instituciones monetarias colombianas en la década de 1950. *Borradores de Economía, 104*, 2–52.

Khanna, T., & Yafeh, Y. (2007). Business groups in emerging markets: Paragons or parasites? *Journal of Economic Literature, 45*(2), 331–372. https://doi.org/10.1257/jel.45.2.331

Kock, C. J., & Guillén, M. (2014). Strategy and structure in developing countries: Business groups as an evolutionary response to opportunities for unrelated diversification. *Industrial and Corporate Change, 10*(1), 77–113. https://doi.org/10.1093/icc/10.1.77

La Porta, R., Lopez-de-Silanes, F., & Shleifer, A. (1999). Corporate ownership around the world. *The Journal of Finance, 54*(2), 471–517. https://doi.org/10.1111/0022-1082.00115

Leff, N. (1978). Industrial organization and entrepreneurship in the developing countries: the economic groups. *Economic Development and Cultural Change, 26*(4), 661–675. https://doi.org/10.1086/451052

Leff, N. (1979). Entrepreneurship and economic development: the problem revisited. *Journal of Economic Literature, XVII*, 46–64.

Llorca-Jana, M., Miller, R., & Barria, D. (Eds.). (2019). *Capitalists, Business and State-Building in Chile.* Palgrave Macmillan.

Marichal, C. (2014). *Presentación las crisis financieras del siglo XX y sus impactos en América Latina. Coloquio del Grupo Iberoamericano de Estudios Empresariales e Historia Económica.* Tijuana, México: Colef.

Marichal, C., & Ludlow, L. (1986). *Banca y poder en México, 1800–1925* (1st ed.). Grijalbo.

Martínez Ruiz, E. (2018). Quinta Sión. Los judíos y la conformación del espacio urbano de Bogotá. Colombia. Editorial Pontificia Universidad Javeriana.

Maurer, N. (2002). *The power and the money: the Mexican financial system, 1876–1932.* Stanford University Press. https://doi.org/10.1086/ahr/109.1.228

Meisel, A. (1990). *El Banco de la República: antecedentes, evolución y estructura.* Banco de la República.

Mejía, D. (1959). Comentarios y recomendaciones. In *Revista Superintendencia de Sociedades Anónimas.* Superintendencia de Sociedades Anónimas.

Miller, R. (2010). Latin American Business History and Varieties of Capitalism. *Business History Review, 84*(4), 653–657.

Misas, G. (1973). *Contribución al estudio del grado de concentración en la industria colombiana.* Instituto Latinoamericano de Investigaciones Sociales.

Morck, R., & Steier, L. (2005). The global history of corporate governance. An introduction. In R. Morck (Ed.), *A history of corporate governance around the world. Family business groups to professional managers* (pp. 1–64). University of Chicago Press.

Musacchio, A. (2009). *Experiments in financial democracy: Corporate governance and financial development in Brazil, 1882–1950.* Cambridge University Press.

Musacchio, A., & Read, I. (2007). Bankers, industrialists, and their cliques: Elite networks in Mexico and Brazil during early industrialization. *Enterprise and Society, 8*(4), 842–880. https://doi.org/10.1093/es/khm079

Ocampo, J. A., Avella, M., Bernal, J., & Errazuriz, M. (2007). La Industrialización y el Intervencionismo Estatal (1945–1980). In J. A. Ocampo (Ed.), *Historia Económica de Colombia.* (pp. 271–340). Planeta - Fedesarrollo. (Original work published 1987)

Pombo, C., & Gutiérrez, L. H. (2011). Outside directors, board interlocks and firm performance: Empirical evidence from colombian business groups. *Journal of Economics and Business, 63*(4), 251–277. https://doi.org/10.1016/j.jeconbus.2011.01.002

Ramírez, M. T. (2007). Efectos de Eslabonamiento de la Infraestructura de Transporte sobre la Economía Colombiana: 1900–1950. In J. Robinson & M. Urrutia (Eds.), *Economía Colombiana en el Siglo XX. Un Análisis Cuantitativo* (pp. 383–458). Banco de la República - Fondo de Cultura Económica.

Reyes, F. (2016). *Derecho societario* (3rd ed.). Editorial Temis.

Rodriguez-Satizabal, B. (2020). Dataset on 25 Colombian Business Groups and Financial Intermediaries, 1949-1980. This dataset is based on public archival and secondary sources, complete list of sources is available from compiler. Unpublished dataset.

Safford, F., & Palacios, M. (2002). *Colombia País Fragmentado, Sociedad Dividida. Su Historia.* Editorial Norma.

Salazar, N. (1996). *Historia Monetaria y Financiera de Colombia, 1940–1970.* Fedesarrollo.

Salvaj, E., & Couyoumdjian, J. P. (2016). Interlocked' business groups and the state in Chile (1970–2010). *Business History*, *58*(1), 129–148. https://doi.org/10.1080/00076791.2015.1044517

Salvaj, E., & Lluch, A. (2012). A comparative study of interlocking directorates at the end of the import-substituting industrialization period in Argentina and Chile. *Revista hispana para el análisis de redes sociales (REDES)*, *23*(2), 80–112. https://doi.org/10.5565/rev/redes.440

Sánchez, F., Fernández, A., & Armenta, A. (2007). Historia monetaria de Colombia en el siglo XX: Grandes tendencias y episodios relevantes. In J. Robinson & M. Urrutia (Eds.), *Economía colombiana del siglo XX. Un análisis cuantitativo* (pp. 313–382). Fondo de Cultura Económica de México - Banco de la República.

Schneider, B. R. (2009). Hierarchical market economies and varieties of capitalism in Latin America. *Journal of Latin American Studies*, *41*(3), 553–575. https://doi.org/10.1017/S0022216X09990186

Touwen, J. (2010). Varieties of capitalism and institutional change in New Zealand, Sweden and the Netherlands in the 1980s and 1990s. In H. Egbert & C. Esser (Eds.), *Aspects in varieties of capitalism: Dynamics, economic crisis, new players*. (Vol. 3, pp. 171–202). US: LAP Lambert Academic Publishing.

Triner, G. D. (2000). *Banking and economic development: Brazil, 1889–1930*. Palgrave. https://doi.org/10.1086/ahr/107.4.1268

Wilkins, M., Thelen, K., Whitley, R., Miller, R. M., Martin, C. J., Berghahn, V. R., Iversen, M. J., Herrigel, G., & Zeitlin, J. (2010). Multinational enterprises and the varieties of capitalism. *Business History Review*, *84*(4), 637–674. https://doi.org/10.1017/S0007680500001975

Varieties of capitalism, competition policy and the UK alcoholic beverages industry

Julie Bower

ABSTRACT
This article informs a key aspect of the business-government interface; the evolution of competition policy and how firms adapt to it. Drawing on an extensive portfolio of inquiries, what constitutes 'the market' and the boundaries of the firm within it is described through the experience of the UK alcoholic beverages industry. In situating competition policy in its historical socio-economic context, this study traces three overlapping eras; family ownership and control, network and conglomerates organisation, and specialisation and financialisation. Issues emerge that inform wider debate, notably the nature of portfolio and network effects, a central and contested theme in contemporary competition policy.

Introduction

Scholars have promoted the Hall and Soskice (2001) Varieties of Capitalism (VoC) framework as a helpful tool in shifting the emphasis in institutional research away from neoclassical orthodoxies such as the self-regulatory power of 'The Market' (Berghahn, 2010), to a more holistic understanding of the role of the political economy in supporting or countering change. Social embeddedness and context are over-riding drivers of structures and processes (Morgan & Kristensen, 2006), with the legal system and approach to establishing the 'rules of the game' in areas such as state ownership and regulation being a major factor (Wilkins, 2005). Competition policy is an important nexus for the state and its legal framework as it seeks to establish and monitor activity at the interface of firm activity and the consumer markets they serve. It is shaped by beliefs about what policy works best for the economy and society (Bartalevich, 2016).

In Hall and Soskice's thesis the distinction is made between two fundamental styles of economic organisation; that of the 'liberal market' economies of the US and UK, and that of the 'coordinated market' economies of mainland European countries such as Germany and the Scandinavian countries. This distinction makes it possible to predict corporate strategic behaviour (Iversen, 2010). However, the distinction is not so discrete as it may appear. Wilkins (2005) observed that the nature of capitalism varies not only between different countries, but also within individual countries over the course of time. Indeed, when looking retrospectively at the supposed 'laissez-faire' approach of the US in the managerial era, there is a distinct difference between the 1960s and the 1980s.[1] In Chandlerian terms, Lazonick (2010), describes this as the old economy business model of the pre-1970s US, breaking down by the 1980s under the weight of financialisaton and the entry of Japanese manufacturers in key industries. Corporations in successful market economies are governed through different combinations of legal protection and concentrated ownership, with banks playing a more significant role in corporate governance in the coordinated economies of both Germany and Japan (Shleifer & Vishny, 1997).[2] In the US model of neoclassical capitalism, the state's role is essentially to remove itself from business and the operation of the market (Berghahn, 2010), although some observers have questioned whether the US conforms to a genuine market economy with a deregulated state (Lazonick, 2010), the UK, and latterly the coordinated economies of continental Europe have tended towards the US model of corporate governance embedded in the 1980s. This owes much to the evolution of competition policy and how it is implemented in a globalised market for many goods and services.

This article focuses on the role of competition policy and the type of capitalism it engenders in market economies. It utilises a long and eventful history of policy oversight and intervention in the UK alcoholic beverages industry, incorporating latterly interactions between UK firms and the competition policy framework of the United States, the Federal Trade Commission (FTC) and Department of Justice (DoJ) and Europe, the European Commission (EC). The history of the UK brewing industry charts a path from family capitalism, with its traditional small-scale vertical tie to public house (pub) ownership and control, to the free market specialisation and financialisation that has characterised the post-Beer Orders environment of the late 1980s. In reaching this deregulated industrial architecture there was a significant albeit short-lived 'detour' of a conglomerate phase in the 1960–1980 period (Shleifer & Vishny, 1991). It adds historical context to the strategic initiatives and structural and ownership changes within an established set of firms as they interacted with legislative changes in the post-War years, new thinking on economic efficiency and the scale and scope of the firm, and the challenges of globalisation of competition policy. There are not hard lines defining each era but overlapping periods of flux where firm adaptation was a work-in-progress running in parallel with changes in the domestic institutional framework, itself subject to external and supra-national factors, such as, for example, the harmonisation of the various competition policy regimes made necessary by the globalisation of markets and industries.

Varieties of capitalism and the competition policy framework

Toms and Wright (2002) pointed to the wide adoption of pre-WWII US management practices and the Chandlerian M-form structure in the UK in the period 1950–80, with Freyer (1992), noting this era was characterised by a series of anti-cartel and merger measures that replaced self-regulation with public control, thereby paving the way for a 'corporate economy'.[3] The period was something of a transition, however, with the UK coming late to the 'wholehearted commitment to competition', something that would only emerge in the 1980s (Wilks, 1999).[4] The move from the use of common law to public policy sought to establish a framework to maintain competition in British industry as part of the pursuit of full employment,[5] with the assumption that post-War reconstruction would be inherently expansionist.[6] In the inter-War years, Cassis (1997) pointed to a growing awareness for modernisation in business practices, something that would be best achieved through the rationalisation opportunities accruing from merger activity.

The 1948 Companies Act was a key staging post in the move to a free market and financialised form of capitalism, bringing a more stringent financial disclosure in company accounts to outside shareholders (Hannah, 1974). In addition to the push for greater corporate disclosure the Monopolies and Restrictive Practices Act of 1948, empowered a so-called Commission to investigate cases where dominant firms might operate against the public interest (Roberts, 1992). Despite this anti-trust legislation, however, it was not until 1965 that merger control was added to the regulatory powers of the re-named Monopolies and Mergers Commission (MMC) meaning that there were no regulatory obstacles to mergers and acquisitions between 1948 and 1965. According to Wilks (1999), competition policy emerged in the UK 'incrementally and piecemeal as a product of consensus building by a powerful civil service heavily influenced by business lobbying, increasingly responding to developments in economic thought and operating under a benign and exceptional mantle of political bi-partisanship',[7] having 'rejected the rigour and dogmatisation of American anti-trust and latterly rejected the comprehensiveness and economisation of the European approach'[8] The market for corporate control remained under-developed, leaving firms largely unchallenged in pursuing value-destroying diversification strategies (Toms & Wright, 2002). The backdrop of dividend restrictions and tax credits led to an over-accumulation of capital that allowed firms with limited dependency on external capital providers to spend freely on an array of expansionary measures (Rowlinson et al., 2007).

Concurrent with these changes in the political economy of the UK, the wider European system of corporatism evolved from an Austrian-German (Ordoliberal) conception of the role of competition and regulation in a market economy, described by Gerber (1998) as 'unlike national competition law systems, its primary objective has not been to obtain the generic benefits associated with competition such as lower prices to consumers or technological progress .... (it is understood) as part of a program for achieving the specific goal of unifying the European market'.[9]Bartalevich (2016) has attributed the Ordoliberal (or Freiburg) School with influencing European competition policy since the 1960s, supporting the EC's practice of taking into account matters 'unrelated to the protection of competition per se'.[10] This represented a competing economic philosophy to neoclassical economic thought associated with the Chicago School,[11] that has dominated US policy since the late 1960s, supplanting the Harvard School's prior role (Hovenkamp, 2010).[12] The US legal base now operates solely in the name of consumer welfare and efficiency, with a decisional framework operating with the ground rule of letting markets work on their own with minimal government intervention (Fox, 2014). The difference between the two jurisdictions has been cast as 'Americans protect competition, while Europeans protect competitors' (Kokkoris, 2014). This emanates from controversial decisions where both jurisdictions have investigated a specific merger, most notably that of US firms, General Electric and Honeywell, and reached different conclusions.[13]

Varieties of capitalism and the UK alcoholic beverages industry

From a theoretic standpoint, the aim of the study is to use historical narrative to integrate interpretations of the past with contemporary knowledge (Rowlinson et al., 2014). Political economists have identified a valuable role for historians in tracking the unintended consequences of policy by comparing intentions of policymakers with what unfolded and in discerning systematic patterns in issues at the heart of the policymaking agenda (Zelizer, 2012). Following Chandler's methodological dictum, business history research can benefit considerably from the VoC approach where history and context is more than incidental in the quest to utilise empirical data collected to explore the boundaries of existing concepts and theories (Iversen, 2010), by marrying contemporary commentary and industrial and political economy insights into a narrative that is attentive to the external environment and context (Maclean et al., 2016; Perchard et al., 2017).

Arguably, competition policy has had a more fundamental impact on the evolution of the UK brewing industry than of any other domestic industry, with entire books dedicated to policy intervention (Spicer et al., 2012), or the internal organisation of its firms (Mutch, 2006). The industry continues to offer important insights to business and economic historians (Bower, 2016a, 2016b; Bower & Cox, 2012; Da Silva Lopes & Casson, 2007, 2012; Higgins et al., 2016), and has informed several empirical studies by industrial and regulatory economists, notably in merger policy (Nalebuff, 2003). Consequently, in addition to the rich dataset provided by a series of regulatory inquiries, shown in Table 1 below, there is an extensive portfolio of prior literature on which to build and enhance the narrative argument.

Family capitalism

In his account of the 'divorce' of ownership and control, Hannah (2007) noted that personally owned or family firms were still the norm in the industrial sector at the start of the twentieth century. Where family firms were engaged with the public market, it was frequently by recourse to preference shares or debenture stock, that reduced voting rights.[14] Very few families, even extended kinship groups were numerous enough, or experienced enough, to manage the scale and scope of national and international markets, and in capital-intensive industries the recruitment of managerial hierarchies was essential for an enterprise to expand market share (Chandler, 1986). Until 1948, all but a small number of the largest UK firms – the producers of branded packaged consumer goods such as Imperial Tobacco, Distillers Company Limited, Unilever and Guinness,[15] - were either family-managed and controlled, or were federations of family firms legally unified under the control of a holding company (Chandler, 1986). Freyer (1992) linked the failure of the British corporate sector to evolve from family ownership into corporate structures at the early part of the twentieth century as reinforcing the view that a lack of managerial centralisation contributed to the UK's relative economic decline.[16]

Da Silva Lopes and Casson (2007) pointed to the stability and consistency in ownership of many of the best-known brands, including those in the alcoholic beverages industry, where most of the firms described were controlled by families, trusts, or a small group of major shareholders. This offered the advantage of rendering the firms relatively immune to pressures from independent shareholders to maximise short-term payment of dividends. Da Silva Lopes and Casson (2012) described how Anglo-Irish brewer Guinness had embarked on a rapid strategy of internationalisation soon after it went public in 1886 by employing the strategy of granting bottling franchises to independent companies in lieu of a restriction of their bottling activities to the eponymous stout beer. Similarly, Weir (1989) described how the Scotch whisky industry developed rapidly from family-related activity into a highly consolidated and dominant producer-marketer in the shape of Distillers Company Limited (DCL).

Table 1. UK alcoholic beverages firms and UK, EC and US competition policy.

Year	Reference	Title of document	Significance of evidence
UK			
1969	MC Inquiry (HC 216)	Beer: A report on the supply of beer	First competition inquiry into the traditional vertically-integrated structure of the UK beer market. No action taken although abuse of market power was identified.
1969	MC Inquiry (HC 297)	Unilever Limited and Allied Breweries Limited: A report on the proposed merger	General observations on mergers attached as an annex. This was also an annex to the Rank Group/De La Rue proposed hostile conglomerate merger.
1989	MMC Inquiry (Cm 651)	The supply of beer: A report on the supply of beer for retail sale in the United Kingdom	Second competition inquiry of the UK beer market led to the 'Beer Orders' – the partial dismantling of the 'Big 6' brewers' vertical tie.
1989	MMC Inquiry (Cm 654)	Elders IXL and Scottish & Newcastle Breweries Plc: A report on the merger situations	Hostile bid blocked following multi-faceted political and regulatory intervention.
1989	DTI Notice (89/745)	Decision on Beer Orders	Partial climb-down on the extent of the 'Beer Orders' after intense lobbying campaign from the Brewers Society.
1990	MMC Inquiry (Cm 1227)	Elders IXL Ltd and Grand Metropolitan Plc: A report on the merger situations	A novel 'breweries-for-pubs' swap of assets with up-front remedies presented and adopted largely in subsequent mergers.
2000	OFT Report (317)	The supply of beer: A report on the review of the Beer Orders by the former DGFT	Admission from UK regulatory authority that the forced separation of brewing and retailing had been draconian.
2001	CC Inquiry (Cm 5014)	Interbrew SA and Bass Plc: A report on the acquisition by Interbrew SA of the brewing interests of Bass PLC	Majority decision that the merger be unwound.
US/EU			
1988	EC Notice (IP-88-512)	Proposed takeover of Irish Distillers	Political interference in a merger through direct lobbying to the European Commission. Described by the UK Takeover Panel as 'a most unusual and long-running saga'.
1997	EC Inquiry (Case IV/M.938)	Guinness/Grand Metropolitan	One of the first transactions subject to multijurisdictional scrutiny under the International Anti-trust Enforcement Assistance Act. Highlighted the different application of economic principles between the US and EC regarding 'portfolio effects' and the definition of relevant markets.
1998	FTC Inquiry (Case C-3801)	Guinness PLC, Grand Metropolitan PLC and Diageo PLC – Complaint	
1998	FTC Notice (opa/98/06/ Diageo)	FTC approves sale of Dewar's Scotch and Bombay Gin to Bacardi for $1.9bn	Largest sale for an FTC-mandated divestiture.
2001	EC Inquiry (Case COMP/M.2268)	Pernod Ricard/Diageo/Seagram Spirits	The discrete economic analysis of Grand Met/ Guinness was upheld by each of the two jurisdictions. As a separation of assets, its significance was the pre- and post-merger cooperation between the parties, and between the regulatory authorities and the parties in the process of devising and concluding remedies to circumvent competition concerns. This became the norm for all subsequent consolidations in the industry
2001	FTC Inquiry (C-4032)	Diageo PLC and Vivendi SA – Complaint	
2001	FTC Notice (opa/01/12/ Diageo)	With conditions, FTC approves joint acquisition of Seagram Spirits and Wine by Diageo PLC and Pernod Ricard SA	
2005	EC Inquiry (Cases COMP/M.3779 and COMP/M.3813)	Pernod Ricard/Allied Domecq (with associated divestment to Fortune Brands)	

By contrast, the UK brewing market remained highly fragmented, and dominated by a large number of families, prior to the great amalgamation of the late 1950s and early 1960s (Gourvish & Wilson, 1994). This was despite an evident erosion of collusive agreements between family firms that emerged in the latter part of the nineteenth century under the financial pressures that accompanied the rush to acquire additional public house outlets and invest in new brewing technology. This was fulfilled by recourse to the public markets, albeit retaining corporate control through issuing low-voting preference and debenture stock (Watson, 1996).[17] Gourvish and Wilson (1994) identified that 'for the great majority of brewers the building up and maintaining of networks of outlets – usually over distances of not much more than a dozen miles – was at the very heart of their business'.[18]The ongoing process of amalgamations resulting in the closure of redundant capacity, and the reassignment of retail outlets within the estates of the acquirers meant that by the time of the 1969 inquiry into the structure and operation of the UK brewing industry, the family origins of the brewers had been lost not only in their surviving names,[19] but also in practical management terms. One possible exception to this was Whitbread, still carrying the name of its founder, and with the direct oversight of Colonel Bill Whitbread and closely aligned family members. The firm retained a unique, and complex dual voting share structure and shareholding relationship with a portfolio of other small family brewers through the Whitbread Investment Company (Bower, 2016b), an arrangement that despite contributing to poor financial performance (Higgins & Toms, 2011), nonetheless endured until the early 1990s.

Family business scholars have pointed to the Chandlerian thesis that the modern economy had rendered family-led enterprise obsolete, while presenting the counterfactual of the prevalent, thriving and ubiquitous family ownership model (Schulze & Gedajlovic, 2010). La Porta et al. (1999) noted that widely held firms are still relatively uncommon, reflecting ownership patterns in a small number of countries, such as the US, or by dint of research focusing on a specific measure of control among a small number of large firms. In much of the rest of the world, legal protection of investors is less substantial, consequently, firms remain family-controlled and, even in some of the richest countries, have difficulty raising outside funds (Shleifer & Vishny, 1997). Contrary to Chandler's prediction, family firms have not disappeared from the ranks of leading publicly listed US firms (Van Essen et al., 2015).

In the context of the UK brewing industry, once the family ownership and control pattern dismantled new business models emerged, conditioned to a great degree by change in the competition policy regime and the structure of the capital markets. It is notable, however, that the 'traditional' UK brewing model is re-emerging with a small but increasingly significant number of newly established firms joining an original set of long-standing family firms in a currently vibrant UK brewing sector. The Independent Family Brewers of Britain (IFBB), established in 1993 with a common goal to preserve the cask ale tradition of the original family sector, is now a dynamic and innovative collective of 29 firms. It includes some well-known names in the brewing industry, such as Brakspear and Fuller, Smith and Turner, that have been in existence for several generations. In aggregate they control 4,000 pubs, 82 per cent of which are tenanted outlets, and unlike those pubs controlled by the pub companies (PubCos) that have characterized the post-Beer Orders era (Bower, 2016a), the name of the brewery is prominent in the signage, including the cask ale associated with the pub. As per tradition, the pubs are close to the breweries that supply them. As Figure 1 shows, there has been a steady decline in the number of pubs per brewery for the major brewery sector since 1990, reflecting both a decline in the number of breweries and number of brewer-owned and operated pubs. However, running in conjunction with the growth in the PubCos and other independent pub operators has been a rapid increase in the number of breweries from just over 200 in 1990 to 1880 by 2015, based on data provided by the British Beer & Pub Association (Statistical Handbook, 2016).

Vertical networks and managerial capitalism

Firms gravitated to opportunities to extract economies of scope during the 1950s (Toms & Wright, 2002), albeit what constituted scope rather than unrelated diversification for which they had no natural competences would become the Achilles heel of all but the most robustly managed industrial conglomerates. Capital market sentiment towards diversified firms changed in the 1980s, and with the deregulation of financial services activity supporting the globalisation of capital flows, the often mentioned conglomerate or 'diversification discount' (Feldman et al., 2014),[20] presented an array of opportunities to well-informed corporate raiders with access to capital in the 1980s merger wave that characterised both the US and UK corporate scene (Herzel & Shepro, 1990).[21]

Analysis of ownership and diversification strategies in the context of the coordinated market VoC model is interesting in that it reveals less distinction versus the liberal market backdrop than might have been predicted. Whittington and Mayer (2000), for example, concluded that in terms of structure, trends in Europe more, or less, tracked the 'Chandlerian' direction albeit there was a time lag. The managerial organisation that was practically unknown in the 1950s, had been adopted by 40 per cent of large industrial firms in France and Germany, and 75 per cent of those in the UK, by the 1970s.[22] In a subsequent refinement, Hautz et al. (2013), considering the diversification strategies of large European firms from 1994 to 2007, found that family ownership concentration was positively related to product diversification and negatively related to international diversification. For financial institutions, accustomed to interacting with the (global) capital markets, strategies are not conditioned by the perceived risk of expanding or acquiring internationally.[23]

The first merger inquiry in the UK brewing sector, and one of the first to be considered following the introduction of the merger regulation in competition policy, was the proposed friendly merger between Allied Breweries and Unilever announced in November 1968. It offers an interesting and informative insight into institutional attitudes to conglomerates and diversification strategies. Unusually, the inquiry report was accompanied by a Monopolies Commission (MC) opinion on 'conglomerate mergers', attached as a 19-page annexe (it was also attached to the concurrent inquiry into the hostile bid of The Rank Organisation Limited for banknote printer The De La Rue Company Limited). Conglomerate mergers in the US had come to prominence in the 1960s,[24] largely as a function of 'the aggressive antitrust enforcement in the '60s and '70s that simply disallowed mergers of firms in the same industry, regardless of the effects of these mergers on competition' (Shleifer & Vishny, 1991).[25] For the MC, investigating mergers that were neither predominantly horizontal nor vertical added to the complexity in establishing market effects, with the decision taken to adopt *de facto* a 'rule of reason', rather than 'per se' illegal stance.[26]

The Unilever/Allied merger gave rise to a considerable amount of public interest. Unilever regarded the merger as a 'product extension ... that is a consolidation of two companies whose activities are related functionally at either the production or marketing level, but whose products are different', and which was a 'natural extension of Unilever's international

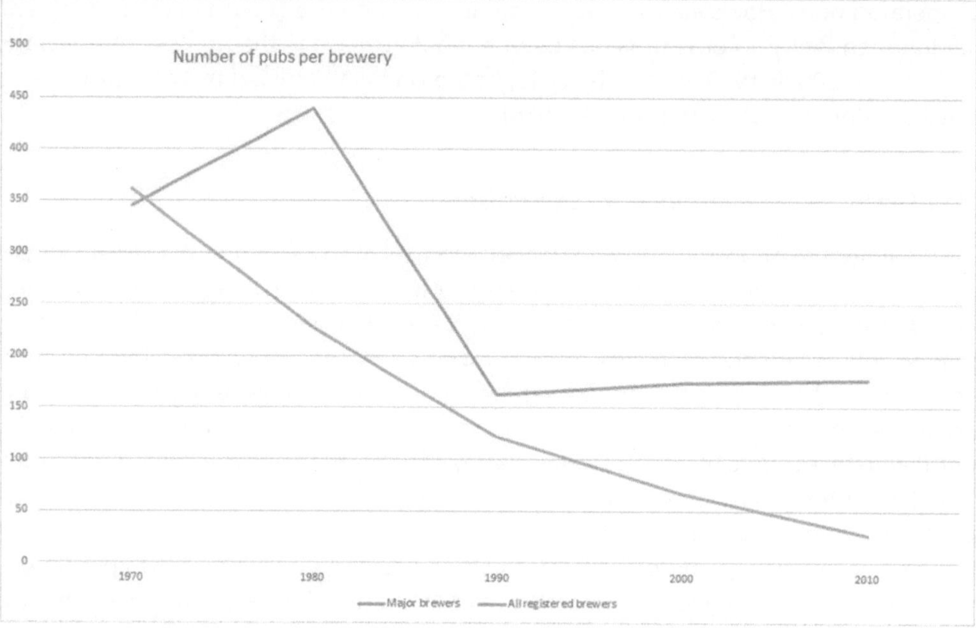

Figure 1. Number of pubs per brewery.

food business'. For Allied, with an ambition to expand rapidly overseas beyond the licensing of home-grown Skol lager,[27] Unilever's presence in brewing joint ventures, primarily in Africa, and its established international position in the food market, 'which was closely related to the drinks market' combined with its expertise and resources in, for example, research and development, would augment Allied's strategic objectives.[28] This was largely dismissed by the MC as 'some exaggeration in the claims made for immediate benefits in this area'.[29]

Also running concurrently with the Unilever/Allied merger was a multi-year investigation of the UK brewing industry, the first of two market inquiries that would lead ultimately to the dismantling of the vertical tie through the 1989 'Beer Orders' (Bower, 2016a). One aspect of the vertical tie that has otherwise attracted limited attention is its impact on the related areas of soft drinks, wine and spirits production and distribution. Indeed the 1969 inquiry highlighted a greater volume of complaints about the tie to spirits sales than any other aspect of the industry's structure and conduct. Tenants, wines and spirits trade associations and others complained about restrictions imposed by the brewers' promotion through wholesale prices and discount structures of their own 'house brands', and their recourse to various underhand practices.[30] Independent brand owners claimed that the retail distribution networks controlled by the brewers were responsible not only for the foreclosure of their brands but that this was also constraining innovation, with the Consumer Council highlighting 'the entry of new producers and new products (other than brewers' own new products) is hindered'.[31]

What started as a noble endeavor to assist their tenants in accessing heavily restricted supplies of wines and spirits that they were previously free to source independently quickly evolved into forced supply contracts when the brewers entered directly into production. Initially the brewers focused on the bulk buying and registration of supplies of whisky, gin, and other wines and spirits to distribute as their own 'house brands' in the late 1950s. By the late 1960s, however, they had expanded such that three major wines and spirits groups were evident in the UK. Allied Breweries, owner of Grants of St. James's Ltd (a wholesale wine and spirit merchant), and Victoria Wine Company Ltd (a national chain of wines and spirits retail shops) acquired brand owner Showerings, Vine Products and Whiteway's Ltd in 1968, making it the largest manufacturer, wholesaler and retailer of wines and spirits in the UK. In 1968, Watney Mann acquired a 38 per cent interest in International Distillers and Vintners Ltd, owner of J&B Rare Scotch whisky and Gilbey's gin, and Whitbread acquired a 33 per cent stake in J R Phillips, a wines and spirits distributor in which Allied also had a shareholding.[32]

The brewers' tie remained unchallenged for a further 20 years before its total elimination for non-alcoholic or low-alcoholic beers, wines, spirits, cider, soft drinks and mineral waters as part of the 1989 'Beer Orders' legislation. Although the brewers had taken steps to slacken the demands on their tenants by this stage,[33] there remained a problem of foreclosure, with the 1989 inquiry noting 'a restriction of consumer choice (that) limits the ability of brand owners of spirits who do not own public houses (in essence, Guinness) to compete in the on-licensed market'.[34] By 1989, the UK brewers were fully-fledged conglomerates of drinks, pub retailing and associated consumer-related activities. Allied-Lyons, Grand Metropolitan (owner of Big 6 brewer Watney Mann), and Guinness were a major force in the international spirits arena, having embraced the mergers and acquisitions market of the 1980s. The Big 6's reach incorporated a wide array of 'related' areas of trade, notably food manufacturing (Allied Breweries' 1978 acquisition of J Lyons), hotels, restaurants and other leisure activities (Bass's acquisition of the Holiday Inn franchise system in 1988/9 added to its existing leisure-related portfolio of bingo clubs, betting shops, and the manufacture, supply and operation of amusement and gaming machines); Scottish & Newcastle's acquisitions of Center Parcs and Pontins in 1989 (paid for by the sale of the home-developed Thistle hotel chain). Headline acquisitions were used in conjunction with, or to support the organic areas of expansion of the 1970s and early 1980s that were the natural response of pub operators to rapid socio-economic change in the UK casual dining and leisure retail market. As Mutch (2006) noted, however, Allied Breweries and Bass were less equipped, or indeed possessed the skills and resources to make the transition away from the traditional style of the working man's pub in the way Whitbread managed successfully.

Deregulation and specialisation

Although a discussion of the economics of competition policy is beyond the scope of this article, it is important to understand that its rules are informed and shaped by economic theories (Bartalevich, 2016). Changes in the 1980s, particularly the free market thinking attributable to the government of Margaret Thatcher, had a lasting impact on the nature and boundaries of 'the market' in the UK, not least, in the structure and operation of the vertically integrated brewing industry. This was supported by the ascendency of Chicago School economics and the associated think-tank movement it promoted, foremost of which was the Mont Pèlerin Society (MPS). Jackson (2012a) attributes the MPS, founded in 1947 by Friedrich Hayek with leading Chicago School economists, Milton Friedman, Frank Knight and George Stigler, to the debate dubbed subsequently as 'neo-liberalism',[35] and the explication and dissemination of the proposition that political interference with market activities was harmful to freedom.[36] The MPS was the first in a number of free-market think tanks, notably the Institute of Economic Affairs (IEA), that would shape the Thatcherite critique of

British social democracy.[37] Business support was crucial in shaping elite opinion in Britain in the 1960s and 1970s, and this prepared the ground for the deregulation of the 1980s that defined Mrs Thatcher's government. Major firms such as British American Tobacco, Marks & Spencer, Unilever, the high street banks, and several City institutions, offered financial support to the IEA and its sister think tanks, the Centre for Policy Studies and the Adam Smith Institute, to neutralise 'the left-wing output of universities (that) was providing ammunition for the unions'.[38]

Notable absences from the list of big business leaders in support of the liberalisation and deregulation of industries were the UK's large brewers. The major brewer-retailers, with the support of their influential trade association, the Brewers' Society, fought hard to preserve the status quo of the vertically integrated arrangement (Bower & Cox, 2012). According to Spicer et al. (2012), in its chapter entitled 'Borrie's bombshell' the brewers believed they had been successful in averting any further intervention when Sir Gordon Borrie, Director General of Fair Trading, indicated he had instructed the UK Government that the Brewers' Society directed swap arrangement that was agreed as part of the 1969 market inquiry had been successful in reducing local pub concentration. Sir Gordon, a lawyer described by Wilks (1999) as a man who 'came squarely from the world of consumer protection, where he had made his mark as an activist, academic and author',[39] however appeared to change his mind.

Change was also evident from within the industry itself as a function of the entry of firms with a more evident managerialist, financially driven approach. Grand Metropolitan (Grand Met), established in 1948 as a hotel and property finance conglomerate, had acquired Watney Mann in the early 1970s, bringing with it a stake in the international spirits industry. Guinness, a brewer without a tied pub estate, and with a portfolio of Scotch whisky assets, had made representations to the MMC during the 1985/6 Scottish & Newcastle/Matthew Brown merger inquiry, in additional to direct approaches to the Office of Fair Trading in the early part of 1986, pressing for an ending of the vertical tie, with its new chief executive, Ernest Saunders, presenting the case in a manner 'altogether more professional than the OFT was accustomed to (from the brewers)'.[40] Finally, there were a series of changes of ownership of Courage, finally settling in the ownership of aggressive Australian conglomerate, Elders IXL.

Grand Met's acquisition of Watney Mann had brought the firm to the edge of bankruptcy in the 1973/4 recession.[41] Founder Maxwell Joseph recruited Allan (later Lord) Sheppard, a seasoned motor industry executive with a background in economics and finance, to salvage the perceived overpayment for Watney Mann and rationalise the brewing operations.[42] Sheppard was the antithesis of the traditional 'Beerage' owner-manager, as 'the epitome of the 1980s' deal-maker', and an early 'conversion to the free-market cause'.[43] He presided over some 70 large acquisitions and disposals, including the 1988 purchase of US bakery firm, Pillsbury/Burger King,[44] and the 1991 innovative 'breweries-for-pubs swap' with Courage/Elders IXL. His legacy, however, is more significant for the expansion into the international spirits industry, marked by the 1987 purchase of Heublein, owner of Smirnoff vodka. Although Grand Met had been successful in its ventures in the US, its aggressive tactics were less than successful in the highly politicised merger market of Europe in the 1980s. Failure to cement an approach for family-controlled Martell Cognac,[45] was followed by political outmanoeuvring in the approach for Irish Distillers when the target lodged a tactical complaint with the EC under both Article 81,[46] and Article 82,[47] prompting 'the Commission's most effective intervention of all'.[48] Perhaps conveniently, the EC Competition Commissioner was high-profile Irish lawyer and politician, Peter Sutherland, at a time when the Irish parliament was under considerable pressure for the retention of the control of Irish Distillers in Ireland.[49]

By the time of the 1989 Beer Orders inquiry, three of the top four international spirits firms were domiciled in the UK (the fourth was Canadian/US firm Seagram); Allied-Lyons (renamed Allied Domecq in 1994), Grand Met (through its IDV subsidiary) and Guinness (the Bell's and DCL acquisitions unified in the UD subsidiary). Despite these acquisitions, however, no firm possessed strength and depth in their international brand portfolios and distribution capabilities. The rationale for the Grand Met and Guinness merger of 1997 that created the global spirits giant Diageo, was to capture the benefits of the complementary nature of their respective spirits operations while eliminating significant costs in marketing and distribution.[50] Key US competitor Seagram commented: 'The industry is suffering from over-capacity, but it is hard for us to imagine a more anti-competitive way of dealing with it than with this deal ... if this deal goes through I believe it will only be after a huge amount of scrutiny and only with major divestitures'.[51] Despite Seagram's concerns the EC cleared the merger in October 1997 with minor remedies,[52] although a different approach from the US regulators in defining 'relevant markets' meant that Diageo was obliged to divest Dewar's Scotch and Bombay gin to an FTC-approved competitor.[53]

Diageo was one of the first mergers to be investigated simultaneously by the FTC and EC as part of the harmonisation of policy initiative.[54] The different approach taken in both defining the relevant market and in establishing the scope of portfolio or network effects aroused wider academic and practitioner interest, culminating in a study undertaken by eminent Yale economist, Barry Nalebuff, on behalf of the UK government, in which the principles of Chicago School economics were criticised (Nalebuff, 2003).[55] In the case of Diageo, the EC had acknowledged that 'the market power deriving from a portfolio of brands exceeds the sum of its parts'.[56] Such an inference, and one which was supported by several leading competitors, stood in 'stark contrast to the Chicago School concept of their being a single monopoly rent'.[57] This added to concerns expressed by both regulators and advisers that US policy, and the underlying economic concepts that supported it such as oligopoly theory (Werden, 2004),[58] were especially inadequate in highly differentiated product mergers (Rubinfeld, 2000).[59] The relative ease with which Diageo had navigated multi-jurisdictional oversight prompted a cascade of subsequent deals, structured similarly; the Diageo/Pernod Ricard joint acquisition of the international spirits portfolio of Seagram, investigated by both the EC,[60] and the FTC,[61] and the Pernod Ricard/Fortune Brands purchase of Allied Domecq's spirits operations in a similar joint carve-out.

Elders IXL's entry into the UK brewing industry was a major catalyst for change in both the economics of brewing and the nature of the brewer-pub retailing relationship that would ensue in the 1990s financialized pub trade (Bower, 2016a): the early prototype lease agreements of the former Inntrepreneur pub estate.[62] The Beer Orders prompted fundamental change in the ownership and governance of relationships between brewers and their tenants.[63] In its assessment of the economic evidence provided by the industry's trade association, the Brewers' Society (conducted on its behalf by two leading University of Oxford economists), the MMC said, 'tenancy agreements have evolved which have a price per barrel above marginal cost and a lower fixed element in the form of a subsidised rent. The Society argues that these agreements give some of the benefits of vertical integration while also reducing the tenant's risk .... We reject this argument'.[64] Lafontaine and Slade (2015) note that the theoretical welfare effects of vertical restraints are almost always ambiguous and historically, competition authorities have treated exclusive dealing more leniently than other forms of vertical restraints.[65] Against this backdrop the intervention into the operation of the UK brewing industry that broke the traditional vertical tie is the more significant for its rarity as for what happened in the evolution of the market subsequently, specifically, the demise of the UK pub industry.[66] Higgins et al. (2016) investigated the matter further as an assessment of the transfer of risk in the PubCo model that was underpinned by a 'full-tie' model. Enterprise Inns, for example, imposed a 'range of exclusive purchasing obligations', that had the effect of maintaining the profit margins available to tenants but at the price of the transfer of a disproportionate amount of risk.[67]

After a ten-year lobbying campaign by The Campaign for Real Ale (CAMRA), a Pubs Code (PCO) came into force in July 2016 to regulate the relationship between all pub companies owning 500 or more tied pubs and their tenants, providing an appeal process to a newly created Pubs Code Adjudicator (PCA).[68] In CAMRA's view, the PubCos had been charging inflated rents and preventing landlords from buying beer at open market prices, thereby forcing them out of business. Moreover, it presented evidence that some PubCos were exploiting gaps in the Code and not abiding by the spirit of the legislation,[69] prompting the first statutory review of the Code and PCA that took place in summer 2019. Both Bower (2016a) and Higgins et al. (2016), allude to the hybrid or unstable nature of the PubCo model regarding transaction cost economics, with Bower (2016a) going further in attributing this to the very nature of the financialisation arrangements that had supported the inexorable rise of the PubCos, and noted that there was evidence of a return to the traditional brewer-retailer tied model. In this respect, it is of note that subsequently Heineken continued its strategy of acquiring pub assets in the UK, having been given clearance by the competition authorities in 2017 to take over Punch Taverns in lieu of selling 30 of Punch's 1,895 pubs. This deal made Heineken the third largest pub owner after brewer Greene King and PubCo Enterprise Inns.[70]

Concluding comments

In seeking further explication of the VoC framework, this study has described three key features of the post-War structure and operation of the UK brewing industry to illustrate how competition policy, a key aspect of the business-government interface, conditions firm strategies. It has drawn on a long and eventful history of policy oversight and intervention in the UK, and latterly considered aspects of the international policy framework of the US and Europe as certain firms embarked on consolidation of the international spirits industry. The narrative account charts a path from family capitalism, with its traditional small-scale vertical tie to pub ownership and control, to the free market specialisation and financialisation that created, Diageo, a firm that dominates the global distribution of many spirits categories, most notably Scotch whisky (McKendrick & Hannan, 2014),[71] and large retail chains of pubs (the PubCos) that, in retaining and advancing many of the more critical aspects of the former brewers vertical tie as they consolidated in the era of seemingly unlimited availability of capital prior to the 2008 Financial Crisis (Lazonick, 2010). The latter have been shown to be fundamentally unstable hybrid constructs designed only to shift risk in the value chain (Bower, 2016a; Higgins et al., 2016). However, highlighting the pros and cons of breaking traditional structures through policy intervention, there is now an invigorated small family brewing sector engaged in traditional practices, and the consolidation of the former PubCos financialisation vehicles in the hands of larger brewers, particularly Heineken. The process of change has not therefore been smooth and one-directional. As Wilkins (2005) established, several types of capitalism can co-exist within the same jurisdiction and this can vary over time.

In reaching the 'final state', there was a significant, albeit short-lived, 'detour' of a conglomerate phase in the 1960–1980 period that charted similar developments in the US (Shleifer & Vishny, 1991). Although the major brewers escaped competition policy intervention in 1969, the implications of the extension of the vertical brewing tie to other types of beverages, notably wines and spirits, was more than a natural extension of scope into related areas when economies of scale in existing lines had been exhausted (Toms & Wright, 2002). The promotion of the brewers 'house brands' of wines and spirits was only possible because of the portfolio or network effects available from their control of distribution into the retail pub market. Heavily criticised by tenants and consumer bodies alike, and fearing perhaps that the competition authorities would have a second look at the structure and operation of the beer market – which they did twenty years later – the brewers embarked on a series of unrelated business distractions that took them further into other areas of the beverages and leisure markets, before the hostile merger market of the 1980s brought conglomerate structures to a virtual end.

The manner in which the Big 6 brewers sought to monopolise the control of the distribution of a wider portfolio of products and services into the retail estates during the 1960s may offer interesting insights for those currently considering the socio-political consequences of the major US technology firms and their reputed monopolisation of information and data networks. This has prompted a wider debate on the fundamental approach adopted by the US to competition policy, specifically the role of Chicago School economic theory, as identified in Khan's (2017) widely cited thesis. Indeed, high-profile politicians in the US have resurrected the idea of a European-style interventionist approach to curtail the 'let the market decide' philosophy of liberal capitalism,[72] referring to the hardening of the EC's stance on potential abuse of dominance in the case of Google. Aktas et al. (2007), described this previously as the US having exported 'its own and possibly flawed antitrust policy to the EC ... the very same policy now hits back at US bidders'.[73]

In the UK, one of the consequences of Brexit means that the UK will have to develop its own independent competition policy regime. Although the trajectory of this is still uncertain, it is notable that the new chairman of the Competition and Markets Authority, Lord Tyrie, has signalled a more interventionist stance, commenting 'in the new regime ... the authority should be "doing and saying a lot more"' as he vowed that the organisation would 'become a more active champion for individuals and small businesses that believe they have lost out to the forces of capitalism'.[74] The backdrop to this was the CMA's controversial decision to block the proposed merger between the supermarket groups, Sainsbury's and ASDA, with the CMA ruling the proposed merger threatened to push up prices and reduce the choice and quality of products on sale in stores.[75] For historians of the UK brewing industry, this sounds ominously similar to reasons cited for the 1989 Beer Orders, 'these measures will increase competition in brewing, wholesaling and retailing, encourage new entry, reduce prices and widen consumer choice'.[76]

Notes

1. Wilkins, 'Multinational enterprises and the varieties of capitalism', p 636, notes '*Many believers in the efficacy of markets, from the 1980s onward, would have been surprised at (Stewart and Simmons's) comments that America in the 1960s had an economy that was relatively laissez-faire*'.
2. Shleifer and Vishny, 'A survey of corporate governance', p 771, notes both Germany and Japan shaped their systems of powerful banks at the end of the 19th century with strong support from the state. The legal system developed to accommodate the prevailing economic power – the banks.
3. Freyer, '*Regulating big business*', p 269.
4. Wilks, '*In the public interest*', p 24-25, comments that the British vocabulary, in common with that of the US, talked about 'monopolies' and 'restrictive practices' but did not regard them as unlawful.
5. Pickering, 'Thoughts on the competition regime' provides a concise historical backdrop to the move from the 'public interest test' in early policy to the 'competition test' of the Enterprise Act 2002 that created an independent Competition Commission.
6. Freyer, '*Regulating big business*', p 234-236, notes that trade associations needed to be dismantled as they were deemed responsible for an unduly rigid industrial structure that stifled new entry, innovation and organisational efficiency.
7. Wilks, '*In the public interest*', p 25.
8. Ibid, p 296.
9. Gerber, '*Law and competition in twentieth century Europe*', p 334.
10. Bartalevich, 'The influence of the Chicago School on the Commission's guidelines', p 270-271, provides an account of the pros and cons of the competing paradigms, Ordoliberal and Chicago School, philosophies.
11. The intellectual movement grounded in the University of Chicago's Economics department of the 1930s and the scholarship of Frank Knight, Jacob Viner and Henry Simons. Later influential scholars of the Chicago School movement include Aaron Director, Milton Friedman, George Stigler, Ronald Coase and Robert Bork.
12. Hovencamp, 'Harvard, Chicago, and transaction cost economics', p 615-617, describes the Harvard or 'structural' school's emergence as the dominant paradigm in US antitrust in the 1930s, and how it viewed with suspicion both ownership vertical integration and vertical contractual practices such as tying, exclusive dealing, resale price maintenance, or related restraints. In contrast, the Chicago School view that displaced it embodied a theory of vertical integration which began with the collapse of the 'leverage' theory in the 1950s and developed into a more general argument that vertical ownership and contract integration should be lawful per se.
13. Kokkoris, 'Introduction: EU and US competition enforcement', p 4, points to a core difference in that the US approach indicates it is not unlawful for a firm with a monopoly in one market to leverage its monopoly power in neighbouring markets per se, whereas under EU law it is viewed as an abuse of dominance.
14. Hannah, 'The "divorce" of ownership from control', p 416, notes that typically families retained absolute voting control with only one-third of the securities.
15. Payne, 'Family business in Britain: An historical and analytical survey', p 185, notes that although Guinness was family-owned and controlled at board level, outside managers had been chosen carefully to run the firm for over 50 years.
16. Freyer, '*Regulating big business*', p 69, attributes shared values and market relationships in providing cohesion among different business interests in contrast to the situation in the US at this time.
17. Watson, 'Banks and industrial finance', notes that by 1900, capital subscribed by the London new issues market accounted for almost 75 per cent of capital invested in brewing.
18. Gourvish and Wilson '*The British brewing industry*', p 127.
19. Gourvish and Wilson, '*The British brewing industry*', p 448-449 noted that the quoted assets of the top five brewers increased from 21 per cent of the industry's total in 1952 to 63 per cent by 1967 as many family names were subsumed in a merger wave precipitated by financial entrepreneurship.

20. Feldman, Gilson and Villalonga, 'Do analysts add value when they most can', studied the role of financial analyst research in aiding investors' understanding of diversified firms. The authors concluded analysts are as challenged by the opacity of diversified firms as investors are.
21. Herzel and Shepro, *'Bidders and targets'*, recounts high-profile hostile bids in the era, including Grand Metropolitan's bid for US food conglomerate, Pillsbury/Burger King.
22. Whittington and Mayer, *'The European Corporation'*, p 13, notes that although the European analysis in the Harvard Programme revealed a steadily rising trend towards the levels of diversification advocated by Chandler, US firms were more likely to have adopted strategies of unrelated (conglomerate) diversification.
23. Hautz, Mayer and Stadler, 'Ownership identity and concentration', p 108, considers that, unlike families, financial institutions are more focused on firm level economic effectiveness.
24. Federal Trade Commission data showed 84 per cent of all mergers in the US during 1968 were of a conglomerate nature.
25. Shleifer and Vishny, 'Takeovers in the '60s and the '80s: evidence and implication', p 52.
26. Monopolies Commission, *'Unilever Limited and Allied Breweries Limited'*, Annex, p 37, notes in conglomerate mergers 'losses in efficiency may in some cases be found sufficiently likely and substantial, even in the absence of anti-competitive consequences, to cause the merger to be regarded as contrary to the public interest'.
27. Ibid, p 11, notes that in 1964 Allied formed Skol International with three overseas brewers to create a world-wide brand of beer, Skol lager. By 1969 Skol lager was manufactured under license in 17 countries and marketed in 50.
28. Ibid, p 15-16.
29. Ibid, p 25.
30. Monopolies Commission, *'Beer: A report on the supply of beer'*, p 61-62, describes the switching of orders, late delivery and various pub-specific financial inducements in lieu of promoting house brands of spirits.
31. Ibid, p 113.
32. Ibid, p 20-24 outlines the already extensive wines and spirits activities of the Big 6 brewers that spanned production and distribution of third-party international brands.
33. Monopolies and Mergers Commission, *'The supply of beer'*, p 63-65, provides evidence of the proportion of optics in various types of outlet by brand, noting that the brands owned by brewers tended to have a higher share in the owning brewer's managed estate, but that the position was different in their tenanted estates.
34. Ibid, p 277
35. Jackson, 'The think-tank archipelago', p 43.
36. Jackson, 'Freedom, the common good, and the rule of law', p 49-50, traces the new economic thinking in criticism of the 1930s New Deal. Critics, such as Walter Lippmann, aligned philosophically with Hayek notwithstanding their polar-extreme political affiliations.
37. Jackson, 'The think-tank archipelago', p 44, quoting Ralph Harris and Arthur Seldon, who had just been entrusted to run the IEA.
38. Ibid, p 48, quoting Sir Nicholas Cayzer's view of the IEA.
39. Wilks, *'In the public interest'*, p 287.
40. Spicer et al, 'Intervention in the modern UK brewing industry', p 42-43.
41. Having been unsuccessful in selling the stake in IDV to Rank Group to reduce the overall cost of the acquisition, Grand Met eventually bought the minorities.
42. Lord Sheppard of Didgemere, Obituary, *The Times* (4 April 2015).
43. Ibid.
44. Herzel and Shepro, *'Bidders and targets'*, refers to this deal as an exemplar of aggressive tactics in the 1980s takeover market.
45. 'Grand Met makes final Martell bid', *The New York Times* (16 January 1988). Seagram was the successful bidder for Martell.
46. Formerly known as Article 85, this deals with agreements between undertakings. For details refer to: http://ec.europa.eu/competition/legislation/treaties/ec/art81_en.html

47. Formerly known as Article 86, this deals with either joint or sole abuse of dominance cases. For details refer to: http://ec.europa.eu/competition/legislation/treaties/ec/art82_en.html
48. Burnside and Meyntjens, 'The EEC merger regulation', p 1373.
49. 'Adjournment Matter – Proposed Takeover of Irish Distillers', Seanad Eireann, Volume 120 (13 July 1988).
50. *'Proposed merger of Guinness PLC and Grand Metropolitan Public Limited Company'*, Listing Particulars (undated), p 14-17 for details on Guinness, and p 18-20 for details on Grand Met (available from the author on request).
51. Cope, 'Grand Met and Guinness in £23bn deal', *The Independent* (13 May 1997), quoting Seagram's vice-chairman, Robert Matschullat.
52. The European Commission analysed broad category, sub-category, price point and brand-specific factors and reached the conclusion: 'the relevant product markets .... are in general no wider than those for each of the individual internationally-recognised main spirit types (whiskey, gin, vodka, rum and so forth) ... Narrower definitions may, however, be appropriate to specific product and geographic areas' (p L 228/28).
53. Various conditions were attached to the remedy, including that Dewar's was sold with inventory of aging whisky to produce 3 million 9-litre cases per annum for a full seven years. Bacardi was the buyer of both brands.
54. Following the passing of the International Anti-trust Enforcement Assistance Act of 1994, the International Competition Policy Advisory Committee (ICPAC) was established under the auspices of the US Attorney General. The International Competition Network (ICN) was borne out of ICPAC, with a mission to 'advocate the adoption of superior standards and procedures in competition policy around the world, formulate proposals for procedural and substantive convergence' (see: http://www.internationalcompetitionnetwork.org/).
55. Nalebuff, *'Bundling, tying, and portfolio effects: part 1-conceptual issues'*, p 21-22 states '(while) the Chicago School argument is persuasive in a static context, it does not take into account the dynamic games that firms play'
56. Case No IV/M.938 Guinness/Grand Metropolitan, p L 288/29.
57. Nalebuff and Majerus, *'Bundling, tying, and portfolio effects: part 2- case studies'*, p 83-84.
58. Werden, 'Economic evidence on the existence of collusion', p 770-771, notes theory does not always provide sufficiently robust predictions of the actions real-world competitors take in pursuit of unilateral self-interest.
59. Rubinfeld, 'Market definition with differentiated products', is an expert witness account of the Post/Nabisco cereal merger of 1992. It criticises econometric models for being calibrated to imply products in the same segment are much closer substitutes than is really the case whereas products categorised in different segments are mathematically seen as insignificant substitutes.
60. EC Case COMP/M.2268. The EC did not identify any situations that would create or strengthen a dominant position or where there was the likelihood of the creation or strengthening of collective dominance.
61. FTC, C-4032. The FTC identified five relevant product markets of concern: premium rum, popular gin, deluxe Scotch, single malt Scotch and Cognac. Diageo agreed to divest its Malibu brand to an approved acquirer.
62. Bower, 'Vertical and financial ownership', p 656 anchors the PubCo business model to the novel 'breweries-for-pubs' swap between Grand Met and Courage, linking competition policy to the subsequent financialisation era.
63. In the case of a managed house the brewer owns the premises and the licensee is an employee of the brewer; the brewer bears all the costs of operating the house and receives all the revenue from it. In the case of a traditional tied tenancy, the brewer owns the premises but lets them to a tenant. The tenancy agreement specifies the rent and various purchasing obligations, usually including the obligation to buy all beer (except, where appropriate, a guest beer) from the brewer concerned. Tenants purchase the fixtures and fittings and stock on taking up the tenancies and sell them on relinquishment. They set retail prices and derive their income from the profit available after meeting costs such as purchase of supplies, rent and staff wages.
64. Monopolies and Mergers Commission, *'The supply of beer'*, p 453-454.

65. Lafontaine and Slade, '*Franchising and exclusive distribution*', p 396.
66. Perrett, 'How have different agreements affected the pub property market', *The Morning Advertiser* (5 March 2019), quotes data from the British Beer & Pub Association. In 1980 there were 69,000 pubs in the UK. By 2017, there were 48,350, of which the brewers controlled 4,000 managed and 7,000 tenanted and leased pubs. PubCos owned 5,400 managed and 9,300 tenanted, with some 22,650 pubs in independent hands.
67. Higgins, Toms and Uddin, 'Vertical monopoly power, profit and risk', p 673, notes that this ranged from a full drinks tie for all alcoholic and non-alcoholic drinks to a partial tie that only applied to beer.
68. The Code's two core principles are fair and lawful dealing by pub-owning businesses in relation to their tied tenants and that tied tenants should be no worse off than they would be if they were not subject to any product or service tie. Tenants can request a Market Rent Only (MRO) option to go free of tie in specific circumstances, including at a rent review or renewal of their tenancy.
69. For details see: https://www.camra.org.uk/pubs/save-our-pubs-campaign/pubs-code-and-adjudicator/
70. Brown, 'Heineken cleared to take over Punch Taverns', *The Financial Times* (18 August 2017).
71. McKendrick and Hannan, 'Oppositional Identities and resource partitioning' p 1273, note 'the near-total domination of the production of an iconic product by global diversified firms', suggesting it is only a matter of time before new entry of specialist traditional distillers will change these metrics. Weir (1989), however, identifies the former DCL as a virtual monopolist following the 1925 mergers that created a vertically integrated DCL group with both whisky production, brand ownership and international distribution arrangements.
72. Prominent Democratic Party senator, Elizabeth Warren, interviewed on the US cable news network CNBC on 24 July 2018 when asked about the fine imposed by the EC on Google said: 'What it shows is that Europe is serious about antitrust laws, Europe is serious about anti-competition laws, and the United States is lagging. We were once the leaders in the world on this, and no more'.
73. Aktas, de Bodt, and Roll, 'Is European M&A regulation protectionist?', p.1118.
74. Kinder, 'Lord Tyrie demands power to police big companies', *The Times* (9 May 2019).
75. Wood, 'Sainsbury's-Asda merger blocked by competition watchdog', *The Guardian* (25 April 2019).
76. Monopolies and Mergers Commission, '*The supply of beer*', p 5.

Disclosure statement

No potential conflict of interest was reported by the author(s).

References

Aktas, N., de Bodt, E., & Roll, R. (2007). Is European M&A regulation protectionist? *The Economic Journal*, *117*, 1096–1121.

Bartalevich, D. (2016). The influence of the Chicago School on the Commission's guidelines, notices and block exemption regulations in EU competition policy. *JCMS: Journal of Common Market Studies*, *54*(2), 267–283. https://doi.org/10.1111/jcms.12292

Berghahn, V. R. (2010). Varieties of capitalism in the "American Century". *Business History Review*, *84*(4), 661–663.

Bower, J. (2016a). Vertical and financial ownership: Competition policy and the evolution of the UK pub market. *Business History, 58*(5), 647–666. https://doi.org/10.1080/00076791.2015.1041380

Bower, J. (2016b). The Whitbread Umbrella: A structural response to shareholder activism. *Enterprise & Society, 17*(4), 874–903. 1https://doi.org/0.1017/eso.2016.3

Bower, J., & Cox, H. (2012). How Scottish & Newcastle became the UK's largest brewer: A case of regulatory capture?*Business History Review, 86*(1), 43–63. https://doi.org/10.1017/S0007680512000037

Burnside, A., & Meyntjens, C. (1990). The EEC merger regulation and its impact on non-EEC businesses. *Brigham Young University Law Review*, (4) 1373–1411.

Cassis, Y. (1997). *Big business: The European experience in the twentieth century*. Oxford University Press.

Chandler, A. D. (1995). Managers, families and financiers. In M. B. Rose (Ed.), *Family business: The international library of critical writings in business history*. 35–63. Edward Elgar.

Da Silva Lopes, T., & Casson, M. (2007). Entrepreneurship and the development of global brands. *Business History Review, 81*(4), 651–680. https://doi.org/10.2307/25097419

Da Silva Lopes, T., & Casson, M. (2012). Brand protection and the globalization of British business. *Business History Review, 86*(2), 287–310. https://doi.org/10.1017/S0007680512000414

Feldman, E. R., Gilson, S. C., & Villalonga, B. (2014). Do analysts add value when they most can? Evidence from corporate spin-offs. *Strategic Management Journal, 35*(10), 1446–1463. https://doi.org/10.1002/smj.2169

Fox, E. M. (2014). Monopolization and abuse of dominance: Why Europe is different. *The Antitrust Bulletin, 59*(1), 129–152. https://doi.org/10.1177/0003603X1405900106

Freyer, A. (1992). *Regulating big business – antitrust in Great Britain and America 1880-1990*. Cambridge University Press. https://doi.org/10.1086/ahr/98.3.838

Gerber, D. J. (1998). *Law and competition in twentieth-century Europe: Protecting prometheus*. Clarendon Press.

Gourvish, T. R., & Wilson, R. G. (1994). *The British brewing industry 1830–1980*. Cambridge University Press. https://doi.org/10.1086/ahr/100.2.520

Hall, P. A., & Soskice, D. (2001). *Varieties of capitalism: The institutional foundations of comparative advantage*. Oxford University Press.

Hannah, L. (1974). Takeover bids in Britain before 1950: An exercise in business 'pre-history. *Business History, 16*(1), 65–77. https://doi.org/10.1080/00076797400000031

Hannah, L. (2007). The 'divorce' of ownership from control from 1900 onwards: Re-calibrating imagined global trends. *Business History, 49*(4), 404–438. https://doi.org/10.1080/00076790701295821

Hautz, J., Mayer, M. C. J., & Stadler, C. (2013). Ownership identity and concentration: A study of their joint impact on corporate diversification. *British Journal of Management, 24*(1), 102–126. https://doi.org/10.1111/j.1467-8551.2011.00792.x

Herzel, L., & Shepro, R. W. (1990). *Bidders & targets: Mergers & acquisitions in the US*. Blackwells.

Higgins, D. M., & Toms, S. (2011). Explaining corporate success: The structure and performance of British firms, 1950–84. *Business History, 53*(1), 85–118. https://doi.org/10.1080/00076791.2011.546668

Higgins, D. M., Toms, S., & Uddin, M. (2016). Vertical monopoly power, profit and risk: The British beer industry, c.1970-c.2004. *Business History, 58*(5), 667–693. https://doi.org/10.1080/00076791.2015.1041381

Hovenkamp, H. (2010). Harvard, Chicago, and transaction cost economics in antitrust analysis. *The Antitrust Bulletin, 55*(3), 613–662. https://doi.org/10.1177/0003603X1005500305

Iversen, M. J. (2010). The "Varieties of Capitalism" approach as an analytical tool for business historians. *Business History Review, 84*(4), 664–666.

Jackson, B. (2012a). The think-tank archipelago: Thatcherism and neo-liberalism. In B. Jackson & R. Saunders (Eds.), *Making Thatcher's Britain*. Cambridge University Press.

Jackson, B. (2012b). Freedom, the common good, and the rule of law: Lippmann and Hayek on economic planning. *Journal of the History of Ideas, 73*(1), 47–68. https://doi.org/10.1353/jhi.2012.0011

Khan, L. M. (2017). Amazon's antitrust paradox. *The Yale Law Journal, 126*, 710–802.

Kokkoris, I. (2014). Introduction: EU and U.S. competition enforcement— Convergence or divergence. *The Antitrust Bulletin, 59*(1), 1–8. https://doi.org/10.1177/0003603X1405900101

La Porta, R., Lopez-de-Silanes, F., & Shleifer, A. (1999). Corporate ownership around the world. *The Journal of Finance, 54*(2), 471–517. https://doi.org/10.1111/0022-1082.00115

Lafontaine, F., Slade, M. E., (2015). Franchising and exclusive distribution: Adaptation and antitrust. In R. D. Blair & D. D. Sokol (Eds.), *Oxford handbook of international antitrust economics, 2* 387–414. Oxford University Press.

Lazonick, W. (2010). Innovative business models and varieties of capitalism: Financialization of the U.S. corporation. *Business History Review, 84*(4), 675–702. https://doi.org/10.1017/S0007680500001987

Maclean, M., Harvey, C., & Clegg, S. R. (2016). Conceptualizing historical organization studies. *Academy of Management Review, 41*(4), 609–632. https://doi.org/10.5465/amr.2014.0133

McKendrick, D. G., & Hannan, M. (2014). Oppositional Identities and resource partitioning: Distillery ownership in Scotch Whisky, 1826–2009. *Organization Science, 25*(4), 1272–1286. https://doi.org/10.1287/orsc.2013.0865

Morgan, G., & Kristensen, P. H. (2006). The contested space of multinationals: Varieties of institutionalism, varieties of capitalism. *Human Relations, 59*(11), 1467–1490. https://doi.org/10.1177/0018726706072866

Mutch, A. (2006). *Strategic and organizational change: From production to retailing in UK brewing 1950–1990*. Routledge.

Nalebuff, A. J. (2006). Bundling, tying and portfolio effects. Part 1, conceptual issues. DTI Economics Paper, Number 1. *Department of Trade and Industry* London UK.

Nalebuff, B. J. (2003). Bundling, tying and portfolio effects. Part 1, conceptual issues. DTI Economics Paper, Number 1. *Department of Trade and Industry*, London UK.

Nalebuff, B. J., & Majerus, D. (2003). Bundling, tying and portfolio effects. Part 2, case studies. DTI Economics Paper, Number 1. *Department of Trade and Industry*, London UK.

Payne, P. L. (1995). Family business in Britain: An historical and analytical survey. In M. B. Rose (Ed.), *Family business: The international library of critical writings in business history*. 171–206. Edward Elgar.

Perchard, A., Mackenzie, N. G., Decker, S., & Favero, G. (2017). Clio in the business school: Historical approaches in strategy, international business and entrepreneurship. *Business History, 59*(6), 904–927. https://doi.org/10.1080/00076791.2017.1280025

Pickering, J. F. (2013). Thoughts on the competition regime. *Utilities Law Review, 17*(1),c.

Roberts, R. (1992). Regulatory responses to the rise in the market for corporate control in Britain in the 1950s. *Business History, 34*(1), 183–200. https://doi.org/10.1080/00076799200000008

Rowlinson, M., Toms, S., & Wilson, J. F. (2007). Competing perspectives on the 'Managerial Revolution': From 'Managerialist' to 'Anti-Managerialist. *Business History, 49*(4), 464–482. https://doi.org/10.1080/00076790701296100

Rowlinson, M., Hassard, J., & Decker, S. (2014). Research strategies for organizational history: A dialogue between historical theory and organizational theory. *Academy of Management Review, 39*(3), 250–274.

Rubinfeld, D. L. (2000). Market definition with differentiated products: The Post/Nabisco cereal merger. *Antitrust Law Journal, 68*, 163–185.

Schulze, W. S., & Gedajlovic, E. R. (2010). Whither family business? *Journal of Management Studies, 47*(2), 191–204. https://doi.org/10.1111/j.1467-6486.2009.00887.x

Shleifer, A., & Vishny, R. W. (1991). Takeovers in the '60s and the '80s: Evidence and implication. *Strategic Management Journal, 12*(S2), 51–59. https://doi.org/10.1002/smj.4250121005

Shleifer, A., & Vishny, R. W. (1997). A survey of corporate governance. *The Journal of Finance, 52*(2), 737–783. https://doi.org/10.1111/j.1540-6261.1997.tb04820.x

Spicer, J., Thurman, C., Walters, J., & Ward, S. (2012). *Intervention in the modern UK brewing industry*. Palgrave Macmillan.

Statistical Handbook (2016). *British Beer & Pub Association*. London.

Toms, S., & Wright, M. (2002). Corporate governance, strategy and structure in British business history, 1950-2000. *Business History, 44*(3), 91–124. https://doi.org/10.1080/713999280

Van Essen, M., Carney, M., Gedajlovic, E. R., & Heugens, P. P. M. A. R. (2015). How does family control influence firm strategy and performance? A meta-analysis of US publicly listed firms. *Corporate Governance: An International Review, 23*(1), 3–24. https://doi.org/10.1111/corg.12080

Watson, K. (1996). Banks and industrial finance: The experience of brewers, 1880-1913. *The Economic History Review*, *49*(1), 58–81. https://doi.org/10.2307/2598448

Weir, R. (1989). Rationalization and diversification in the Scotch whisky industry, 1900-1939. *The Economic History Review*, *42*(3), 375–395. https://doi.org/10.2307/2596439

Werden, G. J. (2004). Economic evidence on the existence of collusion: Reconciling antitrust law with oligopoly theory. *Antitrust Law Journal*, *71*, 719–800.

Whittington, R., & Mayer, M. (2000). *The European corporation: Strategy, structure and social science*. Oxford University Press.

Wilkins, M. (2010). Multinational enterprises and the varieties of capitalism. *Business History Review*, *84*(4), 638–645.

Wilks, S. (1999). *In the public interest: Competition policy and the Monopolies and Mergers Commission*. Manchester University Press.

Zelizer, J. E. (2012). *Governing America: The revival of political history*. Princeton University Press.

'Settlers and comrades'. The variety of capitalism in South Africa, 1910–2016

Grietjie Verhoef

ABSTRACT

The complexities of business in Africa are illustrated through the case study of economic and business development of the different countries. By the time decolonisation brushed across Africa from the late 1950s, South Africa enjoyed political independence under white rule, controlling a viable economy based on mineral and industrial capitalism. This article shows the change in a powerful state-capitalist nexus from mining to the industry to ethnic or race-based 'empowerment'. Contesting nationalisms between Afrikaners and loyal British imperial sympathisers, constituted the rationale for inward-looking economic policies for national economic development. The formation of unstable coalitions for market co-ordination managed market distortion to facilitate the development of the leading modern industrial economy in Africa, while the rest of independent Africa experimented with central planning, socialism and state-capitalism. This study illustrates the peculiarity of capitalist development in Africa, specifically South Africa, considering the particular institutional contexts and broad business environment in which business acts strategically. South African business proactively engaged in a dynamic state/business relationship from national capitalism under minority rule, to an unstable balance of majority black capitalism, socialist worker welfare capitalism and tribal communalism. The manifestation of an unstable but unique state-business nexus involving market and non-market elements, adds innovation to the VoC framework.

Variety of capitalism in Africa

Africa entered the global market through exchange since the eighth century as Muslim trading networks expanded across the Maghreb to trade with African people. The commercial exchange of the trading network connected the northern parts of Africa with other trading networks (Iliffe, 1983; Sender and Smith, 1986; Verhoef, 2017; Wickins, 1981). Trade exchanges did not yet constitute capitalist economic relations in Africa. As the 'History of Capitalism' discourse shows, the concept developed to describe a variety of economic relations (Beaud, 2001; Kocka, 2009, 2010; Neal & Williamson, 2014). Capitalism emerged slowly from different impulses, and manifests in an institutional framework which left a legacy of a distinct 'variety' of capitalism. A critical agreement in this literature is that non-economic contexts are fundamental to understand the history of capitalism. These include social relations, culture, mentalities, politics and religion (Kocka, 2010, p. 24). The history of firms and markets links to the state, in the diverse African political, social, religious, cultural and ethnic traditions. This is the context of emerging capitalism (Wilkins, 2010). Capitalism and entrepreneurial success emerged in Africa in the relationship to a multitude of state configurations – often limiting the success of markets, entrepreneurs and firms (Iliffe, 1983; Sender and Smith, 1986, pp. 130–133; Wickins, 1981).

'African capitalism' is heterogeneous, because of the diversity of contexts of emergence (see Breckenridge, 2018; du Plessis, 2016). A central element is the state, operating in different degrees of participation or intervention in a complex dynamic power relationship between different stakeholders over a period of almost a century. The general view is that the poor African economies do not fit any of the typologies of VoC (Nölke & Vliegenthart, 2009; Rougier & Combarnous, 2017). Africa actually offers a unique case of different dynamisms replacing each other in the quest of market coordination. The state-market nexus shifts around contesting sources of power manipulating the market. In the analysis of global capitalism, comments about Africa remain sceptical. The continent is still considered to reflect 'immeasurable disasters', while 'the lost decade' in Africa is considered the result of take-off factors, such as government corruption, restrictive property regimes and poor education (Radice, 2015, p. 125, 140). Africa is on a highly diverse development path and Austin acknowledges Africa's 'formidable disadvantage of lateness' in the context of the Gerschenkronian latecomer model of development (Austin, 2016). Understanding the variety of capitalism in Africa mandates careful systematic analysis of the specific context of individual states. There is no 'African variety of capitalism' as argued in other limited geographical cases.[1] African economies share the long history of exchange, natural resource endowment, integration in the global economy, colonial and political domination and independence. Responses to the market varied. Post-independence macro-economic policies delivered a variety of political economies. Some were outright centrally planned socialist or command regimes. Some states moved closer to the capitalist market, but with a variety of state-market relations. The development of the market economy in South Africa takes a turn distinct from other African countries.[2] Feinstein argues that three characteristics account for the 'uniqueness' of the South African situation. In the first place, a significant portion of the indigenous population survived European colonisation. By the beginning of the nineteenth century the Khoisan and African population counted around1.5 million, expanding to 4 million by 1904, just after the British conquest in the South African War (1899–1902). Secondly, more European settlers settled permanently in the colonies ultimately consolidating into the Union, than in any other British colony not established as a settler colony. In the third instance, the sheer size of the gold deposits discovered on the Witwatersrand in 1886 compared to none other mineral discoveries in any British colony (Feinstein, 2005). Possible generalisations may deliver superficial similarities, but this article argues that a specific variety of capitalism has evolved in South Africa. This is a racial market economy (RME). This market economy establishes a very special case in the twenty-first century.

This study uses critical historical source analysis of primary and secondary material. The VoC theoretical framework and analytical concepts, encapsulating analytical developments displayed in the literature, inform the analysis of the complex South African history. The bulk of current source material is online documents and newspapers, as private archives of actors are inaccessible to the public.

Varieties theory

The Political Economy discourse on South Africa dismisses the Varieties of Capitalism (VoC) analysis of South African history as 'a-historic', because of the 'firm-centric' approach to developments. This literature offers essentially a class analysis paradigm in the neo-Poulantzian fractions of capital paradigm, referring to relations between finance, industry and the state as the drivers of 'continuity in change' (see Ashman et al., 2010; Fine, 2009; Padyachee, 2013). The discourse about capitalism and the long history of racial segregation in South Africa, followed the French Marxist anthropologist (Claude Meillassoux, Maurice Godelier, with a compendium by David Seddon (Godelier, 1977; Meillassoux, 1971, 1972; Seddon, 1978) literature of the early 1970s. The so-called 'radical' or neo-Marxist revision of South African history sought to 'get beyond the liberal problematic' (Marks & Atmore, 1980, p. 1.) refuting the consensus of the *Oxford History of South Africa (vols 1 & 2, 1969, 1971)* arguing that South African history was one of racial and ethnic conflict (Atmore & Westlake, 1972; Legassick, 1972a, 1972b; Marks, 1972, p. 10). The revisionists argued that race was a class construction (as was ethnicity and nationalism) utilised by the state (aligned to capital) to exploit labour. There was no inherent contradiction between capital and the system of racial segregation in South Africa,[3] as suggested by the liberal historiography. The neo-Marxists maintained that policies of racial and ethnic separation constituted the material reality of a constructed 'white identity' or 'Afrikaner nationalism' by capital, in collaboration with the state, for 'the super exploitation of labour', which was primarily black (Johnstone, 1979). Statutory segregation in urban areas, banning black trade unions, granting voting rights only to whites and control of the physical movement of black persons to 'white' areas, were all class mechanisms of business, in a 'fraction of state capital class' to secure capital accumulation through the exploitation of labour. The British imperial strategy to control the resource wealth of the colonies, caused conflict with settlers and mine-owners, but those differences were set aside to prevent the rise and competing independent African politics (Feinstein, 2005, p. 35). Feinstein nevertheless systematically rejected the neo-Marxist ideological construction, by proving that racial segregation did not benefit the development of a capitalist economy in South Africa. It actually undermined sustained growth (Feinstein, 2005, pp. 244–251). The materialist class analysis did not engage with the VoC literature, but explained intra-sectoral conflict (agriculture, mining, and manufacturing) as Poulantzian fractions of capitalist class cohesion, mitigated through state policies and statutes (Davies et al., 1976; Davies, 1979). Business' agency is reduced to pre-determined class conduct.

The discourse on comparative capitalism of the political economists of the 1990s remains within a systems predetermined analysis, which leaves the perspective of business marginalised. Hall and Soskice's (2001) *Varieties of Capitalism* (Hall & Soskice, 2001) brings the institutional perspective of agents in society and the economy to bear on a dynamically changing relationship of advantage. Business emerges as agents of institutional dynamics and the firm, considered in a relational perspective, is the vehicle of coordination, interaction and performance. The core competencies of firms position them to engage in coordination on five levels. These five areas of coordination are relations between employers and employees in-group (industrial) relations. The next level is relations on the individual level between firm and employees (competencies, selection, information sharing) and the third level of the relationship with labour deals with education or training. The firm is central to these employee relations, but also has to negotiate its relations with its suppliers and with other firms, that is inter-firm relations, that is the dimension of corporate governance. The firm thus operates in markets (for factors of production-capital, labour, resources) and non-market institutions. The business dimension to the development of societies and economies is that the firm takes centre stage in defining the national economy. This perspective then distinguishes between two types of market organization: the 'liberal market economy ' (LME) and the 'coordinated market economy' (CME). Both these forms of market economies operate in the context of institutions, organisations and culture specific to the society. It is especially in the context of coordinated firm behaviour that 'collaborative' action rather than 'competitive' action characterises the market (Hall & Soskice, 2001, VoC, pp. 1–12).

In each national context, the sustainability of the market economy is dependent upon the stability of market relations, with different levels of competition and coordination. The culture of institutions and the specific set of formal institutions affect the nature of coordination required to achieve equilibrium in the economy. It is on this level that nation or country specific contexts are key to explain national developments. The dynamic relationship between market, hierarchies and networks underpin firm behaviour, since firms do not control the overarching institutions of the political economy. This is where the coordination function of firms is fundamental. Hall and Soskice argue that certain institutions seem to complement the specific nature of the market structure, especially in CMEs. Institutional complementarity means mutually reinforcing and supportive functioning of institutions to enhance efficiency returns (Hall & Soskice, 2001, VoC, pp. 12–15). The concepts of 'complementarities' and 'system coordination' are the core VoC tools enabling real historical analysis of social and economic development liberated from the class determinism of political economy. The critical intellectual vibrancy of the VoC offers a dynamic analytical framework of institutional subsystems aligning capital, labour and product markets, driving the development of modern societies. These relations reinforce each other or disrupt equilibria, engendering renewed coordination.

Criticism of a too simplistic and static explanation of the development of market economies, specifically pertaining to a more pronounced role of the state and responses to broad economic shifts and shocks, have led to theoretical refinement of the VoC analytical framework. New developments in the VoC literature have taken into account also the impact of exogenous shocks or pressures (developments outside the national political economy) on the national economy. New attention is devoted to firms not as 'institutional-takers' but as autonomous agents. A wider consideration of firms in other sectors in the economy apart from the manufacturing sector, especially tertiary sector conduct, emerged in specific country analyses. This also allowed for a stronger consideration of the role of the state (Hancké et al., 2007, pp. 1–32).

The critical reflection on the initial VoC framework resulted from the application thereof to a wider range of state systems and geographies. As the world faced the onset of global geo-political reconfiguration following the collapse of the USSR and subsequent emergence of states in Eastern Europe grappling with market reconfigurations, the effects of the global financial crisis and subsequent European credit crises, and the rise of China, the relative simple dual LME and CME models were open to critique. In the post-cold war globalising market, new dimensions of negotiated coordination opened to a critical reflection on earlier or long-established commitments of, for example, employers to workers. Since the 1980s, the impact of the political leadership of Margaret Thatcher and Ronald Reagan pushed towards market deregulation and the renegotiation of coordination. These developments indeed presented a disruption of existing coordination and institutional complementarities, which shifted and displayed institutional flexibility (Hancké et al., 2007, pp. 10–13).

The development in emerging market economies delivered mixed-market political economies, accounting for new dimensions of institutional coordination and relations with the state. Hall and Gingerich (2004) considered the so-called 'mid-spectrum' or mixed-market political economies as developing capacities for coordination under conditions of sub-optimal state coordination. This is an important observation, especially for the analysis of African economies, specifically South Africa. The critique of how the VoC analysis initially dealt with the role of the state enters an enhanced level in the context of the renewed role assumed by the state in the wake of the GFC, as well as in the context of emerging market economies. The critique of the LME/CME dualism went on to ask explanations about emerging market economies, such as India, China and Brazil. The two-tiered VoC model developed around western economies, made way for new models. This included the HME (hierarchical market economy) Schneider identified in Latin American economies. The HME identifies hierarchical coordination between vertically integrated diversified business groups, (*grupo economico)*, MNCs (multinational corporations), low skilled labour and atomistic labour relations (Schneider, 2007, 2009). Another new model is the SME model (state-permeated market economies), which emerged from considering the 'dependent market economies' of East Central Europe (Nölke & Vliegenthart, 2009). This model assigns a strong role to the state in cooperating with the national elite, an omnipresent public sector and competition by state-owned entities. In this model 'clans' or family business interests or the state dominate business and perform the coordinating function. The alliance between families and the state secure a low cost structure for business (see Nölke & Claar, 2013). This SME model describes particular contexts in emerging markets, but the diversity in such market place serious limitations to the usefulness thereof for analysis of the variety of capitalism in emerging markets. These two models seem especially relevant for the South African case, since the nature, organisation and functioning of the business sector is neither 'clan-like' nor class-based, but has vertically integrated diversified business groups and an active state.

The nuanced opening up of the original VoC model in response to empirical evidenced critique, offer a point of departure for considering the case of South Africa. Departing from the observation by Streeck that institutional complementarities in political economies are often the outcome of prolonged class and industrial conflict of the past, the South African case is considered. The solutions to such disputes are in functionally interdependent institutions with the power to distribute and the power to sustain specific sectoral interests (Streeck, 2005). This insight allows an understanding of the dynamic interplay between networks of interests, classes, coalitions and other socio-political formations in societies of deep diversity. In building on the Hall and Soskice acknowledgement of different modes of coordination, Hancké et al note that networks of interests may emerge to effect institutional coordination. These networks may be politically constructed and built on elite networks seeking to control strategic sectors of the economy. A very important extension of the VoC framework is the strategic role that labour assumed in national settlements between labour and capital. These coalitions may either be institutionalised or dissolve as the strategic need disappear. Developments in societies in transition, from centrally planned economies to market economies, or from specific coalitions in CMEs to new coalitions, have displayed a more activist state performing a crucial role in defining, supporting and organising the economic growth model (Hancké et al., 2007, pp. 16–24).

In South Africa, a very specific politically induced coalition between capital, labour and the state developed since the mid-1980s. From this time on the nature of institutional coordination changed fundamentally in response to political shocks. The institutional organisation of South Africa changed radically since 1990. Nattrass and Seekings, and Nattrass (who only consider the post-1980 period) argued that South Africa does not fit 'neatly' into any VoC type, because of the 'heavy hand of the state' (Nattrass, 2014; Nattrass & Seekings, 2010). This is an outdated observation, since the SME model adapted to explain developments in Eastern and Central Europe since the early 1990s, captures exactly that phenomenon. The coordination of institutions, business and labour by the state between 1910 and 1990 was different. The original VoC CME ideal type model may be more useful for the pre-1980s. The South African case plays out in two phases – before and after 1990. This requires an alignment of the CME model to the broader context of globalisation, the end of USSR domination in East and Central Europe and decolonisation in Africa. The extended framework of dynamic operation of business, firms, labour, society and the state has the potential to explain what occurred in South Africa. Specific aspects of the South African development calls for closer explanation.

South Africa in the European sphere

The history of South Africa does not start in 1910 when South Africa became a constitutional Union, but the formation of the Union consolidated political power around a single market economy characterised by social divisions of race and economic means. The capitalist mode of coordination was primarily a LME, with the state at arm's length, formulating a broad policy framework within which business operated. A fragile coalition of mining, industrial and agricultural capital balanced in a political consensus to secure political unification of the four British colonies. The latter was a precondition for economic progress, premised on uniform tariffs, railway connections and unfettered access to ports. The economic disruption and destruction of assets caused by the South African War (1899–1902) in itself forced the two archenemies, the Afrikaner agricultural community and the English/British mining and industrial businesspersons, to devise an economic recovery plan. While much of the post-war recovery was cyclical post-war recovery (Schumann, 1938, p. 112), small industries produced primarily processed agricultural goods and products sheltered by the needs of the gold mining industry (Pearsall, 1937, p. 45). Prior to political unification the logic of market coordination brought political leaders of the four British Colonies (Cape Colony, Transvaal Colony, Orange River Colony, Natal) together in a conference in 1908 to discuss the establishment of a Customs Union. Before the South African War, the Boer republics introduced restrictive tariffs and customs duties on trade from the other colonies, affecting adversely on trade and goods flows to the mining complex on the Witwatersrand. The Customs conference failed to agree on customs duties, tariffs and railway links. The political issues on the location of power in a unified constitutional system, franchise, the 'poor white problem' and a capital city dominated deliberations, while business interests were eager to arrive at an agreement on economic policy to diversify the narrow base of the economy. The formation of the Union was indeed a compromise between Afrikaner nationalist ambitions to restore political independence from Britain, and English-speaking colonists seeking a consolidated market economy, with access to the wider market of the British Empire (Thompson, 1978). The compromise of Union returned political power to Afrikaners and market consolidation to business. An important dimension of the compromise was the exclusion of black franchise, except a small number retaining a qualified vote in the Cape Colony before 1910. During the next two decades, a racially exclusive coalition developed a complex coalition in a market increasingly displaying the characteristics of a CME. The coalition between contesting white 'settlers' – English-speaking British loyalist business, and Afrikaner nationalists refusing to be considered 'settlers' – was fragile. This nationalist-cultural dimension divided the white population, but the 'two (white) races'[4] engaged in strained institutional market coordination. This emerging coalition reflected a cross-nationalist or cross-cultural dimension, as opposed to the cross-class nature identified by Hankcé et al. (p. 23). The state became a strategic tool to facilitate market coordination, albeit unstable. Mutual agreement on the internal reproduction of the business network gained slow momentum as the state implemented inward-oriented industrial policies and mobilised strategic resources though state-owned enterprises (SOEs) to support the local mining and manufacturing industry.

The business coalition remained fragile. English-speaking businesspersons dominated the mining and industrial capital. Afrikaners of the Cape wheat, wool and wine farms and the northern maize belt, constituted agricultural capital. Afrikaners (comprising 51.8 percent of the white population)[5] through the South African Party under the leadership of former Boer General Louis Botha made up a significant portion of the first Union Government as a self-governing Dominion in the British Empire. Foreign banks controlled the financial sector. English-speaking business controlled smaller financial entities, such as building societies. Weak business organisation and growing political animosity between Afrikaner nationalist leadership and English business undermined institutional coordination. A complex disequilibrium existed. Afrikaners made up a slight majority of the white population, but did not control the economy. Extreme poverty amongst a substantial proportion of Afrikaners following the South African War, adverse climatic conditions and a lack of skills to succeed in a new urbanised environment, consolidated Afrikaner nationalist ambitions to secure the upliftment of their people and steady access into the mainstream of the economy. While Afrikaner cultural and church leaders embarked on extended programmes of poverty alleviation and empowerment, the English business fraternity insisted on the resolution of the pre-union unresolved issues on the protection of domestic industries. Uniform customs duties, tariffs and railway links were left unresolved before unification. Having agreed to the Union, business interests secured the appointment of the Cullinan Commission in 1910, to investigate the feasibility of establishing local industries. The passing of the Customs Tariff Act, No 26 of 1914 (shortly before the outbreak of the First World War) was the first manifestation of an emerging fragile coalition between the Afrikaner controlled state and local industrial business interests. The customs duties, which were revenue oriented and relatively low, was enthusiastically supported by the merchant business lobby, represented by the Cape Town merchant J W Jagger, but disappointed industrialists. The latter lobby wanted more comprehensive tariff protection to nurture infant industries. After the interruption of the Great War, a temporary Board of Trade and Industries investigated the protection, sustainability and expansion of existing industries. The state was pro-industry. The Prime Minister called for '...proper and legitimate protection to our industries' (Feinstein, 2005; Jones & Müller, 1992; Lumby, 1981). Responding to higher global tariffs in the wake of the post-war depression in Australia in 1921, and the USA in 1922, the Board of Trade and Industries (BTI) proposed higher tariffs in 1923. These marginally higher tariffs backed by English industrial interests coincided with mounting Afrikaner economic nationalism, which steered the South African LME economy closer to a CME market by the mid-1920s.

Nationalist oriented Afrikaners mobilised in a new political party, the National Party, insisting on British recognition of South African autonomy. General J B M Hertzog, the leader of the National Party championed the slogan 'South Africa first'.[6] As the Statute of Westminster, 1931, finally acknowledged the sovereignty and equality of all Dominions in the British Commonwealth, a strong South Africanism developed around Afrikaner nationalism, providing the basis for the strengthening of the weak coalition between English-speaking and emerging Afrikaner business interests.

By the late 1920s Afrikaner economic empowerment gained momentum since the 1915 establishment of *De Nasionale Pers*, with newspaper *De Burger* entering the media business. Soon followed in 1918 the establishment of short-term and long–term insurance companies: *Suid-Afrikaanse Nasionale Trust en Assuransie Maatskappy (Santam)* and *Suid-Afrikaanse Nasionale Lewensversekerings Maatskappy (Sanlam)*. In 1923 Afrikaners established a commercial bank, *Volkskas,* in 1942 they established an industrial finance house, *Federale Volksbeleggings Beperk (FVB)* and building society, *Saambou Nasionale Bouvereniging,* in 1952 a general bank Trust Bank, and in 1953 a mining house, *Federale Mynbou Beperk (Fedmyn)* (Dommisse, 2005; Giliomee, 2003; Verhoef, 2018). An Afrikaner entrepreneur Anton Rupert established a tobacco company in 1948, with a load from FVB, and built it into the diversified cigarette and spirits conglomerate Rembrandt Corporation. Afrikaner business by the mid-1970s had a presence in all sectors of the economy, but could still only claim a contribution of an aggregate 20.8 percent (excluding agriculture) to the private sector economy in South Africa, as opposed to 9.6 percent in the 1940s (Sadie, 2002, p. 28). Afrikaner political, economic and cultural mobilisation benefitted from the political victory of the National Party and Labour Party election pact in 1924. A cross-class coalition (between Afrikaner nationalist political and economic interests and white labour and English business) developed a precarious equilibrium dependent on the state to sustain this mode of coordination.[7] The ascendancy of Afrikaner business aligned with the nationalist policies of the state and slowly generated a coalition with English industrial and mining power.

Inward-looking industrialisation was administered through two parallel processes: the first was tariff protection, customs duties and later import quotas. The second was domestic state-supported infrastructure and general industry enhancing economic 'infrastructure'. The latter occurred through the establishment of SOEs. These included the Electricity Supply Commission (ESCOM) in 1923, the Iron and Steel Corporation of South Africa (ISCOR) in 1922, the Industrial Development Corporation of South Africa (IDC) in 1942 and the South African Oil and Gas Corporation (SASOL) in 1951. Smaller SOEs were in phosphate development, atomic energy production, and much later armament development (ARMSCOR). The transport sector was always organised in the state Department of Railways and Harbours (SAR&H) and water supply through provincial and municipal entities (see Clarke, 1994; Christie, 1984; Verhoef, 2010, pp. 143–157, 2014, pp. 448–477; 2015, pp. 33–59). SASOL was privatised in 1979, and ISCOR in 1987, and so were parts of ARMSCOR and Telkom, the telecommunication fixed line supplier, after 1994. Transport, electricity and water remain SOE utilities, the typical 'commanding heights' of state intervention (Verhoef, 2014). Private business could acquire shares in the SOEs, but never to a level of control. The state performed a coordinating role through the SOEs in facilitating industrial enterprise through infrastructure delivery and cooperation with business and labour, as suggested in the SME model of state-permeated market economies.

The fragile business coalition, fostered by a shared efficiency-seeking motive, held the CME mode of market coordination together. The state, controlled by the political opponents of English-speaking capital, assisted coordination on four levels. In the sphere of industrial relations statutory regulation of employment conditions, access to categories of work, determinants of wage levels and industrial organisation defined the context of business' relation to labour. Legislation determined racial restrictions to certain categories of work differentiated racial wage levels, access to certain types of vocational training and education and prohibited the organisation of black trade unions. On the level of corporate governance, firms enjoyed access to well-capitalised banks and other specialised financial institutions as well as the local bourse, where a steady flow of foreign investment entered the economy. Foreign shareholders controlled the two largest banks up to the late 1970s. On the level of inter-firm relations, large diversified corporate entities developed interests across all sectors of the economy. These conglomerates often displayed the 'clan' or family control alluded to by Nölke and Vliegenthart (2009), but public listing diversified the shareholder profile. It is on the fourth level of firm relations with employees that state policies of racial segregation finally threatened to derail the business coalition. This article will not engage with the extended statutory apparatus of the state between the 1920s and the mid-1980s seeking to sustain the institutional coordination of the market. What is important for the VoC discourse is that the specific institutional arrangements consciously designed in response to strategic interactions between 'socio-economic actors', as Streeck (2005) formulated it, (or the initially culturally opposing nationalisms of the white business community in South Africa) came under severe pressure (Feinstein, 2005, pp. 200–223; Jones, 2002). This followed economic inefficiencies, macro-economic underperformance, declining manufacturing productivity, collapsing foreign investment, international political pressure and mobilised black domestic opposition. The indigenisation policies of the state (mandating financial institutions to incorporate in South Africa and later to transfer majority shareholding to local shareholders) added to the concentration of business (see Nattrass, 2014, pp. 61–62; Nattrass & Seekings, 2010, pp. 25–27; Jones, 2002, pp. 165–194; Verhoef, 2009, pp. 157–197; Yudelman, 1983, pp. 7–8). What was under pressure, were not the complementarities of the distributive settlements *per se*, but the racial composition thereof.

The dilemma of the South African CME by the 1980s was that the economy switched from 'apparently triumphant progress to distressing decline'.[8] GDP growth (at 1995 constant prices) declined from 4.9 percent between 1951 and 1955, and 6.3 percent between 1961 and 1965, to below 2 percent by the first half of the 1980s.[9] Economic stagnation placed the firm-employee relations under excessive strain. This coincided with mounting international pressure against the white minority government, resulting in the transition to a universal democracy in 1994. Decolonisation occurred systematically in African with the withdrawal of colonial administration since the early 1950s, culminating in the independence of Zimbabwe in 1980. Growing domestic instability finally led to the unbanning of banned black political parties and the return from exile of their leadership. Organised business across all sectors and language orientation mobilised behind negotiations to secure the stability of the institutional equilibrium. The potential contradiction and threat to the CME was fundamental socialism. Marxist- Communist supported exiled black political organisations (the exiled African National Congress (ANC) and the Pan-Africanist Congress (PAC), the South African

Communist party (SACP) and domestic Black Conscious Movement, and United Democratic Front (UDF) alike) mobilised mass support subscribing to the ideologies of their foreign allies, the former USSR, China and newly independent states in the Non-Aligned Movement. The black political parties rallied back to South Africa and in the 1994 elections, the ANC secured an undisputed victory of 62 percent. The elephant in the room was whether South Africa was bound to follow the course of development of many newly independent African states.

Comrades challenge settler market

After independence, private non-indigenous business either disinvested from Africa, were nationalised or experienced that state-led market distortion undermined opportunities to conduct successful business. Without exception, and in different stages of the implementation of national economic strategies, did the new African states introduce policies of indigenisation as a form of economic regulation (Beveridge, 1991, pp. 302–333). Indigenisation meant compulsory transfer of ownership from foreign to local owners. African indigenisation programmes failed to deliver on efficient economic empowerment and sustaining a market economy, partly also because of an incapacity to effect any form of institutional coordination. The extended public sector crowded out private enterprise and state policies seldom embraced the market economy (Grosh & Mukandalala, 1994; Nellis, 2005).

The South African case offers several unique elements. Nowhere in Africa was a European population present in a similar proportion to the indigenous black population, as in South Africa (Feinstein, 2005, p. 1). State policies in support of inward-looking industrialisation enabled business and labour coordination, albeit along racially divided lines.[10] While Afrikaner economic empowerment was self-driven, subsequent state policies restricting full participation in the national economy by black people, generally enjoyed the support of Afrikaner business – at least until such time as market distortion coincided with exogenous factors to cause serious economic inefficiencies and stagnation (Lipton, 1984, pp. 368–376). What is universally ignored (because it could be interpreted as acknowledging an element of justification of racial segregation), is that the policy of separate development encouraged black business development. This occurred in confined racially demarcated markets, in locations of traditional land ownership under the authority of tribal or indigenous authority, or in multi ethnic urban townships. Racial segregation confined the market in which blacks' business could operate, to the demarcated areas, but also excluded established white-owned businesses from competing with the small emerging black-owned businesses. No doubt, prevention from competition in open markets, constitute market distortion and restricted entrepreneurs from taking risks to grow. Since the 1960s the Bantu Investment Corporation Act, No 34 of 1959, established investment corporations for each ethnic homeland,[11] which promoted and subsidised agricultural, mining, industrial and business development in the homelands, as well as in the areas of Indian and Coloured communities. The BICs supported development through subsidies, investments, business planning, business advice and managerial mentorship support (du Toit, 1976; Malan & Hattingh, 1975; Nattrass, 1982, pp. 190–224). While this policy constituted market distortion in seeking to promote development outside the urban core of South Africa, it nevertheless supported the development of an extended network of black-owned enterprises, both in the homelands as well as in urban areas.[12] The BIC operations were a fundamental component of racial segregation and as such undermined the development of a single CME. It aimed at bringing black entrepreneurs into the market, not exclude them from participation.

African peasants responded positively to the opportunities of capitalist surplus production outside the traditional market (Bundy, 1979; Hellmann, 1950), but the state managed a very specific 'variety of capitalism' of racial segregation by preserving the traditional sector alongside the emerging market economy. African and Indian business were initially small owner-managed, geographically confined to statutory prescribed locations, undiversified, generally limited to food distribution and the services sector (limited manufacturing), weak capital base – operating on a cash basis, limited access to banking services, especially credit and little attention to succession planning. The small enterprises formed mutually supportive networks and worked within the structural limitations of racial segregation, albeit consistently opposing the system and calling for the abolition segregation. S J J Lesolang, a leading African businessperson in Johannesburg, acknowledged that the decentralisation policy of Government met with opposition, but had '... created employment facilities for thousands of our people...'[13] Trade associations spread across the country and in April 1964. The National African Chamber of Commerce (NAFCOC) was formed to co-ordinate the activities of its member associations in promoting African business development. The first President was Richard Maponya, a prominent executive from Soweto. As the African buying power strengthened from R487m in 1969, to rise to R7, 5 billion by the end of the twentieth century (Motsuenyane, 2011; NAFCOC Milestones, 1994), the organisation emerged as a champion of African opposition to racial segregation.[14] NAFCOC campaigned to speed up the 'radical upliftment' of Africans through the 'buy-at-home' campaign. Black consumers were encouraged to buy from black business, thereby utilising the policies of racial segregation to foster African business. The success of African business development was that the number of African enterprises in Johannesburg alone rose from1 137 in 1959 to 11 460 in 1969 (Mogotsi, 1977). NAFCOC opposed free access by white and Indian traders to African townships.[15] From radically different ideological positions, the African business community and the Government pragmatically agreed to limit free trade.

A well-organised African business fraternity developed in demarcated urban areas as well as the homelands with NAFCOC as its voice. NAFCOC had no power to oppose state policies but to do so publically. *De facto* the organisation could only use its numbers to support its members, negotiate discounts for bulk buying, or networking entrepreneurs. When economic stagnation set in in the wake of global deregulation, international sanctions against the policy of racial segregation, the fragile business coalition in the CME was at risk. By the late 1970s the state lifted restrictions on the establishment of African trade unions, granted Africans 'right of 99 year leasehold' to own land in urban African townships in 1978,[16] scrapped job reservations by 1982 and abolished influx control in 1986. In 1988, the state repealed all the regulations requiring annual licences, prohibition of land acquisition and operating a second business within a certain radius of his spouse's business.[17] Black enterprise could expand beyond former boundaries, facilitating established business concerns such as that of Richard Maponya, David Tshabalala and the Kunene Brothers to expand, diversify and accumulate extensive capital (Verhoef, 2017, pp. 112–114).

The state-business nexus of the pre-1970s shifted to profound state-business tension. It was apparent that 'the institutionalised compromise that worked relatively well in the past and which persisted because of the potential and actuality of strategic 'functional complementarity', (Hancké et al., 2007, p. 22) had become an institutional arrangement of which the complementarity stemmed from a distributive arrangement of which the *raison d'etre* eroded and declined' (Hancké et al., 2007, p. 22; Streeck, *2005). The benefit that relative political stability brought to business, no longer prevailed. The institutional complementarity between white labour and largely Afrikaner business, disintegrated completely when the state sanctioned black trade unions in 1979. This ushered in a period of unprecedented labour volatility, disruptive strike action and the convergence of black labour activism with the political agenda of black political rights in the Republic of South Africa (see Feinstein, 2005, pp. 240–243; Lipton, 1984, pp. 340–344). The anomalies of seeking selectively to implement the global liberal market tendencies in South Africa while sustaining an exclusionary and discriminatory political system disrupted the state-business nexus. The regulated inclusion of black business aspirations in assigned pockets of the market in order to implement a policy of racial segregation and separate development was untenable.

A series of events and developments between the mid-1980s and the mid-1990s illustrated the reconfiguration of the business coalition, an unprecedented renegotiated state-business nexus and the gradual emergence of a new institutional complementarity between newly configured business and labour. It is significant that business took the initiative to enter into negotiations with the politically marginalised or banned black political leadership, and not the state. Business carefully sculptured a pro-active intra-business coalition. The business sector put pressure on the state to legalise black trade unions, which occurred in 1979. Unprecedented domestic turbulence erupted as domestic opposition mobilised civil protest through the United Democratic Front (UDF), and black trade unions engaged in strike action organised by the newly established Congress of South African Trade Unions (COSATU – finally consolidated in 1985). Since business still displayed a fragile coalition between Afrikaans and English-speaking businesspersons, the domestic instability gave rise to extra-parliamentary organisations, initiated by business, to search for a bridge over the troubled waters. One such organisation was the Urban Foundation (UF), jointly established by Mr Harry Oppenheimer of the Anglo-American Corporation, and Mr Anton Rupert, of Rembrandt – representing English and Afrikaans business. The UF mobilised business (including black business in NAFCOC) to address the needs of the urbanised black population as statutory segregation had been abolished. Sanlam also joined the UF and from 1985 used research capacity in its investment company, Sankorp, to devise strategies to address the explosive situation amongst the urban black population.[18] Business openly challenged the state. Dr A D Wassenaar, CEO of Sanlam, criticised the state in public for excessive intervention in the economy (see Wassenaar, 1977). The state then engaged in public consultation with business (through the so-called Carlton and Good Hope conferences (in 1979 and 1981) on the wisdom of a liberal market-oriented macro-economic policy. Rupert wrote private letters to the President P W Botha, claiming the cost of segregation policies to the economy, as well as expressing concern about the economic mismanagement of the state (see Giliomee, 2003, p. 622). Afrikaans businessmen (*Afrikaanse Handelsinstituut* (AHI)[19] – Afrikaans Chamber of Commerce) and organised English-speaking business[20] criticised the state for the lack of reform in economic and racial policies. Expectations were high that the President P W Botha would announce fundamental steps towards the dismantling of the policy of separate development in August 1985 (his so-called 'Rubicon' address). His failure to articulate wide expectations of reform resulted in external and domestic outrage. In the USA Chase Manhattan Bank refused to roll debt over, followed by other South African creditors, forcing South Africa to declare a debt moratorium and negotiate debt repayments. At home, domestic violence erupted, causing the state twice to declare a state of emergency (Cairncross, 1985; Goedhuys, 1994).

At this crucial point business emerged with a unified 'business' voice, setting language and cultural barriers aside. On the back of Sankorp research, the UF addressed needs of a growing black urban population on education, social and political aspirations of the young black urban population. Business was publically outspoken about the adversity of sanctions, especially to the most vulnerable segment of the population.[21] Business took agency in initiating talks with the black political organisations in exile, first by the Chairman of the Board of Directors of the Anglo American Corporation (AAC), and later by a group of 'eminent persons' (Afrikaans academics), which included business leaders of Sanlam. By 1980 AAC was the largest conglomerate in South Africa, comprising 53.6 percent of the market capitalisation of the Johannesburg Stock Exchange. The first meeting was in Lusaka in September 1986, when Gavin Relly, Chairman of AAC, led a delegation of businessmen to talk to the ANC and 'Comrades' (Adam et al., 1998; Beinart, 2001; Handley, 2008). Then in 1987, the Afrikaans academics and business leaders met with the ANC leaders in Dakar, Senegal (Giliomee, 2003). More meetings followed in Munich in October 1988 and Paris June 1989 and in February 1990, the President F W de Klerk announced the unbanning of exiled black political parties. Negotiations to secure a peaceful transition to a unitary democracy was not about securing democracy, but about securing the market economy. There were no negotiations between the pre-1994 government and the black political leaders in exile. It was organised business in a self-styled coalition going out to those in exile to talk about the future. The final negotiations towards the new democratic elections was a protracted multi-party affair between early 1992 and end 1993 when a final agreement was reached on an election, a draft constitution and a transitional Government of National Unity (GNU) (Beinart, 2001; Davenport & C Saunders, 2000).

On this level of institutional coordination, the new dimension to the VoC debate enters the discourse. The fragile culturally divided business coalition converged into a more unified coordinated entity. Business emerged from direct confrontation with the state, to a position where a future state had to be negotiated with 'Comrades', or people entering the negotiations on a populist, socialist agenda in partnership with the SACP. The policy programme of the ANC, PAC and SACP propagated radical economic transformation, 'redistribution' of assets (nationalisation), and worker empowerment. Business' urgent agency in exerting pressure on the state to abandon the policy of racial segregation and allow the full implementation of a liberal market economy was crucial. The De Klerk government had limited bargaining power. The ANC knew it had the vast majority of the black vote. De Klerk tried to secure 'group rights', the protection of 'minority rights' and the status of the Afrikaans language, but the ANC stalled multi-party negotiations for a democratic election by walking out of negotiations. The ANC refused to allow any pre-conditions to the negotiations. The De Klerk government entered the first democratic elections on 27 April 1994 without any safeguards for minority entities. The 'debate' between the outgoing state and the confident ANC led black majority, was no debate, but an orderly submission to the numerical majority. The stakes were to prevent the country from burning as Africa had after decolonisation. An agreement was signed in September 1993 providing for the election, an interim constitution to be ratified by the new parliament, and that the new parliament would decide on the final new constitution – the ANC assumed it would control that process.

Business' 'political intervention' by entering into talks with exiled black political parties (especially the ANC, the party widely expected to win majority support in the case of a democratic election), was imperative. Business sought to secure institutional coordination with labour, as represented by the black political parties (ANC, 1969, 1994; Jeffrey, 2009). Mention of the protection of human rights, property rights and civil liberties created a sense of confidence going into the 1994 election. In 1995, before the ratification of the final constitution, Thabo Mbeki, deputy-president of the ANC told supporters that the negotiations for an interim constitution were 'contrived elements of a transition' necessary to end white domination, and that the ANC at no time considered those aspects as 'elements of permanence'.[22]

Comrades, chiefs and business

The dilemma was the radically opposed 'settler' minority business interests, property and economic rights, positioned against the majority of 'comrades' backed by tribal aspirations. Business-political stakeholder alliances secured the peaceful transition of power to the black majority, but risked business interests in the economy. The 62 percent majority of the ANC in the first democratic election was the beginning of unilateral internal ANC policy-making and implementation. The institutional coordination of the new ANC state with business rolled out as an elite or ANC cadre enrichment strategy, reversing promises of a redistributive economy, non-racialism, equality before the law and an efficient public administration that is broadly representative of the South African nation.[23] The final constitution provided for the protection of fundamental institutions of the market economy – rule of law, guarantee of private property rights, individual freedom and human rights. It also entrenched the political power of non-democratic inherited tribal authorities, by means of Council of Traditional Leaders, with legislative power. Tribal chiefs control communal land ownership and use. The inherent tension between a market economy, non-freehold land ownership, non-democratic inherited authority and Communist allies in government, constitute a variety of 'capitalism' bound to present exceptional challenges to business. For the black political parties participating in the first unitary democratic election of 1994 the support of the traditional leadership was fundamental. Around 50% of the population of 41.5 million people lived in rural areas in 1995. More than 63% of the black African population lived in non-urban rural areas.[24] The new institutional coordination had to accommodate this essentially non-market element of the socio economic context in negotiating a new coalition. These conditions signalled the dynamic concept of VoC that push the political economy along a distinctive path of adjustment. The political changes in South Africa occurred through the direct business-initiated (business now constituted a new coalition) renegotiated institutional coordination. This new 'equilibrium' was indeed unstable, volatile and dynamic. The nature of the new coordination oscillated (is currently oscillating) between tight coordination and fragile coordination. Hall does not see this dynamic movement to 'eliminating' strategic or market coordination altogether' (Hall, 2007, p. 40). Hall's observation reflected on changes in Europe. The most significant variation of capitalism in the subsequent development in the South African market economy is the co-existence of non-market protection of indigenous authority (with communal property rights), renewed statutory racial exclusivity and entrenchment, and a market economy. In the latter statutory mandated transfer of ownership and control of the economy to black persons, is entrenched. A specific form of 'indigenisation' developed in South Africa.

The ANC entered the first election in 1994 as the leading partner of the Tripartite Alliance – between the ANC, the SACP and COSATU. The populist election programme promised to secure black people a meaningfully large share in the mainstream of the economy through employment. This was motivated as 'dealing with the legacy of Apartheid'.[25] Rural-based traditional leaders constituted a significant constituency of the ANC – the first President of the ANC was Chief Albert Luthuli (Beinart, 2001, pp. 165–169). At this point in the 'national democratic revolution' Nattrass expected a pro-poor coordinated market economy of an institutional alliance between the state, representing the so-called disadvantaged people, and the workers through the ruling Tripartite Alliance, through nationalisation, based on the Reconstruction and Development Plan. The adoption of market oriented macro-economic policies, such as the Growth Employment and Redistribution (GEAR) in 1997 was considered a principled departure from worker alliance towards big business (Jeffrey, 2014, pp. 22–25; Nattrass, 2014; Nattrass & Seekings, 2010).

The policies to transfer ownership of the South African economy to black people[26] passed through different stages of ideological intensity. In a closed meeting of the ANC executive committee and the Black Managers Forum and NAFCOC in 1993, the latter two organisations put pressure on the ANC to speed up the transfer of business to them (Nattrass & Seekings, 2010, p. 31). Black business acted in search of a new coordinated coalition with the ANC, the expected new government after 1994. White business was not privy to this intra-black strategy. Prior to the anticipated political change in government in 1994 private business pro-actively facilitated transactions whereby blacks acquired shares in big business as an 'empowerment' strategy to build a new business coalition or network. Sanlam, through its investment subsidiary Sankorp, concluded the first BEE transaction in 1993 (Chabane et al., 2006; Kruger, 1998; Verhoef, 2003, 2004). By mid-1998 market capitalisation of BEE companies listed on the JSE comprised 6 per cent of the JSE and in January 1999 it stood at R58, 7bn (US$965,61 at 2020 exchange rate), or 5, 5 per cent of the JSE market capitalisation. The decline followed the 1998 Asian market crisis. Debt instruments were the preferred instrument of funding of these BEE transactions. BEE financial engineering encouraged high deal flow and resulted in an unmanageable high debt base rather than an asset base. The 1998 Asian stock market crisis thus left such firms with unsustainable gearing ratios. Furthermore, the Special Purpose Vehicles (SPV's) established to facilitate the empowerment transactions, were premised on a bull market. When the market turned bearish, those companies struggled to meet their financial obligations and had to give up the shares they have only just acquired. The funding vehicles or SPV has protected the empowerment companies from capital risk, thus contributing to the distortion of normal business practise. These funding weaknesses compromised sustained black control (Caygill, 1999, p. 3; Kruger, 1998, pp. 11–16).

It is important to reflect on the ANC policy shift from affirmative action (as per RDP) and BEE. The core policy concept is the 'national democratic revolution' (NDR), which set out to eliminate existing property relations and enforce national demographic representivity across the economy and society. The ANC, and its allies, the SACP and COSATU, are in full agreement that the NDR is the shortest path towards a socialist society. At each of the ANCs, five-year national conferences (Mafikeng, 1997; Stellenbosch, 2002; Polokwane, 2007; Mangaung, 2012; Nasrec, 2017) the party reconfirmed its commitment to the NDR. The stance of the ANC is that a party cannot be bound to pragmatic decisions or agreements, which cannot be changed by mutual consent. A movement such as the ANC cannot be derailed from its long-term objectives by 'tactical concessions' it had to make under certain circumstances.

Therefore, the party may have entered into agreements, which were convenient at a specific conjecture to strengthen its position. If the balance of forces shifts in its favour, that party can disregards or circumvent earlier compromises (Du Toit, 2001; Jeffrey, 2014, pp. 101–102).

After ascent to power, the ruling ANC reneged on the consensus under the draft constitution of non-racism and equality before the law. The final constitution adopted in 1996 was clear that 'non-racialism' constituted a fundamental value of the new democracy. Furthermore, the Bill of Rights, which formed part of the new constitution, proclaimed that all South Africans have 'equality before the law and... the equal protection and benefit of the law'.[27] The deputy President Thabo Mbeki, stated during the debate in Parliament, 'The Constitution whose adoption we celebrate constitutes an unequivocal statement that we refuse to accept that our Africanness shall be defined by our race, colour, gender, or historical origins. It is a firm assertion made by ourselves that South Africa belongs to all who live in it, black and white... It rejoices in the diversity of our people and creates the space for all of us voluntarily to define ourselves as one people'.[28] As the ANC embarked on a systematic roll out of statutes to implement its NDR (in a similar fashion as the National Party government since 1950 systematically enacted statutes to implement its policy of separate development), Mbeki reversed his stance on all South Africans being 'one people'. On 29 May 1998 he claimed, 'We therefore make bold to say that South Africa is a country of two nations. One of these is white [and relatively prosperous]...The second and larger nation of South Africa is black and poor... We are not one nation, but two nations. Ad neither are we becoming one nation' (Kriel, 2006). This position transpired in the shift from non-racialism to the justification for renewed statutory racism.

The ANC affirmative action policy claimed to offer a constructive policy to correct the past and give new opportunities for millions of people, bar racial discrimination and ensure that the state did not become 'an instrument of racially-biased extortion and patronage in which friends are favoured, opponents disadvantaged, and bribes accepted' (ANC, 1994). The consensus amongst all parties in Parliament on so-called 'soft' affirmative action to correct imbalance of the past, was captured in a sub-clause to Section 9 of the Constitution, providing for legislation to 'protect or advance people disadvantaged by unfair discrimination...[in order to] promote the achievement of equality'. The consensus was that excellent education, training and employment opportunities would be the vehicles to achieve that goal. Subsequently the state passed a series of racial laws. The first was the Employment Equity Act, 55 of 1998, set out to implement affirmative action, but based on the national demography.[29] The second was The Public Procurement Act, 1998, as supplemented by the Preferential Procurement Policy Framework Act, No 5 of 2000 and the Mineral and Petroleum Resources Development Act, No of 2002, followed by the Broad-based Black Economic Empowerment Act, No of 2003 (Adam et al., 1998; Jeffrey, 2014, pp. 224–233). An ANC office bearer in Gauteng stated, 'Since ability is randomly distributed among the entire population, black and white South Africans should be represented in the workforce according to their share of the overall population'.[30] The Employment Equity Act mandates the employment of categories of persons according to the national demography, and the definition of a 'historically disadvantaged' person. The Constitution of South Africa (1996) justifies BEE as redistributing the resources of the country equitably amongst the population. These policies are supplemented by skills training laws -the Skills Development Act, No 97 of 1998, and the Skills Development Levies Act, No 9 of 1999. Both statutes mandate business engagement in training and education of the workforce, off course of people of dedicated demographic categories, as prerequisite for compliance with B-BBEE targets and receiving B-BBEE credits in terms of the DTI scorecard. (To be explained below)

In an intra-ANC discourse, reaffirmed at each of the five-year national conferences, the rhetoric was eradication of'apartheid property relations… deracialisation of ownership and control of wealth, including land and equity', and eradicate 'apartheid production relations' (ANC, 2002). This was not part of a public consultation process with business, but the party that had become the state, one-sidedly, planning the enforcement of the NDR. The commitment to the NDR resulted in affirmative action, based on ideas of non-racialism, '… quietly morphing into a complex set of employment equity, BEE, and land reform rules that are cumulatively eroding business autonomy, undermining property rights, crippling public service efficiency, choking off direct investment, retarding economic growth, and adding to a crisis of unemployment…'(Jeffrey, 2014, p. 22) The unfolding of the BEE policy and sanctioning statutes, did not result from a public debate, but emerged from the ruling party's one-sided implementation of the NDR.[31]

Affirmative action became black economic empowerment (BEE). 'Black economic empowerment encompasses, among other things, black entry into business as owners and as managers, advancement in the workplace through the erosion of the industrial colour bar, unionisation, acquisition of equity, redistribution of existing wealth, and the rise of the black consumer' (Sidiripoulos, 1993).[32] The ANC explained BEE as '… economic empowerment for all South Africans – (it) is a very deliberate programme to achieve meaningful participation of disadvantaged South Africans in the mainstream South African economy' (Ramaphosa, 1997). The BEE policy was articulated to reallocate wealth across a broad continuum of society, to transform all sectors of the economy and to deliver improved standards of living, especially to the black population (Burger, 2010; Jeffrey, 2014, 2017). Policy implementation turned out to be prejudicing blacks, and especially the elite. In the foreign press this 'capture' of affirmative action was called *'afgekochte revolutie'* [revolution bought off] (Van Kessel, 1998) by 'Comrade capitalist[s]' (Simon, 2004). The first wave of BEE transaction benefitted only the new black elite as business rushed to gain the favour of the new powerful. Concern over the actual broad empowerment effect of the ownership acquisition deals of corporate entities in South Africa and elite enrichment rather than spreading benefits broadly (Calland, 2006; Nattrass, 2014; Van Kessel, 1998), led to the report by the Department of Trade and Industry DTI) in 2003 outlining proposals for statutory sanctioning of broad-based black economic empowerment (B-BBEE). The state and black business demanded faster and more ownership and management participation to a broader base of the black population. This needed simultaneous skills transfer. The report *South Africa's economic transformation: A Strategy for Broad-based Black Economic Empowerment*[33] led to the passing of the Broad-based Black Economic Empowerment Act, No53 of 2003. This act set out the principle of economic sector based charters to manage the transfer of ownership, managerial control and skills in all sectors of the economy to the broad black community in South Africa. The DTI Code of Good Conduct tracks and assesses the degree of compliance. The incentive to comply with the Code of Good Conduct (See Table 1: DTI General Scorecard) is a B-BBEE score (accreditation).[34] The B-BBEE Code of Good Conduct impacts on the market for factors of production: companies with a high B-BBEE score benefited from preferential procurement by the state, but also with companies doing business with the state.

Securing the market economy depends on statutorily mandated managed transfer of market control in terms of negotiated sectoral charters to black ownership, management

Table 1. DTI Generic BEE Scorecard, 2007.

Element	Weighting 2007	Weighting 2013
Ownership	20	25
Management Control	10	15
Employment Equity	15	
Skills Development	15	20
Preferential Procurement	20	40 Enterprise and supplier development
Enterprise development	15	
Socio-economic Development Initiative	5	5
Total	100	105

Source: DTI Generic Scorecard, 2007: Government Gazette No 29570, Government Printer, Pretoria; DTI Generic Scorecard, 2013: Government Gazette No 38765, Government Printer: Pretoria.

and access to employment and opportunity in all sectors of the economy. This is the South African variety of 'indigenisation' policies implemented in many newly independent African states. This constitutes a very specific 'variety of capitalism', which has no corollary in Africa: entrenched traditional indigenous economic power, a manipulated market economy sanctioning the transfer of property rights in exchange for the privilege to do business with the state, and relative socio-political stability.

BEE effected a transfer of ownership and management of listed companies by 2012 to approximately 15% black persons in executive management and 36% of non-executive directors on the boards of directors of companies (Empowerdex, 2012). The B-BEE policies since 2003 also assisted small black enterprises through the Code of Good Conduct, whereby skills development, enterprise development and preferential procurement invoked statutory compliance with small enterprises, similar to those early African enterprises in the townships. Preferential procurement from black owned enterprises averaged between 16 and 18% by 2012 and as shown in Table 2 below, gradual improvement in skills development, enterprise development and socio-economic development. Institutional coordination thus manifests in the integral framework of ownership and management transfers and broad-based socio-economic development.

The DTI generic scorecard reflects the priorities of ownership and control in BEE implementation. In 2007, the weighting gave effect to the conditions of the Black Economic Empowerment Act, No 53 of 2003. Amendments to the Act in 2013 increased the weighting for ownership and control. The slow progress with compliance under the employment equity and skills development categories, as reflected in Table 2, contributed to the more stringent compliance requirements in the 2013 scorecard. The DTI Code of B-BBEE Conduct is supplemented by the statutory enforced requirements on procurement, employment equity and skills development. Table 2 below illustrates elements of the progress made by 2011.

The broad institutional context and broad business environment embodies a state-business coalition, which is simultaneously a business-employee coalition, although Nattrass disputes the benefits of the policy to labour (Nattrass, 2014). In order to protect the core of a market economy, business agreed to market distortion by statutory enforced ownership and management transfer. This is market distortion on one level. In the relationship with its workforce, legislation compels business to organise employee relations (employment conditions, wage levels, composition of the workforce) according to 'negotiated' sector charters. These charters are incorporated in the DTI Code of Good Governance. All the charters stipulate specific targets for black ownership, management, employment etc. within restricted

Table 2. Attributions by Skills Development (SD), Enterprise Development (ED) and Socio-economic Development (SED), 2008–2011.

Sector	SD 2007	SD 2008	SD 2009	SD 2010	SD 2011	ED 2007	ED 2008	ED 2009	ED 2010	ED 2011	SED 2007	SED 2008	SED 2009	SED 2010	SED 2011
Resources	7.89	6.27	3.51	7.95	8.55	8.71	4.24	2.61	7.26	10.86	4.46	2.41	3.01	4.83	5.21
Financials	6.9	7.1	6.66	7.2	9.12	11.4	11.23	9.56	14.1	14.91	4.46	3.68	3.43	4.25	4.51
ICT	5.43	8.01	5.57	6.42	6.95	10.19	12.62	9.83	12.05	13.63	3.52	3.57	3.77	4.25	4.96
Retail	5.42	8.38	7.27	7.79	8.03	8.43	9.87	10.22	12.93	13.61	4.5	4.57	4.9	5	4.15
Health & Pharm	4.98	8.16	7.49	10.22	10.53	12.93	12.12	8.06	9.19	9.9	3.36	2.94	3.92	4.43	4.63
Travel & Leisure	4.56	4.02	6.01	7.6	8.18	9.72	3.82	3.76	13.59	11.25	4.29	3.5	2.86	5	5
Services	3.03	4.16	4.69	7.61	10.08	5.34	7.17	7.53	11.9	15	2.48	2.79	3.78	3.71	5
Food & Beverage	2.79	3.34	4.03	5.24	8.82	4.69	6.76	10.59	13.47	13.58	3.96	2.99	3.68	3.69	4.49
Basic industrials	2.36	4.92	5.02	7.2	9.2	5.24	7.01	10.91	10.67	14.04	3.17	2.86	2.08	3.72	4.91
General Industrial	2..24	2.26	2.48	7.36	7.82	4.74	3.19	8.02	13.4	13.89	2.82	2.84	2.47	4.33	4.62
Media	1.25	1.28	4.79	6.11	5.53	5	4.86	9.82	12.51	10.03	2.56	2.08	3.25	5	4.32
Transport	1.14	6.45	2.69	7.63	9.26	4.29	10.5	9	15	15	1.71	3.13	2.13	4.49	5

Source: Empowerdex, 2012.

times (Mathura, 2009). A socialist driven worker agenda in alliance with the SACP, thus dictates the relationship between business and its workforce.

The third level of market distortion is on the corporate governance level. The DTI Codes of B-BBEE compliance prescribe business' relationship with shareholders, financial institutions, the stock exchange and foreign investors through the requirement of compliance with sectoral charters. The state only contracts with B-BBEE compliant companies. The Public Procurement Act, 1998, as supplemented by the Preferential Procurement Policy Framework Act, No 5 of 2000, entrenches preferential procurement to companies owned and managed by blacks (Jeffrey, 2014, pp.12–128). Doing business with the state depends on compliance with BEE sector charters. Depending on the level of B-BBEE compliance, an enterprise earns a score, making it eligible to government contracts or tenders. The preferential procurement policy justified state procurement to 'people historically disadvantaged by unfair discrimination on the basis of race, gender or disability'.[35] The state motivates this policy as targeting the development of historically disadvantaged entrepreneurs, and small and medium-sized business. It was therefore not surprising that BEE compliant companies listed on the JSE outperformed the JSE (Mathura, 2009), but failed to deliver on broad-based economic empowerment of the population.

'Comrades capitalists' in the market

An anomaly emerges in the assessment of the impact of the BEE policy on the economic progress, development and improved standards of living of the South African population. Since business with the state is dependent on a high B-BBEE score, companies with a high B-BBEE rating are relatively profitable. Studies have though shown that a high B-BBEE score did not guarantee the highest levels of profitability. Only 21.1% of the variation in operating profit and 9, 9% of turnover have actually been contributed directly to the B-BBEE rating of corporations (Kleynhans & Kruger, 2014). Widespread evidence of corruption in the implementing of the B-BBEE targets and sector charters is endemic.[36] The manipulation and abuse of procurement systems, skills development levies, payment of bribes to secure state contracts and inefficient employment practices to realise so-called 'transformation targets', constitute systematic under-utilisation of human capital resources and a waste of physical and financial capital. In 2009 the former Minister of Finance, Pravin Gordan acknowledged that the state paid excessively high prices to supplies through the preferential procurement system, as procurement policies sheltered suppliers from designated empowerment categories (Jeffrey, 2014). Apart from corruption and mismanagement, the hidden cost to BEE remains obscured. Companies write BEE transaction costs off to restructuring expenditure, or corporate social investment. Most BEE transactions are shrouded in secrecy as strategic repositioning of business through empowerment transactions reflects the fragile nature once again of the new state-business nexus in South Africa. The profound racial nature of the new South African CME is entrenched in, what can be called, a racial market economy (RME). BEE transactions offer participation in share offer schemes exclusively to black employees, to the explicit exclusion of white employees (who have also not been able to afford equity acquisition). Key examples are the Vodacom Yebo Yethu scheme,[37] SASOL Inzalo and Khanyisa schemes,[38] the Discovery Bank's BEE plan,[39] and the Barloworld B-BBEE Khula Sizwe share scheme.[40] The full cost of the BEE transactions to shareholders and investors remains obscured in financial statements. No reliable statistics are available.

Assessing the vision of enhancing economic growth and improve the standards of living of the South African population through B-BBEE, the macro-economic data contradicts the propaganda on empowerment.

The precarious nature of the state seeking to enforce BEE and develop a comprehensive social security framework in South Africa manifests in the threatening fiscal cliff, illustrated by the negative growth of the economy (Table 3). Real growth rates have dropped significantly from 5% in 2005 to 1.3% in 2015. Per capita growth has slumped even further to less than 1% in 2015. At the same time Government deficit has returned to around 4% of GDP, which is almost at the level of 1995. Public debt has risen to 47.3%. The population grows at a rate of around 1.68%, which exceeds economic growth. The escalation in social welfare expenditure at a rate of 17% on average since 2005 indicates a high potential for catapulting off the fiscal cliff (Fedderke, 2009; Moodley & Adam, 2000; Roussouw et al., 2014). The state failed to adhere to economic growth strategies. With social welfare expenditure at 15% of Government expenditure and population growth exceeding economic growth, the domestic economy displays profound failure to generate growth to sustain either empowerment or social welfare.

The trend in state expenditure (based on quarterly data in Table A1 – Appendix A) is reflected in Figure 1.

The rising state expenditure as a proportion of GDP since the 1960s doubled in the scope of 25 years, while government consumption and gross capital formation as a proportion of GDP illustrates the inability of the state to invest in economic growth. As GDP growth almost collapsed by the second decade of the twenty-first century, state expenditure soared. It is clear that there is an uneven burden on business in the fragile coalition. The growing state expenditure on social welfare, as illustrated in Table 4, explains the emphasis on business to fund the B-BBEE project.

Table 3. GDP and Government expenditure, debt, 1995-2015.*

	GDP Real R'bn	% growth	Real GDP per capita	% change	G deficit/ surplus as % GDP	Public debt % GDP
1995	1 704	3.1	43 267	1.09	−5.0	49.5
1996	1 777	4.3	44 193	2.1	−4.8	47.3
1997	1 824	2.6	44 420	0.5	−3.6	46.8
1998	1 834	0.5	43 720	−1.6	−2.7	46.8
1999	1 877	2.4	43 826	0.2	−2.1	44.4
2000	1 955	4.2	45 735	2.1	−1.9	40.9
2001	2 008	2.7	45 075	0.8	−1.4	40.1
2002	2 082	3.7	45 798	1.6	−1.0	34.1
2003	2 143	2.9	46 287	1.1	−2.2	33.5
2004	2 241	4.6	47 605	2.8	−1.4	33.2
2005	2 359.0	5.3	49 335	3.6	−0.3	31.4
2006	2 491	5.6	51 331	4.0	0.7	29.0
2007	2 625	5.4	53 334	3.9	0.9	26.6
2008	2 709	3.2	54 322	1.9	−9.7	26.0
2009	2 667	−1.5	52 838	−2.7	−5.1	31.5
2010	2 748.0	3.1	53 823	1.9	−4.0	35.1
2011	2 836	3.2	54 930	2.1	−4.8	38.6
2012	2 899	2.2	55 508	1.1	−5.3	41.0
2013	2 963	2.2	56 047	1.0	−4.6	43.9
2014	3 009	1.5	56 185	0.2	−4.6	46.2
2015	3 055.1	1.3	56 304		−3.8	47.3

Source: South African reserve bank time series data, www.resbank.co.za accessed 10/10/2016.
*(2010 Prices).

As is illustrated in Table 4, expenditure on social services and welfare [this is transfer payments as social grants within the six categories of social grants outlined above] increased from R16.7 billion in 1995 to R188.1 billion in 2015 – this is an annual compound growth of 113.58% [or simply 1026% overall growth in the twenty years between 1995 and 2015]. Economic growth is insufficient to sustain such transfers – GDP growth rates slumped from 5.2% in 2005 to 1.3% in 2015 (See Table 3). Despite claims to a reduction in poverty, the Gini-coefficient rose since 2002 to between 0.66 and 0.68 by 2016.

Conclusion

The VoC discourse has not considered the developments of market economies in Africa systematically. Many African states did not seek to sustain or develop a market economy after independence. The socialist centrally planning model around a powerful state characterised the general trend of Africa's economic development since the mid-1950s. A slow and often reluctant transition to aspects of the market economy manifested in the post-structural adjustment era in Africa. The development of a market economy in South Africa received more attention in Political Economy. The unfolding of a dynamic nexus between state and business, representing different interest groups, resulted in slowly shifting networks and coalitions through the history of the country since 1910. The cultural or nationalist division

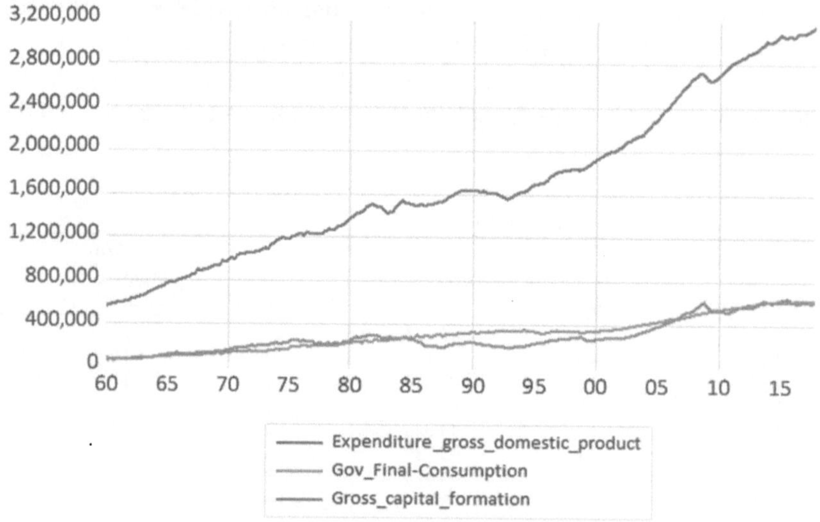

Figure 1. Government Expenditure on GDP, Government consumption and gross capital formation, 1960–2015.

Table 4. Expenditure on Social Services and welfare, 1995-2015.

	R'bn	% Total G expenditure	% of GDP
1995	16.7	11.1	1.1
2000	20.9	15.8	2.4
2005	72.2	16.7	4.8
2010	130.7	15.6	4.8
2015	188.1	15.1	5.0

Source: National Treasury, Budget, 1995 – 2016.

between settlers (people from Europe, with a sense of loyalty to the British Empire) and people of European descent opposing allegiance to the British Empire has been interpreted as a clash of nationalisms or national-socialist tendencies. Despite a deep-seated agricultural grounding, the small Cape-based Afrikaner agricultural/business elite soon forged a coalition with English-speaking business. The unfolding of the market economy in South Africa therefore presents a variety of capitalism, which performed a temporary or interim position between a market system under minority white rule, and the post-1990 black majority coalition. Race was indeed an element of the pre-1990 political order of separate development, but did not use statutory sanctioning to mandate property transfers or sanction the allocation of ownership and management transfers to race-based entities. Responding to Hancké's (2007) call for closer interrogation of a more interventionist state in twenty-first century market economies, this study shows how the post-1994 state embedded race to restructure ownership and control of business and overall economic fundamentals. In developing or emerging market economies (such as in East and Central Europe after 1990), the political reconfiguration gave rise to a highly interventionist redistributive state. In South Africa, this is a race-based market economy (RME), as a variety of a CME. Race has become the cornerstone of state intervention in the market economy. The dynamic nature of this manifestation is the integration of capitalist business into the redistributive market economy based on race-based categories.

This configuration is relevant to the South African experience. The pre-1990 business coalition consciously entered into a market distorting compromise with the anticipated new political leadership as a strategic decision to preserve basic elements of the market. In the good faith of the Constitution of 1996, business anticipated consensus on the preservation of the market based on non-racism, and equality before the law. The new state's commitment to the NDR, undermines that consensus. The integration of non-market traditional systems of authority and a strategic alignment with a Communist political party, to sustain the new state, is a unique development. Race is now more entrenched in society and economy than ever before in the history of South Africa (Adam, 2018; Moodley & Adam, 2000). It calls for a significant openness in market oriented economic thinking towards fragile coalitions with non-market forces. This may lead to further business realignment and a shift in the fragile institutional coordination hardly holding the South African economy afloat.

Notes

1. See Sluyterman (2015), where specific characteristics of the Netherlands are considered; Fellman et al. (2008), presenting the Nordic case; Cassis (1997), presenting a European perspective; and on specifics of the German case, Fear (1997) and Stokes (2009).
2. Breckenridge argues that South Africa is not unique, but shares many common aspects of the African economic landscape, such as tribal authority, infrastructure deficiencies, racial segregation, strong state, resource exports, state-owned enterprises. See Breckenridge (2018): 3. A similar argument is put forward by Padyachee (2013).
3. The early revisionists include Martin Legassick, Frederick A Johnstone, Shula Marks, Harold Wolpe, Stanley Trapido, Colin Bundy and the Sussex Poulantzians (Robert Davies, David Kaplan, Michael Morris and Dan O'Meara), Mike Morris, followed by latecomers such as Peter Richardson, Ian Phimister, William Beinart and Phil Bonner. Off course many more joined the bandwagon, and others matured to moderation after scholarly criticism. For a comprehensive analysis of the Neo-Marxist historiography on South Africa, see Verhoef (1982) and Wright

(1977). Legassick, Johnstone and Wolpe rejected the term 'neo-Marxist', since their analysis was considered to be 'oriented by the approach of Marxist historical materialism, of Marxist political economy and class analysis, of Marxist social science,' Johnstone (1979), 'Most painful to our hearts; South African history through the eyes of the Marxist-school (Revised text of a public lecture, University of the Witwatersrand, April 1979 at Conference on Race Conflict in South Africa: 1.

4. Lord Alfred Milner, British High Commissioner for the Transvaal Colony, referred to the European Boer and English inhabitants of the British colonies in South Africa as 'white races': See De Kiewiet (1941).
5. *Union Statistics for Fifty Year*, 1910–1960. Pretoria: Government Printer: A-3.
6. The formation of the National Party did not unite all Afrikaans-speaking people in one political party, or create a single homogenous cultural entity. Since 1910 Afrikaners were divided on entering the Union under the British monarchy. The National Party established a nationalism driven party on the basis of the primacy of South Africa's interest. This sentiment resonated well with many Afrikaans-speaking people. Despite the National Party, Afrikaners remained divided politically. See H Giliomee (2003) *The Afrikaners;* E Dommisse (2011) *Sir David Pieter de Villiers Graaff. Die erfridder van De Grendel*. Cape Town: Tafelberg; H Giliomee (2012) *Die Laaste Afrikanerleiers. 'n Opperste toets van mag*. Cape Town: Tafelberg. The obsolete deterministic class analysis of so-called 'Afrikanerdom' by D O'Meara (1983), *Volkskapitalisme. Class capital and ideology in the development of Afrikaner nationalism 1934–1948*. Johannesburg: Ravan Press; and (1996) *Forty lost years. The apartheid state and the politics of the National Party, 1948–1994*. Johannesburg: Ravan Press, both fail to capture the multidimensional historical dynamics of adjusting institutional complementarities and systems coordination. O'Meara never consulted any primary documents from archives on the history of Afrikaner people, but digested secondary material trough the deterministic Marxist class paradigm, thus disqualifying it from explaining the dynamic nature of the variety of capitalism in South Africa.
7. This development points to emerging social and economic coordination. It is not the product of capitalist class action fabricating nationalism to defray intra-capitalist class tensions, as suggested by O'Meara (1983, 27–28).
8. Feinstein (2006, p. 200); Jones (2002).
9. Maasdorp (2002).
10. This nature of the coordination was described by the neo-Marxist revisionists as a race-based class domination; See Wolpe (1972) and Lipton (1979).
11. 'Homelands' is the term used to refer to the ethnic tribal lands allocated to the different ethnic African communities under the National Party policy of separate development.
12. BICs engaged extensively with training, support and mentorship in agricultural and industrial enterprise and mining operations. Some examples are irrigation projects along the Letaba River for the farming of cotton, groundnuts, and other winter crops; tea plantations by Tshivasi Tea products near Sibasa in Venda; meat processing businesses, textile weaving (Hillmond Weavers mohair weaving factory in Umtata); radio factory in Lebowa; furniture manufacturing plants in three homelands – Transkei, Venda and Gazankulu; steel cabinet manufacturing in Isithebe in KwaZulu; etc. The cane furniture manufacturing giant of South Africa, Mr Habakuk Shikwane, expanded his cane furniture manufacturing plant in Hammanskraal in the Bophuthatswana homeland, with BIC support; Mr Agrippa Mayapa developed an extensive network of hotels and bakeries in the Transkei with financial and business support of the Transkei Development Corporation. In mining the current Royal Bafokeng Platinum Mines Ltd, originated from mining developments supported by the BIC in the Bophuthatswana homeland. It is impossible to explain the extent if BIC economic and business development in the scope of this article. Suffice to note here that between 1960 and 1976 a total of 124 900 new employment opportunities were created through industrial development in decentralized areas of the homelands. See Viljoen (1976); Verhoef (2017).
13. African Trader, January/March 1967.
14. African Business, August 1980, 31-33; L Mathebe (1994) *Black entrepreneurial activity and the origins of the National African Federation of Chambers of Commerce, (NAFCOC), 1920–1980*. Unpublished limited scope thesis, University of the Witwatersrand, pp. 45–46.

15. African Business, December 1979, p. 5.
16. African Business, April 1979, pp. 11–13.
17. African Business, December/January 1988/1989, p. 23.
18. Cape Archives (KAB) 2562 Archives of the Urban Foundation, 1979–1990; SA: Sanlam Archives: Minutes of the Sankrop Board, 1985–1990.
19. See J N Hamman: "Haal politiek uit ekonomie', *Volkshandel*, 46(68), p. 29.
20. See M Lipton (2007) ; Submissions by the AHI, the Steel and Engineering Industries Federation of South Africa (Seifsa) and the South African Council of Banks to the Truth and Reconciliation Commission underlines the opposition to the policy of racial segregation by increasing cost to industry, undermining productivity and growth since the policy undermined skills development. See Truth and Reconciliation Commission Report, Institutional Healing Culpability submission, 2003: par: 16.
21. See Godsell (1986); see also Jenkins, *Pretoria News*, 23/12/1986, p. 10; Jenkins, *Natal Witness*, 23/12/1985, p. 12.
22. SAPA PR Wire Service: Speech of Thabo Mbeki at ANC National Constitutional Conference, 31 March–2 April 1995; also see Jeffery (2014) and Du Toit (2001).
23. Jeffrey (2014), BEE helping or hurting, pp. 2–122.
24. Central Statistics Service (1996, pp. 5–6).
25. http://www.anc.org.za/ancdocs/history/charter.html.
26. 'Black' here refers to all 'previously disadvantaged persons', which are Africans, Coloured persons and Indians.
27. Section 1.9(1), Constitution of the Republic of South Africa.
28. Statement by Deputy President T M Mbeki, on behalf of the African National Congress on the Occasion of the Adoption by the Constitutional Assembly of the Republic of South Africa Constitution Bill, 1996, Cape Town, 8 May 1996, p. 3: www.anc.org.za.
29. In 1998 blacks made up 77 percent of the South African population of 42.3 million people, Coloured people 8.8 percent, Indians 2.5 percent and whites 10 percent: see http://www.statssa.gov.za/publications/Report-03-01-67/Report-03-01-672011.pdf.
30. Quoted in Jeffrey (2014).
31. There is consensus about the non-consultative intra-party one-sidedness of the ANC economic and BEE policy. See Jeffrey (2014), Moodley and Adam (2000); Nattrass and Seekings (2010), Nattrass (2014).
32. E. Sidiripoulos (1993) 'Black Economic Empowerment', *South African Institute of Race Relations. Spotlight* (2): 1-12.
33. Department of Trade and Industry (DTI) (2003); see also Jack (2003).
34. DTI (2003) , Jack (2007) , and Andrews (2008), Harvard University RWP08-033:33-36.
35. Section 2(d), Preferential Procurement Policy Framework Act, 2000.
36. It is impossible to discuss all the examples of gross corruption in the allocation of procurement and the pricing of tenders in this study. Full detail of endless cases is in A Jeffrey (2014); also see Jeffrey (2016), Mathura (2009), Shava (2016), and Janisch (2018) 'Here's how BEE must change to meet Ramaphosa's vision for South Africa': *SA Investing*, 27/2/2018 (https://www.biznews,com/sa-investing/2018/02/27/bee-must-change-ramaphosa-vision, accessed 28/02/2018).
37. Hogg (2018).
38. https://www.sasolkhanyisa.com/from-inzalo-to-khanyisa/
39. Van Zyl (2018), https://biznews.com/sa-investing/2018/11/22/discovery-ban-bee-plan-adrina-gore-reponds-to-critics.html.
40. Cameron (2019), https://www.biznews.com/transfornation/2019/05/14/khula-sizwe-investment-barloworld.html.

Disclosure statement

No potential conflict of interest was reported by the author.

ORCID

Grietjie Verhoef http://orcid.org/0000-0001-7273-5135

References

Adam, H. (2018). Corruption, race and the future of South Africa. *Canadian Journal of African Affairs, 52*(2), 229–239. https://doi.org/10.1080/00083968.2018.1490193

Adam, H., Van Zyl Slabbert, F., & Moodley, K. (1998). *Comrades in business: Post-liberation politics in South Africa*. International Books.

ANC (1969). Strategy and tactics of the ANC. *Document adopted by the Morogoro Conference of the ANC meeting at Morogoro*, Tanzania, 25 April–1 May.

ANC (1994). Affirmative action and the new constitution, 15 April 1994. www.anc.irg.za.

ANC (1994). *Reconstruction and development program*. ANC.

ANC (2002) Preface to Strategy and tactics of the ANC. *ANC National Conference*, Stellenbosch, pp. 1–2. www.nc.org.za.

Andrews, M. (2008). *Is Black economic empowerment South Africa's growth catalyst, or could it be? John F Kennedy School of Government*. Harvard University RWP08-033.

Ashman, S., Fine, B., & Newman, S. (2010). The Crisis in South Africa: Neoliberalism, Financialization and Uneven and Combined Development', *Socialist Register*, 47, 174–95.

Atmore, A., & Westlake, N. (1972). A liberal dilemma: a critique of the Oxford History of South Africa. *Race, 14*(2), 106–126. https://doi.org/10.1177/030639687201400201

Austin, G. (2016). Is Africa too late for 'Late development'? Gerschenkron south of the Sahara. In Andersson, M. and Axelsson, T. *Diverse development paths and structural transformation in the escape from poverty* (pp. 206–235). Oxford University Press.

Beaud, M. (2001). *A history of capitalism 1500-1980*. New York University Press.

Beinart, W. (2001). *Twentieth century South Africa*. Oxford University Press.

Beveridge, A. C. (1991). Taking control of foreign investment: A case study of indigenization in Nigeria. *The International and Comparative Law Quarterly, 40*(2), 302–333. https://doi.org/10.1093/iclqaj/40.2.302

Breckenridge, K. (2018). *What happened to the theory of African capitalism?* https://wiser.wits.ac.za/content/what-happened-theory-african-capitalism-13042.

Bundy, C. (1979). *The rise and fall of thc South African peasantry*. Heinemann.

Burger, C. (2010). Professional engineering, Ingqandi Consulting. Interview with E Shava, 23 March 2010: East London.

Cairncross (1985). State handling of economic slammed. *Business Day*, 9, 5 October.

Calland, R. (2006). *Anatomy of South Africa: Who holds the power?* Zebra Publishers.

Cameron, J. (2019). *Is Khula Sizwe a good investment? Expert dissects R3.5 bn Barloworld B-BBEE scheme*. https://www.biznews.com/transfornation/2019/05/14/khula-sizwe-investment-barloworld.html.

Cassis, Y. (1997). *Big business: the European experience in the twentieth century. Presenting a European perspective*. Oxford University Press.

Caygill, J. J. (1999). Empowerment 1999. A Moving Experience. *Business Map*, Johannesburg.

Central Statistics Service. (1996). Living in South Africa. *Selected findings of the 1995 October Household Survey. Government Printer: Pretoria*.

Christie, R. (1984). *Electricity, Industry and Class in South Africa*. State University of New York Press.

Clarke, N. L. (1994). *Manufacturing Apartheid. State Corporations in South Africa*. Yale University Press.

Davenport, T. R. H., & Saunders, C. (2000). *South Africa. A modern history*. Macmilllan.

Davies, R. (1979). *Capital, state and white labour in South Africa, 1900–1960. An historical materialist analysis of class formation and class relations*. Harvester Press.
Davies, R., Kaplan, D., Morris, M. & O'Meara, D. (1976). Class struggle and the periodization of the South African state. *Review of African Political Economy*, 7, 4–30. https://doi.org/10.1080/03056247608703298
De Kiewiet, C. W. (1941). *A History of South Africa. Social and economic*. Oxford University Press.
Department of Trade and Industry (DTI) (2003). *South Africa's economic transformation: A strategy for broad-based Black economic Empowerment*. DTI.
Dommisse, E. (2005). *Anton Rupert. 'n Lewensverhaal*. Tafelberg.
Dommisse, E. (2011). *Sir David Pieter de Villiers Graaff. Die erfridder van De Grendel*. Tafelberg.
Du Plessis, W. (2016). Rethinking capitalism in Africa. *Without Prejudice*, September 2016. https://www.howwemadeitinafrica.com/rethinking-capitalism-africa/
Du Toit, S. (ed.). (1976). *Homelands. The role of the Corporations in the Republic of South Africa*. CVR Publishers.
Du Toit, P. (2001). *South Africa's brittle peace: the problems of post-settlement violence*. Palgrave.
Fear, J. (1997). German capitalism. In McCraw, T. K. (Ed.). *Creating modern capitalism: How entrepreneurs, companies and countries triumphed in three industrial revolutions*. Harvard University Press, pp. 135–182.
Feinstein, C. (2005). *An economic history of South Africa. Conquest, discrimination and development*. Cambridge University Press.
Fellman, S., Iversen, M., Thue, M., & Sogren, H. (2008). *Creating Nordic Capitalism: The development of a competitive periphery*. Palgrave.
Fine, B. (2009). Engaging the mineral-energy complex: on a few of my views on a few things. *Transformation*, 71. https://doi.org/10.1353/trn.0.0050
Giliomee, H. (2003). *The Afrikaners. A biography of a people*. Tafelberg.
Giliomee, H. (2012). *Die Laaste Afrikanerleiers. 'n Opperste toets van mag*. Tafelberg.
Godelier, M. (1977). *Perspectives in Marxist Anthropology*. Cambridge University Press (*English translation of 1973 French title*).
Godsell, B. (1986). *The perversity of sanctions*. Johannesburg.
Goedhuys, D. (1994). South African monetary policy in the 1980s: Years of reform and foreign financial aggression. *South African Journal of Economic History*, *9*(2), 145–164. https://doi.org/10.1080/20780389.1994.10417236
Grosh, B., & Mukandalala, R. S. (1994). *State-owned enterprises in Africa*. Lynne Renier Publishers.
Hall, P. A., & Gingerich, D. W. (2004). Spielarten des Kapitalismus und institutionelle Komplementaritäten in der Makroökonomie—Eine empirische Analyse. *Berliner Journal für Soziologie*, *14*(1), 5–31. https://doi.org/10.1007/BF03204694
Hall, P. A. and Soskice, D. (Ed.). (2001). *Varieties of Capitalism. The institutional foundations of comparative advantage*. Oxford University Press.
Hamman, J. N. Haal politiek uit ekonomie. *Volkshandel*, *46*(68), 29.
Hancké, B., Rhodes, M., & Thatcher, M. (2007). *Beyond varieties of capitalism. Conflict, contradictions and complementarities in the European economy*. Oxford University Press.
Handley, A. (2008). *Business and the state in Africa: Economic policy-making in the Neo-liberal era*. Cambridge University Press.
Hart, K. & Padyachee, V. (2013). A history of South Africa capitalism in national and global perspective. *Transformation*, *81/82*, 55–85. https://doi.org/10.1353/trn.2013.0004
Hellmann, E. (1950). The native in the towns. In Schapera, I. (Ed.), *The bantu-speaking tribes of South Africa: An ethnological survey*. Maskew Miller.
Iliffe, J. (1983). *The emergence of African capitalism*. Macmillan.
Jack, V. (2007). Unpacking the different waves of Black Economic Empowerment. In X. Mangcu, G. Marcus, K. Shubane, & A. Hadland (Eds.), *Visions of Black Empowerment* (pp. 108–109). Jacana Press.
Jeffery, A. (2014). *BEE Helping or hurting?* Tafelberg, p. 10
Jeffrey, A. (2009). *People's war: New light on the struggle for South Africa*. Jonathan Ball.
Jeffrey, A. (2012). *BEE is flawed and should be scrapped*. http://mg.co.za/article/2013-01-18-bee-is-flawed-and-should-be-scrapped.

Jenkins, S. (1986). With sanctions the West has missed he mark –yet again. *Pretoria News*, 23 December, p.10.

Jones, F. S. (Ed.) (2002). *The decline of the South African economy*. Edward Elgar.

Jones, F. S., & Müller, A. L. (1992). *The South African economy, 1910–1990*. Macmillan.

Jones, S. (2002). The financial sector. In F. S. Jones (Ed.), *The decline of the South African economy* (pp. 165–194). Edward Elgar.

Kleynhans, E. P. J., & Kruger, M. C. (2014). Effect of Black Economic Empowerment on profit and competitiveness of firms in South Africa. *Acta Commercii*, *14*(1), 1–10. https://doi.org/10.4102/ac.v14i1.200

Kocka, J. (2009). Writing the history of capitalism. *New York Times*, *45*, 29–51.

Kocka, J. (2010). Writing the history of capitalism. *German Historical Institute News*, Fall, 7–24.

Kriel, K. (2006). The revival of racial classification in post-apartheid South Africa. *Fast Facts*, December, pp. 1–2.

Kruger, W. G. (1998). Black Empowerment: An economic evaluation of future investor attractiveness [Unpublished M Com Dissertation]. University of Cape Town.

Legassick, M. (1972a). Review of "Colonialism in Africa, 1870–1960. *The International Journal of African Historical Studies*, *1*(5), 324–326. https://doi.org/10.2307/217555

Legasssick, M. (1972b). Dynamics of modernisation in South Africa. *Journal of African History*, *13*(1), 145–150.

Lipton, M. (1979). The debate about South Africa: neo-Marxists and Neo-Liberals. *African Affairs*, *4*(2), 57–80. https://doi.org/10.1093/oxfordjournals.afraf.a097081

Lipton, M. (1984). *Capitalism and Apartheid, 1910–1984*. New Africa Books.

Lipton, M. (2007). The role of business under apartheid: Revisiting the debate. In H. E. Stolten (Ed.), *History making and present politics: The meaning of collective memory in South Africa*. Nordic Afrikainstituet.

Lumby, A. B. (1981). Industrial development prior to the Second World War. In Coleman, F. L. (Ed), *Economic history of South Africa* (pp. 195–219). HAUM.

Malan, T., & Hattingh, S. (1975). *Black Homelands in South Africa*. Africa Institute.

Marks, S. & Atmore, A. (Eds.). (1980). *Economy and Society in pre-industrial South Africa*. Longman.

Marks, S. (1972). Liberalism, social realities and South African History. *Journal of Commonwealth Political Studies*, *10*(3), 243–249. https://doi.org/10.1080/14662047208447169

Mathebe, L. (1994). Balck entrepreneurial activity and the origins of the national African Federation of Chamber of Commerce (NAFCOC), 1920–1980 [Unpublished limited scope thesis], University of the Witwatersrand.

Mathura, A. (2009). The impact of Broad-based Black economic Empowerment on the financial performance of companies on the JSE [Unpublished MBA dissertation]. GIBS, University of Pretoria.

Mayer, P. (1961). *Tribesmen and Townsmen. Conservatism and the process of urbanisation in a South African city*. Oxford University Press.

Meillassoux, C. (1971). *Development of indigenous trade and markets in West Africa*. Routledge.

Meillassoux, C. (1972). From reproduction to production: A Marxist approach to economic anthropology. *Economy and Society*, 93–105.

Moodley, K., & Adam, H. (2000). Race and nation in post-apartheid South Africa. *Current Sociology*, 48(3), 51–69. https://doi.org/10.1177/0011392100048003005

Motsuenyane, S. (2011). *A Testament of hope: The autobiography of Dr Sam Motsuenyane*. Freedom Foundation, pp. 55–58.

NAFCOC Milestones (1994). NAFCOC: Johannesburg.

Nattrass, J. (1982). *The South African economy. Its growth and change*. Oxford University Press.

Nattrass, N., & Seekings, J. (2010). State, business and growth in Post-Apartheid South Africa. Discussion Paper Series 34, Research Programme Consortium for Improving Institutions for Pro-Poor Growth (IPPG), p. 7. www.ippg.org.

Nattrass, N. (2014). A South African variety of capitalism? *New Political Economy*, *19*(1), 56–78. https://doi.org/10.1080/13563467.2013.768610

Neal, L., & Williamson, J. G. (Eds). (2014). *The Cambridge History of Capitalism. Vol 1 The rise of capitalism: From ancient origins to 1848*. Cambridge University Press.

Nellis, J. (2005). *The evolution of enterprise reform in Africa: From state-owned enterprise to private participation in infrastructure- and back?* World Bank.

Nölke, A., & Vliegenthart, A. (2009). Enlarging the varieties of capitalism: The emergence of dependent market economies in East Central Europe. *World Politics, 61*(4), 670–702. https://doi.org/10.1017/S0043887109990098

Nölke, A., & Claar, S. (2013). Varieties of capitalism in emerging economies. *Transformation, 81*/82, 34–54. https://doi.org/10.1353/trn.2013.0001

O'Meara, D. (1983). *Volkskapitalisme. Class, capital and ideology in the development of Afrikaner nationalism 1934–1948*. Ravan Press.

O'Meara, D. (1996). *Forty lost years. The apartheid state and the politics of the national Party*, 1948–1994. Ravan Press.

Padyachee, V. (2013). Introducing varieties of capitalism into the South Africa debate: uses and limits. *Transformation: Critical perspectives on Southern Africa, 81*/82, 5–32.

Pearsall, C. W. (1937). Some aspects of the development of secondary industry in South Africa. *South African Journal of economics, 5*(4).

Radice, H. (2015). *Global capitalism*. Routledge, p. 125, 140.

Ramaphosa, C. (1997). Empowerment. The Future of Black business. *Boardroom, 2*, 12.

Rougier, E., & Combarnous, F. (2017). Emerging capitalisms and institutional reforms in developing countries. In *The Diversity of Emerging Capitalisms in Developing Countries* (pp. 413–435). Palgrave Macmillan.

Roussouw, J., Joubert, F., & Breytenbach, A. (2014). Suid-Afrika se fiskale afgrond: 'n Blik op die aanwending van owerheidshulpbronne. *Tydskrif vir, 54*(1), 144–162.

Sansom, B. (1974). Traditional economic systems. In W. D. Hammond-Tooke, (Ed.), *The bantu-speaking peoples of southern Africa* (2nd edn). Routledge & Kegan Paul.

Schneider, B. R. (2007). Comparing capitalisms: Liberal, coordinated, network, and hierarchical varieties. Draft published paper.

Schneider, B. R. (2009). Hierarchical market economies and Varieties of Capitalism in Latin America. *Latin American Studies, 41*, 553–575. https://doi.org/10.1017/S0022216X09990186

Schumann, C. G. W. (1938). *Structural change and business cycles in South Africa, 1806–1936*. Staples Press, p. 112. https://doi.org/10.2307/2549096

Seddon, D. (Ed). (1978). *Relations of Production: Marxist approaches to economic anthropology*. Psychology Press.

Sender, J., & Smith, S. (1986). *The Development of capitalism in Africa*. Methuen.

Sidiripoulos, E. (1993). Black Economic Empowerment. *South African Institute of Race Relations. Spotlight 2*, 1–12.

Sluyterman, K. (ed.). (2015). *Varieties of capitalism and Business History: The Dutch case*. Routledge

Stokes, R. G. (2009). *Divide and prosper: the heirs of IG Farben under Allied authority 1945-1951*. Hexagon Press.

Streeck, W. (2005). Rejoinder: on terminology, functionalism, (historical) institutionalism and liberalization. *Socio-Economic Review, 3*(3), 577–587. https://doi.org/10.1093/SER/mwi026

Thompson, L. M. (1978). The Compromise of Union. In M. Wilson & L. M. Thompson (Eds.), *Oxford History of South Africa* (vol. 2, 325–364). Oxford University Press.

Van Zyl, G. (2018). *Discovery Bank's BEE plan: Adrian Gore response to critics*.https://biznews.com/sa-investing/2018/11/22/discovery-ban-bee-plan-adrina-gore-responds-tocritis.html.

Verhoef, G. (1982). Die Radikale Historiografie oor Suid-Afrika [Unpublished MA Dissertation]. Rand Afrikaans University.

Verhoef, G. (2001). Stokvels and economic empowerment: the case of African women in South Africa, c. 1930-1998. In Lemire, B., Pearce, R., & Campbell, G. *Women and Credit. Researching the past, refiguring the future* (pp. 91–116). Berg Publishers.

Verhoef, G. (2003). The Invisible Hand": the roots of Black Economic Empowerment, Sankorp and societal change in South Africa, 1985–2000. *Journal of Contemporary History, 28*(1), 28–47.

Verhoef, G. (2004). Economic empowerment and performance: Strategies towards indigenisation/Black economic Empowerment and the performance of such enterprises in Nigeria and South Africa, since the early 1970's to 2002. *Journal of Contemporary History, 29*(2), 92–118.

Verhoef, G. (2009). Concentration and Competition: The changing landscape of the banking sector in South Africa, 1970–2007. *The South African Journal of Economic History, 24*(2), 157–197. https://doi.org/10.1080/10113430909511222

Verhoef, G. (2010). The chemical industry in South Africa during the 1990s. In R. Vivian & S. Jones (Eds.), *The South African Economy in the 1990s* (pp. 143–157). Manchester University Press.

Verhoef, G. (2014). The South African economy in the twentieth century. In F. Pretorius (Ed.), *A history of South Africa. From the distant past to the present day* (pp. 448–477). Protea Book House.

Verhoef, G. (2015). SASOL: From state-owned enterprise to chemical leader. Management and strategy, 1952–1980. In Felisini, D. (Ed.), *Reassessing the role of management in the Golden Age: An international comparison of public sector managers, 1945-1975. Rivista di Politica Economica, V11-IX,* 33–59.

Verhoef, G. (2017). *The History of Business in Africa*. Springer.

Verhoef, G. (2018). *The Power of your Life. The Sanlam century of insurance empowerment, 1918-2018.* Oxford University Press.

Wassenaar, A. D. (1977). *The Assault on private enterprise. The freeway to communism*. Tafelberg.

Wickins, P. (1981). *An economic history of Africa from earliest times to partition*. Oxford University Press.

Wilkins, M. (2010). Multinational enterprise and the varieties of capitalism. *Business History Review, 84*(4), 638–648.

Wolpe, H. (1972). Capitalism and cheap labour-power in South Africa. From segregation to apartheid. *Economy and Society, 1*(1), 425–456. https://doi.org/10.1080/03085147200000023

Wright, H. M. (1977). The burden of the present. Liberal–Radical controversy over South African history. Cape Town: David Phillip. https://doi.org/10.1086/ahr/84.2.518

Yudelman, D. (1983). *The emergence of modern South Africa. State, capital, and the incorporation of organized labour on the South African gold-fields, 1902–1939.* Greenwood Press.

Appendix A

Table A1. Ratios of national accounts: Quarterly data, 1960-2016 (current prices).

	National accounts: Ratios of selected data: Final consumption expenditure by general government to GDP	National accounts: Ratios of selected data: Gross fixed capital formation to GDP	National accounts: Ratios of selected data: Public sector expenditure to GDP
1960/03/31	9.1	20.9	17.8
1960/06/30	9.8	19.3	17.6
1960/09/30	9.3	19.7	17.3
1960/12/31	9	19.1	16.3
1961/03/31	9.2	19.8	17.2
1961/06/30	9.4	19.3	18
1961/09/30	9.8	18.9	18
1961/12/31	9.9	18.2	18.3
1962/03/31	10.2	18.6	18.3
1962/06/30	10.2	17.9	18.4
1962/09/30	9.9	18.1	17.7
1962/12/31	11.6	18.5	19.8
1963/03/31	10.4	20.2	19.7
1963/06/30	9.9	20.6	19.3
1963/09/30	10.1	20.5	19
1963/12/31	9.6	20.7	19.3
1964/03/31	11	21.1	20.4
1964/06/30	11.1	21.9	20.4
1964/09/30	10.8	23.3	20
1964/12/31	10.8	22.6	19.7
1965/03/31	10.8	24	20.7
1965/06/30	12.4	24	23.3
1965/09/30	12.3	25.1	24.3
1965/12/31	9	26.3	21.3
1966/03/31	11.4	25.1	23.3
1966/06/30	12	23.3	21.1
1966/09/30	10.6	23.9	23.9
1966/12/31	10.6	24.1	22.6
1967/03/31	10.9	23.2	21.9
1967/06/30	10.7	23	22.3
1967/09/30	11	22.6	22.1
1967/12/31	10.7	22.3	21.8
1968/03/31	10.9	22.7	21.4
1968/06/30	11	22.7	22.1
1968/09/30	11.2	21.9	21.3
1968/12/31	11.4	22.3	22.3
1969/03/31	11	23	21.4
1969/06/30	11.5	22.6	21.7
1969/09/30	11.2	22.2	21.7
1969/12/31	11.8	23.2	22.6
1970/03/31	11.4	23.7	23.5
1970/06/30	12	25.1	24.2
1970/09/30	12.4	26.8	25.4
1970/12/31	11.8	25.4	24.2
1971/03/31	13	26.6	25.2
1971/06/30	12.9	26.3	25.1
1971/09/30	12.7	26.5	25.9
1971/12/31	13	27.7	27.4
1972/03/31	12.3	27.6	26.6
1972/06/30	12.8	27.5	26.1
1972/09/30	11.9	28.1	26.5
1972/12/31	11.4	27.2	25.6
1973/03/31	11.1	26.3	24.1
1973/06/30	11.1	26	23.5
1973/09/30	11.3	26.3	23.9
1973/12/31	10.9	26.3	23.1
1974/03/31	11.4	25.9	23.4

(*Continued*)

Table A1. Continued

1974/06/30	10.9	25	22.6
1974/09/30	11.7	26.7	24.1
1974/12/31	11.7	26.5	25.2
1975/03/31	12.4	27.2	26.5
1975/06/30	13.3	31.6	31.3
1975/09/30	12.6	31.5	29.6
1975/12/31	13.2	33.5	32
1976/03/31	13.3	32.5	31.3
1976/06/30	13.9	33	33.2
1976/09/30	14	31.2	30.1
1976/12/31	13.2	31.7	31.6
1977/03/31	13.7	32.9	32.8
1977/06/30	13.6	30.1	30.3
1977/09/30	12.5	30.8	30.6
1977/12/31	12.4	29.9	27.6
1978/03/31	14.3	27.5	28.3
1978/06/30	13.7	29.2	27.5
1978/09/30	13.3	26.3	27.8
1978/12/31	14	28.9	29.6
1979/03/31	13.3	26.7	27.2
1979/06/30	13.6	27.4	27.9
1979/09/30	14.2	29.3	29.8
1979/12/31	13.8	27	27.7
1980/03/31	12.3	25.5	25.9
1980/06/30	13.1	28.5	28.6
1980/09/30	13	28.8	28.4
1980/12/31	13.5	28.3	28.4
1981/03/31	12.5	28.5	28.2
1981/06/30	13.9	28.6	28.4
1981/09/30	14.1	29.7	28.6
1981/12/31	14.1	29.6	27.8
1982/03/31	15.5	29.6	28
1982/06/30	15.5	29.7	29.6
1982/09/30	15	28.6	28.1
1982/12/31	15.5	28.2	27.5
1983/03/31	15	28.2	26.9
1983/06/30	15.3	29.1	30.1
1983/09/30	15	26.7	25.8
1983/12/31	15	27.8	27.4
1984/03/31	15.7	25.8	27.5
1984/06/30	16.8	25.4	27.1
1984/09/30	17.3	25.2	28.1
1984/12/31	17.3	25	27.7
1985/03/31	16.8	25.4	28
1985/06/30	16.6	25.2	27.4
1985/09/30	18.3	24	29.9
1985/12/31	16.7	23.9	28.1
1986/03/31	17.9	22.3	27.8
1986/06/30	18.7	21.7	29.6
1986/09/30	17.6	22	28
1986/12/31	16.1	20.9	25.7
1987/03/31	18.5	20.2	26.5
1987/06/30	18.9	19.6	27.1
1987/09/30	17.6	19.2	25
1987/12/31	18.3	19.4	26.4
1988/03/31	18.1	20.4	26.1
1988/06/30	17.4	20.6	25.1
1988/09/30	17.6	21	25.3
1988/12/31	18.1	21.6	26.8
1989/03/31	18.6	21.6	28.7
1989/06/30	17.3	21.9	26.3
1989/09/30	17.3	22.5	27.1

(Continued)

Table A1. Continued

1989/12/31	17.8	23.3	27.7
1990/03/31	18.1	22.4	25.4
1990/06/30	17.8	21.1	25.9
1990/09/30	18.6	20.5	26.1
1990/12/31	19.7	19.9	27.1
1991/03/31	18.5	20.2	26.6
1991/06/30	19.2	19.3	26.6
1991/09/30	18.3	18.6	25.9
1991/12/31	18.6	18.2	25.3
1992/03/31	19.1	17.8	25.8
1992/06/30	19	17.9	26.2
1992/09/30	18.6	17.9	25.9
1992/12/31	19.1	16.4	25.2
1993/03/31	19.5	16.1	25.6
1993/06/30	19.7	15.9	24.6
1993/09/30	19.7	15.7	24.9
1993/12/31	19.7	15.6	24.1
1994/03/31	19.7	15.7	23.9
1994/06/30	20	16	24.7
1994/09/30	20.2	16.4	24.4
1994/12/31	19.4	16.2	23.7
1995/03/31	18.7	16.8	23.3
1995/06/30	18.4	17.4	23.9
1995/09/30	17.8	17	23
1995/12/31	17.6	16.7	21.8
1996/03/31	18.4	17.1	22.9
1996/06/30	19.1	17.2	23.9
1996/09/30	19.3	17.3	24.3
1996/12/31	19.7	17.2	24.5
1997/03/31	19.6	17.7	24.5
1997/06/30	19.2	17.6	24
1997/09/30	19.2	17.5	24.7
1997/12/31	19.2	17.4	24.6
1998/03/31	19	17.8	24.7
1998/06/30	18.8	17.7	24.7
1998/09/30	19	18.3	25.4
1998/12/31	18.8	18.5	25.8
1999/03/31	18.7	16.9	23.8
1999/06/30	18.8	16.3	23.9
1999/09/30	18.4	15.8	23.1
1999/12/31	18.5	15.6	22.7
2000/03/31	18.6	15.8	22.6
2000/06/30	18.3	15.7	22.6
2000/09/30	18.3	15.4	22.2
2000/12/31	18.3	15.6	22.5
2001/03/31	18.2	15.6	22.3
2001/06/30	18.5	15.5	22.1
2001/09/30	18.7	15.6	22.5
2001/12/31	18.7	15.3	23
2002/03/31	18.6	15.1	22.3
2002/06/30	18.7	15	22.7
2002/09/30	19.1	15.1	23
2002/12/31	18.8	15.4	22.8
2003/03/31	19	15.5	23.3
2003/06/30	18.7	15.9	23.3
2003/09/30	19.1	16	23.4
2003/12/31	19.4	16.4	24.2
2004/03/31	19.1	16.2	23.9
2004/06/30	19.2	16.3	23.6
2004/09/30	19	16.6	23.6
2004/12/31	19.2	16.8	23.2
2005/03/31	19.1	16.8	23.9
2005/06/30	19.1	16.9	23.8

(Continued)

Table A1. Continued

2005/09/30	19.5	17.4	24.1
2005/12/31	20.1	17.8	25
2006/03/31	18.5	18.3	22.3
2006/06/30	17.7	18.6	22.9
2006/09/30	18	19	23
2006/12/31	18.4	19.7	23.5
2007/03/31	17.4	20.3	23
2007/06/30	17.6	20.8	23.5
2007/09/30	18.2	20.9	24.3
2007/12/31	18	20.6	24.5
2008/03/31	18	21.4	24.6
2008/06/30	18.3	22.8	25.7
2008/09/30	18.9	24.4	27
2008/12/31	19.4	25.3	27.6
2009/03/31	19.3	23	28.1
2009/06/30	19.3	22	27.2
2009/09/30	20	20.9	27.4
2009/12/31	20.8	20.3	28.2
2010/03/31	20.6	20	27.9
2010/06/30	19.8	19.4	26.6
2010/09/30	20.1	19.1	26.9
2010/12/31	20.5	18.7	27.2
2011/03/31	19.6	18.8	27.8
2011/06/30	20.1	19	25.2
2011/09/30	20	19.3	25
2011/12/31	19.8	19.4	27.5
2012/03/31	20.2	19.2	28.8
2012/06/30	20.1	19.4	25.3
2012/09/30	20.3	19.1	26
2012/12/31	20.4	19.3	28.5
2013/03/31	20.4	19.6	27.4
2013/06/30	20.6	20.2	28
2013/09/30	20.5	20.7	27
2013/12/31	20.7	21	28.1
2014/03/31	20.7	20.6	27
2014/06/30	21	20.2	29
2014/09/30	20.8	20.2	27.3
2014/12/31	20.7	20.5	27.7
2015/03/31	20.4	20.5	26.7
2015/06/30	20.3	20.3	28.8
2015/09/30	20.6	20.8	28.2
2015/12/31	20.6	20.2	27.8
2016/03/31	20.7	19.8	28.2
2016/06/30	20.9	19.6	27.4
2016/09/30	20.8	19.3	27.9
2016/12/31	20.8	19.4	28.4
2017/03/31	20.9	19.3	27.1
2017/06/30	21	18.7	27.9
2017/09/30	20.9	18.4	26.2
2017/12/31	21	18.6	30.2

Index